# Tottel's Miscellany

# Tottel's Miscellany

## (1557–1587)

EDITED BY

HYDER EDWARD ROLLINS

VOLUME I

Revised Edition

CAMBRIDGE, MASSACHUSETTS

HARVARD UNIVERSITY PRESS

1965

*To*

*THE TWO DEAREST PEOPLE IN TEXAS*

# INTRODUCTORY NOTE

## TO THE SECOND EDITION

THE present reprint of Hyder Rollins' edition of *Tottel's Mis-cellany*, which was first published in 1928–9, is slightly altered and somewhat enlarged. Volume I corrects a few errors which he had noted in his copy.* Volume II includes as an appendix the relevant portion of the article, "Marginalia on Two Elizabethan Poetical Miscellanies," which he contributed to the *Joseph Quincy Adams Memorial Studies* (Folger Shakespeare Library, 1948, pp. 457–74); in this he had assembled additional notes on *Tottel*.

This new edition is a reminder — not that one is needed — both of the immense amount of work accomplished by the editor-general of his age and of the standard of scholarship that he set and maintained. He is described and his publications are listed in Herschel Baker's admirable *Hyder Edward Rollins: A Bibliography* (Harvard, 1960). The variorum edition of Shakespeare's sonnets would alone have been a life-work for anyone else, if indeed anyone else would ever have emerged from that cave of despair; and this was only one of many big undertakings. Hyder's several dozen volumes of Elizabethan miscellanies and ballads and of the letters of Keats and Keats's circle carried such authority that the scholarly reader could always accept texts and apparatus with entire trust; and he also wrote some dozens of articles, monographs, and reviews. We may wish that he could have extended his labors to other Elizabethan and Jacobean texts for which we are still dependent upon Grosart.

One thing that never failed to astonish Hyder's friends was that, in spite of his being always at work, he never seemed to be, and never showed any of the usual signs of disorder; his desk, in his Widener study or at home, was always clear, and if there were a couple of pencils visible, they lay neatly together, parallel with the side of the desk. And he himself was always impeccably elegant in attire; one could not imagine him in the untidy dishabille that is a necessity for most

---

* Only five of these corrections alter the text: *waueryng* for *wauerying* (p. 34, l. 2); *sire* for *fire* (p. 104, l. 23); *here.* for *here,* (p. 105, l. 5); *lest* for *left* (p. 150, l. 24); *bene* for *been* (p. 246, l. 34).

[ vii ]

literary workers.   The photograph in Herschel Baker's memoir, of Hyder in the Keats Room in Houghton Library, is completely typical; he always looked — to borrow Keats's phrase about himself — "like a picture of somebody reading."   This outward orderliness might be taken as a mark of the reserve that was part of his nature.   He had many friends, professional brethren and devoted doctoral students, and he was a genial and lively talker, yet one never felt that one could reach his inner self.   By the same token, he might give the impression that he did not care deeply about the literature he worked with.   Yet I remember that once, when I had expressed lukewarm sentiments about most of Shakespeare's sonnets, he said, with sudden fervor, "They seem to me to say just about everything";   and then, as if conscious of betraying emotion, he began quickly to speak of everyday matters.

Douglas Bush

Cambridge, Massachusetts,
1964.

# CONTENTS

*SONGES AND SONETTES*, June 5, 1557 (*A*)

FACSIMILE TITLE-PAGE . . . . . . . . . . . . . . . . . . . 1

THE PRINTER TO THE READER . . . . . . . . . . . . . . . 2

## POEMS BY HENRY HOWARD, EARL OF SURREY

1. DESCRIPCION OF THE RESTLESSE STATE OF A LOUER, WITH SUTE TO HIS LADIE, TO RUE ON HIS DIYNG HART . . . . . 3

2. DESCRIPTION OF SPRING, WHERIN ECHE THING RENEWES, SAUE ONELIE THE LOUER . . . . . . . . . . . 4

3. DESCRIPCION OF THE RESTLESSE STATE OF A LOUER . . . 5

4. DESCRIPTION OF THE FICKLE AFFECTIONS PANGES AND SLEIGHTES OF LOUE . . . . . . . . . . . . . . . 5

5. COMPLAINT OF A LOUER, THAT DEFIED LOUE, AND WAS BY LOUE AFTER THE MORE TORMENTED . . . . . . . . 7

6. COMPLAINT OF A LOUER REBUKED . . . . . . . . . 8

7. COMPLAINT OF THE LOUER DISDAINED . . . . . . . . 9

8. DESCRIPTION AND PRAISE OF HIS LOUE GERALDINE . . . 9

9. THE FRAILTIE AND HURTFULNES OF BEAUTIE . . . . . . 9

10. A COMPLAINT BY NIGHT OF THE LOUER NOT BELOUED . . 10

11. HOW ECHE THING SAUE THE LOUER IN SPRING REUIUETH TO PLEASURE . . . . . . . . . . . . . . . . . 10

12. VOW TO LOUE FAITHFULLY HOWSOEUER HE BE REWARDED 11

13. COMPLAINT THAT HIS LADIE AFTER SHE KNEW OF HIS LOUE KEPT HER FACE ALWAY HIDDEN FROM HIM . . . . . . 11

14. REQUEST TO HIS LOUE TO IOYNE BOUNTIE WITH BEAUTIE . 12

15. PRISONED IN WINDSOR, HE RECOUNTETH HIS PLEASURE THERE PASSED . . . . . . . . . . . . . . . . . 12

16. THE LOUER COMFORTETH HIMSELF WITH THE WORTHI-NESSE OF HIS LOUE . . . . . . . . . . . . . . . 14

17. COMPLAINT OF THE ABSENCE OF HER LOUER BEING VPON THE SEA . . . . . . . . . . . . . . . . . . . 15

18. COMPLAINT OF A DIYNG LOUER REFUSED VPON HIS LADIES INIUST MISTAKING OF HIS WRITYNG . . . . . . . . 16

[ ix ]

# CONTENTS

19. COMPLAINT OF THE ABSENCE OF HER LOUER BEING VPON
    THE SEA . . . . . . . . . . . . . . . . . . . . . . . . . . . . 18

20. A PRAISE OF HIS LOUE: WHERIN HE REPROUETH THEM THAT
    COMPARE THEIR LADIES WITH HIS . . . . . . . . . . . 19

21. TO THE LADIE THAT SCORNED HER LOUER . . . . . . . 20

22. A WARNING TO THE LOUER HOW HE IS ABUSED BY HIS LOUE 21

23. THE FORSAKEN LOUER DESCRIBETH & FORSAKETH LOUE . 22

24. THE LOUER DESCRIBES HIS RESTLESSE STATE . . . . . . 23

25. THE LOUER EXCUSETH HIMSELF OF SUSPECTED CHANGE . 23

26. A CARELESSE MAN, SCORNING AND DESCRIBING, THE SUTTLE
    VSAGE OF WOMEN TOWARDE THEIR LOUERS . . . . . . 25

27. THE MEANES TO ATTAIN HAPPY LIFE . . . . . . . . . . 26

28. PRAISE OF MEANE AND CONSTANT ESTATE . . . . . . . 26

29. PRAISE OF CERTAIN PSALMES OF DAUID, TRANSLATED BY
    SIR.T.W. THE ELDER . . . . . . . . . . . . . . . . . 27

30. OF THE DEATH OF THE SAME SIR.T.W. . . . . . . . . . 27

31. OF THE SAME . . . . . . . . . . . . . . . . . . . . . . 28

32. OF SARDINAPALUS DISHONORABLE LIFE, AND MISERABLE
    DEATH . . . . . . . . . . . . . . . . . . . . . . . . . 29

33. HOW NO AGE IS CONTENT WITH HIS OWN ESTATE, & HOW THE
    AGE OF CHILDREN IS THE HAPPIEST, IF THEY HAD SKILL TO
    VNDERSTAND IT . . . . . . . . . . . . . . . . . . . . 29

34. BONUM EST MIHI QUOD HUMILIASTI ME . . . . . . . . 30

35. EXHORTACION TO LEARNE BY OTHERS TROUBLE . . . . . 30

36. THE FANSIE OF A WERIED LOUER . . . . . . . . . . . 31

## POEMS BY SIR THOMAS WYATT

37. THE LOUER FOR SHAMEFASTNESSE HIDETH HIS DESIRE
    WITHIN HIS FAITHFULL HART . . . . . . . . . . . . 32

38. THE LOUER WAXETH WISER, AND WILL NOT DIE FOR AFFEC-
    TION . . . . . . . . . . . . . . . . . . . . . . . . . . 32

39. THE ABUSED LOUER SEETH HIS FOLY, AND ENTENDETH TO
    TRUST NO MORE . . . . . . . . . . . . . . . . . . . 33

40. THE LOUER DESCRIBETH HIS BEING STRIKEN WITH SIGHT OF
    HIS LOUE . . . . . . . . . . . . . . . . . . . . . . . 33

41. THE WAUERYNG LOUER WYLLETH, AND DREADETH, TO
    MOUE HIS DESIRE . . . . . . . . . . . . . . . . . . . 34

# CONTENTS

42. THE LOUER HAUING DREAMED ENIOYING OF HIS LOUE, COM-PLAINETH THAT THE DREAME IS NOT EITHER LONGER OR TRUER . . . . . . . . . . . . . . . . . . . . . . . 34

43. THE LOUER VNHAPPY BIDDETH HAPPY LOUERS REIOICE IN MAIE, WHILE HE WAILETH THAT MONETH TO HIM MOST VNLUCKY . . . . . . . . . . . . . . . . . . . . . . . 35

44. THE LOUER CONFESSETH HIM IN LOUE WITH PHILLIS . . . 35

45. OF OTHERS FAINED SORROW, AND THE LOUERS FAINED MIRTH . . . . . . . . . . . . . . . . . . . . . . . 36

46. OF CHANGE IN MINDE . . . . . . . . . . . . . . . 36

47. HOW THE LOUER PERISHETH IN HIS DELIGHT, AS THE FLIE IN THE FIRE . . . . . . . . . . . . . . . . . . . 36

48. AGAINST HIS TONG THAT FAILED TO VTTER HIS SUTES . . . 37

49. DESCRIPTION OF THE CONTRARIOUS PASSIONS IN A LOUER . 37

50. THE LOUER COMPARETH HIS STATE TO A SHIPPE IN PERILOUS STORME TOSSED ON THE SEA . . . . . . . . . . . . 38

51. OF DOUTEOUS LOUE . . . . . . . . . . . . . . . . 38

52. THE LOUER SHEWETH HOW HE IS FORSAKEN OF SUCH AS HE SOMTIME ENIOYED . . . . . . . . . . . . . . . . . 39

53. TO A LADIE TO ANSWERE DIRECTLY WITH YEA OR NAY . . 39

54. TO HIS LOUE WHOM HE HAD KISSED AGAINST HER WILL . . 40

55. OF THE IELOUS MAN THAT LOUED THE SAME WOMAN AND ESPIED THIS OTHER SITTING WITH HER . . . . . . . . 40

56. TO HIS LOUE FROM WHOM HE HADD HER GLOUES . . . . 41

57. OF THE FAINED FREND . . . . . . . . . . . . . . . 41

58. THE LOUER TAUGHT, MISTRUSTETH ALLUREMENTES . . . 41

59. THE LOUER COMPLAYNETH THAT HIS LOUE DOTH NOT PITIE HIM . . . . . . . . . . . . . . . . . . . . . . . 42

60. THE LOUER REIOYSETH AGAINST FORTUNE THAT BY HINDER-ING HIS SUTE HAD HAPPILY MADE HIM FORSAKE HIS FOLLY 42

61. A RENOUNCING OF HARDLY ESCAPED LOUE . . . . . . . 43

62. THE LOUER TO HIS BED, WITH DESCRIBING OF HIS VNQUIET STATE . . . . . . . . . . . . . . . . . . . . . . 44

63. COMPARISON OF LOUE TO A STREAME FALLING FROM THE ALPES . . . . . . . . . . . . . . . . . . . . . . 44

64. WIATES COMPLAINT VPON LOUE, TO REASON: WITH LOUES ANSWER . . . . . . . . . . . . . . . . . . . . . . 45

# CONTENTS

65. THE LOUERS SOROWFULL STATE MAKETH HIM WRITE SOROW-
FULL SONGES, BUT SOUCHE HIS LOUE MAY CHANGE THE
SAME . . . . . . . . . . . . . . . . . . . . . . 48

66. THE LOUER COMPLAINETH HIMSELF FORSAKEN . . . . . 49

67. OF HIS LOUE THAT PRICKED HER FINGER WITH A NEDLE . 50

68. OF THE SAME . . . . . . . . . . . . . . . . 51

69. REQUEST TO CUPIDE, FOR REUENGE OF HIS VNKINDE LOUE 51

70. COMPLAINT FOR TRUE LOUE VNREQUITED . . . . . . . 51

71. THE LOUER THAT FLED LOUE NOW FOLOWES IT WITH HIS
HARME . . . . . . . . . . . . . . . . . . . . 52

72. THE LOUER HOPETH OF BETTER CHANCE . . . . . . . . 52

73. THE LOUER COMPARETH HIS HART TO THE OUERCHARGED
GONNE . . . . . . . . . . . . . . . . . . . . . 53

74. THE LOUER SUSPECTED OF CHANGE PRAIETH THAT IT BE NOT
BELEUED AGAINST HIM . . . . . . . . . . . . . 53

75. THE LOUER ABUSED RENOWNSETH LOUE . . . . . . . . 53

76. THE LOUER PROFESSETH HIMSELF CONSTANT . . . . . . 54

77. THE LOUER SENDETH HIS COMPLAINTES AND TEARES TO SUE
FOR GRACE . . . . . . . . . . . . . . . . . . . 54

78. THE LOUERS CASE CAN NOT BE HIDDEN HOW EUER HE DIS-
SEMBLE . . . . . . . . . . . . . . . . . . . . 55

79. THE LOUER PRAIETH NOT TO BE DISDAINED, REFUSED, MIS-
TRUSTED, NOR FORSAKEN . . . . . . . . . . . . . 56

80. THE LOUER LAMENTETH HIS ESTATE WITH SUTE FOR GRACE 57

81. THE LOUER WAILETH HIS CHANGED IOYES . . . . . . . 58

82. THE LOUER LAMENTETH OTHER TO HAUE THE FRUTES OF
HIS SERUICE . . . . . . . . . . . . . . . . . . 59

83. TO HIS LOUE THAT HAD GEUEN HIM ANSWERE OF RE-
FUSELL . . . . . . . . . . . . . . . . . . . . 60

84. TO HIS LADIE CRUEL OUER HER YELDEN LOUER . . . . . 60

85. THE LOUER COMPLAINETH THAT DEADLIE SICKNESSE CAN
NOT HELPE HIS AFFECCION . . . . . . . . . . . . 61

86. THE LOUER REIOICETH THE ENIOYING OF HIS LOUE . . . 61

87. THE LOUER COMPLAYNETH THE VNKINDNES OF HIS LOUE . 62

88. HOW BY A KISSE HE FOUND BOTH HIS LIFE AND DEATH . . 63

89. THE LOUER DESCRIBETH HIS BEING TAKEN WITH SIGHT OF
HIS LOUE . . . . . . . . . . . . . . . . . . . 63

90. TO HIS LOUER TO LOKE VPON HIM . . . . . . . . . . 64

# CONTENTS

91. THE LOUER EXCUSETH HIM OF WORDES WHERWITH HE WAS VNIUSTLY CHARGED . . . . . . . . . . . . . 64

92. OF SUCH AS HAD FORSAKEN HIM . . . . . . . . 66

93. A DESCRIPTION OF SUCH A ONE AS HE WOULD LOUE . . . 66

94. HOW VNPOSSIBLE IT IS TO FINDE QUIET IN HIS LOUE . . . 66

95. OF LOUE, FORTUNE, AND THE LOUERS MINDE . . . . . . 67

96. THE LOUER PRAYETH HIS OFFRED HART TO BE RECEIUED . 67

97. THE LOUERS LIFE COMPARED TO THE ALPES . . . . . . 68

98. CHARGING OF HIS LOUE AS VNPITEOUS AND LOUING OTHER 68

99. A RENOUNCING OF LOUE . . . . . . . . . . . 69

100. THE LOUER FORSAKETH HIS VNKINDE LOUE . . . . . . 69

101. THE LOUER DESCRIBETH HIS RESTLESSE STATE . . . . . 69

102. THE LOUER LAMENTES THE DEATH OF HIS LOUE . . . . . 70

103. THE LOUER SENDETH SIGHES TO MONE HIS SUTE . . . . 71

104. COMPLAINT OF THE ABSENCE OF HIS LOUE . . . . . . . 71

105. THE LOUER BLAMETH HIS LOUE FOR RENTING OF THE LETTER HE SENT HER . . . . . . . . . . . . . . 74

106. THE LOUER CURSETH THE TYME WHEN FIRST HE FELL IN LOUE . . . . . . . . . . . . . . . . 74

107. THE LOUER DETERMINETH TO SERUE FAITHFULLY . . . . 75

108. THE LOUER SUSPECTED BLAMETH YLL TONGES . . . . . 76

109. THE LOUER COMPLAINETH AND HIS LADY COMFORTETH . . 76

110. WHY LOUE IS BLINDE . . . . . . . . . . . 77

111. TO HIS VNKINDE LOUE . . . . . . . . . . 77

112. THE LOUER BLAMETH HIS INSTANT DESYRE . . . . . . 78

113. THE LOUER COMPLAYNETH HIS ESTATE . . . . . . . 78

114. AGAINST HOURDERS OF MONEY . . . . . . . . 79

115. DISCRIPCION OF A GONNE . . . . . . . . . 79

116. WIAT BEING IN PRISON, TO BRIAN . . . . . . . . 80

117. OF DISSEMBLING WORDES . . . . . . . . . 80

118. OF THE MEANE AND SURE ESTATE . . . . . . . . 80

119. THE COURTIERS LIFE . . . . . . . . . . 81

120. OF DISAPOINTED PURPOSE BY NEGLIGENCE . . . . . . 81

121. OF HIS RETURNE FROM SPAINE . . . . . . . . 81

122. OF SODAINE TRUSTYNG . . . . . . . . . . 82

123. OF THE MOTHER THAT EAT HER CHILDE AT THE SIEGE OF IERUSALEM . . . . . . . . . . . . . . 82

# CONTENTS

124. Of the meane and sure estate written to Iohn
     Poins . . . . . . . . . . . . . . . . . . . . . . 82

125. Of the Courtiers life written to Iohn Poins . . . . 85

126. How to vse the court and him selfe therin, written
     to syr Fraunces Bryan . . . . . . . . . . . . . 88

127. The song of Iopas vnfinished . . . . . . . . . . . 90

POEMS BY NICHOLAS GRIMALD

128. A trueloue . . . . . . . . . . . . . . . . . . . . 93

129. The louer to his dear, of his exceding loue . . . . 93

130. The louer asketh pardon of his dere, for fleeyng
     from her . . . . . . . . . . . . . . . . . . . . 94

131. N. Vincent. to G. Blackwood, agaynst wedding . . . 95

132. G. Blackwood to .N. Vincent, with weddyng . . . . 96

133. The Muses . . . . . . . . . . . . . . . . . . . . 97

134. Musonius the Philosophers saiyng . . . . . . . . . 97

135. Marcus Catoes comparison of mans life with yron . 98

136. Cleobulus the Lydians riddle . . . . . . . . . . . 98

137. Concerning Virgils Eneids . . . . . . . . . . . . 99

138. Of mirth . . . . . . . . . . . . . . . . . . . . . 99

139. To L.I.S. . . . . . . . . . . . . . . . . . . . . 100

140. To maistres D.A. . . . . . . . . . . . . . . . . . 100

141. Of. m. D.A. . . . . . . . . . . . . . . . . . . . 101

142. A neew yeres gift, to the L.M.S. . . . . . . . . . 101

143. An other to. l.M.S. . . . . . . . . . . . . . . . 102

144. To. l. K.S. . . . . . . . . . . . . . . . . . . . 102

145. To. l. E.S. . . . . . . . . . . . . . . . . . . . 103

146. To. m. D.A. . . . . . . . . . . . . . . . . . . . 103

147. To. m. S.H. . . . . . . . . . . . . . . . . . . . 103

148. To his familiar frend . . . . . . . . . . . . . . 104

149. Description of Vertue . . . . . . . . . . . . . . 104

150. Prayse of measure-kepyng . . . . . . . . . . . . . 104

151. Mans life after Possidonius, or Crates . . . . . . 105

152. Metrodorus minde to the contrarie . . . . . . . . 105

153. Of lawes . . . . . . . . . . . . . . . . . . . . . 106

154. Of frendship . . . . . . . . . . . . . . . . . . . 106

# CONTENTS

155. THE GARDEN . . . . . . . . . . . . . . . . . . . . . . 107

156. AN EPITAPH OF SIR IAMES WILFORD KNIGHT . . . . . . 108

157. AN OTHER, OF THE SAME KNIGHTES DEATH . . . . . . . 108

158. AN EPITAPH OF THE LADYE MARGARET LEE. 1555 . . . 108

159. VPON THE TOMB OF A.W. . . . . . . . . . . . . . . . 109

160. VPON THE DECEAS OF W. CH. . . . . . . . . . . . . . 109

161. OF. N. CH. . . . . . . . . . . . . . . . . . . . . . . 110

162. A FUNERALL SONG, VPON THE DECEAS OF ANNES HIS
     MOOTHER . . . . . . . . . . . . . . . . . . . . . . . 111

163. VPON THE DEATH OF THE LORD MAUTRAUERS, OUT OF
     DOCTOR HADDONS LATINE . . . . . . . . . . . . . . 113

164. VPON THE SAYD LORD MAUTRAUERS DEATH . . . . . . 115

165. THE DEATH OF ZOROAS, AN EGIPTIAN ASTRONOMER, IN THE
     FIRST FIGHT, THAT ALEXANDER HAD WITH THE PERSIANS 115

166. MARCUS TULLIUS CICEROES DEATH . . . . . . . . . 118

167. OF M.T. CICERO . . . . . . . . . . . . . . . . . . . 120

## POEMS BY UNCERTAIN AUTHORS

168. THE COMPLAINT OF A LOUER WITH SUTE TO HIS LOUE FOR
     PITYE . . . . . . . . . . . . . . . . . . . . . . . . 121

169. OF THE DEATH OF MASTER DEUEROX THE LORD FERRES
     SONNE . . . . . . . . . . . . . . . . . . . . . . . 122

170. THEY OF THE MEANE ESTATE ARE HAPPIEST. . . . . . 123

171. COMPARISON OF LYFE AND DEATH . . . . . . . . . . 124

172. THE TALE OF PIGMALION WITH CONCLUSION VPON THE
     BEAUTYE OF HIS LOUE . . . . . . . . . . . . . . . 125

173. THE LOUER SHEWETH HIS WOFULL STATE, AND PRAYETH
     PITYE . . . . . . . . . . . . . . . . . . . . . . . . 126

174. VPON CONSIDERACION OF THE STAT[E OF] THIS LYFE HE
     WISHETH DEATH . . . . . . . . . . . . . . . . . . . 127

175. THE LOUER THAT ONCE DISDAINED LOUE IS NOW BECOME
     SUBIECT BEYNG CAUGHT IN HIS SNARE . . . . . . . 127

176. OF FORTUNE, AND FAME . . . . . . . . . . . . . . 129

177. AGAINST WICKED TONGES . . . . . . . . . . . . . . 130

178. NOT TO TRUST TO MUCH BUT BEWARE BY OTHERS CALAMA-
     TIES . . . . . . . . . . . . . . . . . . . . . . . . 130

179. HELL TORMENTETH NOT THE DAMNED GHOSTES SO SORE AS
     VNKINDNESSE THE LOUER . . . . . . . . . . . . . 131

180. OF THE MUTABILITIE OF THE WORLD . . . . . . . . 131

# CONTENTS

181. HARPELUS COMPLAYNT OF PHILLIDAES LOUE BESTOWED ON CORIN, WHO LOUED HER NOT AND DENIED HIM, THAT LOUED HER . . . . . . . . . . . . . . . . . 132

182. VPON SIR IAMES WILFORDES DEATH . . . . . . . . . 135

183. OF THE WRETCHEDNES IN THIS WORLD . . . . . . . . 136

184. THE REPENTANT SINNER IN DURANCE AND ADUERSITIE . . 136

185. THE LOUER HERE TELLETH OF HIS DIUERS IOYES AND ADUERSITIES IN LOUE AND LASTLY OF HIS LADIES DEATH 137

186. OF HIS LOUE NAMED WHITE. . . . . . . . . . . . 145

187. OF THE LOUERS VNQUIET STATE . . . . . . . . . . 145

188. WHERE GOOD WILL IS SOME PROFE WILL APPERE . . . . 146

189. VERSES WRITTEN ON THE PICTURE OF SIR IAMES WILFORD 146

190. THE LADYE PRAIETH THE RETURNE OF OF HER LOUER ABIDYNG ON THE SEAS . . . . . . . . . . . . . 147

191. THE MEANE ESTATE IS BEST . . . . . . . . . . . 147

192. THE LOUER THINKES NO PAYNE TO GREAT, WHERBY HE MAY OBTAINE HIS LADY . . . . . . . . . . . . . . 148

193. OF A NEW MARIED STUDENT . . . . . . . . . . . 150

194. ⟨THE MEANE ESTATE IS TO BE ACCOMPTED THE BEST. . . 150

195. ¶THE LOUER REFUSED LAMENTETH HIS ESTATE . . . . . 151

196. THE FELICITIE OF A MIND IMBRACING VERTUE, THAT BE-HOLDETH THE WRETCHED DESYRES OF THE WORLDE . . 152

197. ALL WORLDLY PLEASURES FADE . . . . . . . . . . 153

198. A COMPLAINT OF THE LOSSE OF LIBERTIE BY LOUE . . . . 154

199. A PRAISE OF HIS LADYE . . . . . . . . . . . . . 155

200. THE PORE ESTATE TO BE HOLDEN FOR BEST . . . . . . 157

201. THE COMPLAINT OF THESTILIS AMID THE DESERT WODDE . 157

202. ⟨THE LOUER PRAIETH PITY SHOWING THAT NATURE HATH TAUGHT HIS DOG AS IT WERE TO SUE FOR THE SAME BY KISSING HIS LADIES HANDES . . . . . . . . . . . 158

203. OF HIS RING SENT TO HIS LADY . . . . . . . . . . 158

204. THE CHANGEABLE STATE OF LOUERS . . . . . . . . . 159

205. A PRAISE OF AUDLEY . . . . . . . . . . . . . . 159

206. TIME TRIETH TRUTH . . . . . . . . . . . . . . 160

207. THE LOUER REFUSED OF HIS LOUE IMBRACETH DEATH . . 160

208. THE PICTURE OF A LOUER . . . . . . . . . . . . 161

[ xvi ]

# CONTENTS

209. OF THE DEATH OF PHILLIPS . . . . . . . . . . . . 162

210. THAT ALL THING SOMETIME FINDE EASE OF THEIR PAINE,
SAUE ONELY THE LOUER . . . . . . . . . . . . . 163

211. THASSAULT OF CUPIDE VPON THE FORT WHERE THE LOUERS
HART LAY WOUNDED AND HOW HE WAS TAKEN . . . . 163

212. THE AGED LOUER RENOUNCETH LOUE . . . . . . . . 165

213. OF THE LADIE WENTWORTHES DEATH . . . . . . . . 166

214. THE LOUER ACCUSING HYS LOUE FOR HER VNFAITHFUL-
NESSE, PURPOSETH TO LIUE IN LIBERTIE . . . . . . . 167

215. THE LOUER FOR WANT OF HIS DESYRE, SHEWETH HIS DEATH
AT HAND . . . . . . . . . . . . . . . . . . 168

216. A HAPPY END EXCEDETH ALL PLEASURES AND RICHES OF THE
WORLDE . . . . . . . . . . . . . . . . . . 169

217. AGAINST AN VNSTEDFAST WOMAN . . . . . . . . . . 169

218. A PRAISE OF PETRARKE AND OF LAURA HIS LADIE . . . . 169

219. THAT PETRARK CANNOT BE PASSED BUT NOTWITHSTANDING
THAT LAWRA IS FAR SURPASSED . . . . . . . . . . 170

220. AGAINST A CRUELL WOMAN . . . . . . . . . . . . 170

221. THE LOUER SHEWETH WHAT HE WOULD HAUE IF IT WERE
GRAUNTED HIM TO HAUE WHAT HE WOULD WISHE . . . 171

222. THE LADY FORSAKEN OF HER LOUER, PRAYETH HIS RE-
TURNE, OR THE END OF HER OWN LIFE . . . . . . . 172

223. THE LOUER YELDEN INTO HIS LADIES HANDES, PRAIETH
MERCIE . . . . . . . . . . . . . . . . . . 173

224. THAT NATURE WHICH WORKETH AL THINGES FOR OUR
BEHOFE, HATH MADE WOMEN ALSO FOR OUR COMFORT
AND DELITE . . . . . . . . . . . . . . . . . 174

225. WHEN ADUERSITIE IS ONCE FALLEN, IT IS TO LATE TO
BEWARE . . . . . . . . . . . . . . . . . . 175

226. OF A LOUER THAT MADE HIS ONELYE GOD OF HIS LOUE . . 176

227. VPON THE DEATH OF SIR ANTONY DENNY . . . . . . . 178

228. A COMPARISON OF THE LOUERS PAINES . . . . . . . . 178

229. OF A ROSEMARY BRAUNCHE SENTE . . . . . . . . . 179

230. TO HIS LOUE OF HIS CONSTANT HART . . . . . . . . 179

231. OF THE TOKEN WHICH HIS LOUE SENT HIM . . . . . . 179

232. MANHODE AUAILETH NOT WITHOUT GOOD FORTUNE . . . 180

233. THAT CONSTANCY OF ALL VERTUES IS MOST WORTHY . . . 180

234. A COMFORT TO THE COMPLAYNT OF THESTILIS . . . . . 180

[ xvii ]

# CONTENTS

235. THE VNCERTAINE STATE OF A LOUER . . . . . . . . . 181

236. THE LOUER IN LIBERTIE SMILETH AT THEM IN THRALDOME,
THAT SOMETIME SCORNED HIS BONDAGE . . . . . . . 182

237. A COMPARISON OF HIS LOUE WYTH THE FAITHFULL AND
PAINFUL LOUE OF TROYLUS TO CRESIDE . . . . . . 183

238. TO LEADE A VERTUOUS AND HONEST LIFE . . . . . . . 185

239. THE WOUNDED LOUER DETERMINETH TO MAKE SUTE TO HIS
LADY FOR HIS RECURE . . . . . . . . . . . . . 186

240. THE LOUER SHEWING OF THE CONTINUALL PAINES THAT
ABIDE WITHIN HIS BREST DETERMINETH TO DIE BECAUSE
HE CAN NOT HAUE REDRESSE . . . . . . . . . . . 187

241. THE POWER OF LOUE OUER GODS THEM SELUES . . . . . 188

242. OF THE SUTTELTYE OF CRAFTYE LOUERS . . . . . . . 188

243. OF THE DISSEMBLING LOUER . . . . . . . . . . 189

244. THE PROMISE OF A CONSTANT LOUER . . . . . . . . 190

245. AGAINST HIM THAT HAD SLAUNDERED A GENTLEWOMAN
WITH HIM SELFE . . . . . . . . . . . . . . . 190

246. A PRAISE OF MAISTRESSE RYCE . . . . . . . . . . 192

247. OF ONE VNIUSTLY DEFAMED . . . . . . . . . . . 193

248. OF THE DEATH OF THE LATE COUNTY OF PENBROKE . . . 194

249. THAT ECHE THING IS HURT OF IT SELFE . . . . . . . 195

250. OF THE CHOISE OF A WIFE . . . . . . . . . . . 195

251. DESCRIPCION OF AN VNGODLYE WORLDE . . . . . . . 196

252. THE DISPAIRYNG LOUER LAMENTETH . . . . . . . . 198

253. AN EPITAPH OF MAISTER HENRY WILLIAMS . . . . . . 199

254. AGAINST A GENTLEWOMAN BY WHOM HE WAS REFUSED . 199

255. AN EPITAPHE WRITTEN BY W.G. TO BE SET VPON HIS OWNE
GRAUE . . . . . . . . . . . . . . . . . . . 200

256. AN AUNSWERE . . . . . . . . . . . . . . . . 201

257. AGAINST WOMEN EITHER GOOD OR BADDE . . . . . . 201

258. AN ANSWERE . . . . . . . . . . . . . . . . 202

259. THE LOUER PRAIETH HIS SERUICE TO BE ACCEPTED AND HIS
DEFAULTES PARDONED . . . . . . . . . . . . . 202

260. DESCRIPTION AND PRAISE OF HIS LOUE . . . . . . . 203

261. AN ANSWERE TO A SONG BEFORE IMPRINTED BEGINNYNG.
TO WALKE ON DOUTFULL GROUNDE . . . . . . . . 204

[ xviii ]

# CONTENTS

ADDITIONAL POEMS BY HENRY HOWARD, EARL OF SURREY

262. THE CONSTANT LOUER LAMENTETH . . . . . . . . . 206

263. A PRAISE OF SIR THOMAS WYATE THELDER FOR HIS EXCELLENT LEARNING . . . . . . . . . . . . . 206

264. ❡A SONG WRITTEN BY THE EARLE OF SURREY BY A LADY THAT REFUSED TO DAUNCE WITH HIM . . . . . . . 207

265. THE FAITHFULL LOUER DECLARETH HIS PAINES AND HIS VNCERTEIN IOIES, AND WITH ONLY HOPE RECOMFORTETH SOMWHAT HIS WOFULL HEART . . . . . . . . . . 209


ADDITIONAL POEMS BY SIR THOMAS WYATT

266. OF HIS LOUE CALLED. ANNA . . . . . . . . . . . 211

267. THAT PLEASURE IS MIXED WITH EUERY PAINE . . . . . 211

268. A RIDDLE OF A GIFT GEUEN BY A LADIE . . . . . . . 211

269. THAT SPEAKING OR PROFERING BRINGES ALWAY SPEDING 212

270. HE RULETH NOT THOUGH HE RAIGNE OUER REALMES THAT IS SUBIECT TO HIS OWNE LUSTES . . . . . . . . . 212

271. WHETHER LIBERTIE BY LOSSE OF LIFE, OR LIFE IN PRISON AND THRALDOME BE TO BE PREFERRED . . . . . . . 213

COLOPHON . . . . . . . . . . . . . . . . . . . 214


POEMS ADDED IN THE SECOND EDITION (B) OF SONGES AND SONETTES, July 31, 1557

272. THE LOUER DECLARETH HIS PAINES TO EXCEDE FAR THE PAINES OF HELL. . . . . . . . . . . . . . . . 217

273. OF THE DEATH OF SIR THOMAS WIATE THE ELDER . . . . 218

274. THAT LENGTH OF TIME CONSUMETH ALL THINGES . . . . 218

275. THE BEGINNING OF THE EPISTLE OF PENELOPE TO VLISSES, MADE INTO VERSE . . . . . . . . . . . . . . . 219

276. THE LOUER ASKETH PARDON OF HIS PASSED FOLLIE IN LOUE 219

277. THE LOUER SHEWETH THAT HE WAS STRIKEN BY LOUE ON GOOD FRIDAY . . . . . . . . . . . . . . . . 220

278. THE LOUER DESCRIBETH HIS WHOLE STATE VNTO HIS LOUE, AND PROMISING HER HIS FAITHFULL GOOD WILL: ASSURETH HIMSELF OF HERS AGAIN . . . . . . . . . 220

279. OF THE TROUBLED COMON WELTH RESTORED TO QUIET BY THE MIGHTY POWER OF GOD . . . . . . . . . . . 227

[ xix ]

# CONTENTS

280. THE LOUER TO HIS LOUE: HAUING FORSAKEN HIM, AND
BETAKEN HER SELF TO AN OTHER . . . . . . . . . . . 229

281. THE LOUER SHEWETH THAT IN DISSEMBLING HIS LOUE
OPENLY HE KEPETH SECRET HIS SECRET GOOD WILL . . 229

282. THE LOUER DISCEIUED BY HIS LOUE REPENTETH HIM OF THE
TRUE LOUE HE BARE HER . . . . . . . . . . . . . 230

283. THE LOUER HAUING ENIOYED HIS LOUE, HUMBLY THANKETH
THE GOD OF LOUE: AND AUOWING HIS HART ONELY TO
HER FAITHFULLY PROMISETH, VTTERLY TO FORSAKE ALL
OTHER . . . . . . . . . . . . . . . . . . . . 231

284. TOTUS MUNDUS IN MALIGNO POSITUS . . . . . . . . 232

285. THE WISE TRADE OF LYFE . . . . . . . . . . . . 234

286. THAT FEW WORDES SHEW WISDOME, AND WORK MUCH
QUIET . . . . . . . . . . . . . . . . . . . . 234

287. THE COMPLAINT OF A HOT WOER, DELAYED WITH DOUTFULL
COLD ANSWERS . . . . . . . . . . . . . . . . . 235

288. THE ANSWER . . . . . . . . . . . . . . . . . 236

289. AN OTHER OF THE SAME . . . . . . . . . . . . . 237

290. THE ANSWERE . . . . . . . . . . . . . . . . . 238

291. THE LOUER COMPLAINETH HIS FAULT, THAT WITH VNGENTLE
WRITING HAD DISPLEASED HIS LADY . . . . . . . . . 239

292. THE LOUER WOUNDED OF CUPIDE, WISHETH HE HAD RATHER
BEN STRIKEN BY DEATH . . . . . . . . . . . . . 241

293. OF WOMENS CHANGEABLE WILL . . . . . . . . . . . 243

294. THE LOUER COMPLAYNETH THE LOSSE OF HIS LADYE . . . 243

295. OF THE GOLDEN MEANE . . . . . . . . . . . . . 244

296. THE PRAISE OF A TRUE FRENDE . . . . . . . . . . 244

297. OF THE VANITIE OF MANS LYFE . . . . . . . . . . 245

298. THE LOUER NOT REGARDED IN EARNEST SUTE, BEING BE-
COME WISER, REFUSETH HER PROFRED LOUE . . . . . 246

299. THE COMPLAINT OF A WOMAN RAUISHED, AND ALSO MOR-
TALLY WOUNDED . . . . . . . . . . . . . . . . 247

300. THE LOUER BEING MADE THRALL BY LOUE, PERCEIUETH
HOW GREAT A LOSSE IS LIBERTYE . . . . . . . . . 247

301. THE DIUERS AND CONTRARIE PASSIONS OF THE LOUER . . 248

302. THE TESTAMENT OF THE HAWTHORNE . . . . . . . . 248

303. THE LOUER IN DISPEIRE LAMENTETH HIS CASE . . . . . 250

304. OF HIS MAISTRESSE .M.B. . . . . . . . . . . . . 251

# CONTENTS

305. THE LOUER COMPLAINETH HIS HARTY LOUE NOT REQUITED  253

306. A PRAISE OF .M.M. . . . . . . . . . . . . . . . 254

307. AN OLD LOUER TO A YONG GENTILWOMAN  . . . . . . 255

308. THE LOUER FORSAKETH HIS VNKINDE LOUE . . . . . . 256

309. THE LOUER PREFERRETH HIS LADY ABOUE ALL OTHER  . . 256

310. THE LOUER LAMENTETH THAT HE WOULD FORGET LOUE, AND
   CAN NOT . . . . . . . . . . . . . . . . . . . 258

VARIANT READINGS AND MISPRINTS (*A — I*)  . . . . . 261

VARIATIONS FROM *A* AND *B* IN ARBER'S REPRINT (1870)  327

INDEX OF FIRST LINES . . . . . . . . . . . . . . 337

# SONGES AND SONETTES,

written by the ryght honorable Lorde
Henry Haward late Earle of Sur=
rey, and other.

Apud Richardum Tottel.
1557.
Cum priuilegio.

## The Printer to the
## Reader.

THat to haue wel written in verse, yea & in small
parcelles, deserueth great praise, the workes of
diuers Latines, Italians, and other, doe proue
sufficiently. That our tong is able in that kynde
to do as praiseworthely as ẙ rest, the honorable stile
of the noble earle of Surrey, and the weightinesse of
the depewitted sir Thomas Wyat the elders verse,
with seuerall graces in sondry good Englishe wri-
ters, doe show abundantly. It resteth nowe (gentle
reder) that thou thinke it not euill doon, to publish,
to the honor of the Englishe tong, and for profit of
the studious of Englishe eloquence, those workes
which the vngentle horders vp of such treasure haue
heretofore enuied thee. And for this point (good re-
der) thine own profit and pleasure, in these presently,
and in moe hereafter, shal answere for my defence. If
parhappes some mislike the statelinesse of stile remo-
ued from the rude skill of common eares: I aske help
of the learned to defend their learned frendes, the au-
thors of this work : And I exhort the vnlearned, by
reding to learne to be more skilfull, and to purge
that swinelike grossenesse, that maketh the swete
maierome not to smell to their delight.

5

10

15

20

25

[1] Descripcion of the restlesse state
of a louer, with sute to his
ladie, to rue on his di-
yng hart.                                                    5

*T*He sonne hath twise brought furth his tender grene,
    And clad the earth in liuely lustinesse:
Ones haue the windes the trees despoiled clene,
And new again begins their cruelnesse,
Since I haue hid vnder my brest the harm                      10
That neuer shall recouer healthfulnesse.
The winters hurt recouers with the warm:
The parched grene restored is with shade.
What warmth (alas) may serue for to disarm
The frosen hart that mine in flame hath made?                15
What colde againe is able to restore
My fresh grene yeares, that wither thus and fade?
Alas, I se, nothing hath hurt so sore,
But time in time reduceth a returne:
In time my harm increaseth more and more,                    20
And semes to haue my cure alwaies in scorne.
Strange kindes of death, in life that I doe trie,
At hand to melt, farre of in flame to burne.
And like as time list to my cure aply,
So doth eche place my comfort cleane refuse.                 25
All thing aliue, that seeth the heauens with eye,
With cloke of night may couer, and excuse
It self from trauail of the dayes vnrest,
Saue I, alas, against all others vse,
That then stirre vp the tormentes of my brest,               30
And curse eche sterre as causer of my fate.
And when the sonne hath eke the dark opprest,
And brought the day, it doth nothing abate
The trauailes of mine endles smart and payn,
For then, as one that hath the light in hate,                35
I wish for night, more couertly to playn,
And me withdraw from euery haunted place,
Lest by my chere my chance appere to playn:
And in my minde I measure pace by pace,
                              𝕬.ii.                    To

[3]

To seke the place where I my self had lost,
That day that I was tangled in the lace,
In semyng slack that knitteth euer most:
But neuer yet the trauaile of my thought                                    5
Of better state coulde catche a cause to bost.
For if I found sometime that I haue sought,
Those sterres by whome I trusted of the porte,
My sayles doe fall, and I aduance right nought,
As ankerd fast, my spretes doe all resorte                                   10
To stande agazed, and sinke in more and more
The deadly harme which she dothe take in sport.
Lo, if I seke, how I doe finde my sore:
And yf I flee I carie with me still
The venomde shaft, whiche dothe his force restore                            15
By hast of flight, and I may plaine my fill
Vnto my selfe, vnlesse this carefull song
Printe in your harte some parcell of my tene
For I, alas, in silence all to long
Of myne olde hurte yet fele the wounde but grene.                            20
Rue on my life: or els your cruell wronge
Shall well appere, and by my death be sene.

## [2] Description of Spring,wherin eche
## thing renewes,saue one-
## lie the louer.                                                             25

The soote season, that bud and blome furth bringes,
With grene hath clad the hill and eke the vale:
The nightingale with fethers new she singes:
The turtle to her make hath tolde her tale:
Somer is come, for euery spray nowe springes,                                30
The hart hath hong his olde hed on the pale:
The buck in brake his winter cote he flinges:
The fishes flote with newe repaired scale:
The adder all her sloughe awaye she slinges:
The swift swalow pursueth the flyes smale:                                   35
The busy bee her honye now she minges:
Winter is worne that was the flowers bale:
And thus I see among these pleasant thinges
Eche care decayes, and yet my sorow springes.

Descripcion

[4]

## [3] Descripcion of the restlesse state of a louer.

When youth had led me halfe the race,
That Cupides scourge me causde to ronne,          5
I loked back to mete the place,
From whence my wery course begonne.
  And then I sawe how my desire
Misguiding me had led the way:
Mine eyen to gredy of their hire,                 10
Had made me lose a better pray.
  For when in sighes I spent the day,
And could not cloke my griefe with game,
The boiling smoke did still bewray
The persaunt heate of secrete flame.              15
  And when salt teares doe bayne my brest,
Where loue his pleasant traines hath sowen
Her bewty hath the fruites opprest,
Ere that the buds were spronge and blowen.
  And when myne eyen dyd styll pursue             20
The flying chace that was their quest,
Their gredy lokes dyd oft renewe.
the hidden wound within my brest.
  When euery loke these chekes might staine,
From deadly pale to glowing red:                  25
By outwarde signes appered plaine,
The woe wherin my hart was fed.
  But all to late loue learneth me,
To painte all kinde of colours new,
To blinde their eyes that els shoulde see,        30
My specled chekes with Cupides hewe.
  And nowe the couert brest I claime,
That worshipt Cupide secretely:
And norished his sacred flame,
From whence no blasing sparkes doe flye.          35

## [4] Description of the fickle affections panges and sleightes of loue.

𝕬.iii.                        Such

[ 5 ]

## Songes.

SVche waiward waies hath loue, that most part in discord
  Our willes do stand, whereby our hartes but seldom doe accord.
    Disceit is his delight, and to begile, and mock
The simple hartes whom he doth strike w̃ froward diuers strok.          5
    He makes the one to rage with golden burning dart,
And doth alay with leaden colde agayn the other hart.
    Whote glemes of burnyng fire, and easy sparkes of flame
In balance of vnegall weight he pondereth by aime.
    From easy forde, where I might wade and passe ful wel,         10
He me withdrawes, and doth me driue into a depe dark hel,
    And me withholdes where I am calde and offred place,
And willes me that my mortall foe I doe beseke of grace:
    He lettes me to pursue a conquest welnere wonne,
To folow where my paines were lost ere that my suite begonne.      15
    So by this meanes I know how soone a hart may turne
From warre to peace, from truce to strife, and so again returne,
    I know how to content my self in others lust,
Of litle stuffe vnto my self to weaue a webbe of trust:
    And how to hide my harmes with soft dissembling chere,         20
When in my face the painted thoughtes would outwardly apere.
    I know how that the blood forsakes the face for dred:
And how by shame it staines again the chekes with flaming red.
    I know vnder the grene the serpent how he lurkes.
The hammer of the restles forge I wote eke how it wurkes.          25
    I know and can by roate the tale that I would tel:
But oft the wordes come furth awrie of him that loueth wel.
    I know in heat and colde the louer how he shakes:
In singing how he doth complain, in slepyng how he wakes:
    To languish without ache, sicklesse for to consume:            30
A thousand thinges for to deuise resoluing all in fume.
    And though he list to se his ladies grace ful sore,
Such pleasures as delight the eye doe not his health restore.
    I know to seke the track of my desired foe,
And feare to finde that I do seke. But chiefly this I know,        35
    That louers must transforme into the thing beloued,
And liue (alas who would beleue?) with sprite from life remoued,
    I know in harty sighes, and laughters of the splene
At once to change my state, my wyll, and eke my coloure clene.
    I know how to deceaue my self with others help:               40
And how the Lion chastised is by beating of the whelp.
    In standyng nere my fire I know how that I freze.
Farre of I burne, in both I wast, and so my life I leze.

                                                              I

I know how loue doth rage vpon a yelding mynde:
How smal a net may take and meash a hart of gentle kinde:
 Or els with seldom swete to season heapes of gall,
Reuiued with a glimse of grace olde sorowes to let fall,    5
 The hidden traines I know, and secret snares of loue:
How soone a loke wil printe a thought, that neuer may remoue.
 The slipper state I know, the sodain turnes from wealth,
The doubtful hope, the certain woe, and sure despeire of health.

## [5] Complaint of a louer, that defied    10
### loue, and was by loue af-
### ter the more tor-
### mented.

WHen sōmer toke in hand the winter to assail,
 With force of might, & vertue gret, his stormy blasts to quail,   15
 And when he clothed faire the earth about with grene,
And euery tree new garmented, that pleasure was to sene:
 Mine hart gan new reuiue, and changed blood dyd stur
Me to withdraw my winter woe, that kept within the dore.
 Abrode, quod my desire: assay to set thy fote,    20
Where thou shalt finde the sauour swete: for sprong is euery rote.
 And to thy health, if thou were sick in any case,
Nothing more good, than in the spring the aire to fele a space.
 There shalt thou here and se all kindes of birdes ywrought,
Well tune their voice ẘ warble smal, as nature hath them tought.   25
 Thus pricked me my lust the sluggish house to leaue:
And for my health I thought it best suche counsail to receaue.
 So on a morow furth, vnwist of any wight,
I went to proue how well it would my heauy burden light.
 And when I felt the aire so pleasant round about,    30
Lorde, to my self how glad I was that I had gotten out.
 There might I se how Ver had euery blossom hent:
And eke the new betrothed birdes ycoupled how they went.
 And in their songes me thought they thanked nature much,
That by her lycence all that yere to loue their happe was such,   35
 Right as they could deuise to chose them feres throughout:
With much reioysing to their Lord thus flew they all about,
 Which when I gan resolue, and in my head conceaue,
What pleasant life, what heapes of ioy these litle birdes receaue,
               And

And sawe in what estate I wery man was brought,
By want of that they had at will, and I reiect at nought:
   Lorde how I gan in wrath vnwisely me demeane.
I curssed loue, and him defied: I thought to turne the streame.    5
   But whan I well behelde he had me vnder awe,
I asked mercie for my fault, that so transgrest his law.
   Thou blinded god (quod I) forgeue me this offense,
Vnwillingly I went about to malice thy pretense.
   Wherewith he gaue a beck, and thus me thought he swore,    10
Thy sorow ought suffice to purge thy faulte, if it were more.
   The vertue of which sounde mine hart did so reuiue,
That I, me thought, was made as hole as any man aliue.
   But here ye may perceiue mine errour all and some,
For that I thought that so it was: yet was it still vndone:    15
   And all that was no more but mine empressed mynde,
That fayne woulde haue some good relefe of Cupide wel assinde.
   I turned home forthwith, and might perceiue it well,
That he agreued was right sore with me for my rebell.
   My harmes haue euer since increased more and more,    20
And I remaine, without his help, vndone for euer more,
   A miror let me be vnto ye louers all:
Striue not with loue: for if ye do, it will ye thus befall,

## [6] Complaint of a louer
## rebuked.    25

*L*Oue, that liueth, and reigneth in my thought,
   That built his seat within my captiue brest,
Clad in the armes, wherin with me he fought,
Oft in my face he doth his banner rest.
She, that me taught to loue, and suffer payne,    30
My doutfull hope, and eke my hote desyre,
With shamefast cloke to shadowe, and refraine,
Her smilyng grace conuerteth straight to yre.
And cowarde Loue then to the hart apace
Taketh his flight, whereas he lurkes, and plaines    35
His purpose lost, and dare not shewe his face.
For my lordes gilt thus faultlesse byde I paynes.
Yet from my lorde shall not my foote remoue.
Swete is his death, that takes his end by loue.

Com-

## [7] Complaint of the louer disdained.

*I* N Ciprus, springes (whereas dame Venus dwelt)
  A well so hote, that whoso tastes the same,
Were he of stone, as thawed yse should melt,         5
And kindled fynde his brest with fired flame.
Whose moyst poyson dissolued hath my hate.
This creeping fire my colde lims so opprest,
That in the hart that harborde freedome late,
Endlesse despeyre longe thraldome hath imprest.     10
An other so colde in frozen yse is founde,
Whose chilling venom of repugnant kynde
The feruent heat doth quenche of Cupides wounde:
And with the spot of change infectes the minde:
Whereof my dere hath tasted, to my paine.        15
My seruice thus is growen into disdaine.

## [8] Description and praise of his loue Geraldine.

*F*Rom Tuskane came my Ladies worthy race:
  Faire Florence was sometyme her auncient seate:     20
The Western yle, whose pleasaunt shore dothe face
Wilde Cambers clifs, did geue her liuely heate:
Fostered she was with milke of Irishe brest:
Her sire, an Erle: her dame, of princes blood.
From tender yeres, in Britain she doth rest,        25
With kinges childe, where she tasteth costly food.
Honsdon did first present her to mine yien:
Bright is her hewe, and Geraldine she hight.
Hampton me taught to wishe her first for mine:
And Windsor, alas, dothe chase me from her sight.    30
Her beauty of kind her vertues from aboue.
Happy is he, that can obtaine her loue.

## [9] The frailtie and hurtfulnes of beautie.

*B*Rittle beautie, that nature made so fraile,       35
  Wherof the gift is small, and short the season,

𝔅                Flow-

[9]

Flowring to day, to morowe apt to faile,
Tickell treasure abhorred of reason,
Daungerous to dele with, vaine, of none auaile,
Costly in keping, past not worthe two peason,     5
Slipper in sliding as is an eles taile,
Harde to attaine, once gotten not geason,
Iewel of ieopardie that perill dothe assaile,
False and vntrue, enticed oft to treason,
Enmy to youth: that moste may I bewaile.     10
Ah bitter swete infecting as the poyson:
Thou farest as frute that with the frost is taken,
To day redy ripe, to morowe all to shaken.

## [10] A complaint by night of the louer<br>not beloued.      15

*A*Las so all thinges nowe doe holde their peace.
   Heauen and earth disturbed in nothing:
The beastes, the ayer, the birdes their song doe cease:
The nightes chare the starres aboute dothe bring:
Calme is the Sea, the waues worke lesse and lesse:     20
So am not I, whom loue alas doth wring,
Bringing before my face the great encrease
Of my desires, whereat I wepe and syng,
In ioye and wo, as in a doutfull ease.
For my swete thoughtes sometyme doe pleasure bring:     25
But by and by the cause of my disease
Geues me a pang, that inwardly dothe sting,
When that I thinke what griefe it is againe,
To liue and lacke the thing should ridde my paine.

## [11] How eche thing saue the louer<br>in spring reuiueth to<br>pleasure.      30

*W*Hen Windsor walles susteyned my wearied arme,
   My hande my chin, to ease my restlesse hed:
The pleasant plot reuested green with warme,     35
The blossomd bowes with lusty Ver yspred,

The

The flowred meades, the wedded birdes so late
Mine eyes discouer: and to my mynde resorte
The ioly woes, the hatelesse shorte debate,
The rakehell lyfe that longes to loues disporte.
Wherewith (alas) the heauy charge of care
Heapt in my brest breakes forth against my will,
In smoky sighes, that ouercast the ayer.
My vapord eyes suche drery teares distill,
The tender spring whiche quicken where they fall,                    10
And I halfebent to throwe me downe withall.

[12] Vow to loue faithfully how-
soeuer he be re-
warded.

S Et me wheras the sunne doth parche the grene,                     15
   Or where his beames do not dissolue the yse:
In temperate heate where he is felt and sene:
In presence prest of people madde or wise.
Set me in hye, or yet in lowe degree:
In longest night, or in the shortest daye:                         20
In clearest skye, or where clowdes thickest be:
In lusty youth, or when my heeres are graye.
Set me in heauen, in earth, or els in hell,
In hyll, or dale, or in the fomyng flood:
Thrall, or at large, aliue where so I dwell:                        25
Sicke, or in health: in euyll fame, or good.
Hers will I be, and onely with this thought
Content my selfe, although my chaunce be nought.

[13] Complaint that his ladie after she
knew of his loue kept her face                                      30
alway hidden from
him.

I Neuer sawe my Ladye laye apart
  Her cornet blacke, in colde nor yet in heate,
Sith first she knew my griefe was growen so great,                  35

**B.ii.**                                    Which

[ 11 ]

Which other fansies driueth from my hart
That to my selfe I do the thought reserue,
The which vnwares did wounde my wofull brest:
But on her face mine eyes mought neuer rest, 5
Yet, sins she knew I did her loue and serue
Her golden tresses cladde alway with blacke,
Her smilyng lokes that hid thus euermore,
And that restraines whiche I desire so sore.
So dothe this cornet gouerne me alacke: 10
In somer, sunne: in winters breath, a frost:
Wherby the light of her faire lokes I lost.

## [14] Request to his loue to ioyne bountie with beautie.

*T*He golden gift that nature did thee geue, 15
  To fasten frendes, and fede them at thy wyll,
With fourme and fauour, taught me to beleue,
How thou art made to shew her greatest skill.
Whose hidden vertues are not so vnknowen,
But liuely domes might gather at the first 20
Where beautye so her perfect seede hath sowen,
Of other graces folow nedes there must.
Now certesse Ladie, sins all this is true,
That from aboue thy gyftes are thus elect:
Do not deface them than with fansies newe, 25
Nor chaunge of mindes let not thy minde infect:
But mercy him thy frende, that doth thee serue,
Who seekes alway thine honour to preserue.

## [15] Prisoned in windsor, he recounteth his pleasure there passed. 30

*S*O cruell prison how coulde betide, alas,
  As proude Windsor? where I in lust and ioye,
With a kinges sonne, my childishe yeres did passe,
In greater feast than Priams sonnes of Troy: 35
Where eche swete place returns a taste full sower,

                                   The

The large grene courtes, where we were wont to houe,
With eyes cast vp into the maydens tower.
And easie sighes, suche as folke drawe in loue:
The stately seates, the ladies bright of hewe:
The daunces shorte, longe tales of great delight:  5
With wordes and lokes, that tygers coulde but rewe,
Where eche of vs did pleade the others right:
The palme play, where, dispoyled for the game,
With dazed eies oft we by gleames of loue,
Haue mist the ball, and got sight of our dame,  10
To baite her eyes, whiche kept the leads aboue:
The grauell grounde, with sleues tyed on the helme:
On fomynge horse, with swordes and frendlye hartes:
With cheare, as though one should another whelme:  15
Where we haue fought, and chased oft with dartes,
With siluer droppes the meade yet spred for ruthe,
In actiue games of nimblenes, and strength,
Where we did straine, trayned with swarmes of youth.
Our tender lymmes, that yet shot vp in length:  20
The secrete groues, which oft we made resounde
Of pleasaunt playnt, and of our ladies prayse,
Recordyng ofte what grace eche one had founde,
What hope of spede, what dreade of long delayes:
The wilde forest, the clothed holtes with grene:  25
With rayns auailed, and swift ybreathed horse,
With crye of houndes, and mery blastes betwene,
Where we did chase the fearfull harte of force,
The wide vales eke, that harborde vs ech night,
Wherwith (alas) reuiueth in my brest  30
The swete accorde: such slepes as yet delight,
The pleasant dreames, the quiet bed of rest:
The secrete thoughtes imparted with such trust:
The wanton talke, the diuers change of play:
The frendship sworne, eche promise kept so iust:  35
Wherwith we past the winter night away.
And, with this thought, the bloud forsakes the face,
The teares berayne my chekes of deadly hewe:
The whiche as sone as sobbyng sighes (alas)
Vpsupped haue, thus I my plaint renewe:  40
O place of blisse, renuer of my woes,
Geue me accompt, where is my noble fere:
Whom in thy walles thou doest eche night enclose,

**B.iii.**          To

[ 13 ]

To other leefe, but vnto me most dere.
Eccho (alas) that dothe my sorow rewe,
Returns therto a hollow sounde of playnte.
Thus I alone, where all my fredome grewe,     5
In prison pyne, with bondage and restrainte,
And with remembrance of the greater greefe
To banishe the lesse, I find my chief releefe.

## [16] The louer comforteth himself with the worthinesse of    10 his loue.

WHen ragyng loue with extreme payne
   Most cruelly distrains my hart:
When that my teares, as floudes of rayne,
Beare witnes of my wofull smart:     15
When sighes haue wasted so my breath,
That I lye at the poynte of death:
  I call to minde the nauye greate,
That the Grekes brought to Troye towne:
And how the boysteous windes did beate    20
Their shyps, and rente their sayles adowne,
Till Agamemnons daughters bloode
Appeasde the goddes, that them withstode.
  And how that in those ten yeres warre,
Full many a bloudye dede was done,    25
And many a lord, that came full farre,
There caught his bane (alas) to sone:
And many a good knight ouerronne,
Before the Grekes had Helene wonne.
  Then thinke I thus: sithe suche repayre,   30
So longe time warre of valiant men,
Was all to winne a ladye fayre:
Shall I not learne to suffer then,
And thinke my life well spent to be,
Seruyng a worthier wight than she?    35
  Therfore I neuer will repent,
But paynes contented stil endure.
For like as when, rough winter spent,
The pleasant spring straight draweth in vre:
                    So

So after ragyng stormes of care
Ioyful at length may be my fare.

## [17] Complaint of the absence of her louer being vpon the sea. 5

*O*Happy dames, that may embrace
    The frute of your delight,
Help to bewaile the wofull case,
And eke the heauy plight 10
Of me, that wonted to reioyce
The fortune of my pleasant choyce:
Good Ladies, help to fill my moorning voyce.
    In ship, freight with rememberance
Of thoughts, and pleasures past, 15
He sailes that hath in gouernance
My life, while it wil last:
With scalding sighes, for lack of gale,
Furdering his hope, that is his sail
Toward me, the swete port of his auail. 20
    Alas, how oft in dreames I se
Those eyes, that were my food,
Which somtime so delited me,
That yet they do me good.
Wherwith I wake with his returne, 25
Whose absent flame did make me burne.
But when I find the lacke, Lord how I mourne?
    When other louers in armes acrosse,
Reioyce their chiefe delight:
Drowned in teares to mourne my losse, 30
I stand the bitter night,
In my window, where I may see,
Before the windes how the cloudes flee.
Lo, what a mariner loue hath made me.
    And in grene waues when the salt flood 35
Doth rise, by rage of winde:
A thousand fansies in that mood
Assayle my restlesse mind.
Alas, now drencheth my swete fo,
That with the spoyle of my hart did go, 40

And

And left me but (alas) why did he so?
  And when the seas waxe calme againe,
To chase fro me annoye.
My doutfull hope doth cause me plaine:                             5
So dreade cuts of my ioye.
Thus is my wealth mingled with wo,
And of ech thought a dout doth growe,
Now he comes, will he come? alas, no no.

## [18] Complaint of a diyng louer re=                            10
### fused vpon his ladies iniust
### mistaking of his
### writyng.

*I* N winters iust returne, when Boreas gan his raigne,
  And euery tree vnclothed fast, as nature taught them plaine:    15
  In misty morning darke, as sheepe are then in holde,
I hyed me fast, it sat me on, my sheepe for to vnfolde.
  And as it is a thing, that louers haue by fittes,
Vnder a palm I heard one crye, as he had lost hys wittes.
  Whose voice did ring so shrill, in vttering of his plaint,      20
That I amazed was to hear, how loue could hym attaint.
  Ah wretched man (quod he) come death, and ridde thys wo:
A iust reward, a happy end, if it may chaunce thee so.
  Thy pleasures past haue wrought thy wo, without redresse.
If thou hadst neuer felt no ioy, thy smart had bene the lesse.    25
  And retchlesse of his life, he gan both sighe and grone,
A rufull thing me thought, it was, to hear him make such mone.
  Thou cursed pen (sayd he) wo worth the bird thee bare,
The man, the knife, and all that made thee, wo be to their share.
  Wo worth the time, and place, where I so could endite.          30
And wo be it yet once agayne, the pen that so can write.
  Vnhappy hand, it had ben happy time for me,
If, when to write thou learned first, vnioynted hadst thou be.
  Thus cursed he himself, and euery other wight,
Saue her alone whom loue him bound to serue both day & night.     35
  Which when I heard, and saw, how he himselfe fordid,
Against the ground with bloudy strokes, himself euen there to rid:
  Had ben my heart of flint, it must haue melted tho:
                                                          For

[ 16 ]

For in my life I neuer saw a man so full of wo.
    With teares, for his redresse, I rashly to him ran,
And in my armes I caught him fast, and thus I spake hym than.
    What wofull wight art thou, that in such heauy case        5
Tormentes thy selfe with such despite, here in this desert place?
    Wherwith, as all agast, fulfild wyth ire, and dred,
He cast on me a staring loke, with colour pale, and ded.
    Nay, what art thou (quod he) that in this heauy plight,
Doest finde me here, most wofull wretch, that life hath in despight?  10
    I am (quoth I) but poore, and simple in degre:
A shepardes charge I haue in hand, vnworthy though I be.
    With that he gaue a sighe, as though the skye should fall:
And lowd (alas) he shryked oft, and Shepard, gan he call,
    Come, hie the fast at ones, and print it in thy hart:        15
So thou shalt know, and I shall tell the, giltlesse how I smart.
    His backe against the tree, sore febled all with faint,
With weary sprite he stretcht him vp: and thus hee told his plaint.
    Ones in my hart (quoth he) it chanced me to loue
Such one, in whom hath nature wrought, her cūning for to proue.   20
    And sure I can not say, but many yeres were spent,
With such good will so recompenst, as both we were content.
    Wherto then I me bound, and she likewise also,
The sonne should runne his course awry, ere we this faith forgo.
    Who ioied then, but I? who had this worldes blisse?      25
Who might compare a life to mine, that neuer thought on this?
    But dwelling in thys truth, amid my greatest ioy,
Is me befallen a greater losse, than Priam had of Troy.
    She is reuersed clene: and beareth me in hand,
That my desertes haue giuē her cause to break thys faithful band.  30
    And for my iust excuse auaileth no defense.
Now knowest thou all: I can no more, but shepard, hye the hense:
    And giue him leaue to die, that may no lenger liue:
Whose record lo I claime to haue, my death, I doe forgiue.
    And eke when I am gone, be bolde to speake it plain:     35
Thou hast seen dye the truest man, that euer loue did pain.
    Wherwith he turned him round, and gasping oft for breath,
Into his armes a tree he raught, and sayd, welcome my death:
    Welcome a thousand fold, now dearer vnto me,
Than should, without her loue to liue, an emperour to be.     40
    Thus, in this wofull state, he yelded vp the ghost:
And little knoweth his lady, what a louer she hath lost.
    Whose death when I beheld, no maruail was it, right

𝕮.i.                 For

For pitie though my heart did blede, to see so piteous sight.
  My blood from heat to colde oft changed wonders sore:
A thousand troubles there I found I neuer knew before.
  Twene dread, and dolour so my sprites were brought in feare,      5
That long it was ere I could call to minde, what I did there,
  But, as eche thing hath end, so had these paynes of mine:
The furies past, and I my wits restord by length of time.
  Then, as I could deuise, to seke I thought it best,
Where I might finde some worthy place, for such a corse to rest.    10
  And in my mind it came: from thence not farre away,
Where Chreseids loue, king Priams sōne, y̆ worthy Troilus lay.
  By him I made his tomb, in token he was treew:
And, as to him belonged well, I couered it with bleew.
  Whose soule, by Angels power, departed not so sone,              15
But to the heauens, lo it fled, for to receiue his dome.

## [19] Complaint of the absence of
## her louer being vpon
## the sea.

*G*Ood Ladies, ye that haue your pleasures in exile,               20
  Step in your foote, come take a place, & moorne with me a while
  And such as by their lordes do set but little price,
Let them sit still: it skilles them not what chance come on y̆ dice.
  But ye whom loue hath bound by ordre of desire
To loue your lords, whose good desertes none other wold require:   25
  Come ye yet ones again, and set your foote by mine,
Whose wofull plight and sorrowes great no tong may wel define.
  My loue and lord, alas, in whom consistes my wealth,
Hath fortune sent to passe the seas in hazarde of his health.
  Whome I was wont tembrace with well contented minde              30
Is now amidde the foming floods at pleasure of the winde.
  Where God well him preserue, and sone him home me send.
Without which hope, my life (alas) wer shortly at an end.
  Whose absence yet, although my hope doth tell me plaine,
With short returne he comes anon, yet ceasith not my payne.        35
  The fearfull dreames I haue, oft times do greue me so:
That when I wake, I lye in doute, where they be true, or no.
  Sometime the roring seas (me semes) do grow so hye:
That my dere Lord (ay me alas) me thinkes I se him die.
  Another time the same doth tell me: he is cumne:                 40
                                                          And

And playeng, where I shall him find with his faire little sonne.
  So forth I go apace to se that leefsom sight.
And with a kisse, me think, I say: welcome my lord, my knight:
  Welcome my swete, alas, the stay of my welfare.                    5
Thy presence bringeth forth a truce atwixt me, & my care.
  Then liuely doth he loke, and salueth me againe,
And saith: my dere, how is it now, that you haue all thys paine?
  Wherwith the heauy cares: that heapt are in my brest,
Breake forth, and me dischargen clene of all my huge vnrest.        10
  But when I me awake, and finde it but a dreme,
The anguishe of my former wo beginneth more extreme:
  And me tormenteth so, that vnneath may I finde
Sum hidden place, wherein to slake the gnawing of my mind.
  Thus euery way you se, with absence how I burn:                    15
And for my wound no cure I find, but hope of good return.
  Saue whan I think, by sowre how swete is felt the more:
It doth abate som of my paines, that I abode before.
  And then vnto my self I say: when we shal meete.
But litle while shall seme this paine, the ioy shal be so sweete.    20
  Ye windes, I you coniure in chiefest of your rage,
That ye my lord me safely sende, my sorowes to asswage:
  And that I may not long abide in this excesse.
Do your good will, to cure a wight, that liueth in distresse.

## [20] A praise of his loue: wherin he                              25
## reproueth them that compare
## their Ladies with his.

GEue place ye louers, here before
  That spent your bostes and bragges in vaine:
My Ladies beawtie passeth more                                       30
The best of yours, I dare well sayen,
Than doth the sonne, the candle light:
Or brightest day, the darkest night.
  And thereto hath a trothe as iust,
As had Penelope the fayre.                                           35
For what she saith, ye may it trust,
As it by writing sealed were.
And vertues hath she many moe,
Than I with pen haue skill to showe.
  I coulde rehearse, if that I wolde,                                40
The whole effect of natures plaint,

When she had lost the perfit mold,
The like to whom she could not paint:
With wringyng handes howe she dyd cry,
And what she said, I know it, I.                          5
   I knowe, she swore with ragyng mynd:
Her kingdom onely set apart,
There was no losse, by lawe of kind,
That could haue gone so nere her hart.
And this was chiefly all her payne:                       10
She coulde not make the lyke agayne.
   Sith nature thus gaue her the prayse,
To be the chiefest worke she wrought:
In faith, me thinke, some better waies
On your behalfe might well be sought,                    15
Then to compare (as ye haue done)
To matche the candle with the sonne.


## [21] To the Ladie that
## scorned her                                            20
## louer.

*A*Lthough I had a check,
   To geue the mate is hard.
For I haue found a neck,
To kepe my men in gard.
And you that hardy ar                                     25
To geue so great assay
Vnto a man of warre,
To driue his men away,
I rede you, take good hede,
And marke this foolish verse:                             30
For I will so prouide,
That I will haue your ferse.
And when your ferse is had,
And all your warre is done:
Then shall your selfe be glad                             35
To ende that you begon.
For yf by chance I winne
Your person the in feeld:
To late then come you in

                        Your

Your selfe to me to yeld.
For I will vse my power,
As captain full of might,
And such I will deuour,
As vse to shew me spight.                                    5
  And for because you gaue
Me checke in such degre,
This vantage loe I haue:
Now checke, and garde to the.                               10
  Defend it, if thou may:
Stand stiffe, in thine estate.
For sure I will assay,
If I can giue the mate.

## [22] A warning to the louer                              15
## how he is abused by
## his loue.

*T*O dearely had I bought my grene and youthfull yeres,
  If in mine age I could not finde when craft for loue apperes.
  And seldom though I come in court among the rest:          20
Yet can I iudge in colours dim as depe as can the best.
  Where grefe tormentes the man that suffreth secret smart,
To breke it forth vnto som frend it easeth well the hart.
  So standes it now with me for my beloued frend.
This case is thine for whom I fele such torment of my minde.  25
  And for thy sake I burne so in my secret brest
That till thou know my hole disseyse my hart can haue no rest.
  I see how thine abuse hath wrested so thy wittes,
That all it yeldes to thy desire, and folowes the by fittes.
  Where thou hast loued so long with hart and all thy power.  30
I se thee fed with fayned wordes, thy fredom to deuour.
  I know, (though she say nay, and would it well withstand)
When in her grace thou held the most, she bare the but in hand.
  I see her pleasant chere in chiefest of thy suite:
Whan thou art gone, I se him come, that gathers vp the fruite. 35
  And eke in thy respect I se the base degre
Of him to whom she gaue the hart that promised was to the.
  I se (what would you more) stode neuer man so sure
On womans word, but wisedome would mistrust it to endure.
                    **C.iii.**                    The

## [23] The forsaken louer descri-
## beth & forsaketh loue.

O Lothsome place where I
   Haue sene and herd my dere,          5
When in my hert her eye
Hath made her thought appere,
By glimsing with such grace
As fortune it ne would,
That lasten any space          10
Betwene vs lenger should.
   As fortune did auance,
To further my desire:
Euen so hath fortunes chance
Throwen all ammiddes the myre.      15
And that I haue deserued
With true and faithful hart,
Is to his handes reserued
That neuer felt the smart.
   But happy is that man,        20
That scaped hath the griefe
That loue well teche him can
By wanting his reliefe.
A scourge to quiet mindes
It is, who taketh hede,         25
A comon plage that bindes,
A trauell without mede.
   This gift it hath also,
Who so enioies it most,
A thousand troubles grow      30
To vexe his weried ghost.
And last it may not long
The truest thing of all
And sure the greatest wrong
That is within this thrall.        35
   But sins thou desert place
Canst giue me no accompt
Of my desired grace
That I to haue was wont,
farewel thou hast me tought      40

                            To

To thinke me not the furst,
That loue hath set aloft.
And casten in the dust.

## [24] The louer describes his restlesse state.

*A*S oft as I behold and se
   The soueraigne bewtie that me bound:
The nier my comfort is to me,
Alas the fresher is my wound.
  As flame doth quenche by rage of fire,
And running stremes consume by raine:
So doth the sight, that I desire,
Appease my grief and deadely paine,
  First when I saw those cristall streames,
whose bewtie made my mortall wound:
I little thought within her beames
So swete a venom to haue found.
  But wilfull will did prick me forth,
And blind Cupide did whippe and guide:
Force made me take my griefe in worth:
My fruitles hope my harme did hide.
  As cruell waues full oft be found
Against the rockes to rore and cry:
So doth my hart full oft rebound
Ageinst my brest full bitterly.
  I fall, and se mine own decay,
As on that beares flame in hys brest,
Forgets in paine to put away
The thing that bredeth mine vnrest.

## [25] The louer excuseth himself of suspected change.

*T*Hough I regarded not
   The promise made by me,
   or passed not to spot
My faith and honeste:

𝕮.iiii.       Yet

# Songes

Yet were my fancie strange,
And wilfull will to wite,
If I sought now to change
A falkon for a kite.                                    5
    All men might well dispraise
My wit and enterprise,
If I estemed a pese
Aboue a perle in price:
Or iudged the oule in sight                             10
The sparehauke to excell,
which flieth but in the night,
As all men know right well:
    Or if I sought to saile
Into the brittle port,                                  15
where anker hold doth faile,
To such as doe resort,
And leaue the hauen sure,
where blowes no blustring winde,
Nor fickelnesse in vre                                  20
So farforth as I finde.
    No, thinke me not so light,
Nor of so chorlish kinde,
Though it lay in my might
My bondage to vnbinde,                                  25
That I would leue the hinde
To hunt the ganders fo.
No no I haue no minde
To make exchanges so:
    Nor yet to change at all.                           30
For think it may not be
That I should seke to fall
From my felicite,
Desyrous for to win,
And loth for to forgo,                                  35
Or new change to begin:
How may all this be so?
    The fire it can not freze:
For it is not his kinde,
Nor true loue cannot lese                               40
The constance of the minde.
Yet as sone shall the fire
want heat to blaze and burn,

                                                    As

[ 24 ]

As I in such desire,
Haue once a thought to turne.

[26] A carelesse man, scorning and
describing, the suttle v=
sage of women to= 5
warde their lo=
uers.

WRapt in my carelesse cloke, as I walke to and fro:
I se, how loue cā shew, what force there reigneth in his bow 10
And how he shoteth eke, a hardy hart to wound:
And where he glanceth by agayne, that litle hurt is found.
For seldom is it sene, he woundeth hartes alike.
The tone may rage, when tothers loue is often farre to seke.
All this I se, with more: and wonder thinketh me: 15
Howe he can strike the one so sore, and leaue the other fre.
I se, that wounded wight, that suffreth all this wrong:
How he is fed with yeas, and nayes, and liueth all to long.
In silence though I kepe such secretes to my self:
Yet do I se, how she somtime doth yeld a loke by stelth: 20
As though it seemd, ywys I will not lose the so.
When in her hart so swete a thought did neuer truely go.
Then say I thus: alas, that man is farre from blisse:
That doth receiue for his relief none other gayn, but this.
And she, that fedes him so, I fele, and finde it plain: 25
Is but to glory in her power, that ouer such can reign.
Nor are such graces spent, but when she thinkes, that he,
A weried man is fully bent such fansies to let flie:
Then to retain him stil she wrasteth new her grace,
And smileth lo, as though she would forthwith the man embrace. 30
But when the proofe is made to try such lokes withall:
He findeth then the place all voyde, and fraighted full of gall.
Lorde what abuse is this? who can such women praise?
That for their glory do deuise to vse such crafty wayes.
I, that among the rest do sit, and mark the row, 35
Fynde, that in her is greater craft, then is in twenty mo.
Whose tender yeres, alas, with wyles so well are spedde:
What will she do, when hory heares are powdred in her hedde?
D.i.                    The

[ 25 ]

## [27] The meanes to attain happy life.

*M*Artiall, the thinges that do attayn
The happy life, be these, I finde.                5
The richesse left, not got with pain:
The frutefull ground: the quiet mynde:
The egall frend, no grudge, no strife:
No charge of rule, nor gouernance:
Without disease the healthfull lyfe:              10
The houshold of continuance:
The meane diet, no delicate fare:
Trew wisdom ioyned with simplenesse:
The night discharged of all care,
Where wine the wit may not oppresse:              15
The faithful wife, without debate:·
Suche slepes, as may begyle the night:
Contented with thine owne estate,
Ne wish for death, ne feare his might.

## [28] Praise of meane and constant estate.

*O*F thy lyfe, Thomas, this compasse well mark:   20
Not aye with full sayles the hye seas to beat:
Ne by coward dred, in shonning stormes dark,
On shalow shores thy keel in perill freat.        25
Who so gladly halseth the golden meane,
Voyde of dangers aduisdly hath his home
Not with lothsom muck, as a den vncleane:
Nor palacelyke, wherat disdayn may glome.
The lofty pyne the great winde often riues:       30
With violenter swey falne turrets stepe:
Lightninges assault the hye mountains, and cliues,
A hart well stayd, in ouerthwartes depe,
Hopeth amendes: in swete, doth feare the sowre.
God, that sendeth, withdraweth winter sharp.      35
Now ill, not aye thus: once Phebus to lowre
With bow vnbent shall cesse, and frame to harp.
His voyce. In straite estate appere thou stout:
And so wisely, when lucky gale of winde

All

All thy puft sailes shall fil, loke well about:
Take in a ryft: hast is wast, profe doth finde.

## [29] Praise of certain psalmes
### of Dauid,translated by
### sir. T. w. the elder.

5

*T*He great Macedon, that out of Persie chased
   Darius, of whose huge power all Asie rong,
In the rich ark dan Homers rimes he placed,
Who fayned gestes of heathen princes song.
What holy graue? what worthy sepulture
To Wiattes Psalmes should Christians then purchase?
Where he doth paint the liuely faith, and pure,
The stedfast hope, the swete returne to grace
Of iust Dauid, by perfite penitence.
Where rulers may se in a mirrour clere
The bitter frute of false concupiscence:
How Iewry bought Vrias death full dere.
In princes hartes gods scourge imprinted depe,
Ought thcm awake, out of their sinfull slepe.

10

15

20

## [30] Of the death of the same
### sir. T. w.

*D*Yuers thy death doe diuersly bemone.
   Some, that in presence of thy liuelyhed
Lurked, whose brestes enuy with hate had swolne,
Yeld Ceasars teares vpon Pompeius hed.
Some, that watched with the murdrers knife,
With egre thirst to drink thy giltlesse blood,
Whose practise brake by happy ende of lyfe,
Wepe enuious teares to heare thy fame so good.
But I, that knew what harbred in that hed:
What vertues rare were temperd in that brest:
Honour the place, that such a iewell bred,
And kisse the ground, whereas thy corse doth rest,
With vapord eyes: from whence such streames auayl,
As Pyramus dyd on Thisbes brest bewail.

25

30

35

                            **D.ii.**        Of

## [31] Of the same.

W. resteth here, that quick could neuer rest:
  Whose heauenly giftes encreased by disdayn,
And vertue sank the deper in his brest.          5
Such profit he by enuy could obtain.
  A hed, where wisdom misteries did frame:
Whose hammers bet styll in that liuely brayn,
As on a stithe: where that some work of fame
Was dayly wrought, to turne to Britaines gayn.   10
  A visage, stern, and myld: where bothe did grow,
Vice to contemne, in vertue to reioyce:
Amid great stormes, whom grace assured so,
To lyue vpright, and smile at fortunes choyce.
  A hand, that taught, what might be sayd in ryme:   15
That reft Chaucer the glory of his wit:
A mark, the which (vnparfited, for time)
Some may approche, but neuer none shall hit.
  A toung, that serued in forein realmes his king:
Whose courteous talke to vertue did enflame.   20
Eche noble hart: a worthy guide to bring
Our English youth, by trauail, vnto fame.
  An eye, whose iudgement none affect could blinde,
Frendes to allure, and foes to reconcile:
Whose persing loke did represent a mynde   25
With vertue fraught, reposed, voyd of gyle.
  A hart, where drede was neuer so imprest,
To hyde the thought, that might the trouth auance:
In neyther fortune loft, nor yet represt,
To swell in wealth, or yeld vnto mischance.   30
  A valiant corps, where force, and beawty met:
Happy, alas, to happy, but for foes:
Liued, and ran the race, that nature set:
Of manhodes, shape where she the molde did lose.
  But to the heauens that simple soule is fled:   35
Which left with such, as couet Christ to know,
Witnesse of faith, that neuer shall be ded:
Sent for our helth, but not receiued so.
Thus, for our gilte, this iewel haue we lost:
The earth his bones, the heauens possesse his gost.   40
        Of

## [32] Of Sardinapalus dishonora-
## ble life,and miserable
## death.

*T*Hassirian king in peace, with foule desire,          5
  And filthy lustes, that staynd his regall hart
In warre that should set princely hartes on fire:
Did yeld, vanquisht for want of marciall art.
The dint of swordes from kisses semed strange:
And harder, than his ladies syde, his targe:          10
From glutton feastes, to souldiars fare a change:
His helmet, farre aboue a garlands charge.
Who scace the name of manhode did retayn,
Drenched in slouth, and womanish delight,
Feble of sprite, impacient of pain:          15
When he had lost his honor, and his right:
Proud, time of wealth, in stormes appalled with drede,
Murthered himself, to shew some manful dede.

## [33] How no age is content with his
## own estate,& how the age of          20
## children is the happiest,if
## they had skill to vn-
## derstand it.

*L*Ayd in my quiet bed, in study as I were,
  I saw within my troubled head, a heape of thoughtes appere:          25
  And euery thought did shew so liuely in myne eyes,
That now I sighed, & thē I smilde, as cause of thought doth ryse.
  I saw the lytle boy in thought, how oft that he
Did wish of god, to scape the rod, a tall yongman to be.
  The yongman eke that feles, his bones with paines opprest,          30
How he would be a rich olde man, to lyue, and lye at rest.
  The rich old man that sees his end draw on so sore,
How he would be a boy agayn, to liue so much the more.
  Wherat full oft I smilde, to se, how all these three,
From boy to man, from man to boy, would chop & change degree.          35

𝕯.iii.          And

[ 29 ]

And musyng thus I thynk, the case is very strange,
That man from welth, to lyue in wo, doth euer seke to change.
   Thus thoughtfull as I lay, I saw my wytherd skyn,
How it doth show my dented chewes, the flesh was worne so thyn:    5
   And eke my tothelesse chaps, the gates of my rightway,
That opes and shuts, as I do speake, doe thus vnto me say:
   Thy white and hoarish heares, the messengers of age,
That shew, like lines of true belief, that this life doth asswage,
   Byds thee lay hand, and fele them hanging on thy chin:    10
The whiche do write two ages past, the third now comming in.
   Hang vp therfore the bit of thy yong wanton tyme:
And thou that therin beaten art, the happiest life define.
   Wherat I sighed, and sayd, farewell, my wonted ioy:
Trusse vp thy pack, and trudge from me to euery litle boy:    15
   And tell them thus from me, theyr tyme most happy is:
If, to their time, they reason had to know the trueth of this.

## [34] Bonum est mihi quod humiliasti me.

*T*He stormes are past these cloudes are ouerblowne,    20
  And humble chere great rygour hath represt:
For the defaute is set a paine foreknowne,
And pacience graft in a determed brest.
And in the hart where heapes of griefes were growne,
The swete reuenge hath planted mirth and rest,    25
No company so pleasant as myne owne.
Thraldom at large hath made this prison fre,
Danger well past remembred workes delight:
Of lingring doutes such hope is sprong pardie,
That nought I finde displeasaunt in my sight:    30
But when my glasse presented vnto me.
The curelesse wound that bledeth day and nyght,
To think (alas) such hap should graunted be
Vnto a wretch that hath no hart to fight,
To spill that blood that hath so oft bene shed,    35
For Britannes sake (alas) and now is ded.

## [35] Exhortacion to learne by o= thers trouble.

My

*M*Y Ratclif, when thy rechlesse youth offendes:
   Receue thy scourge by others chastisement.
For such callyng, when it workes none amendes:
Then plages are sent without aduertisement.          5
Yet Salomon sayd, the wronged shall recure:
But Wiat said true, the skarre doth aye endure.

## [36] The fansie of a weried
## louer.

*T*He fansy, which that I haue serued long,         10
   That hath alway bene enmy to myne ease,
Semed of late to rue vpon my wrong,
And bad me flye the cause of my misease.
And I forthwith dyd prease out of the throng,
That thought by flight my painfull hart to please     15
Som other way: tyll I saw faith more strong:
And to my self I sayd: alas, those dayes
In vayn were spent, to runne the race so long.
And with that thought, I met my guyde, that playn
Out of the way wherin I wandred wrong,         20
Brought me amiddes the hylles, in base Bullayn:
Where I am now, as restlesse to remayn,
Against my will, full pleased with my payn.

                                 𝔇.iiii.

# *SVRREY.*

*Songes.*

## [37] The louer for shamefastnesse hideth his desire within his faith= full hart.

*T*He longe loue, that in my thought I harber,     5
  And in my hart doth kepe his residence,
Into my face preaseth with bold pretence,
And there campeth, displaying his banner.
She that me learns to loue, and to suffer,
And willes that my trust, and lustes negligence     10
Be reined by reason, shame, and reuerence,
With his hardinesse takes displeasure.
Wherwith loue to the hartes forest he fleeth,
Leauyng his enterprise with paine and crye,
And there him hideth and not appeareth.     15
What may I do? when my maister feareth,
But in the field with him to liue and dye,
For good is the life, endyng faithfully.

## [38] The louer waxeth wiser, and will not die for affe=     20
## ction

*Y* Et was I neuer of your loue agreued,
  Nor neuer shall, while that my life doth last:
But of hatyng my self, that date is past,
And teares continual sore haue me weried.     25
I will not yet in my graue be buried,
Nor on my tombe your name haue fixed fast,
As cruel cause, that did my sprite sone hast.
From thunhappy boones by great sighes stirred.
Then if an hart of amorous fayth and will     30
Content your minde withouten doyng grief:
Please it you so to this to do relief.
If otherwise you seke for to fulfill
Your wrath: you erre, and shal not as you wene,
And you your self the cause therof haue bene.     35

The

[ 32 ]

## [39] The abused louer seeth his foly, and entendeth to trust no more.

W As neuer file yet half so well yfiled,                    5
  To file a file for any smithes intent,
As I was made a filyng instrument,
To frame other, while that I was begiled.
But reason, loe, hath at my foly smiled,
And pardoned me, sins that I me repent              10
Of my lost yeres, and of my time mispent.
For youth led me, and falshod me misguided.
Yet, this trust I haue of great apparence:
Sins that disceit is ay returnable,
Of verye force it is agreable,                              15
That therwithall be done the recompence.
Then gile begiled playnd should be neuer,
And the reward is little trust for euer.

## [40] The louer describeth his being striken with sight of his loue.                    20

*T*He liuely sparkes, that issue from those eyes,
  Against the which there vaileth no defence,
Haue perst my hart, and done it none offence,
With quakyng pleasure, more then once or twise.    25
Was neuer man could any thing deuise,
Sunne beames to turne with so great vehemence
To dase mans sight, as by their bright presence
Dased am I, much like vnto the gise
Of on striken with dint of lightenyng,             30
Blind with the stroke, and erryng here and there.
So call I for helpe, I not when, nor where,
The payne of my fall paciently bearyng.
For streight after the blase (as is no wonder)
Of deadly noyse heare I the fearfull thunder.      35

                            ℭ                    The

[ 33 ]

## [41] The waueryng louer wylleth, and dreadeth,to moue his desire.

SVch vain thought, as wonted to mislead me 5
  In desert hope by well assured mone,
Makes me from company to liue alone,
In folowyng her whom reason bids me fle.
And after her my hart would faine be gone:
But armed sighes my way do stop anone, 10
Twixt hope and dread lockyng my libertie.
So fleeth she by gentle crueltie.
Yet as I gesse vnder disdainfull brow
One beame of ruth is in her cloudy loke:
Which comfortes the mind, that erst for fear shoke. 15
That bolded straight the way then seke I how
To vtter forth the smart I bide within:
But such it is, I not how to begyn.

## [42] The louer hauing dreamed enioy-ing of his loue,complaineth that the dreame is not either longer or truer.
20

VNstable dreame, accordyng to the place,
  Be stedfast ones, or els at least be true.
By tasted swetenesse, make me not to rew 25
The soden losse of thy false fained grace.
By good respect in such a dangerous case
Thou broughtest not her into these tossing seas,
But madest my sprite to liue my care tencrease,
My body in tempest her delight timbrace. 30
The body dead, the sprite had his desire.
Painelesse was thone, the other in delight.
Why then alas did it not kepe it right,
But thus return to leape in to the fire:
And where it was at wishe, could not remayne? 35
Such mockes of dreames do turne to deadly payne.
                            The

## [43] The louer vnhappy biddeth happy louers reioice in Maie, while he waileth that moneth to him most vnlucky.

*Y* E that in loue finde luck and swete abundance,
  And lyue in lust of ioyfull iolitie,
Aryse for shame, do way your sluggardy:
Arise I say, do May some obseruance:
Let me in bed lye, dreamyng of mischance.
Let me remember my missehappes vnhappy,
That me betide in May most commonly:
As one whom loue list little to aduance.
Stephan said true, that my natiuitie
Mischanced was with the ruler of May.
He gest (I proue) of that the veritie.
In May my wealth, and eke my wittes, I say,
Haue stand so oft in such perplexitie.
Ioye: let me dreame of your felicitie.

## [44] The louer confesseth him in loue with Phillis.

*I* F waker care: if sodayn pale colour:
  If many sighes, with litle speach to plaine:
Now ioye, now wo: if they my chere distayne:
For hope of small, if much to fear therfore,
To haste, or slack: my pace to lesse, or more:
Be signe of loue: then do I loue agayne.
If thou aske whom: sure sins I did refrayne
Brunet, that set my welth in such a rore,
Thunfayned chere of Phillis hath the place,
That Brunet had: she hath, and euer shall:
She from my self now hath me in her grace:
She hath in hand my wit, my will, and all:
My hart alone welworthy she doth stay,
Without whose helpe skant do I liue a day.
𝕮.ii.

Of

[45] Of others fained sorrow, and
the louers fained
mirth.

CEsar, when that the traytour of Egypt                           5
  With thonorable hed did him present,
Coueryng his hartes gladnesse, did represent
Plaint with his teares outward, as it is writ.
Eke Hannibal, when fortune him outshyt
Clene from his reigne, and from all his entent,                10
Laught to his folke, whom sorow did torment,
His cruel despite for to disgorge and quit.
So chanceth me, that euery passion
The minde hideth by colour contrary,
With fayned visage, now sad, now mery.                         15
Wherby, if that I laugh at any season:
It is because I haue none other way
To cloke my care, but vnder sport and play.

[46] Of change in minde.

ECHe man me telth, I change most my deuise:                     20
  And, on my faith, me thinke it good reason
To change purpose, like after the season.
For in ech case to kepe still one guise
Is mete for them, that would be taken wise.
And I am not of such maner condicion:                          25
But treated after a diuers fashion:
And therupon my diuersnesse doth rise.
But you, this diuersnesse that blamen most,
Change you no more, but still after one rate
Treat you me well: and kepe you in that state.                 30
And while with me doth dwell this weried gost,
My word nor I shall not be variable,
But alwaies one, your owne both firme and stable.

[47] How the louer perisheth in his
delight,as the flie in                                          35
the fire.

Some

[ 36 ]

S Ome fowles there be, that haue so perfit sight
   Against the sunne their eies for to defend:
And some, because the light doth them offend,
Neuer appeare, but in the darke, or night.
Other reioyce, to se the fire so bryght,           5
And wene to play in it, as they pretend:
But find contrary of it, that they intend.
Alas, of that sort may I be, by right.
For to withstand her loke I am not able:      10
Yet can I not hide me in no dark place:
So foloweth me remembrance of that face:
That with my teary eyn, swolne, and vnstable,
My desteny to beholde her doth me lead:
And yet I knowe, I runne into the glead.      15

## [48] Against his tong that failed to
## vtter his sutes.

B Ecause I still kept thee fro lyes, and blame,
   And to my power alwayes thee honoured,
Vnkind tongue, to yll hast thou me rendred,    20
For such desert to do me wreke and shame.
In nede of succour most when that I am,
To aske reward: thou standst like one afraied,
Alway most cold: and if one word be sayd,
As in a dreame, vnperfit is the same.      25
And ye salt teares, agaynst my wyll eche nyght,
That are wyth me, when I would be alone:
Then are ye gone, when I should make my mone.
And ye so ready sighes, to make me shright,
Then are ye slacke, when that ye should outstart.    30
And onely doth my loke declare my hart.

## [49] Description of the contra-
## rious passions in a
## louer.

I Find no peace, and all my warre is done:    35
  I feare, and hope: I burne, and frese like yse:

𝕮.iii.           I

I flye aloft, yet can I not arise:
And nought I haue, and all the worlde I season.
That lockes nor loseth, holdeth me in pryson,
And holdes me not, yet can I scape no wise:                    5
Nor lettes me lyue, nor dye, at my deuise,
And yet of death it geueth me occasion.
Without eye I se, without tong I playne:
I wish to perysh, yet I aske for helth:
I loue another, and thus I hate my selfe.                      10
I fede me in sorow, and laugh in all my payne.
Lo, thus displeaseth me both death and life.
And my delight is causer of this strife.

X

## [50] The louer compareth his state
## to a shippe in perilous storme                              15
## tossed on the sea.

*M*Y galley charged with forgetfulnesse,
    Through sharpe seas, in winter nightes doth passe,
Twene rocke, and rocke: and eke my fo (alas)
That is my lord, stereth with cruelnesse:                      20
And euery houre, a thought in readinesse,
As though that death were light, in such a case.
An endlesse wynd doth teare the sayle apace
Of forced sighes, and trusty fearfulnesse.
A rayne of teares, a clowde of darke disdayne                  25
Haue done the weried coardes great hinderance,
Wrethed with errour, and wyth ignorance.
The starres be hidde, that leade me to this payne.
Drownde is reason that should be my comfort:
And I remayne, dispearyng of the port.                         30

## [51] Of douteous loue.

*A*Visyng the bright beames of those fayre eyes,
    Where he abides that mine oft moistes and washeth:
The weried mynd streight from the hart departeth,
To rest within hys worldly Paradise,                           35
                       And

And bitter findes the swete, vnder this gyse.
What webbes there he hath wrought, well he perceaueth
Wherby then with him self on loue he playneth,
That spurs wyth fire, and brydleth eke with yse.          5
In such extremity thus is he brought:
Frosen now cold, and now he standes in flame:
Twixt wo, and welth: betwixt earnest, and game:
With seldome glad, and many a diuers thought:
In sore repentance of hys hardinesse.                     10
Of such a roote lo cometh frute frutelesse.

[52] The louer sheweth how he is
        forsaken of such as he som-
            time enioyed.

*T*Hey flee from me, that somtime did me seke            15
    With naked fote stalkyng within my chamber.
Once haue I seen them gentle, tame, and meke,
That now are wild, and do not once remember
That sometyme they haue put them selues in danger,
To take bread at my hand, and now they range,           20
Busily sekyng in continuall change.
    Thanked be fortune, it hath bene otherwise
Twenty tymes better: but once especiall,
In thinne aray, after a pleasant gyse,
When her loose gowne did from her shoulders fall,        25
And she me caught in her armes long and small,
And therwithall, so swetely did me kysse,
And softly sayd: deare hart, how like you this?
    It was no dreame: for I lay broade awakyng.
But all is turnde now through my gentlenesse.            30
Into a bitter fashion of forsakyng:
And I haue leaue to go of her goodnesse,
And she also to vse newfanglenesse.
But, sins that I vnkyndly so am serued:
How like you this, what hath she now deserued?           35

[53] To a ladie to answere directly
        with yea or nay.

                                            Madame

[ 39 ]

*M*Adame, withouten many wordes:
  Once I am sure, you will, or no.
And if you will: then leaue your boordes,
And vse your wit, and shew it so:                                    5
For with a beck you shall me call.
And if of one, that burns alway,
Ye haue pity or ruth at all:
Answer hym fayer with yea, or nay.
If it be yea: I shall be faine.                                     10
Yf it be nay: frendes, as before.
You shall another man obtayn:
And I mine owne, and yours no more.


[54] To his loue whom he
        had kissed against                                         15
              her will.


*A*Las, Madame, for stealing of a kisse,
  Haue I so much your mynde therin offended?
Or haue I done so greuously amisse:
That by no meanes, it may not be amended?                           20
Reuenge you then, the rediest way is this:
Another kisse my life it shall haue ended.
For, to my mouth the first my hart did suck:
The next shall clene out of my brest it pluck.


[55] Of the Ielous man that loued                                  25
      the same woman and espied
          this other sitting
              with her.


*T*He wandring gadling, in the sommer tyde,
  That findes the Adder with his rechlesse foote                    30
Startes not dismaid so sodeinly aside,
As iealous despite did, though there were no boote,
When that he saw me sitting by her syde,
That of my health is very crop, and roote,

                                                                   It

It pleased me then to haue so fayre a grace,
To styng the hart, that would haue had my place.

## [56] To his loue from whom he hadd her gloues.

5

WHat nedes these threatnyng woordes, and wasted wynd?
   All this can not make me restore my pray,
To robbe your good ywis is not my minde:
Nor causelesse your faire hand did I display.
Let loue be iudge: or els whom next we finde: 10
That may both hear, what you and I can say.
She reft my hart: and I a gloue from her:
Let vs se then if one be worth the other.

## [57] Of the fained frend.

RIght true it is, and sayd full yore ago: 15
   Take hede of him, that by the backe thee claweth.
For, none is worse, then is a frendly fo.
Thought he seme good, all thing that thee deliteth,
Yet know it well, that in thy bosome crepeth.
For, many a man such fire oft times he kindleth: 20
That with the blase his berd him self he singeth.

## [58] The louer taught, mistrusteth allurementes.

IT may be good like it who list:
   But I do dout, who can me blame?
For oft assured, yet haue I mist: 25
And now againe I fear the same.
The wordes, that from your mouth last came,
Of sodayn change make me agast.
For dread to fall, I stand not fast. 30
   Alas I tread an endlesse mase:
That seke taccord two contraries:
And hope thus styll, and nothing hase:

F                    Im-

Imprisoned in liberties,
As one vnheard, and styll that cryes:
Always thirsty, and naught doth taste,
For dreade to fall, I stand not fast.                               5
  Assured I dout I be not sure,
Should I then trust vnto such suretie?
That oft haue put the proufe in vre,
And neuer yet haue found it trustie?
Nay syr in fayth, it were great folly.                              10
And yet my life thus do I waste,
For dreade to fall I stand not fast.

## [59] The louer complayneth that his loue doth not pitie him.

RЕsownde my voyce ye woodes, that heare me plaine:       15
  Both hilles and vales causyng reflexion,
And riuers eke, record ye of my paine:
Which haue oft forced ye by compassion,
As iudges lo to heare my exclamacion.
Amonge whom, such (I finde) yet doth remaine.                       20
Where I it seke, alas, there is disdaine.
  Oft ye riuers, to hear my wofull sounde,
Haue stopt your cours, and plainely to expresse,
Many a teare by moisture of the grounde
The earth hath wept to hear my heauinesse:                          25
Which causelesse I endure without redresse.
The hugy okes haue rored in the winde,
Ech thing me thought complayning in their kinde.
  Why then alas doth not she on me rew,
Or is her hart so hard that no pitie                                30
May in it sinke, my ioye for to renew?
O stony hart who hath thus framed thee
So cruell? that art cloked with beauty,
That from thee may no grace to me procede,
But as reward death for to be my mede.                              35

## [60] The louer reioyseth against fortune that by hindering his sute had happily made him forsake his folly.

If

*I*N fayth I wot not what to say,
　Thy chaunces ben so wonderous,
Thou fortune with thy diuers play
That makst the ioyfull dolourous,　　　　　　　　5
And eke the same right ioyous.
Yet though thy chayne hath me enwrapt,
Spite of thy hap, hap hath well hapt.
　Though thou hast set me for a wonder,
And sekest by change to do me payne:　　　　　10
Mens mindes yet mayst thou not so order,
For honestie if it remayne,
Shall shine for all thy cloudy rayne.
In vayne thou sekest to haue me trapt,
Spite of thy hap, hap hath well hapt.　　　　　15
　In hindryng me, me didst thou further,
And made a gap where was a style.
Cruell willes ben oft put vnder,
Wenyng to lower, then didst thou smile.
Lord, how thy selfe thou didst begyle,　　　　　20
That in thy cares wouldst me haue wrapt?
But spite of thy hap, hap hath well hapt.


## [61] A renouncing of hardly
## escaped loue.


*F*Arewell the hart of crueltie.　　　　　　　25
　Though that with payne my libertie
Deare haue I bought, and wofully
Finisht my fearfull tragedy.
Of force I must forsake such pleasure:
A good cause iust, sins I endure　　　　　　　30
Therby my wo, whiche be ye sure,
Shall therwith go me to recure.
　I fare as one escapt that fleeth,
Glad he is gone, and yet styll feareth
Spied to be caught, and so dredeth　　　　　　35
That he for nought his paine leseth.
In ioyfull payne reioyce my hart,
Thus to sustaine of ech a part.

**F.ii.**　　　　　　　　　Let

Let not this song from thee astart.
Welcome among my pleasant smart.

## [62] The louer to his bed , with describing of his vnquiet state.

*T*He restfull place, renewer of my smart:
  The labours salue, encreasyng my sorow:
The bodyes ease, and troubler of my hart:
Quieter of minde, myne vnquiet fo:
Forgetter of payne, remembrer of my wo:
The place of slepe, wherin I do but wake:
Besprent with teares, my bed, I thee forsake.
  The frosty snowes may not redresse my heat:
Nor heat of sunne abate my feruent cold.
I know nothing to ease my paynes so great.
Ech cure causeth encrease by twenty fold,
Renewyng cares vpon my sorowes old.
Such ouerthwart effectes in me they make.
Besprent with teares my bedde for to forsake.
  But all for nought: I finde no better ease
In bed, or out. This most causeth my paine:
Where I do seke how best that I may please,
My lost labour (alas) is all in vaine.
My hart once set, I can not it refrayne.
No place from me my grief away can take.
Wherfore with teares, my bed, I thee forsake.

## [63] Comparison of loue to a streame falling from the Alpes.

*F*Rom these hie hilles as when a spring doth fall,
  It trilleth downe with still and suttle course,
Of this and that it gathers ay and shall,
Till it haue iust downflowed to streame and force:
Then at the fote it rageth ouer all.
So fareth loue, when he hath tane a sourse.
Rage is his raine. Resistance vayleth none.
The first eschue is remedy alone.

Wiates

Line numbers: 5, 10, 15, 20, 25, 30, 35

[64] wiates complaint vpon
Loue, to Reason: with
Loues answer.

MYne olde dere enmy, my froward maister,
    Afore that Quene, I causde to be accited,      5
Which holdeth the diuine part of our nature,
That, like as golde, in fire he mought be tryed.
Charged with dolour, there I me presented
With horrible feare, as one that greatly dredeth      10
A wrongfull death, and iustice alway seketh.
    And thus I sayd: once my left foote, Madame,
When I was yong, I set within his reigne:
Wherby other than fierly burning flame
I neuer felt, but many a greuous pain.      15
Torment I suffred, angre, and disdain:
That mine oppressed pacience was past,
And I mine owne life hated, at the last.
    Thus hitherto haue I my time passed
In pain and smart. What wayes profitable:      20
How many pleasant dayes haue me escaped,
In seruing this false lyer so deceauable?
What wit haue wordes so prest, and forceable,
That may conteyn my great mishappinesse,
And iust complaintes of his vngentlenesse?      25
    So small hony, much aloes, and gall,
In bitternesse, my blinde life hath ytasted.
His false semblance, that turneth as a ball:
With fair and amorous daunce, made me be traced,
And, where I had my thought, and mynde araced,      30
From earthly frailnesse, and from vayn pleasure,
Me from my rest he toke, and set in errour:
    God made he me regard lesse, than I ought,
And to my self to take right litle hede:
And for a woman haue I set at nought      35
All other thoughtes: in this onely to spede.
And he was onely counseler of this dede:
Whettyng always my youthly frayle desire
On cruell whetston, tempered with fire.
    But (Oh alas) where, had I euer wit?      40
                    **F.iii.**                    Or

[45]

Or other gift, geuen to me of nature?
That sooner shalbe changed my weried sprite:
Then the obstinate wyll, that is my ruler.
So robbeth he my fredom with displeasure,                    5
This wicked traytour, whom I thus accuse:
That bitter life hath turned in pleasant vse.
　　He hath me hasted, thorough diuers regions:
Through desert wodes, and sharp hye mountaines:
Through froward people, and through bitter passions:        10
Through rocky seas, and ouer hilles and plaines:
With wery trauell, and with laborous paynes:
Always in trouble and in tediousnesse:
All in errour, and dangerous distresse,
　　But nother he, nor she, my tother fo,                   15
For all my flight, dyd euer me forsake:
That though my timely death hath been to slow
That me as yet, it hath not ouertake:
The heauenly goddes of pity doe it slake.
And, note they this his cruell tiranny,                      20
That fedes him, with my care, and misery.
　　Since I was his, hower rested I neuer,
Nor loke to do: and eke the waky nightes
The banished slepe may in no wise recouer.
By guile, and force, ouer my thralled sprites,              25
He is ruler: since which bel neuer strikes,
That I heare not as sounding to renue
My plaintes. Himself, he knoweth, that I say true.
　　For, neuer wormes olde rotten stocke haue eaten:
As he my hart, where he is resident,                         30
And doth the same with death dayly threaten.
Thence come the teares, and thence the bitter torment:
The sighes: the wordes, and eke the languishment:
That noy both me, and parauenture other.
Iudge thou: that knowest the one, and eke the tother.       35
　　Mine aduersair, with such greuous reproofe,
Thus he began. Heare Lady, thother part:
That the plain troth, from which he draweth aloofe,
This vnkinde man may shew, ere that I part.
In his yong age, I toke him from that art,                   40
That selleth wordes, and makes a clatteryng Knight:
And of my wealth I gaue him the delight.
　　Now shames he not on me for to complain,

That

That held him euermore in pleasant gain,
From his desyre, that might haue been his payn.
Yet therby alone I brought him to some frame:
Which now, as wretchednes, he doth so blame:
And towarde honor quickned I his wit:                                5
Where:as a daskard els he mought haue sit.
   He knoweth, how grete Atride that made Troy freat,
And Hanniball, to Rome so troubelous:
Whom Homer honored, Achilles that great,
And Thaffricane Scipion the famous:                                 10
And many other, by much nurture glorious:
Whose fame, and honor did bring them aboue:
I did let fall in base dishonest loue.
   And vnto him, though he vnworthy were:
I chose the best of many a Milion:                                  15
That, vnder sonne yet neuer was her pere,
Of wisdom, womanhod, and of discrecion:
And of my grace I gaue her such a facion,
And eke such way I taught her for to teache,
That neuer base thought his hart so hye might reche,                20
   Euermore thus to content his maistresse,
That was his onely frame of honesty,
I stirred him still, toward gentlenesse:
And causde him to regard fidelity.                                  25
Pacience I taught him in aduersity.
Such vertues learned, he in my great schole:
Wherof repenteth, now the ignorant foole.
   These, were the same deceites, and bitter gall,
That I haue vsed, the torment, and the anger:                       30
Sweter, then euer dyd to other fall,
Of right good sede yll frute loe thus I gather.
And so shall he, that the vnkinde dothe further.
A Serpent nourish I vnder my wing:
And now of nature, ginneth he to styng.                             35
   And for to tell, at last, my great seruise.
From thousand dishonesties haue I him drawen:
That, by my meanes, him in no maner wyse.
Neuer vile pleasure once hath ouerthrowen.
Where, in his dede, shame hath him alwaies gnawen:                  40
Doutyng report, that should come to her eare:
Whom now he blames, her wonted he to feare.
   What euer he hath of any honest custome:

𝔉.iiii,                Of

Of her, and me: that holdes he euerywhit,
But, lo, yet neuer was there nightly fantome
So farre in errour, as he is from his wit.
To plain on vs, he striueth with the bit,                          5
Which may rule him, and do him ease, and pain:
And in one hower, make all his grief his gayn.
   But, one thing yet there is, aboue all other:
I gaue him winges, wherwith he might vpflie
To honor, and fame: and if he would to higher          10
Than mortall thinges, aboue the starry skie:
Considering the pleasure, that an eye
Might geue in earth, by reason of the loue:
What should that be that lasteth still aboue?
   And he the same himself hath sayd, ere this.       15
But, now, forgotten is both that and I,
That gaue her him, his onely wealth and blisse.
And, at this word, with dedly shreke and cry:
Thou gaue her once: quod I, but by and by,
Thou toke her ayen from me: that wo worth the.         20
Not I but price: more worth than thou (quod he.)
   At last: eche other for himself, concluded:
I, trembling still: but he, with small reuerence.
Lo, thus, as we eche other haue accused:
Dere Lady: now we waite thyne onely sentence.          25
She smiling, at the whisted audience:
It liketh me (quod she) to haue hard your question:
But, lenger time doth ask a resolucion.

## [65] The louers sorowfull state maketh
## him write sorowfull songes, but          30
## Souche his loue may
## change the same.

*M* Aruell no more altho
    The songes, I sing do mone:
For other lyfe then wo,                                           35
I neuer proued none.
   And in my hart, also,
Is grauen with letters depe
A thousand sighes and mo:
A flood of teares to wepe.                                        40
                            How

How may a man in smart
Finde matter to reioyce?
How may a moornyng hart
Set foorth a pleasant voice.                                    5
   Play who so can, that part:
Nedes must in me appere:
How fortune ouerthwart
Doth cause my moorning chere.
   Perdy there is no man,                              10
If he saw neuer sight:
That perfitly tell can
The nature of the light.
   Alas: how should I than,
That neuer taste but sowre:                                    15
But do, as I began,
Continually to lowre.
   But yet, perchance some chance
May chance to change my tune:
And, when (Souch) chance doth chance:                          20
Then, shall I thank fortune?
   And if I haue (Souch) chance:
Perchance ere it be long:
For (Souch) a pleasant chance,
To sing some pleasant song.                                    25

## [66] The louer complaineth him⸗
## self forsaken.

WHere shall I haue, at myne owne wyll,
   Teares to complain? Where shall I fet
Such sighes? that I may sigh my fyll:                          30
And then agayne my plaintes repete.
For, though my plaint shall haue none end:
My teares cannot suffise my wo.
To mone my harm, haue I no frend.
For fortunes frend is mishaps fo.                              35
Comfort (God wot) els haue I none:
But in the winde to wast my wordes,
Nought moueth you my dedly mone:
But stil you turne it into bordes.

                          G.i.       I

I speake not, now, to moue your hart,
That you should rue vpon my payn:
The sentence geuen may not reuert:
I know, such labour were but vayn.                              5
But since that I for you (my dere)
Haue lost that thyng, that was my best:
A right small losse it must appere,
To lese these wordes, and all the rest.
But, though they sparcle in the winde:                         10
Yet, shall they shew your falsed faith:
Which is returned to his kynde:
For lyke to like: the prouerb sayeth,
Fortune, and you did me auance.
Me thought, I swam, and could not drowne:                      15
Happiest of all, but my mischance
Did lift me vp, to throw me downe.
And you, with her, of cruelnesse,
Dyd set your foote vpon my neck,
Me, and my welfare to oppresse:                                20
Without offence, your hart to wreck,
Where are your pleasant wordes? alas:
Where is your faith? your stedfastnesse?
There is no more: but all doth passe:
And I am left all comfortlesse.                                25
But since so much it doth you greue,
And also me my wretched life:
Haue here my troth: Nought shall releue,
But death alone my wretched strife.
Therfore, farewell my life, my death,                          30
My gayn, my losse: my salue, my sore:
Farewell also, with you my breath:
For, I am gone for euermore.

## [67] Of his loue that pricked
## her finger with a                                            35
## nedle.

SHe sat, and sowed: that hath done me the wrong:
Wherof I plain, and haue done many a day:
And, whilst she herd my plaint, in piteous song:

She

She wisht my hart the samplar, that it lay.
The blinde maister, whom I haue serued so long:
Grudgyng to heare, that he did heare her say:
Made her owne weapon do her finger blede:     5
To fele, if pricking wer so good in dede.

### [68] Of the same.

WHat man hath hard such cruelty before?
   That, when my plaint remembred her my wo,
That caused it: she cruell more, and more,     10
Wished eche stitche, as she did sit, and sow,
Had prickt my hart, for to encrease my sore.
And, as I think, she thought, it had bene so.
For as she thought, this is his hart in dede:
She pricked hard: and made her self to blede.     15

### [69] Request to Cupide, for re-
### uenge of his vnkinde
### loue.

BEhold, Loue, thy power how she despiseth:
   My greuous payn how litle she regardeth,     20
The solemne othe, wherof she takes no cure,
Broken she hath: and yet, she bydeth sure,
Right at her ease, and litle thee she dredeth.
Weaponed thou art, and she vnarmed sitteth:
To the disdainful, all her life she leadeth:     25
To me spitefull, without iust cause, or measure.
Behold Loue, how proudly she triumpheth,
I am in hold, but if thee pitie meueth:
Go, bend thy bow, that stony hartes breaketh:
And with some stroke reuenge the great displeasure     30
Of thee, and him that sorow doth endure,
And as his Lord thee lowly here entreateth.

### [70] Complaint for true loue
### vnrequited.

**G.ii.**        What

WHat vaileth troth? or by it, to take payn?
  To striue by stedfastnesse, for to attayn
How to be iust: and flee from doublenesse?
Since all alyke, where ruleth craftinesse,                              5
Rewarded is both crafty false, and plain.
Soonest he spedes, that most can lye and fayn.
True meaning hart is had in hye disdain.
Against deceyt, and cloked doublenesse,
What vaileth troth, or parfit stedfastnesse.                          10
Deceaud is he, by false and crafty trayn,
That meanes no gyle, and faithfull doth remayn
Within the trap, without help or redresse.
But for to loue (lo) such a sterne maistresse,
Where cruelty dwelles, alas it were in vain.                          15

## [71] The louer that fled loue now folowes it with his harme.

SOmtime I fled the fire, that me so brent,
  By sea, by land, by water, and by wynde:
And now, the coales I folow, that be quent,                           20
From Douer to Calais, with willing minde,
Lo, how desire is both furth sprong, and spent:
And he may see, that whilom was so blinde:
And all his labour, laughes he now to scorne,
Meashed in the breers, that erst was onely torne.                     25

## [72] The louer hopeth of better chance.

HE is not dead, that somtime had a fall.
  The Sonne returnes, that hid was vnder clowd.
And when Fortune hath spit out all her gall,                          30
I trust, good luck to me shall be alowd.
For, I haue seen a ship in hauen fall,
After that storme hath broke both maste, and shroude.
The willowe eke, that stoupeth with the winde,
Doth rise againe, and greater wood doth binde.                        35
                                                        The

[73] The louer compareth his
hart to the ouercharged
gonne.

*T*He furious goonne, in his most ragyng yre,
  When that the boule is rammed in to sore:                    5
And that the flame cannot part from the fire,
Crackes in sunder: and in the ayer doe rore
The sheuered peces.  So doth my desyre,
Whose flame encreaseth ay from more to more.                  10
Which to let out, I dare not loke, nor speake:
So inward force my hart doth all to breake.

[74] The louer suspected of change
praieth that it be not be=
leued against him.                                            15

*A* Ccused though I be, without desert:
  Sith none can proue, beleue it not for true.
For neuer yet, since that you had my hert,
Intended I to false, or be vntrue.
Sooner I would of death sustayn the smart,                   20
Than breake one word of that I promised you.
Accept therfore my seruice in good part.
None is alyue, that can yll tonges eschew.
Hold them as false: and let not vs depart
Our frendship olde, in hope of any new.                      25
Put not thy trust in such as vse to fayn,
Except thou mynde to put thy frend to payn.

[75] The louer abused re=
nowneth loue.

*M*Y loue to skorne, my seruice to retayne,                  30
  Therin (me thought) you vsed crueltie.
                                        𝕲.iii.      Since

Since with good will I lost my libertie,
Might neuer wo yet cause me to refrain,
But onely this, which is extremitie,
To geue me nought (alas) nor to agree, 5
That as I was, your man I might remain.
But synce that thus ye list to order me,
That would haue bene your seruant true, and fast:
Displease you not: my doting time is past.
And with my losse to leaue I must agree. 10
For as there is a certayn time to rage:
So is there time such madnes to aswage.

## [76] The louer professeth
## himself con-
## stant. 15

WIthin my brest I neuer thought it gain,
 Of gentle mynde the fredom for to lose.
Nor in my hart sanck neuer such disdain,
To be a forger, faultes for to disclose.
Nor I can not endure the truth to glose, 20
To set a glosse vpon an earnest pain.
Nor I am not in nomber one of those,
That list to blow retrete to euery train.

## [77] The louer sendeth his com-
## plaintes and teares to sue 25
## for grace.

PAsse forth my wonted cryes,
 Those cruell eares to pearce,
Which in most hatefull wyse
Doe styll my plaintes reuerse. 30
Doe you, my teares, also
So wet her barrein hart:
That pitye there may grow,
And crueltie depart.
 For though hard rockes among 35
 She

She semes to haue bene bred:
And of the Tigre long
Bene nourished, and fed.
Yet shall that nature change,                          5
If pitie once win place.
Whom as vnknowen, and strange,
She now away doth chase.
  And as the water soft,
Without forcyng or strength,                          10
Where that it falleth oft,
Hard stones doth perse at length:
So in her stony hart
My plaintes at last shall graue,
And, rygour set apart,                                15
Winne grant of that I craue.
  Wherfore my plaintes, present
Styll so to her my sute,
As ye, through her assent,
May bring to me some frute.                           20
And as she shall me proue,
So bid her me regarde,
And render loue for loue:
Which is a iust reward.

[78] The louers case can not be            25
      hidden how euer he
            dissemble.


*Y*Our lokes so often cast,
    Your eyes so frendly rolde,
Your sight fixed so fast,
Alwayes one to behold.                                30
Though hyde it fayn ye would:
It plainly doth declare,
Who hath your hart in hold,
And where good will ye bare,                          35
  Fayn would ye finde a cloke
Your brennyng fire to hyde:
Yet both the flame, and smoke
Breakes out on euery syde.

G.iiii.                                          Ye

[ 55 ]

Yee can not loue so guide,
That it no issue winne.
Abrode nedes must it glide,
That brens so hote within. 5
   For cause your self do wink,
Ye iudge all other blinde:
And secret it you think,
Which euery man doth finde.
In wast oft spend ye winde 10
Your self in loue to quit:
For agues of that kinde
Will show, who hath the fit.
   Your sighes yow fet from farre,
And all to wry your wo: 15
Yet are ye nere the narre,
Men ar not blinded so.
Depely oft swere ye no:
But all those othes ar vaine.
So well your eye doth showe, 20
Who puttes your hert to paine.
   Thinke not therfore to hide,
That still it selfe betrayes:
Nor seke meanes to prouide
To darke the sunny daies. 25
Forget those wonted waies:
Leaue of such frowning chere:
There will be found no stayes
To stoppe a thing so clere.

## [79] The louer praieth not to be disdai- 30
## ned, refused, mistrusted,
## nor forsaken.

𝒟Isdaine me not without desert:
   Nor leaue me not so sodenly:
Sins well ye wot, that in my hert 35
I meane ye not but honestly.
   Refuse me not without cause why:
Nor think me not to be vniust:

Since

Sins that by lotte of fantasy,
This carefull knot neades knit I must.
 Mistrust me not, though some there be,
That faine would spot my stedfastnesse:
Beleue them not, sins that ye se,                      5
The profe is not, as they expresse.
 Forsake me not, till I deserue:
Nor hate me not, tyll I offend.
Destroy me not, tyll that I swerue.                    10
But sins ye know what I intend:
 Disdaine me not that am your owne:
Refuse me not that am so true:
Mistrust me not till all be knowne:
Forsake me not, ne for no new.                         15


[80] The louer lamenteth his estate
        with sute for grace.


*F*Or want of will, in wo I playne:
  Vnder colour of sobernesse.
Renewyng with my sute my payne,                        20
My wanhope with your stedfastnesse.
Awake therfore of gentlenesse.
Regard at length, I you require,
The sweltyng paynes of my desire.
 Betimes who geueth willingly,                         25
Redoubled thankes aye doth deserue.
And I that sue vnfaynedly,
In frutelesse hope (alas) do sterue.
How great my cause is for to swerue:
And yet how stedfast is my sute:                       30
Lo, here ye see, where is the frute?
 As hounde that hath his keper lost,
Seke I your presence to obtayne:
In which my hart deliteth most,
And shall delight though I be slayne.                  35
You may release my band of payne.
Lose then the care that makes me crye,
For want of helpe or els I dye.

                                𝕳.i.            I

I dye, though not incontinent,
By processe yet consumingly
As waste of fire, which doth relent.
If you as wilfull wyll denye.                                    5
Wherfore cease of such crueltye:
And take me wholy in your grace:
Which lacketh will to change his place.


## [81] The louer waileth his
## changed ioyes.                                               10

IF euer man might him auaunt
  Of fortunes frendly chere:
It was my selfe I must it graunt,
For I haue bought it dere.
And derely haue I helde also                                    15
The glory of her name:
In yelding her such tribute, lo,
As did set forth her fame.
  Sometyme I stode so in her grace:
That as I would require,                                        20
Ech ioy I thought did me imbrace,
That furdered my desire.
And all those pleasures (lo) had I,
That fansy might support:
And nothing she did me denye,                                   25
That was to my comfort.
  I had (what would you more perdee?)
Ech grace that I did craue.
Thus fortunes will was vnto me
All thing that I would haue.                                    30
But all to rathe alas the while,
She built on such a ground:
In little space, to great a guyle
In her now haue I found.
  For she hath turned so her whele:                             35
That I vnhappy man
May waile the time that I did fele
Wherwith she fedde me than.
For broken now are her behestes:
And pleasant lokes she gaue:                                    40

                                                        And

And therfore now all my requestes,
From perill can not saue.
  Yet would I well it might appere
To her my chiefe regard:
Though my desertes haue ben to dere     5
To merite such reward.
Sith fortunes will is now so bent
To plage me thus pore man:
I must my selfe therwith content:     10
And beare it as I can.

## [82] The louer lamenteth other to haue the frutes of his seruice.

S Ome men would thinke of right to haue     15
  For their true meaning some reward.
But while that I do crye and craue:
I se that other be preferd.
I gape for that I am debard.
I fare as doth the hounde at hatch:     20
The worse I spede, the lenger I watch.
  My wastefull will is tried by trust:
My fond fansie is mine abuse.
For that I would refrayne my lust:
For mine auayle I can not chuse,     25
A will, and yet no power to vse.
A will, no will by reason iust,
Sins my will is at others lust.
  They eat the hony, I hold the hyue.
I sowe the sede, they reape the corne.     30
I waste, they winne, I draw, they driue.
Theirs is the thanke, mine is the skorne.
I seke, they spede, in waste my winde is worne.
I gape, they get, and gredely I snatch:
Till wurse I spede, the lenger I watch.     35
  I fast, they fede: they drynke, I thurst.
They laugh, I wayle: they ioye, I mourne.
They gayne, I lose: I haue the worst.
They whole, I sicke: they cold, I burne.
                  **H.ii.**           They

They leape, I lye: they slepe, I tosse and turne,
I would, they may: I craue, they haue at will.
That helpeth them, lo, cruelty doth me kyll.

## [83] To his loue that had geuen
## him answere of
## refusell.

*T*He answere that ye made to me my deare,
  When I did sue for my pore hartes redresse:
Hath so appalde my countenance and my chere:
That in this case, I am all comfortlesse:
Sins I of blame no cause can well expresse.
  I haue no wrong, where I can clayme no right.
Nought tane me fro, where I haue nothing had.
Yet of my wo, I can not so be quite.
Namely, sins that another may be glad
With that, that thus in sorow makes me sad.
  Yet none can claime (I saie) by former graunt,
That knoweth not of any graunt at all.
And by desert, I dare well make auaunt,
Of faithfull will, there is no where that shall
Bear you more trouth, more ready at your call.
  Now good then, call againe that bitter word:
That toucht your frende so nere with panges of paine:
And saie my dere that it was sayd in bord.
Late, or to sone, let it not rule the gaine,
Wherwith free will doth true desert retayne.

## [84] To his ladie cruel ouer her
## yelden louer.

*S*Vch is the course, that natures kinde hath wrought,
  That snakes haue time to cast away their stynges.
Ainst chainde prisoners what nede defence be sought:
The fierce lyon will hurt no yelden thinges:
Why shoulde such spite be nursed then in thy thought?
Sith all these powers are prest vnder thy winges:

And

5

10

15

20

25

30

35

And eke thou seest, and reason thee hath taught:
What mischief malice many waies it bringes.
Consider eke, that spight auaileth naught,
Therfore this song thy fault to thee it singes:  5
Displease thee not, for saiyng thus (me thought.)
Nor hate thou him from whom no hate forth springes,
For furies, that in hell be execrable,
For that they hate, are made most miserable.

## [85] The louer complaineth that deadlie  10
## sicknesse can not helpe his
## affeccion.

*T*He enmy of life, decayer of all kinde,
  That with his cold wythers away the grene:
This other night, me in my bed did finde:  15
And offerd me to ryd my feuer clene.
And I did graunt: so did dispayre me blinde.
He drew his bow, with arrowes sharpe and kene:
And strake the place, where loue had hit before:
And draue the first dart deper more and more.  20

## [86] The louer reioiceth the enioying
## of his loue.

*O*Nce as me thought, fortune me kist:
  And bade me aske, what I thought best:
And I should haue it as me list,  25
Therewith to set my hart in rest.
  I asked but my ladies hart
To haue for euermore myne owne:
Then at an end were all my smart:
Then should I nede no more to mone.  30
  Yet for all that a stormy blast
Had ouerturnde this goodly day:
And fortune semed at the last,
That to her promise she said nay.
  But like as one out of dispayre  35
To sodain hope reuiued I.

                                    Now

Now fortune sheweth her selfe so fayre,
That I content me wondersly.
  My most desire my hand may reach:
My will is alway at my hand.           5
Me nede not long for to beseche
Her, that hath power me to commaunde.
  What earthly thing more can I craue?
What would I wishe more at my will?
Nothing on earth more would I haue,     10
Saue that I haue, to haue it styll.
  For fortune hath kept her promesse,
In grauntyng me my most desire.
Of my soueraigne I haue redresse,
And I content me with my hire.       15

## [87] The louer complayneth the vn-kindnes of his loue.

*M*Y lute awake performe the last
    Labour that thou and I shall waste:
And end that I haue now begonne:     20
And when this song is song and past:
My lute be styll for I haue done.
  As to be heard where eare is none:
As lead to graue in marble stone:
My song may pearse her hart as sone.   25
Should we then sigh? or singe, or mone?
No, no, my lute for I haue done.
  The rockes do not so cruelly
Repulse the waues continually,
As she my sute and affection:      30
So that I am past remedy,
Wherby my lute and I haue done.
  Proude of the spoile that thou hast gotte
Of simple hartes through loues shot:
By whom vnkinde thou hast them wonne,   35
Thinke not he hath his bow forgot,
Although my lute and I haue done.
  Vengeaunce shall fall on thy disdaine
That makest but game on earnest payne.

Thinke

[ 62 ]

Thinke not alone vnder the sunne
Vnquit to cause thy louers plaine:
Although my lute and I haue done.
   May chance thee lie witherd and olde,         5
In winter nightes that are so colde,
Playning in vaine vnto the mone:
Thy wishes then dare not be tolde.
Care then who list, for I haue done.
   And then may chance thee to repent         10
The time that thou hast lost and spent
To cause thy louers sigh and swowne.
Then shalt thou know beauty but lent,
And wish and want as I haue done.
   Now cease my lute this is the last,         15
Labour that thou and I shall wast,
And ended is that we begonne.
Now is this song both song and past,
My lute be still for I haue done.

## [88] How by a kisse he found both       20
## his life and death.

NAture that gaue the Bee so feat a grace,
  To finde hony of so wondrous fashion:
Hath taught the spider out of the same place
To fetch poyson by strange alteracion.         25
Though this be strange, it is a stranger case,
With one kisse by secrete operacion,
Both these at once in those your lippes to finde,
In change wherof, I leaue my hart behinde.

## [89] The louer describeth his being       30
## taken with sight of
## his loue.

VNwarely so was neuer no man caught,
  With stedfast loke vpon a goodly face:
As I of late: for sodainely me thought,         35
My hart was torne out of his proper place.
   Thorow mine eye the stroke from hers did slide,
Directly downe into my hart it ranne:

                                    In

In helpe wherof the blood therto did glide,
And left my face both pale and wanne.
   Then was I like a man for wo amased:
Or like the fowle that fleeth into the fire.        5
For while that I vpon her beauty gased:
The more I burnde in my desire.
   Anone the bloud start in my face agayne,
Inflamde with heat, that it had at my hart.
And brought therwith through out in euery vaine,    10
A quakyng heat with pleasant smart.
   Then was I like the straw, when that the flame
Is driuen therin, by force, and rage of winde.
I can not tell, alas, what I shall blame:
Nor what to seke, nor what to finde.       15
   But well I wot: the griefe doth hold me sore
In heat and cold, betwixt both hope and dreade:
That, but her helpe to health do me restore:
This restlesse life I may not lead.


## [90] To his louer to loke vpon    20
## him.


*A*L in thy loke my life doth whole depende.
   Thou hydest thy self, and I must dye therfore.
But sins thou mayst so easily helpe thy frend:
Why doest thou stick to salue that thou madest sore?    25
Why do I dye? sins thou mayst me defend?
And if I dye, thy life may last no more.
For ech by other doth liue and haue reliefe,
I in thy loke, and thou most in my griefe.


## [91] The louer excuseth him of wordes    30
## wherwith he was vniustly
## charged.


*P* Erdy I sayd it not:
   Nor neuer thought to do.

                As

As well as I ye wot:
I haue no power therto,
And if I did, the lot,
That first did me enchayne:     5
May neuer slake the knot,
But strayght it to my payne.
  And if I did ech thing,
That may do harme or wo:
Continually may wring     10
My hart where so I go.
Report may always ring
Of shame on me for aye:
If in my hart did spring
The wordes that you do say     15
  And if I did ech starre,
That is in heauen aboue,
May frowne on me to marre
The hope I haue in loue.
And if I did such warre,     20
As they brought vnto Troye,
Bring all my life as farre
From all his lust and ioye.
  And if I did so say:
The beautie that me bounde,     25
Encrease from day to day
More cruell to my wounde:
With all the mone that may,
To plaint may turne my song:
My life may sone decay,     30
Without redresse by wrong.
  If I be cleare from thought,
Why do you then complayne?
Then is this thing but sought.
To turne my hart to payne,     35
Then this that you haue wrought,
You must it now redresse,
Of right therfore you ought
Such rigour to represse.
  And as I haue deserued:     40
So graunt me now my hire:
You know I neuer swerued,
You neuer founde me lyer.

J.i.     For

[ 65 ]

For Rachel haue I serued,
For Lea cared I neuer:
And her I haue reserued
Within my hart for euer.                                    5

## [92] Of such as had forsaken him.

*L* Vx, my faire fawlcon, and thy felowes all:
  How wel pleasant it were your libertie:
Ye not forsake me, that faire mought you fall.
But they that sometime liked my company:              10
Like lice away from dead bodies they crall.
Loe, what a proufe in light aduersitie?
But ye my birdes, I sweare by all your belles,
Ye be my frendes, and very few elles.

## [93] A description of such a one as        15
## he would loue.

*A* Face that should content me wonderous well,
  Should not be faire, but louely to beholde:
Of liuely loke, all griefe for to repell:
With right good grace, so would I that it should      20
Speake without word, such wordes as none can tell.
The tresse also should be of crisped gold.
With wit, and these perchance I might be tryde,
And knit againe with knot, that should not slide.

## [94] How vnpossible it is to finde          25
## quiet in his loue.

*E* Ver my hap is slack and slowe in commyng
  Desire encreasyng ay my hope vncertaine:
That loue or wait it, alike doth me payne.
And Tygre like so swift it is in partyng.             30
Alas the snow black shal it be and scalding,
The sea waterles, and fishe vpon the mountaine:
The Temis shal backe returne into his fountaine:
And where he rose the sunne shall take his lodgyng.

                                              Ere

Ere I in this finde peace or quietnesse.
Or that loue or my lady rightwisely
Leaue to conspire against me wrongfully.
And if I haue after such bitternesse,                5
Any thing swete, my mouth is out of taste:
That all my trust and trauell is but waste.

## [95] Of Loue, Fortune, and the louers minde.

*L*Oue, Fortune, and my minde which do remember      10
  Eke that is now, and that that once hath bene:
Torment my hart so sore that very often
I hate and enuy them beyonde all measure.
Loue sleeth my hart while Fortune is depriuer
Of all my comfort: the folishe minde than:           15
Burneth and playneth: as one that sildam
Liueth in rest. Still in displeasure
My pleasant daies they flete away and passe.
And dayly doth myne yll change to the worse.
While more then halfe is runne now of my course.     20
Alas not of stele, but of brittle glasse,
I se that from my hand falleth my trust:
And all my thoughtes are dasshed into dust.

## [96] The louer prayeth his offred hart to be receiued.                                  25

*H*Ow oft haue I, my deare and cruell fo:
  With my great pain to get som peace or truce,
Geuen you my hart? but you do not vse,
In so hie thinges, to cast your minde so low.
If any other loke for it, as you trow,               30
Their vaine weake hope doth greatly them abuse.
And that thus I disdayne, that you refuse.
It was once mine, it can no more be so.
If you it chase, that it in you can finde,
In this exile, no maner of comfort:                  35
Nor liue alone, nor where he is calde, resort,
He may wander from his naturall kinde.

**J.ii.**                                            So

So shall it be great hurt vnto vs twayne,
And yours the losse, and mine the deadly payne.

## [97] The louers life compared to
## the Alpes.

*L*Yke vnto these vnmesurable mountaines,
  So is my painefull life, the burden of yre.
For hye be they, and hye is my desire.
And I of teares, and they be full of fountaines.
Vnder craggy rockes they haue barren plaines,
Hard thoughtes in me my wofull minde doth tyre,
Small frute and many leaues their toppes do attire,
With small effect great trust in me remaines.
The boystous windes oft their hye boughes do blast:
Hote sighes in me continually be shed.
Wilde beastes in them, fierce loue in me is fed.
Vnmoueable am I: and they stedfast.
Of singing birdes they haue the tune and note:
And I alwaies plaintes passing through my throte.

## [98] Charging of his loue as vnpiteous
## and louing other.

*I*F amourous fayth, or if an hart vnfained
  A swete languor, a great louely desire:
If honest will, kindled in gentle fire:
If long errour in a blinde mase chained,
If in my visage ech thought distayned:
Or if my sparkelyng voyce, lower, or hier,
Which fear and shame, so wofully doth tyre:
If pale colour, which loue alas hath stayned:
If to haue another then my self more dere,
If wailyng or sighyng continually,
With sorowfull anger fedyng busily,
If burnyng a farre of, and fresyng nere,
Are cause that by loue my selfe I stroy:
Yours is the fault, and mine the great annoy.

A renouncyng

## [99] A renouncing of loue.

*F*Arewell, Loue, and all thy lawes for euer.
  Thy bayted hokes shall tangle me no more.
Senec, and Plato call me from thy lore: 5
To parfit wealth my wit for to endeuer.
In blinde errour when I dyd parseuer:
Thy sharp repulse, that pricketh aye so sore:
Taught me in trifles that I set no store:
But scape forth thence: since libertie is leuer. 10
Therfore, farewell: go trouble yonger hartes:
And in me claime no more auctoritie.
With ydle youth go vse thy propartie:
And theron spend thy many brittle dartes.
For, hytherto though I haue lost my tyme: 15
Me lyst no lenger rotten bowes to clime.

## [100] The louer forsaketh his
## vnkinde loue,

*M*Y hart I gaue thee, not to do it pain:
  But, to preserue, lo it to thee was taken. 20
I serued thee not that I should be forsaken:
But, that I should receiue reward again,
I was content thy seruant to remain:
And, not to be repayd after this fashion.
Now, since in thee is there none nother reason: 25
Displease thee not, if that I do refrain.
Vnsaciat of my wo, and thy desyre.
Assured by craft for to excuse thy fault.
But, since it pleaseth thee to fain defaut:
Farewell, I say, departing from the fire. 30
For, he, that doth beleue bearyng in hand:
Ploweth in the water: and soweth in the sand.

## [101] The louer describeth his
## restlesse state.

**I.iii.**        The

*T*He flaming sighes that boyle within my brest
   Sometime breake forth and they can well declare
The hartes vnrest and how that it doth fare,
The pain therof the grief and all the rest.            5
The watred eyen from whence the teares doe fall,
Do fele some force or els they would be drye:
The wasted flesh of colour ded can trye,
and somthing tell what swetenesse is in gall.
And he that lust to see and to disarne,            10
How care can force within a weried minde:
Come he to me I am that place assinde.
But for all this no force it doth no harme.
The wound alas happe in some other place:
From whence no toole away the skar can race.       15
   But you that of such like haue had your part,
Can best be iudge wherfore my frend so deare:
I thought it good my state should now appeare,
To you and that there is no great desart.
And wheras you in weighty matters great:         20
Of fortune saw the shadow that you know,
For trifling thinges I now am striken so
That though I fele my hart doth wound and beat:
I sit alone saue on the second day:
My feuer comes with whom I spend my time,       25
In burning heat while that she list assigne.
And who hath helth and libertie alway:
Let him thank god and let him not prouoke,
To haue the like of this my painfull stroke.

## [102] The louer lamentes the       30
## death of his loue.

*T*He piller perisht is wherto I lent,
   The strongest stay of mine vnquiet minde:
The like of it no man again can finde:
From East to West still seking though he went.      35
To mine vnhappe for happe away hath rent,
Of all my ioy the very bark and rynde:
And I (alas) by chance am thus assinde.
Daily to moorne till death do it relent,
But since that thus it is by desteny,            40
                                   What

What can I more but haue a wofull hart,
My penne, in plaint, my voyce in carefull crye:
My minde in wo, my body full of smart.
And I my self, my selfe alwayes to hate,                               5
Till dreadfull death do ease my dolefull state.


## [103] The louer sendeth sighes to
## mone his sute.


$G$O burning sighes vnto the frosen hart,
  Go breake the yse which pities painfull dart.                        10
Myght neuer perce and yf that mortall prayer,
In heauen be herd, at lest yet I desire.
That death or mercy end my wofull smart.
Take with thee payn, wherof I haue my part,
And eke the flame from which I cannot start,                           15
And leaue me then in rest, I you require:
Go burning sighes fulfil that I desire.
I must go worke I see by craft and art,
For truth and faith in her is laid apart:
Alas, I can not therfore assaile her,                                  20
With pitefull complaint and scalding fier,
That from my brest disceiuably doth start.


## [104] Complaint of the absence
## of his loue.


$S$O feble is the threde, that doth the burden stay,                  25
  Of my poore life: in heauy plight, that falleth in decay:
That, but it haue elswhere some ayde or some succours:
The running spindle of my fate anone shall end his course.
For since thunhappy hower, that dyd me to depart,
From my swete weale: one onely hope hath stayed my life, apart:  30
Which doth perswade such wordes vnto my sored minde:
Maintain thy self, O wofull wight, some better luck to finde.
For though thou be depriued from thy desired sight:
Who can thee tell, if thy returne be for thy more delight?

𝕴.iiii.                    Or

[ 71 ]

Or, who can tell, thy losse if thou mayst once recouer?
Some pleasant hower thy wo may wrappe: & thee defend, & couer.
Thus in this trust as yet it hath my life sustained:
But now (alas) I see it faint: and I, by trust, am trayned.     5
The tyme doth flete, and I se how the howers, do bend
So fast: that I haue scant the space to mark my commyng end.
Westward the sonne from out the East scant shewes his light:
When in the West he hides him strayt, within the dark of nyght.
And comes as fast, where he began, his path awry.     10
From East to West, from West to East so doth his iourney ly.
The life so short, so fraile, that mortall men liue here:
So great a weight, so heauy charge the bodies, that we bere:
That, when I think vpon the distaunce, and the space:
That doth so farre deuide me from my dere desired face:     15
I know not, how tattain the winges, that I require,
To lift me vp: that I might flie, to folow my desyre.
Thus of that hope, that doth my life somethyng sustayne,
Alas: I feare, and partly fele: full litle doth remain.
Eche place doth bring me griefe: where I do not behold     20
Those liuely eyes: which of my thoughts wer wont ẏ keys to hold
Those thoughtes were pleasāt swete: whilst I enioyed that grace:
My pleasure past, my present pain, when I might well embrace.
And, for because my want should more my wo encrease:
In watch, and slepe, both day, and night, my will doth neuer cease  25
That thing to wish: wherof since I did leese the sight:
Was neuer thing that mought in ought my woful hart delight,
Thunesy lyfe, I lead, doth teach me for to mete
The floodes, the seas, the land, the hylles: that doth thē entermete
Twene me, and those shene lightes: that wonted for to clere     30
My darked panges of cloudy thoughts, as bright as Pheb⁹ spere,
It teacheth me, also, what was my pleasant state:
The more to fele, by such record, how that my wealth doth bate.
If such record (alas) prouoke thenflamed mynde:
Which sprong that day, that I did leaue the best of me behynde:     35
If loue forget himself, by length of absence, let:
Who doth me guyde (O wofull wretch) vnto this bayted net?
Where doth encrease my care: much better wer for me,
As dumme, as stone, all thyng forgot, still absent for to be.
Alas: the clere cristall, the bright transplendant glasse     40
Doth not bewray the colours hidde, which vnderneth it hase:
As doth thaccumbred sprite the thoughtfull throwes discouer,
Of feares delite, of feruent loue: that in our hartes we couer.
Out by these eyes, it sheweth that euermore delight.     In

In plaint, and teares to seke redresse: and eke both day and night.
These kindes of pleasures most wherein men so reioyce,
To me they do redubble still of stormy sighes the voyce.
For, I am one of them, whom playnt doth well content:        5
It sits me well: myne absent wealth me semes for to lament:
And with my teares, tassay to charge myne eies twayn:
Lyke as my hart aboue the brink is fraughted full of payn.
And forbecause, therto, of those fair eyes to treate
Do me prouoke: I wyll returne, my plaint thus to repeate.        10
For, there is nothing els, that toucheth me so within:
Where they rule all: and I alone nought but the case, or skin.
Wherefore, I shall returne to them, as well, or spring:
From whom descendes my mortall wo, aboue all other thing.
So shall myne eyes in pain accompany my hart:        15
That were the guides, that did it lead of loue to fele the smart.
The crisped golde, that doth surmount Apollos pride:
The liuely streames of pleasant starres that vnder it doth glyde:
Wherein the beames of loue doe styll encrease theyr heate:
Which yet so farre touch me so nere, in colde to make me sweate.        20
The wyse and pleasant talk, so rare, or els alone:
That gaue to me the curteis gift, that erst had neuer none:
Be farre from me, alas: and euery other thyng
I might forbeare with better wyll: then this that dyd me bryng,
With pleasant worde and chere, redresse of lingred pain:        25
And wonted oft in kindled will to vertue me to trayn.
Thus, am I forst to heare, and harken after newes.
My comfort scant my large desire in doutfull trust renewes.
And yet with more delite to mone my wofull case:
I must complain those handes, those armes: ẙ firmely do embrace        30
Me from my self: and rule the sterne of my poore lyfe:
The swete disdaines, the pleasant wrathes, and eke ẙ louely strife:
That wonted well to tune in temper iust, and mete,
The rage: that oft dyd make me erre, by furour vndiscrete.
All this is hydde me fro, with sharp, and ragged hylles:        35
At others will, my long abode my depe dispaire fullfils.
And if my hope sometime ryse vp, by some redresse:
It stumbleth straite, for feble faint: my feare hath such excesse.
Such is the sort of hope: the lesse for more desyre:
And yet I trust ere that I dye to see that I require:        40
The restyng place of loue: where vertue dwelles and growes
There I desire, my wery life, somtime, may take repose.
My song: thou shalt attain to finde that pleasant place:

                                  𝕶.i.        Where

Where she doth lyue, by whō I liue: may chance, to haue this grace
When she hath red, and sene the grief, wherin I serue:
Betwene her brestes she shall thee put: there, shall she thee reserue
Then, tell her, that I cumme: she shall me shortly see:      5
And if for waighte the body fayle, the soule shall to her flee.

## [105] The louer blameth his loue
## for renting of the letter he
## sent her.

S Vffised not (madame) that you did teare,      10
  My wofull hart, but thus also to rent:
The weping paper that to you I sent.
Wherof eche letter was written with a teare.
Could not my present paines, alas suffise,
Your gredy hart? and that my hart doth fele,      15
Tormentes that prick more sharper then the stele,
But new and new must to my lot arise.
Vse then my death. So shal your cruelty:
Spite of your spite rid me from all my smart,
And I no more such tormentes of the hart:      20
Fele as I do. This shalt thou gain thereby.

## [106] The louer curseth the tyme
## when first he fell in loue.

W Hen first mine eyes did view, and marke,
  Thy faire beawtie to beholde:      25
And when mine eares listned to hark:
The pleasant wordes, that thou me tolde:
I would as then, I had been free,
From eares to heare, and eyes to see.
And when my lips gan first to moue,      30
Wherby my hart to thee was knowne:
And when my tong did talk of loue,
To thee that hast true loue down throwne:
I would, my lips, and tong also:

                                         Had

Had then bene dum, no deale to go.
And when my handes haue handled ought,
That thee hath kept in memorie:
And when my fete haue gone, and sought                    5
To finde and geat thy company:
I would, eche hand a foote had bene,
And I eche foote a hand had sene.
And when in mynde I did consent
To folow this my fansies will:                            10
And when my hart did first relent,
To tast such bayt, my life to spyll:
I would, my hart had bene as thyne:
Or els thy hart had bene, as mine.

## [107] The louer determineth to                         15
## serue faithfully.


SYnce loue wyll nedes, that I shall loue:
Of very force I must agree.
And since no chance may it remoue:
In welth, and in aduersitie,                              20
I shall alway my self apply
To serue, and suffer paciently.
  Though for good will I finde but hate:
And cruelty my life to wast:
And though that still a wretched state                    25
Should pine my dayes vnto the last:
Yet I professe it willingly.
To serue, and suffer paciently.
  For since my hart is bound to serue:
And I not ruler of mine owne:                             30
What so befall, tyll that I sterue.
By proofe full well it shall be knowne:
That I shall still my selfe apply
To serue, and suffer paciently.
  Yea though my grief finde no redresse:                  35
But still increase before mine eyes:
Though my reward be cruelnesse,
With all the harme, happe can deuise:
Yet I professe it willingly

**K.ii.**          To

To serue, and suffer paciently.
  Yea though fortune her pleasant face
Should shew, to set me vp a loft:
And streight, my wealth for to deface,          5
Should writhe away, as she doth oft:
Yet would I styll my self apply
To serue and suffer paciently.
  There is no grief, no smart, no wo:
That yet I fele, or after shall:          10
That from this mynde may make me go,
And whatsoeuer me befall:
I do professe it willingly
To serue and suffer paciently.

## [108] The louer suspected bla-     15
## meth yll tonges.

*M*Ystrustfull mindes be moued
  To haue me in suspect.
The troth it shalbe proued:
Which time shall once detect.          20
  Though falshed go about
Of crime me to accuse:
At length I do not doute,
But truth shall me excuse.
  Such sawce, as they haue serued          25
To me without desart:
Euen as they haue deserued:
Therof god send them part.

## [109] The louer complaineth and his
## lady comforteth.          30

[Lou]er.  *I*T burneth yet, alas, my hartes desire.
[Lad]y.   What is the thing, that hath inflamde thy hert?
[Lo.]     A certain point, as feruent, as the fyre.
[La.]     The heate shall cease, if that thou wilt conuert.
[Lo.]      I cannot stoppe the feruent raging yre.          35
                                                What

La.  What may I do, if thy self cause thy smart?
Lo.      Heare my request, alas, with weping chere.
La.  With right good wyll, say on: lo, I thee here.
Lo.      That thing would I, that maketh two content.                5
La.  Thou sekest, perchance, of me, that I may not.
Lo.      Would god, thou wouldst, as thou maist, well assent.
La.  That I may not, thy grief is mine: God wot.
Lo.      But I it fele, what so thy wordes haue ment.
La.  Suspect me not: my wordes be not forgot.                      10
Lo.      Then say, alas: shall I haue help? or no.
La.  I see no time to answer, yea, but no.
Lo.      Say ye, dere hart: and stand no more in dout.
La.  I may not grant a thing, that is so dere.
Lo.      Lo, with delayes thou drieues me still about.             15
La.  Thou wouldest my death: it plainly doth appere.
Lo.      First, may my hart his bloode, and life blede out.
La.  Then for my sake, alas, thy will forbere.
Lo.      From day to day, thus wastes my life away.
La.  Yet, for the best, suffer some small delay.                   20
Lo.      Now, good, say yea: do once so good a dede.
La.  If I sayd yea: what should therof ensue?
Lo.      An hart in pain of succour so should spede,
Twixt yea, and nay, my doute shall styll renew.
My swete, say yea: and do away this drede.                         25
La.  Thou wilt nedes so: be it so: but then be trew.
Lo.      Nought would I els, nor other treasure none.
Thus, hartes be wonne, by loue, request and mone.

## [110] why loue is blinde.

OF purpose, loue chose first for to be blinde:                     30
  For, he with sight of that, that I beholde,
Vanquisht had been, against all godly kinde.
His bow your hand, and trusse should haue vnfolde.
And he with me to serue had bene assinde.
But, for he blinde, and recklesse would him holde:                 35
And still, by chance, his dedly strokes bestowe:
With such, as see, I serue, and suffer wo.

## [111] To his vnkinde loue.

𝕶.iii.        What

WHat rage is this? what furor? of what kinde?
  What power, what plage doth wery thus my minde:
Within my bones to rankle is assinde
What poyson pleasant swete?                  5
  Lo, see, myne eyes flow with continuall teares:
The body still away slepelesse it weares:
My foode nothing my fainting strength repayres,
Nor doth my limmes sustain.
  In depe wide wound, the dedly stroke doth turne:     10
To cureles skarre that neuer shall returne.
Go to: triumph: reioyce thy goodly turne:
Thy frend thou doest oppresse.
  Oppresse thou doest: and hast of him no cure:
Nor yet my plaint no pitie can procure.           15
Fierce Tigre, fell, hard rock without recure:
Cruell rebell to Loue,
  Once may thou loue, neuer beloued again:
So loue thou styll, and not thy loue obtain:
So wrathfull loue, with spites of iust disdain,     20
May thret thy cruell hart.

## [112] The louer blameth his in=
### stant desyre.

DEsire (alas) my master, and my fo:
  So sore altred thy self how mayst thou see?     25
Sometime thou sekest, that drieues me to and fro
Sometime, thou leadst, that leadeth thee, and me.
What reason is to rule thy subiectes so?
By forced law, and mutabilitie.
For where by thee I douted to haue blame:     30
Euen now by hate again I dout the same.

## [113] The louer complayneth
### his estate.

I see, that chance hath chosen me
  Thus secretely to liue in paine:     35
And to an other geuen the fee

Of

Of all my losse to haue the gayn.
By chance assinde thus do I serue:
And other haue, that I deserue.
   Vnto my self sometime alone             5
I do lament my wofull case.
But what auaileth me to mone?
Since troth, and pitie hath no place
In them: to whom I sue and serue:
And other haue, that I deserue.          10
   To seke by meane to change this minde:
Alas, I proue, it will not be.
For in my hart I cannot finde
Once to refrain, but still agree,
As bounde by force, alway to serue:     15
And other haue, that I deserue.
   Such is the fortune, that I haue
To loue them most, that loue me lest:
And to my pain to seke, and craue
The thing, that other haue possest.     20
So thus in vain alway I serue.
And other haue, that I deserue.
   And till I may apease the heate:
If that my happe will happe so well:
To waile my wo my hart shall freate:     25
Whose pensif pain my tong can tell.
Yet thus vnhappy must I serue:
And other haue, that I deserue.

## [114] Against hourders of money.

*F*Or shamefast harm of great, and hatefull nede:     30
  In depe despayre, as did a wretch go,
With ready corde, out of his life to spede:
His stumbling foote did finde an hoorde, lo,
Of golde, I say: where he preparde this dede:
And in eschange, he left the corde, tho.     35
He, that had hidde the golde, and founde it not:
Of that, he founde, he shapte his neck a knot.

## [115] Discripcion of a gonne.

𝕶.iii.         Vulcane

$V$ Vlcane begat me: Minerua me taught:
   Nature, my mother: Craft nourisht me yere by yere:
Three bodyes are my foode: my strength is in naught:
Angre, wrath, wast, and noyce are my children dere.     5
Gesse, frend, what I am: and how I am wraught:
Monster of sea, or of land, or of els where.
Know me, and vse me: and I may thee defend:
And if I be thine enmy, I may thy life end.

## [116] wiat being in prison, to     10
### Brian.

$S$ Yghes are my foode: my drink are my teares.
   Clinkyng of fetrers would such Musick craue,
Stink, and close ayer away my life it weares.
Pore innocence is all the hope, I haue.     15
Rayn, winde, or wether iudge I by mine eares.
Malice assaultes, that righteousnesse should haue.
Sure am I, Brian, this wound shall heale again:
But yet alas, the skarre shall still remayn.

## [117] Of dissembling wordes.     20

$T$ Hrough out the world if it wer sought,
   Faire wordes ynough a man shall finde:
They be good chepe they cost right nought.
Their substance is but onely winde:
But well to say and so to mene,     25
That swete acord is seldom sene.

## [118] Of the meane and sure
### estate.

$S$ Tond who so list vpon the slipper whele,
   Of hye astate and let me here reioyce.     30
And vse my life in quietnesse eche dele,
Vnknowen in court that hath the wanton toyes.

             In

In hidden place my time shall slowly passe
And when my yeres be past withouten noyce
Let me dye olde after the common trace
For gripes of death doth he to hardly passe                          5
That knowen is to all: but to him selfe alas,
He dyeth vnknowen, dased with dreadfull face.

## [119] The courtiers life.

*I*N court to serue decked with freshe aray,
  Of sugred meates felyng the swete repast:                          10
The life in bankets, and sundry kindes of play,
Amid the presse of lordly lokes to waste,
Hath with it ioynde oft times such bitter taste.
That who so ioyes such kinde of life to holde,
In prison ioyes fettred with cheines of gold.                       15

## [120] Of disapointed purpose by negligence.

*O*F Carthage he that worthy warriour
  Could ouercome, but could not vse his chaunce
And I likewise of all my long endeuour                              20
The sharpe conquest though fortune did aduance,
Ne could I vse.  The holde that is geuen ouer,
I vnpossest. so hangeth in balance
Of warre, my peace, reward of all my paine,
At Mountzon thus I restlesse rest in Spaine.                        25

## [121] Of his returne from Spaine.

*T*Agus farewel that westward with thy stremes
  Turnes vp the graines of gold already tried,
For I with spurre and saile go seke the temmes,
Gaineward the sunne that sheweth her welthy pride,                  30
And to the towne that Brutus sought by dreames,
Like bended mone that leanes her lusty side.
My king, my countrey, I seke for whom I liue,
O mighty Ioue the windes for this me geue.
                                    𝕷.i.                        Of

[ 81 ]

*Songes.*

## [122] Of sodaine trustyng.

*D*Riuen by desire I did this dede
To danger my self without cause why:
To trust thuntrue not like to spede,                        5
To speake and promise faythfully:
But now the proufe doth verifie,
That who so trusteth ere he know.
Doth hurt him self and please his foe.

## [123] Of the mother that eat her                        10
### childe at the siege of
### Ierusalem.

*I*N doubtfull breast whiles motherly pity
With furious famine standeth at debate,
The mother sayth: O childe vnhappy                         15
Returne thy bloud where thou hadst milke of late
Yeld me those lymmes that I made vnto thee,
And enter there where thou were generate.
For of one body agaynst all nature,
To an other must I make sepulture.                         20

## [124] Of the meane and sure estate
### written to Iohn Poins.

*M*Y mothers maides when they do sowe and spinne:
They sing a song made of the feldishe mouse:
That forbicause her liuelod was but thinne,                25
Would nedes go se her townish sisters house,
She thought, her selfe endured to greuous payne,
The stormy blastes her caue so sore did sowse:
That when the furrowes swimmed with the rayne:
She must lie colde, and wet in sory plight.                30
And worse then that, bare meat there did remaine
To comfort her, when she her house had dight:
Sometime a barly corne: sometime a beane:

For

[ 82 ]

For which she laboured hard both day and night,
In haruest tyme, while she might go and gleane.
And when her store was stroyed with the floode:
Then weleaway for she vndone was cleane. 5
Then was she faine to take in stede of fode,
Slepe if she might, her honger to begyle.
My sister (quod she) hath a liuyng good:
And hence from me she dwelleth not a myle.
In colde and storme, she lieth warme and dry, 10
In bed of downe: the durt doth not defile
Her tender fote, she labours not as I,
Richely she fedes, and at the richemans cost:
And for her meat she nedes not craue nor cry.
By sea, by land, of delicates the most 15
Her cater sekes, and spareth for no perill:
She fedes on boyle meat, bake meat, and on rost:
And hath therfore no whit of charge nor trauell.
And when she list the licour of the grape
Doth glad her hart, till that her belly swell. 20
And at this iourney makes she but a iape:
So forth she goes, trusting of all this wealth,
With her sister her part so for to shape:
That if she might there kepe her self in health:
To liue a Lady while her life doth last. 25
And to the dore now is she come by stealth:
And with her fote anone she scrapes full fast.
Thother for fear, durst not well scarse appere:
Of euery noyse so was the wretch agast.
At last, she asked softly who was there. 30
And in her language as well as she could,
Pepe (quod the other) sister I am here.
Peace (quod the towne mouse) why speakest thou so loude?
And by the hand she toke her fayre and well.
Welcome (quod she) my sister by the rode. 35
She feasted her that ioye it was to tell
The fare they hadde, they dranke the wine so clere:
And as to purpose now and then it fell:
She chered her, with how sister what chere?
Amid this ioye be fell a sory chance: 40
That (weleaway) the stranger bought full dere
The fare she had.  For as she lookt a scance:
Vnder a stole she spied two stemyng eyes.

L.ii In

[ 83 ]

# Songes.

In a rounde head, with sharpe eares: in Fraunce
Was neuer mouse so ferde, for the vnwise
Had not ysene such a beast before.
Yet had nature taught her after her gise,                    5
To know her fo: and dread him euermore.
The townemouse fled: she knew whither to go:
The other had no shift, but wonders sore
Ferde of her life, at home she wisht her tho:
And to the dore (alas) as she did skippe:                    10
The heauen it would, lo: and eke her chance was so:
At the threshold her sely fote did trippe:
And ere she might recouer it agayne:
The traytour cat had caught her by the hippe:
And made her there against hir will remayne:                 15
That had forgot her power, surety and rest,
For semyng welth, wherin she thought to raine.
Alas (my Poyns) how men do seke the best,
And finde the worst, by errour as they stray,
And no maruell, when sight is so opprest,                    20
And blindes the guide, anone out of the way
Goeth guide and all in seking quiet life.
O wretched mindes, there is no golde that may
Graunt that you seke, no warre, no peace, no strife.
No, no, although thy head were hoopt with golde,            25
Sergeant with mace, with hawbart, sword, nor knife,
Can not repulse the care that folow should.
Ech kinde of life hath with him his disease.
Liue in delite, euen as thy lust would:
And thou shalt finde, when lust doth most thee please:      30
It irketh straight, and by it selfe doth fade.
A small thing is it, that may thy minde appease.
None of you al there is, that is so madde,
To seke for grapes on brambles, or on bryers:
Nor none I trow that hath his witte so badde,               35
To set his haye for conies ouer riuers:
Nor ye set not a dragge net for an hare.
And yet the thing, that most is your desire,
You do misseke, with more trauell and care.
Màke plaine thine hart, that it be not knotted              40
With hope or dreade, and se thy will be bare
From all affectes, whom vice hath euer spotted.
Thy selfe content with that is thee assinde:

And

[ 84 ]

And vse it well that is to thee alotted.
Then seke no more out of thy selfe to finde
The thing that thou hast sought so long before.
For thou shalt feele it stickyng in thy minde,                     5
Madde if ye list to continue your sore.
Let present passe, and gape on time to come:
And depe your selfe in trauell more and more.
Henceforth (my Poins) this shalbe all and summe
These wretched foles shall haue nought els of me:              10
But, to the great God and to his dome,
None other paine pray I for them to be:
But when the rage doth leade them from the right:
That lokyng backward, Vertue they may se,
Euen as she is, so goodly fayre and bright.                      15
And whilst they claspe their lustes in armes a crosse:
Graunt them good Lord, as thou maist of thy might,
To freate inward, for losyng such a losse.

## [125] Of the Courtiers life written
### to Iohn Poins.                                              20

*M*Yne owne Iohn Poyns: sins ye delite to know
    The causes why that homeward I me draw,
And fle the prease of courtes, where so they go:
Rather then to liue thrall vnder the awe,
Of lordly lokes, wrapped within my cloke,                       25
To will and lust learnyng to set a law:
It is not, because I scorne or mocke
The power of them: whom fortune here hath lent
Charge ouer vs, of ryght to strike the stroke.
But true it is that I haue alwayes ment                          30
Lesse to esteme them, then the common sort
Of outward thinges: that iudge in their entent,
Without regard, what inward doth resort.
I graunt, sometime of glory that the fire
Doth touch my hart. Me list not to report                        35
Blame by honour, and honour to desire.
But how may I this honour now attaine?
That can not dye the colour blacke a lyer.
My Poyns, I can not frame my tune to fayne:
To cloke the truth, for prayse without desert,                   40
Of them that list all nice for to retaine.
                        L.iii.                            I am

## Songes.

I can not honour them, that set their part
With Venus, and Bacchus, all their life long:
Nor holde my peace of them, although I smart.
I can not crouch nor knele to such a wrong:                    5
To worship them like God on earth alone:
That are as wolues these sely lambes among.
I can not with my wordes complaine and mone,
And suffer nought: nor smart without complaynt:
Nor turne the worde that from my mouth is gone.              10
I can not speake and loke like as a saynt:
Vse wiles for wit, and make disceyt a pleasure:
Call craft counsaile, for lucre still to paint.
I can not wrest the law to fill the coffer:
With innocent bloud to fede my selfe fatte:                    15
And do most hurt: where that most helpe I offer.
I am not he, that can alowe the state
Of hye Ceasar, and damne Cato to dye:
That with his death did scape out of the gate,
From Ceasars handes, if Liuye doth not lye:                    20
And would not liue, where libertie was lost,
So did his hart the common wealth apply.
I am not he, such eloquence to bost:
To make the crow in singyng, as the swanne:
Nor call the lyon of coward beastes the most.                  25
That can not take a mouse, as the cat can.
And he that dieth for honger of the golde,
Call him Alexander, and say that Pan
Passeth Appollo in musike manifold:
Praise syr Topas for a noble tale,                             30
And scorne the story that the knight tolde:
Prayse him for counsell, that is dronke of ale:
Grinne when he laughes, that beareth all the sway:
Frowne, when he frownes: and grone when he is pale:
On others lust to hang both night and day.                    35
None of these poyntes would euer frame in me.
My wit is nought, I can not learne the way.
And much the lesse of thinges that greater be,
That asken helpe of colours to deuise
To ioyne the meane with ech extremitie:                       40
With nearest vertue ay to cloke the vice.
And as to purpose likewise it shall fall:
To presse the vertue that it may not rise.

And

[ 86 ]

And as to purpose likewise it shall fall,
To presse the vertue that it may not rise.
As dronkennesse good felowship to call:
The frendly foe, with his faire double face, 5
Say he is gentle and curties therewithall.
Affirme that fauell hath a goodly grace,
In eloquence: And cruelty to name
Zeale of Iustice: And change in time and place.
And he that suffreth offence withoutt blame: 10
Call him pitifull, and him true and plaine,
That rayleth rechlesse vnto ech mans shame.
Say he is rude, that can not lye and faine:
The letcher a louer, and tyranny
To be the right of a Prynces rayghne. 15
I can not, I no, no, it will not be.
This is the cause that I could neuer yet
Hang on their sleues, that weygh (as thou mayst se)
A chippe of chance more then a pounde of wit.
This maketh me at home to hunt and hauke: 20
And in fowle wether at my boke to sit:
In frost and snow, then with my bow to stalke.
No man doth marke where so I ride or go.
In lusty leas at libertie I walke:
And of these newes I fele nor weale nor wo: 25
Saue that a clogge doth hang yet at my heele.
No force for that, for it is ordred so:
That I may leape both hedge and dike full wele,
I am not now in Fraunce, to iudge the wine:
With savry sauce those delicates to fele. 30
Nor yet in Spaine where one must him incline,
Rather then to be, outwardly to seme.
I meddle not with wyttes that be so fine,
Nor Flaunders chere lettes not my syght to deme
Of blacke and white, nor takes my wittes away 35
With beastlinesse: such do those beastes esteme.
Nor I am not, where truth is geuen in pray,
For money, poyson, and treason: of some
A common practise, vsed nyght and day.
But I am here in kent and christendome: 40
Among the Muses, where I reade and ryme,
Where if thou list myne owne Iohn Poyns to come:
Thou shalt be iudge, how I do spende my time.

How

*Songes.*

[126] How to vse the court and him
selfe therin,written to syr
Fraunces Bryan.

*A* Spendyng hand that alway powreth out,          5
   Had nede to haue a bringer in as fast.
And on the stone that styll doth turne about,
There groweth no mosse.  These prouerbes yet do last:
Reason hath set them in so sure a place:
That length of yeres their force can neuer waste.          10
When I remember this, and eke the case,
Wherin thou standst: I thought forthwith to write
(Brian) to thee? who knowes how great a grace
In writyng is to counsaile man the right.
To thee therfore that trottes still vp and downe:          15
And neuer restes, but runnyng day and night,
From realme to realme, from citye strete, and towne.
Why doest thou weare thy body to the bones?
And mightest at home slepe in thy bedde of downe:
And drinke good ale so noppy for the nones:          20
Fede thy selfe fatte, and heape vp pounde by pounde.
Likest thou not this? No.  Why?  For swine so groines
In stye, and chaw dung moulded on the ground.
And driuell on pearles with head styll in the manger,
So of the harpe the asse doth heare the sound.          25
So sackes of durt be filde.  The neate courtier
So serues for lesse, then do these fatted swine.
Though I seme leane and drye, withouten moysture:
Yet will I serue my prince, my lord and thine.
And let them liue to fede the paunch that lyst:          30
So I may liue to fede both me and myne.
By God well said.  But what and if thou wist
How to bring in, as fast as thou doest spend.
That would I learne.  And it shall not be mist,
To tell thee how.  Now harke what I intende.          35
Thou knowest well first, who so can seke to please,
Shall purchase frendes: where trouth, shall but offend.
Flee therefore truth, it is both welth and ease.
For though that trouth of euery man hath prayse:
Full neare that winde goeth trouth in great misease.          40
                                          Vse

Vse vertue, as it goeth now a dayes:
In worde alone to make thy language swete:
And of the dede, yet do not as thou saies.
Els be thou sure: thou shalt be farre vnmete                    5
To get thy bread, ech thing is now so skant.
Seke still thy profite vpon thy bare fete.
Lende in no wise: for feare that thou do want:
Vnlesse it be, as to a calfe a chese:
By which returne be sure to winne a cant                        10
Of halfe at least.  It is not good to leese.
Learne at the ladde, that in a long white cote,
From vnder the stall, withouten landes or feese,
Hath lept into the shoppe: who knowes by rote
This rule that I haue told thee here before.                    15
Sometime also riche age beginnes to dote,
Se thou when there thy gaine may be the more.
Stay him by the arme, where so he walke or go:
Be nere alway, and if he coughe to sore:
What he hath spit treade out, and please him so.                20
A diligent knaue that pikes his masters purse,
May please him so, that he withouten mo
Executour is.  And what is he the wurs?
But if so chance, thou get nought of the man:
The wydow may for all thy charge deburs.                        25
A riueld skynne, a stinkyng breath, what than?
A tothelesse mouth shall do thy lippes no harme.
The golde is good, and though she curse or banne:
Yet where thee list, thou mayest lye good and warme.
Let the olde mule bite vpon the bridle:                         30
Whilst there do lye a sweter in thine arme.
In this also se thou be not idle:
Thy nece, thy cosyn, thy sister, or thy daughter,
If she bee faire: if handsome be her middle:
If thy better hath her loue besought her:                       35
Auaunce his cause, and he shall helpe thy nede.
It is but loue, turne it to a laughter.
But ware I say, so gold thee helpe and spede:
That in this case thou be not so vnwise,
As Pandar was in such a like dede.                              40
For he the fole of conscience was so nice:
That he no gaine would haue for all his payne.
Be next thy selfe for frendshyp beares no price.

                      𝔐          Laughest

Laughest thou at me, why? do I speake in vaine?
No not at thee, but at thy thrifty iest.
Wouldest thou, I should for any losse or gayne,
Change that for golde, that I haue tane for best          5
Next godly thinges: to haue an honest name?
Should I leaue that? then take me for a beast.
Nay then farewell, and if thou care for shame:
Content thee then with honest pouertie:
With free tong, what thee mislikes, to blame.          10
And for thy trouth sometime aduersitie.
And therwithall this thing I shall thee giue,
In this world now litle prosperitie:
And coyne to kepe, as water in a siue.

## [127] The song of Iopas vn⸗          15
### finished.

W Hen Dido feasted first the wanderyng Troian knight:
    whō Iunos wrath w̄ stormes did force in Libyk sāds to light
That mighty Atlas taught, the supper lastyng long,
With crisped lockes on golden harpe, Iopas sang in song.          20
That same (quod he) that we the world do call and name:
Of heauen and earth with all contents, it is the very frame.
Or thus, of heauenly powers by more power kept in one
Repungnant kindes, in mids of whō the earth hath place alone:
Firme, round, of liuing thinges, the mother place and nourse:          25
Without the which in egal weight, this heuen doth hold his course
And it is callde by name, the first and mouyng heauen,
The firmament is placed next, conteinyng other seuen,
Of heauenly powers that same is planted full and thicke:
As shinyng lightes which we call stars, that therin cleue & sticke.          30
With great swift sway, the first, & with his restlesse sours,
Carieth it self, and al those eyght, in euen continuall cours.
And of this world so round within that rollyng case,
Two points there be that neuer moue, but firmely kepe their place
The tone we see alway, the tother standes obiect          35
Against the same, deuidyng iust the grounde by line direct.
Which by imaginacion, drawen from the one to thother
Toucheth the centre of the earth, for way there is none other.
And these be callde the Poles, discriyde by starres not bright.
Artike the one northward we see: Antartike thother hyght.          40

                                                    The

The line, that we deuise from thone to thother so:
As axel is, vpon the which the heauens about do go
Which of water nor earth, of ayre nor fire haue kinde.
Therfore the substance of those same were harde for man to finde.   5
But they bene vncorrupt, simple and pure vnmixt:
And so we say been all those starres, that in those same be fixt.
And eke those erryng seuen, in circle as they stray:
So calld, because agaynst that first they haue repungnant way:
And smaller bywayes to, skant sensible to man:   10
To busy worke for my pore harpe: let sing them he, that can.
The wydest saue the first, of all these nine aboue
One hundred yere doth aske of space, for one degree to moue.
Of which degrees we make, in the first moouyng heauen,
Three hundred and threscore in partes iustly deuided euen.   15
And yet there is another betwene those heauens two:
Whose mouyng is so sly so slack: I name it not for now.
The seuenth heauen or the shell, next to the starry sky,
All those degrees that gatherth vp, with aged pase so sly:
And doth performe the same, as elders count hath bene,   20
In nine and twenty yeres complete, and daies almost sixtene:
Doth cary in his bowt the starre of Saturne old:
A threatner of all liuyng things, with drought & with his cold.
The sixt whom this conteyns, doth stalke with yoonger pase:
And in twelue yere doth somwhat more then thothers viage was.   25
And this in it doth bear the starre of Ioue benigne,
Twene Saturns malice and vs men, frendly defendyng signe.
The fift bears bloudy Mars, that in three hundred daies,
And twise eleuen with one full yere, hath finisht all those wayes.
A yere doth aske the fourth, and howers therto sixe,   30
And in the same the dayes eie the sunne, therin her styckes.
The third, that gouernd is by that, that gouerns mee:
And loue for loue, and for no loue prouokes: as oft we see:
In like space doth performe that course, that did the tother.
So dothe the next vnto the same, that second is in order.   35
But it doth bear the starre, that calld is Mercury:
That many a crafty secrete steppe doth tread, as Calcars try.
That sky is last, and fixt next vs, those wayes hath gone,
In seuen and twenty cōmon dayes, and eke the third of one:
And beareth with his sway, the diuers Moone about:   40
Now bright, now brown, now bēt, now ful, & now her light is out
Thus haue they of their owne two mouynges al these seuen
One, wherin they be caried still, ech in his seueral heuen.

              **M.ii.**         An

An other of them selues, where their bodyes be layed
In bywayes, and in lesser rowndes, as I afore haue sayd.
Saue of them all the sunne doth stray lest from the streight,
The starry sky hath but one cours, that we haue calde the eight.      5
And all these moouynges eight are ment from west to the east:
Although they seme to clime aloft, I say from east to west.
But that is but by force of the first mouyng sky:
In twise twelue houres frō east to east y̆ᵗ carieth thē by and by.
But marke we well also, these mouinges of these seuen,      10
Be not about the axell tree of the first mouyng heuen.
For they haue their two poles directly tone to the tother. &c.


*T. VV YAT E the elder.*

## [128] A trueloue.

WHat sweet releef the showers to thirstie plants we see:
  What dere delite, the blooms to beez: my trueloue is to mee.
  As fresh, and lusty vere foule winter doth exceed:
As morning bright, with scarlet sky, doth passe the euenings weed:   5
  As melow peares aboue the crabs esteemed be:
So doth my loue surmount them all, whom yet I hap to se.
  The oke shall oliues bear: the lamb, the lion fray:
The owle shall match the nightingale, in tuning of her lay:   10
  Or I my loue let slip out of mine entiere hert:
So deep reposed in my brest is she, for her desert.
  For many blessed giftes, O happy, happy land:
Where Mars, and Pallas striue to make their glory most to stand
  Yet, land, more is thy blisse: that, in this cruell age,   15
A Venus ymp, thou hast brought forth, so stedfast, and so sage.
  Among the Muses nyne, a tenth yf Ioue would make:
And to the Graces three, a fourth: her would Apollo take.
  Let some for honour hoont, and hourd the massy golde:
With her so I may liue, and dye, my weal cannot be tolde.   20

## [129] The louer to his dear, of his exceding loue.

PHebe twise took her horns, twise layd them by:
  I, all the while, on thee could set no yie.
Yet doo I liue: if life you may it call,   25
Which onely holds my heauy hert, as thrall.
Certesse for death doo I ful often pray,
To rid my wo, and pull these pangs away.
So plaines Prometh, his womb no time to faile:
And, ayelife left, had leefer, he might quaile.   30
I erre, or els who this deuise first found,
By that gripes name he cleped loue vnsound.
In all the town, what streat haue I not seen?
In all the town, yet hath not Carie been.
Eyther thy sier restraines thy free outgate,   35
O woman, worthy of farre better state:

Or peeplepesterd London lykes thee nought,
But pleasant ayr, in quiet countrie sought.
Perchaunce, in olds our loue thou doest repeat,
And in sure place woldst euery thing retreat.                          5
Forth shall I go, ne will I stay for none,
Vntyll I may somwhere finde thee alone.
Therwhile, keep you of hands, and neck the heew:
Let not your cheeks becoom or black, or bleew.
Go with welcouerd hed: for you in case                                10
Apollo spied, burn wold he on your face.
Daphne, in groue, clad with bark of baytree:
Ay mee, if such a tale should ryse of thee.
Calisto found, in woods, Ioues force to fell:
I pray you, let him not like you so well.                             15
Eigh, how much dreed? Here lurks of theeus a haunt:
Whoso thou beest, preyseeker prowd, auaunt.
Acteon may teach thee Dictynnaes ire:
Of trouth, this goddesse hath as fiers a fire.
What doo I speak? O chief part of my minde,                           20
Vnto your eares these woords no way doo finde.
Wold god, when you read this, obserue I might
Your voyce, and of your countinaunce haue sight,
Then, for our loue, good hope were not to seek:
I mought say with myself, she will be meek.                           25
Doutlesse I coom, what euer town you keep,
Or where you woon, in woods, or mountanes steep:
I coom, and if all pear not in my face,
Myself will messenger be of my case.
If to my prayer all deaf, you dare saye, no:                          30
Streight of my death agilted shall you go.
Yet in mid death, this same shall ease my hart:
That Carie, thou wert cause of all the smart.


[130] **The louer asketh pardon
of his dere, for flee-                                                 35
yng from
her.**

Louers

*L*Ouers men warn the corps beloued to flee,
From the blinde fire in case they wold liue free.
Ay mee, how oft haue I fled thee, my Day?
I flee, but loue bides in my brest alway.                                5
Lo yet agayn, I graunt, I gan remoue:
But both I could, and can say still, I loue.
If woods I seek, cooms to my thought Adone:
And well the woods do know my heauy mone.
In gardens if I walk: Narcissus there                                   10
I spy, and Hyacints with weepyng chere:
If meads I tred, O what a fyre I feel?
In flames of loue I burn from hed to heel.
Here I behold dame Ceres ymp in flight:
Here bee, methynk, black Plutoes steeds in sight.                       15
Stronds if I look vpon, the Nymphs I mynde:
And, in mid sea, oft feruent powrs I fynde.
The hyer that I clyme, in mountanes wylde,
The nearer mee approcheth Venus chylde.
Towns yf I haunt: in short, shall I all say?                            20
There soondry fourms I view, none to my pay.
Her fauour now I note, and now her yies:
Her hed, amisse: her foot, her cheeks, her guyse.
· In fyne, where mater wants, defautes I fayn:
Whom other, fayr: I deem, she hath soom stayn.                          25
What boots it then to flee, sythe in nightyde,
And daytyme to, my Day is at my side?
A shade therfore mayst thou be calld, by ryght:
But shadowes, derk, thou, Day, art euer bright.
Nay rather, worldly name is not for thee:                              30
Sithe thou at once canst in twoo places bee.
Forgiue me, goddesse, and becoom my sheeld:
Euen Venus to Anchise herself dyd yeeld.
Lo, I confesse my flight: bee good therfore:
Ioue, oftentimes, hath pardond mee for more.                          35
Next day, my Day, to you I coom my way:
And, yf you suffer mee, due payns wyll pay.

[131] N. Vincent. to G. Black
wood, agaynst wed=
ding.                                                                 40

𝔐.iiii.                              Sythe

[ 95 ]

SYthe, Blackwood, you haue mynde to wed a wife:
I pray you, tell, wherefore you like that life.
What? that henceforth you may liue more in blisse?
I am beguylde, but you take mark amisse. 5
Either your fere shall be defourmd: (and can
You blisful be, with flower of frying pan?
Or els, of face indifferent: (they say,
Face but indifferent will soone decay.)
Or faire: who, then, for many men semes fine: 10
Ne can you say, she is all holly mine.
And be she chaste (if no man chaunce to sew)
A sort of brats she bringes, and troubles new:
Or frutelesse will so passe long yeres with thee,
That scant one day shall voyd of brawlyng bee. 15
Hereto heap vp vndaunted hed, stif hart,
And all the rest: eche spouse can tell a part.
Leaue then, this way, to hope for happy life:
Rather be your bed sole, and free from strife.
Of blessed state if any path be here: 20
It lurketh not, where women wonne so nere.

## [132] G.Blackwood to.N.Vincent, with weddyng.

SYthe, Vincent, I haue minde to wed a wife:
You bid me tell, wherfore I like that life. 25
Foule will I not, faire I desire: content,
If faire me fayle, with one indifferent.
Fair, you alledge, a thousand will applie:
But, nere so oft requirde, she will denie.
Meane beautie doth soone fade: therof playn hee, 30
Who nothing loues in woman, but her blee.
Frute if she bring, of frute is ioyfull sight:
If none, what then? our burden is but light.
The rest, you ming, certesse, we graunt, be great:
Stif hert, vndaunted hed cause soom to freat. 35
But, in all thinges, inborne displeasures be:
Yea pleasure we, full of displeasure, se.
And maruail you, I looke for good estate,
Hereafter if a woman be my mate?

Or

Oh straight is vertues path, if sooth men say:
And likewise, that I seek, straight is the way.

## [133] The Muses.

*I*Mps of king Ioue, and quene Remembrance lo,                    5
  The sisters nyne, the poets pleasant feres.
Calliope doth stately style bestow,
And worthy prayses payntes of princely peres.
Clio in solem songes, reneweth old day,
With present yeres conioynyng age bypast.                    10
Delitefull talke loues Comicall Thaley:
In fresh green youth, who dothe like laurell last.
With voyces Tragicall sowndes Melpomen,
And, as with cheyns, thallured eare shee bindes.
Her stringes when Terpsichor dothe touche, euen then        15
Shee toucheth hartes, and raigneth in mens mindes.
Fine Erato, whose look a liuely chere
Presents, in dauncyng keeps a comely grace.
With semely gesture doth Polymnie stere:
Whose wordes holle routes of renkes doo rule in place,      20
Vranie, her globes to view all bent,
The ninefolde heauen obserues with fixed face.
The blastes Euterpe tunes of instrument,
With solace sweet hence heauie dumps to chase.
Lord Phebus in the mids (whose heauenly sprite             25
These ladies dothe enspire) embraceth all.
The graces in the Muses weed, delite
To lead them forth, that men in maze they fall.

## [134] Musonius the Philosophers
## saiyng.                    30

*I*N workyng well, if trauell you sustaine:
  Into the winde shall lightly passe the payne:
But of the deed the glory shall remaine,
And cause your name with worthy wightes to raigne.
In workyng wrong, if pleasure you attaine:                  35
The pleasure soon shall vade, and uoide, as vaine:
𝔑.i.

But

[ 97 ]

But of the deed, throughout the life, the shame
Endures, defacyng you with fowl defame:
And stil torments the minde, bothe night and daye:
Scant length of time the spot can wash awaye.                    5
Flee then ylswading pleasures baits vntreew:
And noble vertues fayr renown purseew.

## [135] Marcus Catoes comparison of mans life with yron.

W Ho wold beleeue mans life like yron to bee,            10
   But proof had been, great Cato, made by thee?
For if, long time, one put this yron in vre,
Folowing ech day his woork, with bysye cure:
With dayly vse, hee may the metall wear,
And bothe the strength, and hardnesse eke impaire.    15
Again, in case his yron hee cast aside,
And carelesse long let it vntoucht abide:
Sythe, cankerd rust inuades the mettall sore,
And her fowl teeth there fastneth more and more.
So man, in case his corps hee tyre, and faint           20
With labor long: his strength it shall attaint.
But if in sluggard slothe the same dothe lye:
That manly might will fall away, and dye:
That bodies strength, that force of wit remooue:
Hee shall, for man, a weaklyng woman prooue.          25
Wherfore, my childe, holde twene these twaine the waye:
Nother with to much toyl thy lyms decaye,
In idle ease nor giue to vices place:
In bothe who measure keeps, hee hath good grace.

## [136] Cleobulus the Lydians riddle.                     30

O Ne is my sire: my soons, twise six they bee,
   Of daughters ech of them begets, you see,
Thrise ten: wherof one sort be fayr of face,
The oother doth vnseemly black disgrace.              35
Nor this holl rout is thrall vnto deathdaye,
Nor worn with wastful time, but liue alwaye:

And

And yet the same alwaies (straunge case) do dye.
The sire, the daughters, and the soons distry.
In case you can so hard a knot vnknit:
You shall I count an Edipus in wit. 5

## [137] Concerning Virgils Eneids.

*B*Y heauens hye gift, in case reuiued were
  Lysip, Apelles, and Homer the great:
The moste renowmd, and ech of them sance pere,
In grauyng, paintyng, and the Poets feat: 10
Yet could they not, for all their vein diuine,
In marble, table, paper more, or lesse,
With cheezil, pencil, or with poyntel fyne,
So graue, so paynt, or so by style expresse
(Though they beheld of euery age, and land 15
The fayrest books, in euery toung contriued,
To frame a fourm, and to direct their hand)
Of noble prince the liuely shape descriued:
As, in the famous woork, that Eneids hight,
The naamkouth Virgil hath set forth in sight. 20

## [138] Of mirth.

*A*Heauy hart, with wo encreaseth euery smart:
  A mirthfull minde in time of need, defendeth sorowes dart.
The sprite of quicnesse seems, by drery sadnesse slayn:
By mirth, a man to liuely plight, reuiued is agayn. 25
Dolour dryeth vp the bones: the sad shall sone be sick:
Mirth can preserue the kyndly helth, mirth makes the body quick.
Depe dumps do nought, but dull, not meet for man but beast:
A mery hert sage Salomon countes his continuall feast.
Sad soll, before thy time, brings thee vnto deaths dore: 30
That fond condicions haue bereft, late daye can not restore.
As, when the couered heauen, showes forth a lowryng face,
Fayr Titan, with his leam of light, returns a goodly grace:
So, when our burdened brest is whelmd with clowdy thought,
A pleasant calm throughout the corps, by chereful hart is brought 35
Enioye we then our ioyes, and in the lorde reioyce:
Faith makyng fast eternall ioye, of ioyes while wee haue choyce.

𝕹.ii.            To

## [139] To L. I. S.

*C*Haris the fourth, Pieris the tenth, the second Cypris, Iane,
One to assemblies thre adioynd: whom Phebus fere, Diane,
Among the Nymphs Oreades, might wel vouchsafe to place:     5
But you as great a goddesse serue, the quenes most noble grace:
Allhayle, and while, like Terpsichor, much melody you make:
Which if the field, as doth the court, enioyd, the trees wold shake:
While latine you, and french frequent: while English tales you tel:
Italian whiles, and Spanish you do hear, and know full well:     10
Amid such peares, and solemne sightes, in case conuenient tyme
You can (good Lady) spare, to read a rurall poets ryme:
Take here his simple sawes, in briefe: wherin no need to moue
Your Ladishyp, but thus lo speakes thabundance of his loue.
The worthy feates that now so much set forth your noble name,     15
So haue in vre, they still encreast, may more encrease your fame.
For though diuine your doings be, yet thews w^t yeres may grow:
And if you stay, streight now adayes fresh wits will ouergo.
Wherfore the glory got maintayne, maintayne the honour great.
So shal the world my doom approue, and set you in that seat,     20
Where Graces, Muses, and Ioues ymp, the ioyful Venus, raigne:
So shall the bacheler blessed bee, can such a Nymph obtaine.

## [140] To maistres D. A.

*W*Hat cause, what reasō moueth me: what fansy fils my brains
That you I minde of virgins al, whō Britan soile sustains     25
Bothe when to lady Mnemosynes dere daughters I resort,
And eke whē I y̆ season slow deceaue, w̆ glad disport?  (late foūd,
What force, what power haue you so great, what charms haue you
To pluck, to draw, to rauish hartes, & stirre out of ther stownd?
To you, I trow, Ioues daughter hath the louely gyrdle lent,     30
That Cestos hight: wherin there bee all maner graces blent,
Allurementes of conceits, of wordes the pleasurable taste:
That same, I gesse, hath she giuen you, and girt about your waste
Beset with sute of precious pearl, as bright as sunny day.
But what? I am beguilde, and gone (I wene) out of the way.     35
These causes lo do not so much present your image prest,
That will I, nill I, night and day, you lodge within this brest:
Those gifts of your right worthy minde, those goldē gifts of mind
Of

Of my fast fixed fansiefourm first moouing cause I finde:
Loue of the one, and threefold powr: faith sacred, sound, sincere:
A modest maydens mood: an hert, from clowd of enuy clere:
Wit, fed with Pallas food diuine: will, led with louely lore:    5
Memorie, conteining lessons great of ladies fiue, and fowr:
Woords, sweeter, than the sugar sweet,with heauenly nectar drest:
Nothing but coomly can they carp, and wonders well exprest.
Such damsels did the auncient world, for Poets penns, suffise:
Which, now a dayes, welnye as rare, as Poets fyne, aryse.    10
Wherfore,by gracious gifts of god, you more than thrise yblest:
And I welblest myself suppose: whom chastefull loue imprest,
In frendships lace, with such a lasse, doth knit, and fast combine:
Which lace no threatning fortune shall, no length of tyme vntwine:
And I that daye, with gem snowwhite, will mark, & eke depaynt    15
With pricely pen: which, Awdley, first gan mee with you acquaint.

## [141] Of. m.  D. A.

*D* Eserts of Nymphs, that auncient Poets showe,
  A r not so kouth, as hers: whose present face,
M ore, than my Muse, may cause the world to knowe    20
A nature nobly giuen: of woorthy race:
S o trayned vp, as honour did bestowe.
C yllene, in sugerd speech, gaue her a grace.
E xcell in song Apollo made his dere.
N o fingerfeat Minerue hid from her sight.    25
E xprest in look, she hath so souerain chere,
  A s Cyprian once breathed on the Spartan bright.
W it, wisdom, will, woord, woork, and all, I ween,
D are no mans pen presume to paint outright.
L o luyster and light: which if old tyme had seen,    30
E ntroned, shyne she should, with goddesse Fame.
Y eeld, Enuie, these due prayses to this dame.

## [142] A neew yeres gift,to
## the l. M. S.

*N* Ow flaming Phebus, passing through his heauenly regiō hye,    35
  The vttrest Ethiopian folk with feruent beams doth frye:
And with the soon, the yere also his secret race doth roon:
And Ianus, with his double face, hath it again begoon:

𝔑.iii.    O

O thou, that art the hed of all, whom mooneths, and yeres obey:
At whose commaund bee bothe the sterres, and surges of the sea:
By powr diuine, now prosper vs this yere with good successe:
This well to lead, and many mo, vs with thy fauour blesse.          5
Graunt, with sound soll in body sound that here we dayly go:
And, after, in that conntrey lyue, whence bannisht is all wo:
Where hoonger, thirst, and sory age, and sicknesse may not mell:
No sense perceius, no hert bethinks the ioyes, that there do dwel.


## [143] An other to.l.M.S.          10


ᔕO happy bee the course of your long life:
 So roon the yere intoo his circle ryfe:
That nothyng hynder your welmeanyng minde:
Sharp wit may you, remembrans redy fynde,
Perfect intelligence, all help at hand:          15
Styll stayd your thought in frutefull studies stand.
Hed framed thus may thother parts well frame,
Diuine demeanour wyn a noble name:
By payzed doom with leasure, and good heed:
By vpright dole, and much auayling deed:          20
By hert vnthirld, by vndiscoomfite chere,
And brest discharged quite of coward fere:
By sober mood, and orders coomly rate:
In weal, and wo, by holdyng one estate.
And to that beauties grace, kynde hath you lent,          25
Of bodies helth a perfite plight bee blent.
Dame fortunes gifts may so stand you in sted,
That well, and wealfully your lyfe be led.
And hee, who giues these graces not in vayn,
Direct your deeds, his honour to maintain.          30


## [144] To.l. K.S.


TO you, madame, I wish, bothe now, and eke from yere to yere,
 Strēgth w̃ Debore, w̃ Iudith faith, w̃ Maudlē zeal, Anns chere
With blessed Mary modest moode: like Sibill, life full long:
A mynde with sacred sprite enspired, wit fresh, and body strong:          35
And, when of your forepointed fate you haue outroon the race:
Emong all these, in Ioues hye raygn of blisses full, a place.
                                                        To

## [145] To .l. E. S.

*A*S this first daye of Ianus youthe restores vnto the yere:
  So bee your minde in coorage good reuiued, and herty chere.
And as dame Tellus labreth now her frutes conceiued to breed:      5
Right so of your most forward wit may great auail proceed.
So lucky bee the yere, the mooneths, the weeks, ẙ dayes, ẙ howrs
That them, with long recours, you may enioy in blisfull bowrs.

## [146] To. m. D. A.

*G*Orgeous attire, by art made trym, and clene,      10
  Cheyn, bracelet, perl, or gem of Indian riuer,
To you I nil, ne can (good Damascene)
This time of Ianus Calends, here deliuer.
But, what? My hert: which, though long sins certain
Your own it was, aye present at your hest:      15
Yet here itself doth it resigne agayn,
Within these noombers closde. Where, think you best
This to repose? There, I suppose, where free
Minerue you place. For it hath you embraste,
As thHeliconian Nymphs: with whom, euen hee,      20
That burn for soom, Apollo liueth chaste.
Presents in case by raarnesse you esteem:
O Lord, how great a gift shall this then seem?

## [147] To. m. S. H.

*T*O you this present yere full fayre, and fortunable fall,      25
  Returning now to his prime part: and, good luck therwithall,
May it proceed: and end, and oft return, to glad your hert:
O Susan, whom among my frendes I count, by your desert.
Ioy may your heauenly sprite: endure fresh wit, in ẙ fyne brayn:
Your knowledge of good things encreas: your body, safe remain:      30
A body, of such shape, as showeth a worthy wight by kynde:
A closet, fit for to contein the vertues of that minde.
What shall I yet moreouer add? God graunt, w̃ pleasaunt mate
A pleasaunt life you lead. Well may that man reioyse his fate.

                                    **𝔫.iiii.**      To

### [148] To his familiar frend.

NO image carued with coonnyng hand, no cloth of purple dye,
No precious weight of metall bright, no siluer plate gyue I:
Such gear allures not heuēly herts: such gifts no grace they bring:     5
I lo, ỹ know your minde, will send none such, what then? nothing.

### [149] Description of Ver:
### tue.

WHat one art thou, thus in torn weed yclad?
Vertue, in price whom auncient sages had.                               10
Why, poorely rayd? For fadyng goodes past care.
Why doublefaced? I mark eche fortunes fare.
This bridle, what? Mindes rages to restrain.
Tooles why beare you? I loue to take great pain.
Why, winges? I teach aboue the starres to flye.                        15
Why tread you death? I onely cannot dye.

### [150] Prayse of measure:
### kepyng.

THe auncient time commended, not for nought,
The mean: what better thing can ther be sought?                        20
In mean, is vertue placed: on either side,
Bothe right, and left, amisse a man shall slide.
Icar, with sire hadst thou the mid way flown,
Icarian beck by name had no man known.
If middle path kept had proud Phaeton,                                 25
No burning brand this erth had falln vpon.
Ne cruell powr, ne none to soft can raign:
That keeps a mean, the same shall styll remain.
Thee, Iulie, once did too much mercy spill:
Thee, Nero stern, rigor extreem did kill.                              30
How could August so many yeres well passe?
Nor ouermeek, nor ouerferse he was.
Worship not Ioue with curious fansies vain,
Nor him despise: hold right atween these twayn.

No

No wastefull wight, no greedy goom is prayzd.
Stands largesse iust, in egall balance payzd.
So Catoes meal surmountes Antonius chere,
And better fame his sober fare hath here.                                5
To slender buildyng, bad: as bad, to grosse:
One, an eyesore, the tother falls to losse.
As medcines help, in measure: so (God wot)
By ouermuch, the sick their bane haue got.
Vnmeet mee seems to vtter this, mo wayes:                                10
Measure forbids vnmeasurable prayse.

## [151] Mans life after Possidonius, or Crates.

W Hat path list you to tred? what trade will you assaye?
  The courts of plea, by braul, & bate, driue gentle peace away.        15
In house, for wife, and childe, there is but cark, and care:
With trauail, and with toyl ynough, in feelds wee vse to fare.
Vpon the seas lieth dreed: the riche, in foraine land,
Doo fear the losse: and there, the poore, like misers poorly stand.
Strife, with a wife, without, your thrift full hard to see:              20
Yong brats, a trouble: none at all, a maym it seems to bee:
Youth, fond: age hath no hert, and pincheth all to nye.
Choose then the leefer of these twoo, no life, or soon to dye.

## [152] Metrodorus minde to the contrarie.                               25

W Hat race of life ronne you? what trade will you assaye?
  In courts, is glory gott, and witt encreased daye by daye.
At home, wee take our ease, and beak our selues in rest:
The feelds our nature doo refresh with pleasures of the best.
On seas, is gayn to gett: the straunger, hee shall bee                   30
Esteemed, hauing much: if not, none knoweth his lack, but hee.
A wife will trym thy house: no wife? then art thou free.
Brood is a louely thing: without, thy life is loose to thee.
Yong bloods be strong: old sires in double honour dwell.
Doo waye that choys, no life, or soon to dye: for all is well.           35

®.i.                     Of

## [153] Of lawes.

W Hen princes lawes, w̃ reuerend right, do keep ỹ cõmons vnder
   As meek as lãbes, thei do their charge, & scatter not asunder.
But if they raise their heades aloft, and lawe her brydle slake:    5
Then, like a tyger fell, they fare, and lust for law they take.
Where water dothe preuail, and fire, no mercy they expresse:
But yet the rage of that rude rout is much more mercilesse.

## [154] Of frendship.

O F all the heauenly gifts, that mortall men commend,    10
   What trusty treasure in the world can coũteruail a frend?
Our helth is soon decayd: goodes, casuall, light, and vain:
Broke haue we seen the force of powr, and honour suffer stain.
In bodies lust, man doth resemble but base brute:
True vertue gets, and keeps a frend, good guide of our pursute:    15
Whose harty zeal with ours accords, in euery case:
No terme of time, no space of place, no storme can it deface.
When fickle fortune fayls, this knot endureth still:
Thy kin out of their kinde may swarue, when frẽds owe thee good
What sweeter solace shall befall, than one to finde,   (wil.  20
Vpon whose brest thou mayst repose the secrets of thy minde?
Hee wayleth at thy wo, his tears with thine be shed:
With thee dothe hee all ioyes enioye: so leef a life is led.
Behold thy frend, and of thy self the pattern see:
One soull, a wonder shall it seem, in bodies twain to bee.    25
In absence, present, riche in want, in sickenesse sownd,
Yea, after death aliue, mayst thou by thy sure frend be found.
Ech house, ech towne, ech realm by stedfast loue dothe stand:
Where fowl debate breeds bitter bale, in eche diuided land.
O frendship, flowr of flowrs: O liuely sprite of life,    30
O sacred bond of blisfull peace, the stalworth staunch of strife:
Scipio with Lelius didst thou conioyn in care,
At home, in warrs, for weal and wo, with egall faith to fare.
Gesippus eke with Tite, Damon with Pythias,
And with Menetus sonne Achill, by thee combined was.    35
Euryalus, and Nisus gaue Virgil cause to sing:
Of Pylades doo many rymes, and of Orestes ring.
                                  Down

Down Theseus went to hell, Pirith, his frend to finde:
O y̆ the wiues, in these our dayes, were to their mates so kinde.
Cicero, the frendly man, to Atticus, his frend,
Of frendship wrote: such couples lo dothe lott but seeldom lend.    5
Recount thy race, now ronne: how few shalt thou there see,
Of whome to saye: This same is hee, that neuer fayled mee.
So rare a iewel then must nedes be holden dere:
And as thou wilt esteem thyself, so take thy chosen fere.
The tyrant, in dispayre, no lack of gold bewayls:    10
But, Out I am vndoon (sayth hee) for all my frendship fayls.
Wherfore sins nothing is more kindely for our kinde:
Next wisdome, thus that teacheth vs, loue we the frendful minde.

## [155] The Garden.

*T*He issue of great Ioue, draw nere you, Muses nine:    15
   Help vs to praise the blisfull plott of garden ground so fine.
The garden giues good food, and ayd for leaches cure:
The garden, full of great delite, his master dothe allure.
Sweet sallet herbs bee here, and herbs of euery kinde:
The ruddy grapes, the seemly frutes bee here at hand to finde.    20
Here pleasans wanteth not, to make a man full fayn:
Here marueilous the mixture is of solace, and of gain.
To water sondry seeds, the forow by the waye
A ronning riuer, trilling downe with liquor, can conuay.
Beholde, with liuely heew, fayr flowrs that shyne so bright:    25
With riches, like the orient gems, they paynt the molde in sight.
Beez, humming with soft sound, (their murmur is so small)
Of blooms and blossoms suck the topps, on dewed leaues they fall
The creping vine holds down her own bewedded elms:
And, wādering out w̆ branches thick, reeds folded ouerwhelms.    30
Trees spred their couerts wyde, with shadows fresh and gaye:
Full well their branched bowz defend the feruent sonne awaye.
Birds chatter, and some chirp, and some sweet tunes doo yeeld:
All mirthfull, w̆ their songs so blithe, they make both ayre, & feeld.
The garden, it allures, it feeds, it glads the sprite:    35
Frō heauy harts all doolfull dumps the garden chaseth quite.
Strength it restores to lims, drawes, and fulfils the sight:
With chere reuiues the senses all, and maketh labour light.
O, what delites to vs the garden ground dothe bring?
Seed, leaf, flowr, frute, herb, bee, and tree, & more, then I may sing.    40

                                  P.ii.              An

## [156] An epitaph of sir Iames
## wilford knight.

*T*He worthy Wilfords body, which alyue,
  Made both the Scot, and Frenchman sore adrad:       5
A body, shapte of stomake stout to striue
With forein foes: a corps, that coorage had
So full of force, the like nowhere was ryfe:
With hert, as free, as ere had gentle knight:
Now here in graue (thus chaungeth ay, this lyfe)       10
Rests, with vnrest to many a wofull wight.
Of largesse great, of manhod, of forecast
Can ech good English souldiour bear record.
Speak Laundersey, tell Muttrel maruails past:
Crye Musselborough: prayse Haddington thy lord,       15
From thee that held both Scots, and frekes of Fraunce:
Farewel, may England say, hard is my chaunce.

## [157] An other, of the same
## knightes death.

*F*Or Wilford wept first men, then ayr also,       20
  For Wilford felt the wayters wayfull wo.
The men so wept: that bookes, abrode which bee,
Of moornyng meeters full a man may see.
So wayld the ayr: that, clowds consumde, remaynd
No dropes, but drouth the parched erth sustaynd.       25
So greeted floods: that, where ther rode before
A ship, a car may go safe on the shore.
Left were no mo, but heauen, and erth, to make,
Throughout the world, this greef his rigor take.
But sins the heauen this Wilfords goste dothe keep,       30
And earth, his corps: saye mee, why shold they weep?

## [158] An Epitaph of the ladye
## Margaret Lee.
## 1 5 5 5.

Man

*M*An, by a woman lern, this life what we may call:
   Blod, frēdship, beauty, youth, attire, welth, worship, helth & al
Take not for thine: nor yet thy self as thine beknow.
For hauing these, with full great prayse, this lady did but show     5
Her self vnto the world: and in prime yeres (bee ware)
Sleeps doolfull sister, who is wont for no respect to spare,
Alas, withdreew her hence: or rather softly led:
For with good will I dare well saye, her waye to him shee sped:
Who claymed, that he bought: and took that erst hee gaue:     10
More meet than any worldly wight, such heauenly gems to haue.
Now wold shee not return, in earth a queen to dwell.
As shee hathe doon to you, good frend, bid lady Lee, farewell.

## [159] Vpon the tomb of A. w.

*M*Yrrour of matrones, flowr of spouslike loue,     15
   Of fayr brood frutefull norsse, poor peoples stay,
Neybours delite, true hert to him aboue,
In yeelding worlds encreas took her decaye:
Who printed liues yet in our hertes alway:
Whose closet of good thews, layd here a space,     20
Shall shortly with the soull in heauen haue place.

## [160] Vpon the deceas of w. Ch.

*N*Ow, blythe Thaley, thy feastfull layes lay by:
   And to resound these doolfull tunes apply.
Cause of great greef the tyrant death imports:     25
Whose vgsoom idoll to my brayns resorts.
A gracefull ymp, a flowr of youth, away
Hath she bereft (alas) before his daye.
Chambers, this lyfe to leaue, and thy dear mates,
So soon doo thee constrayn enuyous fates?     30
Oh, with that wit, those maners, that good hert,
Woorthy to lyue olde Nestors yeres thou wert.
You wanted outward yies: and yet aryght
In stories, Poets, oratours had sight.
Whatso you herd, by liuely voyce, exprest,     35
Was soon reposde within that mindefull brest.
To mee more pleasant Plautus neuer was,
Than those conceits, that from your mouth did passe.

                           **O̶.iii.**         Our

Our studiemates great hope did hold alway,
You wold be our schooles ornament, one day.
Your parents then, that thus haue you forgone,
Your brethren eke must make theyr heauy mone:5
Your louyng feres cannot theyr teares restrayn:
But I, before them all, haue cause to playn:
Who in pure loue was so conioynd with thee,
An other Grimald didst thou seem to bee.
Ha lord, how oft wisht you, with all your hart,10
That vs no chaunce a sonder might depart?
Happy were I, if this your prayer tooke place:
Ay mee, that it dothe cruell death deface.
Ah lord, how oft your sweet woords I repeat,
And in my mynde your woonted lyfe retreat?15
O Chambers, O thy Grimalds mate moste dere:
Why hath fell fate tane thee, and left him here?
But wherto these complaintes in vain make wee?
Such woords in wyndes to waste, what mooueth mee?
Thou holdst the hauen of helth, with blisfull Ioue:20
Through many waues, and seas, yet must I roue.
Not woorthy I, so soon with thee to go:
Mee styll my fates reteyn, bewrapt in wo.
Liue, our companion once, now lyue for aye:
Heauens ioyes enioy, whyle wee dye day by daye.25
You, that of faith so sure signes here exprest,
Do triumph now, no dout, among the blest:
Haue changed sea for porte, darknesse for light,
An inn for home, exile for countrey right,
Trauail for rest, straunge way for citie glad,30
Battail for peas, free raign for bondage bad.
These wretched erthly stounds who can compare
To heauenly seats, and those delites moste rare?
We frayl, you firm: we with great trouble tost,
You bathe in blisse, that neuer shall bee lost.35
Wherfore, Thaley, reneew thy feastfull layes:
Her doolfull tunes my chered Muse now stayes.

## [161] Of. N. Ch.

WHy, Nicolas, why doest thou make such haste
After thy brother? Why goest thou so? To taste40

Of

Of changed lyfe with hym the better state?
Better? yea best of all, that thought can rate.
Or, did the dreed of wretched world driue thee
Leste thou this afterfall should hap to see:         5
Mauortian moods, Saturnian furies fell,
Of tragicall turmoyls the haynous hell?
O, whose good thews in brief cannot be told,
The hartiest mate, that euer trod the mold:
If our farewell, that here liue in distresse,        10
Auayl, farewell: the rest teares do suppresse.

## [162] A funerall song, vpon the deceas of Annes his moother.

*Y*Ea, and a good cause why thus should I playn.    15
   For what is hee, can quietly sustayn
So great a grief, with mouth as styll, as stone?
My loue, my lyfe, of ioye my ieewell is gone.
This harty zeale if any wight disprooue,
As womans work, whom feeble minde doth mooue:   20
Hee neither knowes the mighty natures laws,
Nor touching elders deeds hath seen old saws.
Martius, to vanquish Rome, was set on fire:
But vanquisht fell, at moothers boon, his ire.
Into Hesperian land Sertorius fled,        25
Of parent aye cheef care had in his hed.
Dear weight on shoulders Sicil brethren bore,
While Etnaes gyant spouted flames full sore.
Not more of Tyndars ymps hath Sparta spoke,
Than Arge of charged necks with parents yoke.   30
Nor onely them thus dyd foretyme entreat:
Then, was the noorsse also in honour great.
Caiet the Phrygian from amid fireflame
Rescued, who gaue to Latine stronds the name.
Acca, in dubble sense Lupa ycleaped,      35
To Romane Calendars a feast hath heaped.
His Capra Ioue among the sterres hath pight:
In welkin clere yet lo she shineth bryght.
Hyades as gratefully Lyai did place,

                                  ℗.iiii.        Whom

Songes.

Whom, in primetide, supports the Bulls fayr face.
And should not I expresse my inward wo,
When you, most louyng dam, so soon hence go?
I, in your frutefull woomb conceyued, born was,          5
Whyle wanderyng moon ten moonths did ouerpasse.
Mee, brought to light, your tender arms sustaynd:
And, with my lips, your milky paps I straynd.
You mee embraced, in bosom soft you mee
Cherished, as I your onely chylde had bee.              10
Of yssue fayr with noombers were you blest:
Yet I, the bestbeloued of all the rest.
Good luck, certayn forereadyng moothers haue,
And you of mee a speciall iudgement gaue.
Then, when firm pase I fixed on the ground:             15
When toung gan cease to break the lispyng sound:
You mee streightway did too the Muses send,
Ne suffered long a loyteryng lyfe to spend,
What gayn the wooll, what gayn the wed had braught,
It was his meed, that me there dayly taught.            20
When with Minerue I had acquaintance woon:
And Phebus seemd to loue mee, as his soon:
Browns hold I bad, at parents hest, farewell:
And gladly there in schools I gan to dwell:
Where Granta giues the ladies nyne such place,          25
That they reioyse to see theyr blisfull case.
With ioyes at hert, in this pernasse I bode,
Whyle, through his signes, fiue tymes great Titan glode:
And twyse as long, by that fayr foord, whereas
Swanfeeder Temms no furder course can passe.            30
O, what desire had you, therwhile, of mee?
Mid doutfull dreeds, what ioyes were wont to bee?
Now linnen clothes, wrought with those fyngers fyne,
Now other thynges of yours dyd you make myne:
Tyll your last thredes gan Clotho to vntwyne,           35
And of your dayes the date extreem assygne.
Hearyng the chaunce, your neybours made much mone:
A dearworth dame, they thought theyr coomfort gone.
Kinswoomen wept: your charge, the maydens wept:
Your daughters wept, whom you so well had kept.         40
But my good syre gaue, with soft woords, releef:
And clokes, with outward chere, his inward greef:
Leste, by his care, your sicknes should augment,

And

[ 112 ]

And on his case your thoughtfull hert be bent.
You, not forgetting yet a moothers mood,
When at the dore dartthirling death there stood,
Did saye: Adeew, dear spouse, my race is roon:                    5
Wher so he bee, I haue left you a soon,
And Nicolas you naamd, and naamd agayn:
With other speech, aspiring heauenly raign:
When into ayre your sprite departed fled,
And left the corps a cold in lukewarm bed.                        10
Ah, could you thus, deare mother, leaue vs all?
Now, should you liue: that yet, before your fall,
My songs you might haue soong, haue heard my voyce,
And in commodities of your own reioyce.
My sisters yet vnwedded who shall guide?                          15
With whose good lessons shall they bee applyed?
Haue, mother, monumentes of our sore smart:
No costly tomb, areard with curious art:
Nor Mausolean masse, hoong in the ayre:
Nor loftie steeples, that will once appayre:                      20
But waylful verse, and doolfull song accept.
By verse, the names of auncient peres be kept:
By verse, liues Hercules: by verse, Achil:
Hector, Ene, by verse, be famous still.
Such former yeres, such death hath chaūced thee:                 25
Closde, with good end, good life is woont to bee.
But now, my sacred parent, fare you well:
God shall cause vs agayn togither dwell,
What time this vniuersall globe shall hear
Of the last troomp the rynging voyce: great fear                 30
To soom, to such as you a heauenly chear.
Til then, reposde rest you in gentle sleep:
While hee, whom to you are bequeathd, you keep.

## [163] Vpon the death of the lord Mautra-<br>uers,out of doctor Haddons     35<br>latine.

*T*He noble Henry, he, that was the lord Mautrauers named:
  Heyr to the house of thArundels, so long a time now famed:

𝔓          Who

Who from Fitzalens doth recount discent of worthy race,
Fitzalens, earls of hye estate, men of a goodly grace:
Whom his renowmed father had seen florish, and excell,
In arms, in arts, in witt, in skill, in speaking wonders well:     5
Whose yeres, to timely vertue had, and manly grauenesse caught:
With soden ruine is downfalln, and into ashes braught:
While glory his coragious hert enflames to trauail great:
And, in his youthly brest ther raigns an ouerferuent heat.
The perelesse princesse, Mary quene, her message to present,     10
This Britan lord, as one moste meet, to Cesars broother sent.
On coursing steeds hee rids the waye: in ship hee fleeteth fast:
To royall Cesars court he comes, the payns, and perils past:
His charge enioynd perfourmeth hee, attaind exceeding prayse:
His name, and fame so fully spred, it dures for afterdayes.     15
But lo, a feruent feeuer doth, amid his triumphs, fall:
And, with hertgripyng greef, consumes his tender lyms and all.
O rufull youth, thy helth too far forgot, and too much heed
To countrie, and too parent yeuen: why makest thou such speed?
O, staye your self: your country so to serue dothe right require,     20
That often serue you may: and then, at length, succeed your sire.
But thee perchaunce it likes, thy life the price of praise to paye:
Nor deth doest dreed, where honor shines, as bright, as sonny day.
Certesse no greater glory could, than this, to thee betide:
Though Ioue, six hundred yeres, had made thy fatall thread abide     25
Of iourneys, and of trauails huge the cause thy country was:
Thy funerall to honour, forth great Cesars court gan passe.
And thus, O thus (good lord) this ymp, of heuē most worthy wight
His happy life with blisfull death concluded hath aright:
When, in fourt yere quene Maries raign proceeded: & what day,     30
Was last of Iulie moneth, the same his last took him awaye.
From yeres twise ten if you in count wil but one yere abate:
The very age then shall you finde of lord Mautrauers fate.
Likewise, was Titus Cesar hence withdrawn, in his prime yeres:
Likewise, the yong prince Edward went: and diuers other peres.     35
Father, forbear thy wofull tears, cease, England, too lament:
Fates fauour none, the enmie death to all alike is bent.
The onely mean, that now remains, with eloquence full fine,
Hath Shelley vsed, in setting forth this barons name diuine.
Your Haddon eke, who erst in your life time, bore you good hart,     40
Presenteth you this monument, of woonted zeal some part.
And now farewell: of English youth most chosen gem, farewell:
A worthyer wight, saue Edward, did in England neuer dwell.

                                        Vpon

[164] Vpon the sayd lord Mautra-
uers death.

MEe thought, of late when lord Mautrauers dyed,
  Our common weal, thus, by her self shee cryed:       5
Oft haue I wept for mine, so layd a sleep,
Yet neuer had I iuster cause to weep.

[165] The death of Zoroas,an Egiptian
Astronomer,in the first fight,
that Alexander had with       10
the Persians.

NOw clattering arms, now ragyng broyls of warr
  Gan passe the noyes of taratantars clang:
Shrowded with shafts, the heuen: with clowd of darts,
Couered, the ayre: against fulfatted bulls,       15
As forceth kindled ire the Lions keen:
Whose greedy gutts the gnawing hoonger pricks:
So Macedoins against the Persians fare.
Now corpses hide the purpurde soyl with blood:
Large slaughter, on ech side: but Perses more       20
Moyst feelds bebledd: their herts, and noombers bate.
Fainted while they giue back, and fall to flight:
The lightning Macedon, by swoords, by gleaus,
By bands, and trowps, of fotemen with his garde,
Speeds to Darie: but him, his nearest kyn,       25
Oxate preserues, with horsemen on a plump
Before his carr: that none the charge could giue.
Here grunts, here grones, echwhere strong youth is spent:
Shaking her bloody hands, Bellone, among
The Perses, soweth all kindes of cruel death.       30
With throte ycutt, hee roores: hee lyeth along,
His entrails with a launce through girded quite:
Him down the club, him beats farstryking bowe,
And him the slyng, and him the shinand swoord:
Hee dieth, hee is all dedd, hee pants, hee rests.       35
Right ouer stood, in snowwhite armour braue,

**P.ii.**       The

# Songes.

The Memphite Zoroas, a cooning clerk:
To whom the heauen lay open, as his book:
And in celestiall bodyes hee could tell
The moouyng, meetyng, light, aspect, eclyps,　　　　5
And influence, and constellations all:
What earthly chaunces wold betide: what yere
Of plenty storde, what signe forwarned derth:
How winter gendreth snow: what temperature
In the primetide dothe season well the soyl:　　　　10
Why soomer burns: why autum hath ripe grapes:
Whether the circle, quadrate may becoom:
Whether our tunes heauens harmony can yeeld:
Of fowr begynns, among them selues how great
Proportion is: what swaye the erring lightes　　　　15
Dothe send in course gayn that first moouing heauen:
What grees, one from an other distant bee:
What sterr dothe lett the hurtfull sire to rage,
Or him more mylde what opposition makes:
What fire dothe qualifie Mauorses fire:　　　　20
What house echone doth seek: what planet raigns
Within this hemisphere, or that: small things
I speak: holl heauen hee closeth in his brest.
This sage then, in the starrs had spied: the fates
Threatned him death, without delaye: and sithe　　　　25
Hee saw, hee could not fatall order change:
Forward hee preast, in battayl that hee might
Meet with the ruler of the Macedoins:
Of his right hand desirous to be slayn,
The boldest beurn, and worthiest in the feeld:　　　　30
And, as a wight now weary of his life,
And seeking death: in first front of his rage,
Cooms desperatly to Alisanders face:
At him, with darts, one after other, throwes:
With reckles woords, and clamour him prouokes:　　　　35
And sayth, Nectanabs bastard, shameful stain
Of mothers bed: why losest thou thy strokes,
Cowards emong? Turn thee to mee, in case
Manhod ther bee so much left in thy hert:
Coom fight with mee: that on my helmet wear　　　　40
Apolloes laurel, bothe for learnings laude,
And eke for Martiall prayse: that, in my shield,
The seuenfold sophie of Minerue contein:

　　　　　　　　　　　　　　　　　　A match

A match, more meet, sir king, than any here.
The noble prince amoued, takes ruthe vpon
The wilfull wight: and, with soft woords, ayen,
O monstrous man (quod he) whatso thou art,     5
I praye thee, lyue: ne do not, with thy death,
This lodge of lore, the Muses mansion marr.
That treasure house this hand shall neuer spoyl:
My swoord shall neuer bruze that skylfull brayn,
Longgatherd heapes of science soon to spyll.     10
O, how faire frutes may you to mortall men
From wisdoms garden, giue? How many may,
By you, the wyser, and the better proue?
What error, what mad moode, what phrenzey thee
Persuades to bee downsent to deep Auern:     15
Where no artes florish, nor no knowledge vails?
For all these sawes, when thus the souerain sayde,
Alighted Zoroas: with swoord vnsheathed,
The carelesse king there smote, aboue the greaue,
At thopening of his quishes: wounded him     20
So, that the blood down reyled on the ground.
The Macedon, perceyuing hurt, gan gnash:
But yet his minde he bent, in any wyse,
Hym to forbear: set spurrs vnto his steed,
And turnd away: leste anger of the smart     25
Should cause reuenger hand deal balefull blowes.
But of the Macedonian chieftanes knights
One, Meleager, could not bear this sight:
But ran vpon the sayd Egyptian renk:
And cut him in both kneez: hee fell to ground:     30
Wherwith a hole route came of souldiours stern,
And all in peeces hewed the silly seg.
But happyly the soll fled to the sterres:
Where, vnder him, he hath full sight of all,
Wherat hee gazed here, with reaching looke.     35
The Persians wayld such sapience to forgo:
The very fone, the Macedonians wisht,
Hee wold haue lyued: kyng Alisander self
Deemd him a man, vnmeet to dye at all:
Who woon lyke prayse, for conquest of his ire,     40
As for stout men in feeld that daye subdeewd:
Who princes taught, how to discern a man,

                    **P.iii.**               That

That in his hed so rare a iewell beares.
But ouer all, those same Camenes, those same
Diuine Camenes, whose honour he procurde,
As tender parent dothe his daughters weal:           5
Lamented: and, for thanks, all that they can,
Do cherish him deceast, and set hym free
From derk obliuion of deuouryng death.

## [166] Marcus Tullius Ciceroes death.

*T*Herfore, when restlesse rage of wynde, and waue     10
    Hee saw: By fates, alas calld for (quod hee)
Is haplesse Cicero: sayl on, shape course
To the next shore, and bryng me to my death.
Perdie these thanks, reskued from ciuil swoord,
Wilt thou, my countrey, paye?  I see mine end:        15
So powrs diuine, so bid the gods aboue,
In citie saued that Consul Marcus shend.
Speakyng no more, but drawyng from deep hert
Great grones, euen at the name of Room reherst:
His yies, and cheeks, with showrs of teares, hee washt. 20
And (though a route in dayly daungers worn)
With forced face, the shipmen held theyr teares:
And, striuyng long the seas rough floods to passe,
In angry wyndes, and stormy stowrs made waye:
And at the last, safe anchord in the rode.           25
Came heauy Cicero a land: with payn,
His faynted lyms the aged sire dothe draw:
And, round about their master, stood his band:
Nor greatly with theyr own hard hap dismayd,
Nor plighted fayth, prone in sharp time to break:    30
Soom swoords prepare: soom theyr deare lord assist:
In littour layd, they lead hym vnkouth wayes:
If so deceaue Antonius cruell gleaus
They might, and threats of folowing routs escape.
Thus lo, that Tullie, went, that Tullius,            35
Of royall robe, and sacred Senate prince:
When hee afar the men approche espyeth,
And of his fone the ensignes dothe aknow:
And, with drawn swoord, Popilius threatnyng death:
Whose life, and holl estate, in hazard once,         40
                                              He

Hee had preserud: when Room as yet to free
Herd hym, and at his thundryng voyce amazde.
Herennius eek, more eyger than the rest,
Present enflamde with furie, him purseews.
What might hee doo? Should hee vse in defense 5
Disarmed hands? or pardon ask, for meed?
Should hee with woords attempt to turn the wrath
Of tharmed knyght, whose safegard hee had wrought?
No, age, forbids, and fixt within deep brest
His countreys loue, and falling Rooms image. 10
The charret turn, sayth hee, let loose the rayns:
Roon to the vndeserued death: mee, lo,
Hath Phebus fowl, as messanger, forwarnd:
And Ioue desires a neew heauensman to make.
Brutus, and Cassius soulls, liue you in blisse: 15
In case yet all the fates gaynstriue vs not,
Neyther shall wee perchaunce dye vnreuenged.
Now haue I liued, O Room, ynough for mee:
My passed lyfe nought suffreth mee to dout
Noysom obliuion of the lothesom death. 20
Slea mee: yet all thofspring to coom shall know:
And this deceas shall bring eternall lyfe.
Yea and (onlesse I fayl, and all in vain
Room, I soomtyme thy Augur chosen was)
Not euermore shall frendly fortune thee 25
Fauour, Antonius: once the day shall coom:
When her deare wights, by cruell spight, thus slayn,
Victorious Room shall at thy hands require.
Mee likes, therwhyle, go see the hoped heauen.
Speech had he left: and therwith hee, good man, 30
His throte preparde, and held his hed vnmoued.
His hastyng too those fates the very knights
Be lothe to see: and, rage rebated, when
They his bare neck beheld, and his hore heyres:
Scant could they hold the teares, that forth gan burst: 35
And almost fell from bloody hands the swoords.
Onely the stern Herennius, with grym look,
Dastards, why stand you styll? he sayth: and streight,
Swaps of the hed, with his presumptuous yron. 40
Ne with that slaughter yet is hee not fild:
Fowl shame on shame to heap, is his delyte.
Wherfore the hands also doth hee of smyte,

**P.iiii.** Which

[ 119 ]

Which durst Antonius life so liuely paynt.
Him, yeldyng strayned goste, from welkin hye,
With lothly chere, lord Phebus gan behold:
And in black clowd, they saye, long hid his hed.                    5
The latine Muses, and the Grayes, they wept:
And, for his fall, eternally shall weep.
And lo, hertpersyng Pitho (straunge to tell)
Who had to him suffisde bothe sense, and woords,
When so he spake: and drest, with nectar soote,                    10
That flowyng toung: when his wyndpype disclosde,
Fled with her fleeyng frend: and (out alas)
Hath left the erth, ne wil no more return.
Popilius flyeth, therwhyle: and, leauyng there
The senslesse stock, a gryzely sight doth bear               15
Vnto Antonius boord, with mischief fed.

## [167] Of  M. T.  Cicero.

*F*Or Tullie, late, a toomb I gan prepare:
  When Cynthie, thus, bad mee my labour spare:
Such maner things becoom the ded, quoth hee:               20
But Tullie liues, and styll alyue shall bee.

                                    *N. G.*

## [168] The complaint of a louer
## with sute to his loue
## for pitye.

*I*F euer wofull man might moue your hartes to ruthe,          5
  Good ladies here his woful plaint, whose deth shal try his truth
  And rightfull iudges be on this his true report:
If he deserue a louers name among the faithfull sort.
  Fiue hundred times the sonne hath lodged him in the West:
Since in my hart I harbred first of all the goodlyest gest.          10
  Whose worthinesse to shew my wittes are all to faint.
And I lack cunnyng of the scoles, in colours her to paynt.
  But this I briefly say in wordes of egall weight.
So void of vice was neuer none, nor with such vertues freyght.
  And for her beauties prayse, no wight, that with her warres.          15
For, where she comes, she shewes her self as sonne amōg ẙ starres.
  But Lord, thou wast to blame, to frame such parfitenesse:
And puttes no pitie in her hart, my sorowes to redresse.
  For yf ye knew the paynes, and panges, that I haue past:
A wonder would it be to you, how that my life hath last.          20
  When all the Goddes agreed, that Cupide with his bow
Should shote his arrowes frō her eies, on me his might to show
  I knew it was in vain my force to trust vpon:
And well I wist, it was no shame, to yelde to such a one.
  Then did I me submit with humble hart, and minde,          25
To be her man for euermore: as by the Goddes assinde.
  And since that day, no wo, wherwith loue might torment,
Could moue me frō this faithfull band: or make me once repent.
  Yet haue I felt full oft the hottest of his fire:
The bitter teares, the scalding sighes, the burning hote desyre.          30
  And with a sodain sight the trembling of the hart:
And how the blood doth come, and go, to succour euery part.
  When that a pleasant loke hath lift me in the ayer:
A frowne hath made me fall as fast into a depe despayer.
  And when that I, er this, my tale could well by hart:          35
And that my tong had learned it, so that no worde might start:
  The sight of her hath set my wittes in such a stay:
That to be lord of all the world, one word I could not say.
  And many a sodayn cramp my hart hath pinched so:
                            Q.i.      That

That for the time, my senses all felt neither weale, nor wo.
　Yet saw I neuer thing, that might my minde content:
But wisht it hers, and at her will, if she could so consent.
　Nor neuer heard of wo: that did her will displease: 5
But wisht the same vnto my self, so it might do her ease.
　Nor neuer thought that fayre, nor neuer liked face:
Vnlesse it did resemble her, or some part of her grace.
　No distance yet of place could vs so farre deuide:
But that my hert, and my good will did still with her abide. 10
　Nor yet it neuer lay in any fortunes powre,
To put that swete out of my thought, one minute of an howre.
　No rage of drenching sea, nor woodenesse of the winde,
Nor cannōs wͭ their thundryng cracks could put her frō my minde
　For when bothe sea and land asunder had vs set: 15
My hole delite was onely then, my self alone to get.
　And thitherward to loke, as nere as I could gesse:
Where as I thought, that shee was then, ẙ might my wo redresse.
　Full oft it did me good, that waies to take my winde:
So pleasant ayre in no place els, me thought I could not finde. 20
　I saying to my self, my life is yonder waye:
And by the winde I haue here sent, a thousand sighes a daye.
　And sayd vnto the sunne, great gifts are geuen thee:
For thou mayst see mine earthly blisse, where euer that she bee.
　Thou seest in euery place, wold God I had thy might: 25
And I the ruler of my self, then should she know no night.
　And thus from wish to wishe my wits haue been at strife:
And wantyng all that I haue wisht, thus haue I led my life.
　But long it can not last, that in such wo remaines.
No force for that: for death is swete to him, that feles such paines. 30
　Yet most of all me greues: when I am in my graue,
That she shall purchase by my death a cruell name to haue.
　Wherfore all you that heare this plaint, or shall it see:
Wish, that it may so perce her hert, that she may pitie mee.
　For and it were her will: for bothe it were the best, 35
To saue my life, to kepe her name, and set my hert at rest.

## [169] Of the death of master Deuerox
## the lord Ferres
## sonne.

Who

WHo iustly may reioyce in ought vnder the skye?
  As life, or lands: as frends, or frutes: which only liue to dye.
Or who dothe not well know all worldly works are vaine?
And geueth nought but to the lendes, to take the same againe.          5
For though it lift some vp: as wee long vpward all:
Such is the sort of slipper welth: all things do rise to fall.
Thuncertentie is such: experience teacheth so:
That what things men do couet most, them sonest they forgo.
Lo Deuorox where he lieth: whose life men heeld so deare          10
That now his death is sorowed so, that pitie it is to heare.
His birth of auncient blood: his parents of great fame:
And yet in vertue farre before the formost of the same.
His king, and countrye bothe he serued to so great gaine:
That with the Brutes record doth rest, and euer shall remaine.          15
No man in warre so mete, an enterprise to take:
No man in peace that pleasurd more of enmies frends to make.
A Cato for his counsell: his head was surely such.
Ne Theseus frenship was so great, but Deuorox was as much.
A graffe of so small grothe so much good frute to bring:          20
Is seldome heard, or neuer sene: it is so rare a thing.
A man sent vs from God, his life did well declare:
And now sent for by god again, to teach vs what we are.
Death, and the graue, that shall accompany all that liue,
Hath brought hī heuē, though sōewhat sone, which life could neuer          25
God graunt well all, that shall professe as he profest:          (geue
To liue so well, to dye no worse: and send his soule good rest.


## [170] They of the meane estate
##          are happiest.


IF right be rackt, and ouerronne:          30
  And power take part with open wrong:
If fear by force do yelde to soone,
The lack is like to last to long.
  If God for goodes shalbe vnplaced:
If right for riches lose his shape:          35
If world for wisdome be embraced:
The gesse is great, much hurt may happe.
  Among good things, I proue and finde,
The quiet life dothe most abound:

**Q.ii.**                    And

And sure to the contented minde
There is no riches may be found.
   For riches hates to be content:
Rule is enmy to quietnesse.            5
Power is most part impacient:
And seldom likes to liue in pease.
   I hard a herdman once compare:
That quiet nightes he had mo slept:
And had mo mery daies to spare:       10
Then he, which ought the beastes, he kept.
   I would not haue it thought hereby
The dolphin swimme I meane to teach:
Nor yet to learne the Fawcon flie:
I rowe not so farre past my reache.     15
   But as my part aboue the rest,
Is well to wish and well to will:
So till my breath shall fail my brest,
I will not ceasse to wish you styll.

## [171] Comparison of lyfe    20
### and death.

*T*He lyfe is long, that lothsumly doth last:
   The dolefull dayes draw slowly to theyr date:
The present panges, and paynfull plages forepast
Yelde griefe aye grene to stablish this estate.    25
So that I fele, in this great storme, and strife,
The death is swete that endeth such a life.
   Yet by the stroke of this strange ouerthrow,
At which conflict in thraldom I was thrust:
The Lord be praysed: I am well taught to know,   30
From whence man came, and eke whereto he must:
And by the way vpon how feble force
His term doth stand, till death doth end his course.
   The pleasant yeres that seme, so swifte that runne:
The mery dayes to end, so fast that flete:    35
The ioyfull nightes, of which day daweth so soone:
The happy howers, which mo do misse, then mete,
Doe all consume: as snow against the sunne:
And death makes end of all, that life begunne.

Since

Since death shall dure, tyll all the world be wast.
What meaneth man to drede death then so sore?
As man might make, that life should alway last.
Without regard, the lord hath led before                                5
The daunce of death, which all must runne on row:
Though how, or when, the lord alone doth know.
　　If man would minde, what burdens life doth bring:
What greuous crimes to god he doth commit:
What plages, what panges, what perilles therby spring:        10
With no sure hower in all his dayes to sit:
He would sure think, as with great cause I do:
The day of death were better of the two.
　　Death is a port, wherby we passe to ioy,
Life is a lake, that drowneth all in pain.                              15
Death is so dere, it ceaseth all annoy.
Life is so leude, that all it yeldes is vayn.
And as by life to bondage man is braught:
Euen so likewise by death was fredome wraught.
　　Wherfore with Paul let all men wish, and pray           20
To be dissolude of this foule fleshy masse:
Or at the least be armed against the day:
That they be found good souldiers, prest to passe
From life to death: from death to life agayn
To such a life, as euer shall remain.                                    25

## [172] The tale of Pigmalion with conclusion vpon the beau- tye of his loue.

*I*N Grece somtime there dwelt a man of worthy fame:
　　To graue in stone his connyng was: Pygmaliō was his name.      30
　　To make his fame endure, when death had him bereft:
He thought it good, of his owne hand some filed work were left.
　　In secrete studie then such work he gan deuise,
As might his conning best commend, and please the lokers eyes.
　　A courser faire he thought to graue, barbd for the field:          35
And on his back a semely knight, well armd with speare & shield:
　　Or els some foule, or fish to graue he did deuise:
And still, within his wandering thoughtes, new fansies did aryse.
　　　　　　　　　　　　　　　　　℞.iii.　　　　　　Thus

[ 125 ]

Thus varyed he in mynde, what enterprise to take:
Till fansy moued his learned hand a woman fayre to make.
    Whereon he stayde, and thought such parfite fourm to frame:
Whereby he might amaze all Greece, and winne immortall name.    5
    Of Yuorie white he made so faire a woman than:
That nature scornd her perfitnesse so taught by craft of man.
    Welshaped were her lyms, full cumly was her face:
Eche litle vayn most liuely coucht, eche part had semely grace.
    Twixt nature, & Pygmalion, there might appeare great stryfe.    10
So semely was this ymage wrought, it lackt nothyng but life.
    His curious eye beheld his own deuised work:
And, gasyng oft thereon, he found much venome there to lurke.
    For all the featurde shape so dyd his fansie moue:
That, with his idoll, whom he made, Pygmalion fell in loue.    15
    To whom he honour gaue, and deckt with garlandes swete,
And did adourn with iewels riche, as is for louers mete.
    Somtimes on it he fawnd: some time in rage would crye:
It was a wonder to beholde, how fansy bleard his eye.
    Since that this ymage dum enflamde so wyse a man:    20
My dere, alas since I you loue, what wonder is it than?
    In whom hath nature set the glory of her name:      (frame.
And brake her mould, in great dispayre, your like she could not

## [173] The louer sheweth his wofull
## state, and prayeth pitye.    25

*L*Yke as the lark within the marlians foote
   With piteous tunes doth chirp her yelden lay:
So syng I now, seyng none other boote,
My renderyng song, and to your wyll obey.
Your vertue mountes aboue my force so hye.    30
And with your beautie seased I am so sure:
That there auails resistance none in me,
But paciently your pleasure to endure
For on your wyll my fansy shall attend:
My lyfe, my death, I put both in your choyce:    35
And rather had this lyfe by you to end,
Than lyue, by other alwayes to reioyce.
And if your crueltie doe thirst my blood:
Then let it forth, if it may doe you good.
                             Vpon

[174] Vpon consideracion of the stat[e of]
this lyfe he wisheth death.

*T*He lenger lyfe, the more offence:
  The more offence, the greater payn:          5
The greater payn, the lesse defence:
The lesse defence, the lesser gayn.
The losse of gayn long yll doth trye:
Wherefore come death, and let me dye.
  The shorter life, lesse count I fynde:        10
The lesse account, the sooner made:
The count soon made, the meryer minde:
The mery minde doth thought euade.
Short lyfe in truth this thing doth trye:
Wherefore come death, and let me dye:      15
  Come gentle death, the ebbe of care,
The ebbe of care, the flood of lyfe,
The flood of lyfe, the ioyfull fare,
The ioyfull fare, the end of strife.
The end of strife, that thing wishe I:       20
Wherefore come death, and let me dye.

[175] The louer that once disdained loue
is now become subiect beyng
caught in his snare.

*T*O this my song geue eare, who list:       25
  And mine intent iudge, as you wyll:
The tyme is cume, that I haue mist,
The thyng, wheron I hoped styll,
And from the top of all my trust,
Myshap hath throwen me in the dust.        30
  The time hath been, and that of late:
My hart and I might leape at large.
And was not shut within the gate
Of loues desyre: nor toke no charge
Of any thyng, that dyd pertain          35
                  **Q.iiii.**             As

As touching loue in any payn.
  My thought was free, my hart was light:
I marked not, who lost, who saught.
I playde by day, I slept by night.          5
I forced not, who wept, who laught.
My thought from all such thinges was free:
And I my self at libertee.
  I toke no hede to tauntes, nor toyes:
As leefe to see them frowne as smile:      10
Where fortune laught I scorned their ioyes:
I found their fraudes and euery wile.
And to my self oft times I smiled:
To see, how loue had them begiled.
  Thus in the net of my conceit        15
I masked styll among the sort
Of such as fed vpon the bayt,
That Cupide laide for his disport.
And euer as I saw them caught:
I them beheld, and therat laught.        20
  Till at the length when Cupide spied
My scornefull will and spitefull vse
And how I past not who was tied.
So that my self might still liue lose:
He set himself to lye in wait:        25
And in my way he threw a bait.
  Such one, as nature neuer made,
I dare well say saue she alone.
Such one she was as would inuade
A hart, more hard then marble stone.    30
Such one she is, I know, it right,
Her nature made to shew her might.
  Then as a man euen in a maze,
When vse of reason is away:
So I began to stare, and gaze.        35
And sodeinly, without delay,
Or euer I had the wit to loke:
I swalowed vp both bayt, and hoke.
  Which daily greues me more and more
By sondry sortes of carefull wo:      40
And none aliue may salue the sore,
But onely she, that hurt me so.
In whom my life doth now consist,

To

To saue or slay me as she list.
  But seing now that I am caught,
And bounde so fast, I cannot flee:
Be ye by mine ensample taught,                       5
That in your fansies fele you free.
Despise not them, that louers are:
Lest you be caught within his snare.

## [176] Of Fortune, and Fame.

*T*He plage is great, where fortune frownes:       10
  One mischief bringes a thousand woes
Where trumpets geue their warlike sownes:
The weake sustain sharp ouerthrowes.
No better life they taste, and fele:
That subiect are to fortunes whele.               15
  Her happy chance may last no time:
Her pleasure threatneth paines to come.
She is the fall of those, that clime:
And yet her whele auanceth some.
No force, where that she hates, or loues:    20
Her ficle minde so oft remoues.
  She geues no gift, but craues as fast.
She soone repentes a thankful dede.
She turneth after euery blast.
She helpes them oft, that haue no nede.    25
Where power dwelles, and riches rest:
False fortune is a common gest,
  Yet some affirm, and proue by skyll:
Fortune is not as fleyng Fame,
She neither can do good, nor yll.          30
She hath no fourme, yet beares a name.
Then we but striue agaynst the streames,
To frame such toyes on fansies dreames.
  If she haue shape, or name alone:
If she do rule, or beare no sway:         35
If she haue bodie, lief, or none:
Be she a sprite I cannot say.
But well I wot, some cause there is:
That causeth wo, and sendeth blisse.
  The cause of things I will not blame:    40

𝕽.i.              Lest

Lest I offend the prince of peas.
But I may chide, and braule with Fame:
To make her crye, and neuer cease.
To blow the trump within her eares:                                    5
That may apease my wofull teares.

## [177] Against wicked tonges.

O Euyll tonges, which clap at euery winde:
  Ye slea the quick, and eke the dead defame:
Those that liue well, som faute in them ye fynde.          10
Ye take no thought, in slaundring theyr good name.
Ye put iust men oft times to open shame.
Ye ryng so loude, ye sound vnto the skyes:
And yet in proofe ye sowe nothyng, but lyes.
  Ye make great warre, where peace hath been of long,      15
Ye bring rich realmes to ruine, and decay.
Ye pluck down right: ye doe enhaunce the wrong.
Ye turne swete myrth to wo, and welaway
Of mischiefes all ye are the grounde, I say.
Happy is he, that liues on such a sort:                    20
That nedes not feare such tonges of false report.

## [178] Not to trust to much but beware
## by others calamaties.

TO walke on doubtfull ground, where danger is vnseen
  Doth double men that carelesse be in depe dispaire I wene,   25
For as the blynde dothe feare, what footing he shall fynde:
So doth the wise before he speak, mistrust the strangers mynde.
For he that blontly runnes, may light among the breers,
And so be put vnto his plunge where danger least apperes:
The bird that selly foole, doth warn vs to beware,         30
Who lighteth not on euery bushe, he dreadeth so the snare.
The mouse that shonnes the trap, doth shew what harme doth ly:
Within the swete betraying bait, that oft disceiues the eye.
The fish auoides the hoke, though hunger byds him bite,
And houereth still about the worme, whereon is his delyte.  35
Yf birdes and beastes can see, where their vndoyng lies:
                                                    How

How should a mischief scape our heades, ẙ haue both wit and eyes.
What madnesse may be more, then plow the barreyn field:
Or any frutefull wordes to sow, to eares that are vnwyld.
They here and than mislyke, they like and than they lothe,                    5
Thei hate, thei loue, thei skorn, thei praise, yea sure thei cā do both
We see what falles they haue, that clyme on trees vnknowne:
As they that truste to rotten bowes, must nedes be ouerthrowne.
A smart in silence kept, doth ease the hart much more,
Than for to plain where is no salue, for to recure the sore.                   10
Wherfore my grief I hide, within a holow hart:
Vntill the smoke thereof be spied, by flaming of the smart.

## [179] Hell tormenteth not the damned ghostes so sore as vnkindnesse the louer.                                                             15

The restlesse rage of depe deuouryng hell,
The blasing brandes, that neuer do consume,
The roryng route, in Plutoes den that dwell:
The fiery breath, that from those ymps doth fume:
The dropsy dryeth, that Tantale in the flood                                  20
Endureth aye, all hopelesse of relief:
He hongersteruen, where frute is ready food:
So wretchedly his soule doth suffer grief:
The liuer gnawne of gylefull Promethus,
Which Vultures fell with strayned talant tyre:                                25
The labour lost of wearyed Sisiphus:
These hellish houndes, with paines of quenchlesse fyre,
Can not so sore the silly soules torment,
As her vntruth my hart hath alltorent.

## [180] Of the mutabilitie of the world.                                    30

*B*Y fortune as I lay in bed, my fortune was to fynde
  Such fāsies, as my carefull thought had brought into my minde
And when eche one was gone to rest, full soft in bed to lye:
I would haue slept: but then the watch did folow still myne eye.             35
And sodeinly I saw a sea of wofull sorowes prest:
                                        ℜ.ii.            Whose

Whose wicked wayes of sharp repulse bred mine vnquiet rest.
I saw this world: and how it went, eche state in his degree:
And that from wealth ygraunted is, both lyfe, and libertee.
I saw, how enuy it did rayne, and beare the greatest price:     5
Yet greater poyson is not found within the Cockatrice.
I saw also, how that disdayn oft times to forge my wo,
Gaue me the cup of bitter swete, to pledge my mortall fo.
I saw also, how that desire to rest no place could finde
But styll constrainde in endlesse pain to folow natures kynde.     10
I saw also most straunge of all how nature did forsake
The blood, that in her womb was wrought: as doth y̆ lothed snake
I saw, how fansy would retayn no lenger then her lust:
And as the winde how she doth change: and is not for to trust.
I saw, how stedfastnesse did fly with winges of often change:     15
A fleyng birde, but seldom seen, her nature is so strange.
I saw, how pleasant times did passe, as flowers doe in the mede:
To day that ryseth red as rose: to morow falleth ded.
I saw, my tyme how it did runne, as sand out of the glasse.
Euen as eche hower appointed is from tyme, and tyde to passe.     20
I saw the yeares, that I had spent, and losse of all my gayn:
And how the sport of youthfull playes my foly dyd retayn.
I saw, how that the litle ant in somer still dothe runne
To seke her foode, wherby to liue in winter for to come,
I saw eke vertue, how she sat the threde of life to spinne.     25
Which sheweth the end of euery work, before it doth beginne.
And when all these I thus beheld with many mo pardy:
In me, me thought, eche one had wrought a parfite proparty.
And then I said vnto my self: a lesson this shalbe
For other: that shall after come, for to beware by me.     30
Thus, all the night I did deuise, which way I might constrayn.
To fourme a plot, that wit might work these branches in my brain.

## [181] Harpelus complaynt of Phillidaes
### loue bestowed on Corin, who
### loued her not and denied     35
### him, that loued her.

*P*Hylida was a fayer mayde,
  And fresh as any flowre:

     Whom

Whom Harpalus the herdman prayed
To be his paramour.
   Harpalus and eke Corin
Were herdmen both yfere:
And Phillida could twist and spin           5
And therto sing full clere.
   But Phillida was all to coy
For Harpelus to winne.
For Corin was her onely ioye,           10
Who forst her not a pynne.
   How often would she flowers twine
How often garlandes make:
Of Couslippes and of Colombine,
And all for Corins sake.           15
   But Corin he had haukes to lure
And forced more the field:
Of louers lawe he toke no cure
For once he was begilde.
   Harpalus preualed nought           20
His labour all was lost:
For he was fardest from her thought
And yet he loued her most.
   Therfore waxt he both pale and leane
And drye as clot of clay:           25
His fleshe it was consumed cleane
His colour gone away.
   His beard it had not long be shaue,
His heare hong all vnkempt:
A man most fitte euen for the graue           30
Whom spitefull loue had spent.
   His eyes were red and all forewatched
His face besprent with teares:
It semde vnhap had him long hatched.
In middes of his dispayres.           35
   His clothes were blacke and also bare
As one forlorne was he:
Vpon his heade alwaies he ware,
A wreath of wilow tree.
   His beastes he kept vpon the hyll,           40
And he sate in the dale:
And thus with sighes and sorowes shryll,
He gan to tell his tale.

**R.iii.**           O Har-

# Songes.

O Harpelus thus would he say,
Vnhappiest vnder sunne:
The cause of thine vnhappy day
By loue was first begone. 5
  For thou wentest first by sute to seeke
A Tygre to make tame:
That sets not by thy loue a leke
But makes thy grefe her game.
  As easye it were, for to conuert 10
The frost into the flame:
As for to turne a froward hert
Whom thou so fain wouldst frame.
  Corin he liueth carelesse
He leapes among the leaues: 15
He eates the frutes of thy redresse
Thou reapes he takes the sheaues.
  My beastes a while your fode refrayne
And herken your herdmans sounde:
Whom spitefull loue alas hath slaine 20
Throughgirt with many a wounde.
  Oh happy be ye beastes wilde
That here your pasture takes:
I se that ye be not begylde
Of these your faythfull face. 25
  The Hart he fedeth by the Hynde
The Bucke hard by the Doo,
The Turtle Doue is not vnkinde
To him that loues her so.
  The Ewe she hath by her the Ramme 30
The yong Cow hath the Bulle:
The calf with many a lusty lamme
Do feede their honger full.
  But wellaway that nature wrought
Thee Phillida so faire: 35
For I may say that I haue bought
Thy beauty all to deare.
  What reason is it that cruelty
With beauty should haue part,
Or els that such great tyranny 40
Should dwell in womans hart.
  I see therfore to shape my death
She cruelly is prest:

To

To thend that I may want my breathe
My dayes been at the best.
   O Cupide graunt this my request
And do not stoppe thine eares:            5
That she may fele within her brest
The paynes of my dispayres.
   Of Corin that is carelesse
That she may craue her fee:
As I haue done in great distresse        10
That loued her faythfully.
   But sins that I shall die her slaue
Her slaue and eke her thrall:
Write you my frendes, vpon my graue
This chance that is befall.          15
   Here lieth vnhappy Harpelus
Whom cruell loue hath slayne:
By Phillida vniustly thus
Murdred with false disdaine.

## [182] Vpon sir Iames wilfordes    20
## death.

*L*O here the end of man the cruell sisters three
   The web of Wilfords life vnethe had half ysponne,
When rash vpon misdede they all accorded bee
To breke vertues course er half the race were ronne   25
And trip him on his way that els had won the game
And holden highest place within the house of fame.
   But yet though he be gone, though sence with him be past
Which trode the euen steppes that leaden to renowne
We that remaine aliue ne suffer shall to waste    30
The fame of his deserts, so shall he lose but sowne.
The thing shall aye remaine, aye kept as freshe in store
As if his eares shold ring of that he wrought before.
   Waile not therfore his want sith he so left the stage
Of care and wretched life, with ioye and clap of hands   35
Who plaieth lenger partes may well haue greater age
But few so well may passe the gulfe of fortunes sandes
So triedly did he treade ay prest at vertues beck
That fortune found no place to geue him once a check.

                **R.iiii.**          The

The fates haue rid him hence, who shall not after go,
Though earthed be his corps, yet florish shall his fame,
A gladsome thing it is that er he step vs fro,
Such mirrours he vs left our life therby to frame,     5
Wherfore his praise shall last aye freshe in Brittons sight,
Till sunne shall cease to shine, and lende the earth his light.

## [183] Of the wretchednes in this world.

WHo list to liue vpright, and holde him self content,     10
   Shall se such wonders in this world, as neuer erst was sent.
Such gropyng for the swete, such tastyng of the sower
Such wandryng here for wordly welth that lost is in one houre.
And as the good or badde gette vp in hye degre,
So wades the world in right or wrong it may none other be.     15
And loke what lawes they make, ech man must them obay,
And yoke himself with pacient hart to driue and draw ẙ way.
For such as long ago, great rulers were assinde
Both liues & lawes are now forgot & worne clene out of minde
So that by this I se, no state on earth may last     20
But as their times appointed be, to rise and fall as fast.
The goodes that gotten be, by good and iust desart,
Yet vse them so that neady handes may helpe to spend the part
For loke what heape thou hordst, of rusty golde in store,
Thine enemies shall waste the same, that neuer swat therfore.     25

## [184] The repentant sinner in durance and aduersitie.

VNto the liuyng Lord for pardon do I pray,
   From whō I graunt euen frō the shell, I haue run styl astray.
And other liues there none (my death shall well declare)     30
On whom I ought to grate for grace, as faulty folkes do fare.
But thee O Lorde alone, I haue offended so,
That this small scourge is much to scant for mine offence I know
I ranne without returne, the way the world liekt best
And what I ought most to regard, that I respected lest     35
The throng wherin I thrust, hath throwen me in such case
                               That

That Lorde my soule is sore beset without thy greater grace
My giltes are growen so great, my power doth so appayre
That with great force they argue oft, and mercy much dispayre.
But then with fayth I flee to thy prepared store
Where there lieth help for euery hurt, and salue for euery sore. 5
My loste time to lament, my vaine waies to bewaile,
No day no night no place no houre no moment I shal faile
My soule shall neuer cease with an assured faith
To knock, to craue, to call to cry to thee for helpe which sayth 10
Knocke and it shalbe heard, but aske and geuen it is
And all that like to kepe this course, of mercy shall not misse
For when I call to minde how the one wandryng shepe,
Did bring more ioye with his returne, then all the flocke did kepe.
It yeldes full hope and trust my strayed and wandryng ghost 15
Shalbe receiued and held more dere then those were neuer lost.
O Lord my hope beholde, and for my helpe make haste
To pardon the forpassed race that carelesse I haue past.
And but the day draw neare that death must pay the det,
For lone of life which thou hast lent and time of payment set. 20
From this sharpe shower me shilde which threatened is at hand,
Wherby thou shalt great power declare & I the storme withstand.
Not my will lord but thyne, fulfilde be in ech case,
To whose gret wil & mighty power al powers shal once geue place
My fayth my hope my trust, my God and eke my guide 25
Stretch forth thy hand to saue the soule, what so the body bide.
Refuse not to receiue that thou so dere hast bought,
For but by thee alone I know all safety in vaine is sought.
I know and knowledge eke albeit very late,
That thou it is I ought to loue and dreade in ech estate. 30
And with repentant hart do laude thee Lord on hye,
That hast so gently set me straight, that erst walkt so awry.
Now graunt me grace my God to stand thine strong in sprite,
And let ẙ world thē work such wayes, as to the world semes mete.

[185] The louer here telleth of his diuers 35
ioyes and aduersities in loue
and lastly of his
ladies death.

S Ythe singyng gladdeth oft the hartes
Of them that fele the panges of loue: 40

S.i. And

And for the while doth ease their smartes:
My self I shall the same way proue.
   And though that loue hath smit the stroke,
Wherby is lost my libertie:                      5
Which by no meanes I may reuoke:
Yet shall I sing, how pleasantly.
   Ny twenty yeres of youth I past:
Which all in libertie I spent:
And so from fyrst vnto the last,              10
Er aught I knew, what louing ment.
   And after shall I syng the wo,
The payne, the greefe, the deadly smart:
When loue this lyfe did ouerthrowe,
That hydden lyes within my hart.          15
   And then, the ioyes, that I did feele.
When fortune lifted after this,
And set me hye vpon her whele:
And changed my wo to pleasant blisse,
   And so the sodeyn fall agayne       20
From all the ioyes, that I was in.
All you, that list to heare of payne,
Geue eare, for now I doe beginne.
   Lo, fyrst of all, when loue began
With hote desyres my heart to burne:     25
Me thought, his might auailde not than
From libertie my heart to turne.
   For I was free: and dyd not knowe,
How much his might mannes hert may greue.
I had profest to be his fo:               30
His law I thought not to beleue.
   I went vntyed in lusty leas,
I had my wish alwayes at will:
Ther was no wo, might me displease:
Of pleasant ioyes I had my fill.         35
   No paynfull thought dyd passe my hart:
I spilt no teare to wet my brest:
I knew no sorow, sigh, nor smart.
My greatest grefe was quyet rest.
   I brake no slepe, I tossed not:      40
Nor dyd delyte to syt alone.
I felt no change of colde, and hote:
Nor nought a nightes could make me mone.
                          For

For all was ioy that I did fele:
And of voide wandering I was free.
I had no clogge tied at my hele:
This was my life at libertie.
    That yet me thinkes it is a blisse, 5
To thinke vpon that pleasure past.
But forthwithall I finde the misse,
For that it might no lenger last.
    Those dayes I spent at my desire,
Without wo or aduersitie: 10
Till that my hart was set a fire,
With loue, with wrath, and ielousie.
    For on a day (alas the while)
Lo, hear my harme how it began:
The blinded Lord, the God of guile 15
Had list to end my fredome than.
    And through mine eye into my hart,
All sodenly I felt it glide.
He shot his sharped fiery dart,
So hard, that yet vnder my side 20
    The head (alas) dothe still remaine,
And yet since could I neuer know,
The way to wring it out againe:
Yet was it nye three yere ago. 25
    This soden stroke made me agast:
And it began to vexe me sore.
But yet I thought, it would haue past,
As other such had done before.
    But it did not that (wo is me) 30
So depe imprinted in my thought,
The stroke abode: that yet I see,
Me thynkes my harme how it was wrought.
    Kinde taught me streight that this was loue
And I perceiued it perfectlye. 35
Yet thought I thus: Nought shall me moue:
I will not thrall my libertie.
    And diuers waies I did assay,
By flight, by force, by frend, by fo,
This fyrye thought to put away. 40
I was so lothe for to forgo
    My libertie: that me was leuer,
Then bondage was, where I heard saie:

                        S.ii.           Who

Who once was bounde, was sure neuer
Without great paine to scape away.
   But what for that, there is no choyce,
For my mishap was shapen so:                   5
That those my dayes that did reioyce,
Should turne my blisse to bitter wo.
   For with that stroke my blisse toke ende.
In stede wherof forthwith I caught,
Hotte burnyng sighes, that sins haue brend,      10
My wretched hart almost to naught.
   And sins that day, O Lord my life,
The misery that it hath felt.
That nought hath had, but wo and strife,
And hotte desires my hart to melt.             15
   O Lord how sodain was the change
From such a pleasant liberty?
The very thraldome semed strange:
But yet there was no remedy.
   But I must yeld, and geue vp all,          20
And make my guide my chiefest fo.
And in this wise became I thrall.
Lo loue and happe would haue it so.
   I suffred wrong and helde my peace,
I gaue my teares good leaue to ronne:      25
And neuer would seke for redresse,
But hopt to liue as I begonne.
   For what it was that might me ease,
He liued not that might it know.
Thus dranke I all mine owne disease:      30
And all alone bewailde my wo.
   There was no sight that might mee please,
I fled from them that did reioyce.
And oft alone my hart to ease,
I would bewayle with wofull voyce        35
   My life, my state, my miserie,
And curse my selfe and all my dayes.
Thus wrought I with my fantasie,
And sought my helpe none other waies.
   Saue sometime to my selfe alone,      40
When farre of was my helpe God wot:
Lowde would I cry: My life is gone,
My dere, if that ye helpe me not.

                            Then

Then wisht I streight, that death might end
These bitter panges, and all this grief.
For nought, methought, might it amend.
Thus in dispaire to haue relief, 5
  I lingred forth: tyll I was brought
With pining in so piteous case:
That all, that saw me, sayd, methought:
Lo, death is painted in his face.
  I went no where: but by the way 10
I saw some sight before mine eyes:
That made me sigh, and oft times say:
My life, alas I thee despyse.
  This lasted well a yere, and more:
Which no wight knew, but onely I: 15
So that my life was nere forlore:
And I dispaired vtterly.
  Tyll on a day, as fortune would:
(For that, that shalbe, nedes must fall)
I sat me down, as though I should 20
Haue ended then my lyfe, and all.
  And as I sat to wryte my plaint,
Meaning to shew my great vnrest:
With quaking hand, and hart full faint,
Amid my plaintes, among the rest, 25
  I wrote with ynk, and bitter teares:
I am not myne, I am not mine:
Behold my lyfe, away that weares:
And if I dye the losse is thyne.
  Herewith a litle hope I caught: 30
That for a whyle my life did stay.
But in effect, all was for naught.
Thus liued I styll: tyll on a day,
  As I sat staring on those eyes:
I meane, those eyes, that first me bound: 35
My inward thought tho cryed: Aryse:
Lo, mercy where it may be found.
  And therewithall I drew me nere:
With feble hart, and at a braide,
(But it was softly in her eare) 40
Mercy, Madame, was all, I sayd.
  But wo was me, when it was tolde.
For therewithall fainted my breath.

                  **S.iii.**           And

And I sate still for to beholde,
And heare the iudgement of my death.
   But Loue nor Hap would not consent,
To end me then, but welaway:                         5
There gaue me blisse: that I repent
To thinke I liue to see this day.
   For after this I playned still
So long, and in so piteous wise:
That I my wish had at my will                      10
Graunted, as I would it deuise.
   But Lord who euer heard, or knew
Of halfe the ioye that I felt than?
Or who can thinke it may be true,
That so much blisse had euer man?            15
   Lo, fortune thus set me aloft:
And more my sorowes to releue,
Of pleasant ioyes I tasted oft:
As much as loue or happe might geue.
   The sorowes olde, I felt before           20
About my hart, were driuen thence:
And for eche greefe, I felt afore,
I had a blisse in recompence.
   Then thought I all the time well spent:
That I in plaint had spent so long.           25
So was I with my life content:
That to my self I sayd among.
   Sins thou art ridde of all thine yll:
To showe thy ioyes set forth thy voyce.
And sins thou hast thy wish at will:         30
My happy hart, reioyce, reioyce.
   Thus felt I ioyes a great deale mo,
Then by my song may well be tolde:
And thinkyng on my passed wo,
My blisse did double many folde.           35
   And thus I thought with mannes blood,
Such blisse might not be bought to deare.
In such estate my ioyes then stode:
That of a change I had no feare.
   But why sing I so long of blisse?         40
It lasteth not, that will away,
Let me therfore bewaile the misse:
And sing the cause of my decay.
                                       Yet

Yet all this while there liued none,
That led his life more pleasantly:
Nor vnder hap there was not one,
Me thought, so well at ease, as I.                                      5
   But O blinde ioye, who may thee trust?
For no estate thou canst assure?
Thy faithfull vowes proue all vniust:
Thy faire behestes be full vnsure.
   Good proufe by me: that but of late                          10
Not fully twenty dayes ago:
Which thought my life was in such state:
That nought might worke my hart this wo.
   Yet hath the enemy of my ease,
Mishappe I meane, that wretched wight:                                  15
Now when my life did moste me please:
Deuised me such cruel spight.
   That from the hiest place of all,
As to the pleasyng of my thought,
Downe to the deepest am I fall,                                         20
And to my helpe auaileth nought,
   Lo, thus are all my ioyes gone:
And I am brought from happinesse,
Continually to waile, and mone.
Lo, such is fortunes stablenesse.                                       25
   In welth I thought such suretie,
That pleasure should haue ended neuer.
But now (alas) aduersitie,
Doth make my singyng cease for euer.
   O brittle ioye, O slidyng blisse,                            30
O fraile pleasure, O welth vnstable:
Who feles thee most, he shall not misse
At length to be made miserable.
   For all must end as doth my blisse:
There is none other certentie.                                          35
And at the end the worst is his,
That most hath knowen prosperitie.
   For he that neuer blisse assaied,
May well away with wretchednesse:
But he shall finde that hath it sayd,                                   40
A paine to part from pleasantnesse:
   As I doe now, for er I knew
What pleasure was: I felt no griefe,

                                             Like

Like vnto this, and it is true,
That blisse hath brought me all this mischiefe.
  But yet I haue not songen, how
This mischiefe came: but I intend              5
With wofull voice to sing it now:
And therwithall I make an end.
  But Lord, now that it is begoon,
I feele, my sprites are vexed sore.
Oh, geue me breath till this be done:       10
And after let me liue no more,
  Alas, the enmy of my life,
The ender of all pleasantnesse
Alas, he bringeth all this strife,
And causeth all this wretchednesse.       15
  For in the middes of all the welth,
That brought my hart to happinesse:
This wicked death he came by stelthe,
And robde me of my ioyfulnesse.
  He came, when that I little thought     20
Of ought, that might me vexe so sore:
And sodenly he brought to nought
My pleasantnesse for euermore,
  He slew my ioye (alas, the wretch)
He slew my ioye, or I was ware:       25
And now (alas) no might may stretch
To set an end to my great care.
  For by this cursed deadly stroke,
My blisse is lost, and I forlore:
And no help may the losse reuoke:      30
For lost it is for euermore.
  And closed vp are those faire eyes,
That gaue me first the signe of grace:
My faire swete foes, myne enemies,
And earth dothe hide her pleasant face.     35
  The loke which did my life vpholde:
And all my sorowes did confounde:
With which more blisse then may be tolde:
Alas, now lieth it vnder ground.
  But cease, for I will syng no more:     40
Since that my harme hath no redresse:
But as a wretche for euermore,
My life will waste with wretchednesse.
                              And

And ending thys my wofull song,
Now that it ended is and past:
I wold my life were but as long:
And that this word might be my last.                5
  For lothsome is that life (men saye)
That liketh not the liuers minde:
Lo, thus I seke myne owne decaye,
And will, till that I may it finde.

## [186] Of his loue named white.                10

*F*Vll faire and white she is, and White by name:
  Whose white doth striue, the lillies white to staine:
Who may contemne the blast of blacke defame:
Who in darke night, can bring day bright againe.
The ruddy rose inpreaseth, with cleare heew,          15
In lips, and chekes, right orient to behold:
That the nere gaser may that bewty reew,
And fele disparst in limmes the chilling cold:
For White, all white his bloodlesse face wil be:
The asshy pale so alter will his cheare.              20
But I that do possesse in full degree
The harty loue of this my hart so deare:
So oft to me as she presents her face,
For ioye do fele my hart spring from his place.

## [187] Of the louers vnquiet                25
### state.

WHat thing is that which I bothe haue and lacke,
  With good will graunted yet it is denyed
How may I be receiued and put abacke
Alway doing and yet vnoccupied,                       30
Most slow in that which I haue most applied,
Still thus to seke, and lese all that I winne,
And that was ready is newest to begyn.
  In riches finde I wilfull pouertie,
In great pleasure liue I in heauinesse,               35
In much freedome I lacke my libertie,
             **T.i.**          Nothing

Thus am I bothe in ioye and in distresse.
And in few wordes, if that I shall be plaine,
In Paradise I suffer all this paine.

## [188] where good will is some profe will appere. 5

$I$T is no fire that geues no heate,
  Though it appeare neuer so hotte:
And they that runne and can not sweate,
Are very leane and dry God wot. 10
  A perfect leche applieth his wittes,
To gather herbes of all degrees:
And feuers with their feruent fittes,
Be cured with their contraries.
   New wine will search to finde a vent, 15
Although the caske be neuer so strong:
And wit will walke when will is bent,
Although the way be neuer so long.
  The rabbets runne vnder the rockes,
The snailes do clime the highest towers: 20
Gunpowder cleaues the sturdy blockes,
A feruent will all thing deuowers.
  When witte with will and diligent
Apply them selues, and match as mates,
There can no want of resident, 25
From force defende the castell gates.
  Forgetfulnesse makes little haste,
And slouth delites to lye full soft:
That telleth the deaf, his tale dothe waste,
And is full drye that craues full oft. 30

## [189] Verses written on the picture of sir Iames wilford.

$A$Las that euer death such vertues should forlet,
  As compast was within his corps, whose picture is here set.
Or that it euer laye in any fortunes might, 35
Through depe disdaine his life to traine y̆ was so worthy a wight
                       For

For sith he first began in armour to be clad,
A worthier champion then he was yet Englande neuer had.
And though recure be past, his life to haue againe,
Yet would I wish his worthinesse in writyng to remaine.      5
That men to minde might call how farre he did excell,
At all assayes to wynne the praise, which were to long to tell.
And eke the restlesse race that he full oft hath runne,
In painfull plight frō place to place, where seruice was to doon
Then should men well perceiue, my tale to be of trouth,      10
And he to be the worthiest wight that euer nature wrought.


[190] The ladye praieth the returne of
        of her louer abidyng on
            the seas.


S Hall I thus euer long, and be no whit the neare,      15
   And shal I styll complayn to thee, the which me will not here?
Alas say nay, say nay, and be no more so dome,
But open thou thy manly mouth, and say that thou wilt come.
Wherby my hart may thinke, although I see not thee,
That thou wilt come thy word so sware, if thou a liues man be.      20
The roaryng hugy waues, they threaten my pore ghost,
And tosse thee vp and downe the seas, in daunger to be lost.
Shall they not make me feare that they haue swalowed thee,
But as thou art most sure aliue so wilt thou come to me.
Wherby I shall go see thy shippe ride on the strande      25
And thinke and say lo where he comes, and sure here will he land.
And then I shall lift vp to thee my little hande,
And thou shalt thinke thine hert in ease, in helth to se me stand.
And if thou come in dede (as Christ the send to do,)
Those armes which misse thee now shall then imbrace thee to.      30
Ech vaine to euery ioynt, the liuely bloud shall spred,
Which now for want of thy glad sight, doth show full pale & dead.
But if thou slip thy trouth and do not come at all,
As minutes in the clocke do strike so call for death I shall.
To please bothe thy false hart, and rid my self from wo,      35
That rather had to dye in trouth then liue forsaken so.


[191] The meane estate is best.
                    T.ii.              The

*T*HE doutfull man hath feuers strange
   And constant hope is oft diseased,
Dispaire can not but brede a change,
Nor fletyng hartes can not be pleasde.         5
Of all these badde, the best I thinke,
Is well to hope, though fortune shrinke.
   Desired thinges are not ay prest,
Nor thinges denide left all vnsought,
Nor new things to be loued best,         10
Nor all offers to be set at nought,
Where faithfull hart hath bene refusde,
The chosers wit was there abusde.
   The woful shyppe of carefull sprite,
Fletyng on seas of wellyng teares,         15
With sayles of wishes broken quite,
Hangyng on waues of dolefull feares,
By surge of sighes at wrecke nere hand,
May fast no anker holde on land.
   What helps the dyall to the blinde,         20
Or els the clock without it sound,
Or who by dreames dothe hope to finde,
The hidden gold within the ground:
Shalbe as free from cares and feares,
As he that holds a wolfe by the eares.         25
   And how much mad is he that thinkes
To clime to heauen by the beames,
What ioye alas, hath he that winkes,
At Titan or his golden stremes,
His ioyes not subiect to reasons lawes,         30
That ioyeth more then he hath cause.
   For as the Phenix that climeth hye,
The sonne lightly in ashes burneth,
Againe, the Faulcon so quicke of eye,
Sone on the ground the net masheth.         35
Experience therfore the meane assurance,
Prefers before the doutfull pleasance.

[192] The louer thinkes no payne to
    great, wherby he may ob-
       taine his lady.         40

                             Sith

SIth that the way to welth is woe,
  And after paynes pleasure prest,
Whie should I than dispaire so.
Ay bewailling mine vnrest,                                    5
Or let to lede my liefe in paine,
So worthy a lady to obtayne,
  The fisher man doth count no care,
To cast hys nets to wracke or wast,
And in reward of eche mans share.                            10
A gogen gift is much imbrast,
Should I than grudge it grief or gall,
That loke at length to whelm a whall.
  The pore mā ploweth his groūd for graine,
And soweth his seede increase to craue,                      15
And for thexpence of all hys paine.
Oft holdes it hap his seede to saue,
These pacient paines my part do show,
To long for loue er that I know.
  And take no skorne to scape from skill,                    20
To spende my spirites to spare my speche,
To win for welth the want of will.
And thus for rest to rage I reche,
Running my race as rect vpright:
Till teares of truth appease my plight.                      25
  And plant my plaint within her brest,
Who doubtles may restore againe,
My harmes to helth my ruthe to rest.
That laced is within her chayne,
For earst ne are the grieues so gret:                        30
As is the ioy when loue is met.
  For who couets so high to clim,
As doth the birde that pitfoll toke,
Or who delightes so swift to swim.
As doth the fishe that scapes the hoke,                      35
If these had neuer entred woe:
How mought they haue reioysed so.
  But yet alas ye louers all,
That here me ioy thus lesse reioyce,
Iudge not amys whatso befall.                                40
In me there lieth no power of choyse,
It is but hope that doth me moue:
Who standerd bearer is to loue.
                          **T.iii.**                On

[ 149 ]

On whose ensigne when I beholde,
I se the shadowe of her shape,
Within my faith so fast I folde:
Through dread I die, through hope I scape,                    5
Thus ease and wo full oft I finde,
What will you more she knoweth my minde.

## [193] Of a new maried Student.

*A* Student at his boke so plast,
    That welth he might haue wonne:                       10
From boke to wife did flete in haste,
From wealth to wo to runne.
Now, who hath plaied a feater cast,
Since iuglyng first begoon?
In knittyng of him selfe so fast,                            15
Him selfe he hath vndoon.

## [194] ❡ The meane estate is to be accompted the best.

W Ho craftly castes to stere his boate
    and safely skoures the flattering flood:             20
He cutteth not the greatest waues
    for why that way were nothing good.
Ne fleteth on the crocked shore
    lest harme him happe awayting lest.
But wines away betwene thē both,                             25
    as who would say the meane is best.
Who waiteth on the goldē meane,
    he put in point of sickernes:
Hides not his head in sluttishe coates,
    ne shroudes himself in filthines.                    30
Ne sittes aloft in hye estate,
    where hatefull hartes enuie his chance:
But wisely walkes betwixt them twaine,
    ne proudly doth himself auance
The highest tree in all the woode                            35
    is rifest rent with blustring windes:

The

The higher hall the greater fall
    such chance haue proude and lofty mindes.
When Iupiter from hie doth threat
    with mortall mace and dint of thunder         5
the highest hilles ben batrid eft
    when they stand still that stoden vnder
The man whose head with wit is fraught
    in welth will feare a worser tide
When fortune failes dispaireth nought         10
    but constantly doth stil abide
For he that sendith grisely stormes
    with whisking windes and bitter blastes
And fowlth with haile the winters face
    and frotes the soile with hory frostes         15
Euen he adawth the force of colde
    the spring in sendes with somer hote
The same full oft to stormy hartes
    is cause of bale: of ioye the roote.
Not always il though so be now         20
    when cloudes ben driuen then rides the racke
Phebus the fresh ne shoteth still
    sometime he harpes his muse to wake
Stand stif therfore pluck vp thy hart
    lose not thy port though fortune faile         25
Againe whan wind doth serue at will
    take hede to hye to hoyse thy saile.

## [195] ¶ The louer refused lamen=
## teth his estate.

*I*Lent my loue to losse and gaged my life in vaine,         30
    If hate for loue and death for life of louers be the gaine.
    And curse I may by course the place eke time and howre
That nature first in me did forme to be a liues creature
    Sith that I must absent my selfe so secretly
In place desert where neuer man my secretes shall discrye         35
    In dolling of my dayes among the beastes so brute
Who with their tonges may not bewray the secretes of my sute
    Nor I in like to them may once to moue my minde
But gase on them and they on me as bestes are wont of kinde
    Thus ranging as refusde to reche some place of rest,         40

               **T.iiii.**                             All

All ruff of heare, my nayles vnnocht, as to such semeth best.
  That wander by theyr wittes, deformed so to be,
That men may say, such one may curse the tyme he first gan se,
  The beauty of her face, her shape in such degree,      5
As god himself may not discerne, one place mended to be.
  Nor place it in lyke place, my fansy for to please,
Who would become a heardmans hyre one howre to haue of ease.
  Wherby I might restore, to me some stedfastnes,
That haue mo thoughts hept in my head then life may lōg disges.   10
  As oft to throw me downe vpon the earth so cold,
Wheras with teares most rufully, my sorowes do vnfold.
  And in beholding them, I chiefly call to mynd,
What woman could find in her heart, such bondage for to bynd.
  Then rashly furth I yede, to cast me from that care,    15
Lyke as the byrd for foode doth flye, and lighteth in the snare.
  From whence I may not meue, vntil my race be roon,
So trayned is my truth through her, ẙ thinkes my life well woon.
  Thus tosse I too and fro, in hope to haue reliefe,
But in the fine I fynd not so, it doubleth but my grief.    20
  Wherfore I will my want, a warning for to be,
Vnto all men, wishing that they, a myrrour make of me.

## [196] The felicitie of a mind imbracing ver‑
## tue, that beholdeth the wretched
## desyres of the worlde.     25

WHē dredful swelling seas, through boisterous windy blastes
  So tosse the shippes, that al for nought, serues ancor sayle &
Who takes not pleasure then, safely on shore to rest,   (mastes.
And see with dreade & depe despayre, how shipmen are distrest.
  Not that we pleasure take, when others felen smart,    30
Our gladnes groweth to see their harmes, & yet to fele no parte.
  Delyght we take also, well ranged in aray,
When armies meete to see the fight, yet free be from the fray.
  But yet among the rest, no ioy may match with this,
Taspayre vnto the temple hye, where wisdom troned is.    35
  Defended with the saws of hory heades expert,
Which clere it kepe frō errours myst, that myght the truth peruert.
  From whence thou mayst loke down, and see as vnder foote,
Mans wādring wil & doutful life, frō whēce they take their roote.
                                  Howe

How some by wit contend by prowes some to rise
Riches and rule to gaine and hold is all that men deuise.
O miserable mindes O hertes in folly drent
Why se you not what blindnèsse in thys wretched life is spent.    5
Body deuoyde of grefe mynde free from care and dreede
Is all and some that nature craues wherwith our life to feede.
So that for natures turne few thinges may well suffice
Dolour and grief clene to expell and some delight surprice:
Yea and it falleth oft that nature more contente    10
Is with the lesse, then when the more to cause delight is spent.

## [197] All worldly pleasures fade.

*T*He winter with his griesly stormes no lenger dare abyde,
  The plesant grasse, with lusty grene, the earth hath newly dyde.
The trees haue leues, ẏ bowes don spred, new chāged is ẏ yere.    15
The water brokes are cleane sonke down, the plesāt bākes apere.
The spring is come, the goodly nimphes now daūce in euery place
Thus hath the yere most plesantly of late ychangde his face.
Hope for no immortalitie, for welth will weare away,
As we may learne by euery yere, yea howres of euery day.    20
For Zepharus doth mollifye the colde and blustering windes:
The somers drought doth take away ẏ spryng out of our minds.
And yet the somer cannot last, but once must step asyde,
Thē Autumn thinkes to kepe hys place, but Autumn cānot bide.
For when he hath brought furth his fruits & stuft ẏ barns w̃ corn,    25
The winter eates & empties all, and thus is Autumn worne.
Then hory frostes possesse the place, thē tēpestes work much harm,
Thē rage of stormes done make al colde whiche somer had made so
Wherfore let no man put his trust in that, that will decay,  (warm
For slipper welth will not cūtinue, plesure will weare away.    30
For when that we haue lost our lyfe, & lye vnder a stone,
What are we then, we are but earth, then is our pleasure gon.
No man can tell what god almight of euery wight doth cast,
No man can say to day I liue, till morne my lyfe shall last.
For when thou shalt before thy iudge stand to receiue thy dome,    35
What sentence Minos dothe pronounce that must of thee become.
Then shall not noble stock and blud redeme the frō his handes,
Nor surged talke with eloquence shal lowse thee frō his bandes.
Nor yet thy lyfe vprightly lead, can help thee out of hell,
For who descendeth downe so depe, must there abyde & dwell.    40
                  **U.i.**            Diana

Diana could not thence deliuer chaste Hypolitus,
Nor Theseus could not call to life his frende Periothous.

## [198] A complaint of the losse of libertie
## by loue.

5

*I*N sekyng rest vnrest I finde,
  I finde that welth is cause of wo:
Wo worth the time that I inclinde,
To fixe in minde her beauty so.
   That day be darkened as the night,        10
Let furious rage it cleane deuour:
Ne sunne nor moone therin geue light,
But it consume with storme and shower.
   Let no small birdes straine forth their voyce,
With pleasant tunes ne yet no beast:        15
Finde cause wherat he may reioyce,
That day when chaunced mine vnrest.
   Wherin alas from me was raught,
Mine owne free choyse and quiet minde:
My life my death in balance braught        20
And reason rasde through barke and rinde.
   And I as yet in flower of age,
Bothe witte and will did still aduaunce:
Ay to resist that burnyng rage:
But when I darte then did I glaunce.        25
   Nothing to me did seme so hye,
In minde I could it straight attaine:
Fansy persuaded me therby,
Loue to esteme a thing most vaine.
   But as the birde vpon the brier,        30
Dothe pricke and proyne her without care:
Not knowyng alas pore fole how nere
She is vnto the fowlers snare,
   So I amid disceitfull trust,
Did not mistrust such wofull happe:        35
Till cruell loue er that I wist
Had caught me in his carefull trappe.
   Then did I fele and partly know,
How little force in me did raigne:

So

So sone to yelde to ouerthrow,
So fraile to flit from ioye to paine.
  For when in welth will did me leade
Of libertie to hoyse my saile:
To hale at shete and cast my leade,        5
I thought free choise wold still preuaile
  In whose calme streames I sayld so farre
No ragyng storme had in respect:
Vntyll I raysde a goodly starre,        10
Wherto my course I did direct.
  In whose prospect in doolfull wise,
My tackle failde my compasse brake:
Through hote desires such stormes did rise,
That sterne and toppe went all to wrake.      15
  Oh cruell happe oh fatall chaunce,
O Fortune why were thou vnkinde:
Without regard thus in a traunce,
To reue fro me my ioyfull minde.
  Where I was free now must I serue,     20
Where I was lose now am I bounde:
In death my life I do preserue,
As one through girt with many a wound.

## [199] A praise of his La-
## dye.        25

*G*Eue place you Ladies and be gon,
  Boast not your selues at all:
For here at hande approcheth one
Whose face will staine you all.
  The vertue of her liuely lokes,       30
Excels the precious stone:
I wishe to haue none other bokes
To read or loke vpon.
  In eche of her two cristall eyes,
Smileth a naked boye:        35
It would you all in hart suffise
To see that lampe of ioye.
  I thinke nature hath lost the moulde,
Where she her shape did take:

**U.ii.**              Or

## Songes

Or els I doubt if nature could,
So faire a creature make.
    She may be well comparde
Vnto the Phenix kinde:                                    5
Whose like was neuer sene nor heard,
That any man can finde.
    In life she is Diana chast,
In trouth Penelopey:
In word and eke in dede stedfast,                         10
What will you more we sey.
    If all the world were sought so farre,
Who could finde such a wight:
Her beauty twinkleth like a starre,
Within the frosty night.                                  15
    Her rosiall colour comes and goes,
With such a comely grace:
More redier to then doth the rose,
Within her liuely face.
    At Bacchus feast none shall her mete,                 20
Ne at no wanton play:
Nor gasyng in an open strete,
Nor gaddyng as a stray.
    The modest mirth that she dothe vse,
Is mixt with shamefastnesse:                              25
All vice she dothe wholy refuse,
And hateth ydlenesse.
    O lord it is a world to see,
How vertue can repaire:
And decke in her such honestie,                           30
Whom nature made so fayre.
    Truely she dothe as farre excede,
Our women now adayes:
As dothe the Ielifloure a wede,
And more a thousande wayes.                               35
    How might I do to get a graffe:
Of this vnspotted tree.
For all the rest are plaine but chaffe,
Which seme good corne to be.
    This gift alone I shall her geue                      40
When death doth what he can:
Her honest fame shall euer liue,
Within the mouth of man.
                                                    The

[ 156 ]

## [200] The pore estate to be holden for best.

*E* Xperience now doth shew what God vs taught before,
   D esired pompe is vaine, and seldome dothe it last:     5
W ho climbes to raigne with kinges, may rue his fate full sore.
A las the wofull ende that comes with care full fast,
R eiect him dothe renowne his pompe full lowe is caste.
D eceiued is the birde by swetenesse of the call
E xpell that pleasant taste, wherein is bitter gall.     10
  S uch as with oten cakes in pore estate abides,
O f care haue they no cure, the crab with mirth they rost,
M ore ease fele they then those, that from their height downe slides
E xcesse doth brede their wo, they saile in scillas cost,
R emainyng in the stormes till shyp and all be lost.     15
S erue God therfore thou pore, for lo, thou liues in rest,
E schue the golden hall, thy thatched house is best.

## [201] The complaint of Thestilis amid the desert wodde.

*T* Hestilis a sely man, when loue did him forsake,     20
  In mourning wise, amid y̆ woods thus gan his plaint to make.
Ah wofull man (quod he) fallen is thy lot to mone
And pyne away w̃ carefull thoughts, vnto thy loue vnknowen.
Thy lady thee forsakes whom thou didst honor so
That ay to her thou wer a frend, and to thy self a foe.     25
Ye louers that haue lost your heartes desyred choyse,
Lament with me my cruell happe, & helpe my trembling voyce.
Was neuer man that stode so great in fortunes grace:
Nor with his swete alas to deare possest so high a place.
As I whose simple hart aye thought him selfe full sure,     30
But now I se hye springyng tides they may not aye endure.
She knowes my giltelesse hart, and yet she lets it pine,
Of her vntrue professed loue so feble is the twine.
What wonder is it than, if I berent my heeres,
And crauyng death continually do bathe my selfe in teares,     35
When Cresus king of Lide was cast in cruell bandes,
And yelded goodes and life also into his enemies handes.
𝕬.iii,           What

What tong could tell hys wo yet was hys griefe much lesse:
Then mine for I haue lost my loue which might my woe redresse.
Ye woodes that shroud my limes giue now your holow sound,
That ye may helpe me to bewaile the cares that me confound.          5
Ye riuers rest a while and stay the stremes that runne,
Rew Thestilis most woful man that liueth vnder sunne.
Transport my sighes ye windes vnto my pleasant foe,
My trickling teares shall witnesse bear of this my cruell woe.
O happy man wer I if all the goddes agreed:                          10
That now the susters three should cut in twaine my fatall threde.
Till life with loue shall ende I here resigne all ioy:
Thy pleasant swete I now lament whose lack bredes myne anoy
Farewell my deare therfor farewell to me well knowne
If that I die it shalbe sayd that thou hast slaine thine owne.       15

[202] ¶ The louer praieth pity showing that
nature hath taught his dog as it
were to sue for the same by
kissing his ladies handes.

NAture that taught my silly dog god wat:                             20
    Euen for my sake to like where I do loue,
Inforced him wheras my lady sat
With humble sute before her falling flat.
As in his sorte he might her play and moue
To rue vpon his lord and not forgete                                 25
The stedfast faith he beareth her and loue,
Kissing her hand whom she could not remoue.
Away that would for frowning nor for threte
As though he would haue sayd in my behoue.
Pity my lord your slaue that doth remaine                            30
Lest by his death you giltles slay vs twaine.

[203] Of his ring sent to his lady.

SInce thou my ring mayst goe where I ne may.
    Since thou mayst speake where I must hold my peace.
Say vnto her that is my liues stay.                                  35
Grauen the within which I do here expresse:
That sooner shall the sonne not shine by day,
And with the raine the floodes shall waxen lesse.
                                                        Sooner

Sooner the tree the hunter shall bewray,
Then I for change or choyce of other loue,
Do euer seke my fansy to remoue.

## [204] The changeable state
of louers.

5

*F*Or that a restles head must somewhat haue in vre
  Wherwith it may acquaynted be, as falcon is with lure.
  Fansy doth me awake out of my drowsy slepe,
In seeing how the little mouse, at night begyns to crepe.　　　10
  So the desyrous man, that longes to catch hys pray,
In spying how to watch hys tyme, lyeth lurkyng styll by day.
  In hopyng for to haue, and fearyng for to fynde
The salue that should recure his sore, & soroweth but the mynde,
  Such is the guyse of loue, and the vncertain state,　　　15
That some should haue theyr hoped happe, and other hard estate.
  That some should seme to ioy in that they neuer had,
And some agayn shall frown as fast, where causeles they be sad.
  Such trades do louers vse when they be most at large,
That gyde the stere when they themselues lye fettred in y̆ barge.　20
  The grenes of my youth cannot therof expresse
The proces, for by profe vnknowen, all this is but by gesse.
  Wherfore I hold it best, in tyme to hold my peace,
But wanton will it cannot hold, or make my pen to cease.
  A pen of no auayle, a fruitles labour eke,　　　25
My troubled head with fansies fraught, doth payn it self to seke.
  And if perhappes my wordes of none auayle do pricke,
Such as do fele the hidden harmes, I would not they shold kicke.
  As causeles me to blame which thinketh them no harme,
Although I seme by others fyre, sometime my self to warme.　　30
  Which clerely I denye, as gyltles of that cryme,
And though wrong demde I be therin, truth it will trye in tyme.

## [205] A praise of Audley.

*W* Hen Audley had runne out his race and ended wer his days,
  His fame stept forth & bad me write of hī some worthy praise.　35
What life he lad, what actes he did: his vertues & good name,
Wherto I calde for true report, as witnes of the same.

Well

Wel born he was wel bent by kinde, whose mind did neuer swarue
A skilfull head, a valiant hert, a ready hand to serue.
Brought vp & trained in feats of war long time beyond the seas
Cald home again to serue his prince whō styll he sought to please.     5
What tornay was there he refusde, what seruice did he shone,
Where he was not nor his aduice, what great exploit was done,
In towne a lambe in felde full fierce a lyon at the nede,
In sober wit a Salomon, yet one of Hectors sede.
Then shame it were that any tong shold now defame his dedes     10
That in his life a mirror was to all that him succedes.
No pore estate nor hie renowne his nature could peruart,
No hard mischaunce that him befel could moue his constant hart.
Thus long he liued loued of all as one mislikt of none,
And where he went who cald him not the gentle Peragon.     15
But course of kinde doth cause eche frute to fall whē it is ripe,
And spitefull death will suffer none to scape his greuous gripe.
Yet though the ground receiued haue his corps into her wombe,
This epitaphe ygraue in brasse, shall stand vpon his tombe.
Lo here he lies that hateth vice, and vertues life imbrast,     20
His name in earth his sprite aboue deserues to be well plast.

## [206] Time trieth truth.

*E* Che thing I se hath time which time must trye my truth,
   Which truth deserues a special trust, on trust gret frēdship gro-
And frendship may not faile where faithfulnesse is founde,     (weth     25
And faithfulnesse is ful of frute, & fruteful thinges be sounde.
And sound is good at proufe, and proufe is prince of praise,
And precious praise is such a pearle as seldome ner decayes.
All these thinges time tries forth, which time I must abide,
How shold I boldly credite craue till time my truth haue tryed.     30
For as I found a time to fall in fansies frame,
So I do wishe a lucky time for to declare the same.
If hap may answere hope and hope may haue his hire,
Then shall my hart possesse in peace the time that I desire.

## [207] The louer refused of his loue     35
## imbraceth death.

My

*M*Y youthfull yeres are past,
  My ioyfull dayes are gone:
My life it may not last,
My graue and I am one.                                        5
  My mirth and ioyes are fled,
And I a man in wo:
Desirous to be dedde,
My mischiefe to forgo.
  I burne and am a colde,                                     10
I frise amids the fire:
I see she dothe withholde
That is my most desire.
  I see my helpe at hand,
I see my lyfe also:                                           15
I see where she dothe stande
That is my deadly foe.
  I see how she dothe see,
And yet she will be blinde:
I se in helpyng me                                            20
She sekes and will not finde.
  I see how she doth wry,
When I begyn to mone:
I see when I come nie,
How faine she wold be gone.                                   25
  I see what will ye more
She will me gladly kyll:
And you shall see therfore
That she shall haue her will.
  I can not liue with stones                                  30
It is to hard a fode:
I will be dead at once
To do my Lady good.


[208] The Picture of a
        louer.                                                35


*B*Ehold my picture here well portrayed for the nones,
  With hart consumed and fallyng flesshe, lo here the very bones.
Whose cruell chaunce alas and desteny is such,
Onely because I put my trust in some folke all to much.
                           X.i.                        For

For since the time that I did enter in this pine,
I neuer saw the risyng sunne but with my wepyng eyen.
Nor yet I neuer heard so swete a voice or sounde,
But that to me it did encrease the dolour of my wounde.          5
Nor in so soft a bedde, alas I neuer laye,
But that it semed hard to me or euer it was daye.
Yet in this body bare that nought but life retaines,
The strength wherof clene past away the care yet still remaines.
Like as the cole in flame dothe spende it selfe you se,          10
To vaine and wretched cinder dust till it consumed be.
So dothe this hope of mine inforce my feruent sute,
To make me for to gape in vaine, whilst other eate the frute.
And shall do till the death do geue me such a grace,
To rid this sillye wofull spirite out of this dolefull case.    15
And then wold God were writte in stone or els in leade,
This Epitaphe vpon my graue, to shew why I am deade.
Here lieth the louer loe, who for the loue he aught,
Aliue vnto his ladye dere, his death therby he caught.
And in a shielde of blacke, loe here his armes appeares,        20
With weping eies as you may see, well poudred all with teares.
Loe here you may beholde, aloft vpon his brest,
A womans hand strainyng the hart of him that loued her best.
Wherfore all you that se this corps for loue that starues,
Example make vnto you all, that thankelesse louers sarues.      25

## [209] Of the death of Phillips.

*B*Ewaile with me all ye that haue profest,
Of musicke tharte by touche of coarde or winde:
Laye downe your lutes and let your gitterns rest,
Phillips is dead whose like you can not finde.                  30
Of musicke much exceadyng all the rest,
Muses therfore of force now must you wrest.
Your pleasant notes into an other sounde,
The string is broke, the lute is dispossest,
The hand is colde, the bodye in the grounde.                    35
The lowring lute lamenteth now therfore,
Phillips her frende that can her touche no more.

                                                      That

[210] That all thing sometime finde
ease of their paine, saue
onely the louer.

*I*See there is no sort,                                      5
  Of thinges that liue in griefe:
Which at sometime may not resort,
Wheras they haue reliefe.
  The striken dere by kinde,
Of death that standes in awe:                        10
For his recure an herbe can finde,
The arrow to withdrawe.
  The chased dere hath soile,
To coole him in his het:
The asse after his wery toyle,                        15
In stable is vp set.
  The conye hath his caue,
The little birde his nest:
From heate and colde them selues to saue,
At all times as they lyst.                                 20
  The owle with feble sight,
Lieth lurkyng in the leaues:
The sparrow in the frosty nyght,
May shroude her in the eaues.
  But wo to me alas,                                 25
In sunne nor yet in shade.
I can not finde a restyng place,
My burden to vnlade.
  But day by day still beares,
The burden on my backe:                               30
With wepyng eyen and watry teares,
To holde my hope abacke.
  All thinges I see haue place,
Wherin they bowe or bende:
Saue this alas my wofull case,                        35
Which no where findeth ende.

[211] Thassault of Cupide vpon the fort
where the louers hart lay wounded
and how he was taken.

                𝒳.ii.            When

## Songes.

WHen Cupide scaled first the fort,
   Wherin my hart lay wounded sore:
The battry was of such a sort
That I must yelde or dye therfore.         5
   There saw I loue vpon the wall,
How he his banner did display:
Alarme alarme he gan to call,
And bad his souldiours kepe aray.
   The armes the which that Cupide bare     10
Were pearced harts with teares besprent:
In siluer and sable to declare
The stedfast loue he alwayes ment.
   There might you se his band all drest,
In colours like to white and blacke:     15
With powder and with pellets prest,
To bring the fort to spoile and sacke.
   Good will the master of the shot,
Stode in the rampyre braue and proud:
For spence of powder he spared not,     20
Assault assault to crye aloude.
   There might you heare the cannons rore
Eche pece discharged a louers loke:
Which had the power to rent, and tore
In any place whereas they toke.     25
   And euen with the trumpets sowne,
The scalyng ladders were vp set:
And beauty walked vp and downe
With bow in hand and arrowes whet.
   Then first desire began to scale,     30
And shrowded him vnder his targe:
As on the worthiest of them all,
And aptest for to geue the charge.
   Then pusshed souldiers with their pikes
And holbarders with handy strokes:     35
The hargabushe in fleshe it lightes,
And dims the ayre with misty smokes.
   And as it is the souldiers vse,
When shot and powder gins to want:
I hanged vp my flagge of truce,     40
And pleaded for my liues graunt.
   When fansy thus had made her breach
And beauty entred with her bande:

                                With

With bag and baggage selyc wretch,
I yelded into beauties hand.
    Then beawty bad to blow retrete,
And euery soldiour to retire.                                    5
And mercy wilde with spede to fet:
Me captiue bound as prisoner.
    Madame (quoth I) sith that thys day,
Hath serued you at all assaies:
I yeld to you without delay,                                    10
Here of the fortresse all the kaies.
    And sith that I haue ben the marke,
At whom you shot at with youe eye:
Nedes must you with your handy warke,
Or salue my sore or let me dye.                                15

## [212] The aged louer renounceth loue.

*I*Lothe that I did loue,
    In youth that I thought swete:
As time requires for my behoue                                 20
Me thinkes they are not mete,
    My lustes they do me leaue,
My fansies all be fledde:
And tract of time begins to weaue,
Gray heares vpon my hedde.                                     25
    For age with stelyng steppes,
Hath clawed me with his cowche:
And lusty life away she leapes,
As there had bene none such.
    My muse dothe not delight                                  30
Me as she did before:
My hand and pen are not in plight,
As they haue bene of yore.
    For reason me denies,
This youthly idle rime:                                        35
And day by day to me she cryes,
Leaue of these toyes in time.
    The wrincles in my brow,
The furrowes in my face:

**X.iii.**                                    Saye

Say limpyng age will hedge him now,
Where youth must geue him place.
   The harbinger of death,
To me I see him ride: 5
The cough, the colde, the gaspyng breath,
Dothe bid me to prouide.
   A pikeax and a spade,
And eke a shrowdyng shete,
A house of claye for to be made, 10
For such a gest most mete.
   Me thinkes I heare the clarke,
That knols the careful knell:
And bids me leaue my wofull warke,
Er nature me compell. 15
   My kepers knit the knot,
That youth did laugh to scorne:
Of me that clene shalbe forgot,
As I had not ben borne.
   Thus must I youth geue vp, 20
Whose badge I long did weare:
To them I yelde the wanton cup
That better may it beare.
   Loe here the bared scull,
By whose balde signe I know: 25
That stoupyng age away shall pull,
Which youthfull yeres did sowe.
   For beauty with her bande
These croked cares hath wrought:
And shipped me into the lande, 30
From whence I first was brought.
   And ye that bide behinde,
Haue ye none other trust:
As ye of claye were cast by kinde,
So shall ye waste to dust. 35

## [213] Of the ladie wentworthes death.

*T*O liue to dye, and dye to liue againe,
  With good renowne of fame well led before

Here

Here lieth she that learned had the lore,
Whom if the perfect vertues wolden daine.
To be set forth with foile of worldly grace,
Was noble borne and matcht in noble race,                    5
Lord Wentworthes wife, nor wāted to attain
In natures giftes her praise among the rest,
But that that gaue her praise aboue the best
Not fame her wedlocks chastnes durst distain
Wherein with child deliueryng of her wombe,                  10
Thuntimely birth hath brought them both in
So left she life by death to liue again. (tombe

## [214] The louer accusing hys loue for her vnfaithfulnesse, purposeth to liue in libertie.                              15

*T*He smoky sighes the bitter teares,
  That I in vaine haue wasted:
The broken slepes, the wo and feares,
That long in me haue lasted:
The loue and all I owe to thee,                              20
Here I renounce and make me free.
  Which fredome I haue by thy guilt,
And not by my deseruing,
Since so vnconstantly thou wilt,
Not loue, but still be swaruyng.                             25
To leue me oft which was thine owne,
Without cause why as shalbe knowen.
  The frutes were faire the which did grow,
Within thy garden planted,
The leaues were grene of euery bough,                        30
And moysture nothing wanted,
Yet or the blossoms gan to fall,
The caterpiller wasted all.
  Thy body was the garden place,
And sugred wordes it beareth,                                35
The blossomes all thy faith it was,
Which as the canker wereth.
The caterpiller is the same,
That hath wonne thee and lost thy name.

                                        I meane

I meane thy louer loued now,
By thy pretended folye,
　Which will proue lyke, thou shalt fynd how,
Vnto a tree of holly:　　　　　　　　　　　　　　　5
That barke and bery beares alwayes,
The one, byrdes feedes, the other slayes.
　And right well mightest thou haue thy wish
Of thy loue new acquaynted:
For thou art lyke vnto the dishe　　　　　　　　　10
That Adrianus paynted:
Wherin wer grapes portrayd so fayre
That fowles for foode did there repayre.
　But I am lyke the beaten fowle
That from the net escaped,　　　　　　　　　　　15
And thou art lyke the rauening owle
That all the night hath waked.
For none intent but to betray
The sleping fowle before the day.
　Thus hath thy loue been vnto me　　　　　　　20
As pleasant and commodious,
As was the fyre made on the sea
By Naulus hate so odious.
Therwith to trayn the grekish host
From Troyes return where they wer lost.　　　　25

# [215] The louer for want of his de⸗
## syre, sheweth his death
## at hand.

*A*S Cypres tree that rent is by the roote.
　As branch or slyppe bereft from whēce it growes　　30
As well sowen seede for drought that can not sproute
As gaping ground that raineles can not close
As moules that want the earth to do them bote
As fishe on lande to whom no water flowes,
As Chameleon that lackes the ayer so sote.　　　　35
As flowers do fade when Phebus rarest showes.
As salamandra repulsed from the fyre:
So wanting my wishe I dye for my desyre
　　　　　　　　　　　　　　　A happy

[ 168 ]

[216] A happy end excedeth all plea=
sures and riches of the
worlde,

*T*He shinyng season here to some,                    5
  The glory in the worldes sight,
Renowmed fame through fortune wonne
The glitteryng golde the eyes delight.
The sensuall life that semes so swete,
The hart with ioyfull dayes replete,               10
The thing wherto eche wight is thrall,
The happy ende exceadeth all.

[217] Against an vnstedfast

woman.

*O* Temerous tauntres that delights in toyes        15
  Tumbling cockboat tottryng to and fro,
Ianglyng iestres depraueres of swete ioyes,
Ground of the graffe whence al my grief dothe
Sullen serpent enuironned wͨ dispite,      (grow
That yll for good at all times doest requite.       20

[218] A praise of Petrarke and of Lau=
ra his ladie.

*O* Petrarke hed and prince of poets all,
  Whose liuely gift of flowyng eloquence,
Wel may we seke, but finde not how or whence       25
So rare a gift with thee did rise and fall,
Peace to thy bones, and glory immortall
Be to thy name, and to her excellence.
Whose beauty lighted in thy time and sence
So to be set forth as none other shall.             30
Why hath not our pens rimes so p̃fit wrought
Ne why our time forth bringeth beauty such
To trye our wittes as golde is by the touche,
                𝔓.i.                    If to

If to the stile the matter aided ought.
But ther was neuer Laura more then one,
And her had petrarke for his paragone,

[219] That petrark cannot be passed          5
          but notwithstanding that
       Lawra is far surpassed.

WIth petrarke to compare there may no wight,
      Nor yet attain vnto so high a stile,
But yet I wote full well where is a file.            10
To frame a learned man to praise aright:
Of stature meane of semely forme and shap,
Eche line of iust proporsion to her height:
Her colour freshe and mingled with such sleight:
As though the rose sate in the lilies lap.           15
In wit and tong to shew what may be sed,
To euery dede she ioynes a parfit grace,
If Lawra liude she would her clene deface.
For I dare say and lay my life to wed
That Momus could not if he downe discended,          20
Once iustly say lo this may be amended.

[220] Against a cruell woman.

CRuell and vnkind whom mercy cannot moue,
     Herbour of vnhappe where rigours rage doth raigne,
The ground of my griefe where pitie cannot proue:    25
To tickle to trust of all vntruth the traine,
thou rigorous rocke that ruth cannot remoue.
Daungerous delph depe dungeon of disdaine:
The sacke of selfe will the chest of craft and change,
What causeth the thus so causels for to change.      30
   Ah piteles plante whome plaint cannot prouoke,
Darke den of disceite that right doth still refuse,
Causles vnkinde that carieth vnder cloke
Cruelty and craft me onely to abuse,
Statelye and stubberne withstanding cupides stroke,  35
Thou merueilouse mase that makest men to muse,

                                        Solleyn

Solleyn by selfe will, most stony stiffe and straunge,
What causeth thee thus causelesse for to chaunge.
Slipper and secrete where surety can not sowe
Net of newelty, neast of newfanglenesse,                                    5
Spring of very spite, from whence whole fluddes do flow,
Thou caue and cage of care and craftinesse
Waueryng willow that euery blast dothe blowe
Graffe withouten grothe and cause of carefulnesse.
The heape of mishap of all my griefe the graunge,                          10
What causeth thee thus causelesse for to chaunge.
　　Hast thou forgote that I was thine infeft,
By force of loue haddest thou not hart at all,
Sawest thou not other that for thy loue were left
Knowest thou vnkinde, that nothing mught befall                            15
From out my hart that could haue the bereft.
What meanest thou then at ryot thus to raunge,
And leauest thine owne that neuer thought to chaūge.


[221] The louer sheweth what he would
　　haue if it were graunted him to                                          20
　　haue what he would
　　　wishe.


*I*F it were so that God would graunt me my request,
　And that I might of earthly thinges haue ẙ I liked best.
I would not wishe to clime to princely hye astate,                         25
which  slipper is and slides so oft, and hath so fickle fate.
Nor yet to conquere realmes with cruell sworde in hande,
And so to shede the giltlesse bloude of such as would withstand.
Nor I would not desire in worldly rule to raigne,
Whose frute is all vnquietnesse, and breakyng of the braine.              30
Nor richesse in excesse of vertue so abhorde,
I would not craue which bredeth care and causeth all discorde.
But my request should be more worth a thousand folde:
That I might haue and her enioye that hath my hart in holde.
Oh God what lusty life should we liue then for euer,                       35
In pleasant ioy and perfect blisse, to length our liues together.
With wordes of frendlye chere, and lokes of liuely loue,
To vtter all our hotte desires, which neuer should remoue.
　　　　　　　　　　　　　𝔇.ii.　　　　　　　　But

But grose and gredie wittes which grope but on the ground.
To gather muck of worldly goodes which oft do them confounde.
Can not attaine to knowe the misteries deuine
Of perfite loue wherto hie wittes of knowledge do incline          5
A nigard of his gold suche ioye can neuer haue
which gettes w<sup>t</sup> toile and kepes with care and is his money slaue.
As they enioy always that taste loue in his kinde,
For they do holde continually a heauen in their minde.
No worldly goodes could bring my hart so great an ease,          10
As for to finde or do the thing that might my ladye please.
For by her onely loue my hart should haue all ioye,
And with the same put care away, and all that coulde annoy.
As if that any thyng shold chance to make me sadde,
The touching of her corall lippes would straighteways make me          15
And when that in my heart I fele that dyd me greue     (gladde,
With one imbracing of her armes she might me sone releue:
And as the Angels all which sit in heauen hye
With presence and the sight of god haue theyr felicitie.
So lykewyse I in earth, should haue all earthly blis,          20
With presence of that paragon, my god in earth that is.

### [222] The lady forsaken of her louer, prayeth his returne, or the end of her own life.

*T*O loue, alas, who would not feare          25
   That seeth my wofull state,
For he to whom my heart I beare
Doth me extremely hate,
And why therfore I cannot tell,
He will no lenger with me dwell.          30
   Did you not sewe and long me serue
Ere I you graunted grace?
And will you this now from me swarue
That neuer did trespace?
Alas poore woman then alas,          35
A wery lyfe here must I passe.
   And is there now no remedy
But that you will forgeat her,
Ther was a tyme whcn that perdy
You

You would haue heard her better.
But now that time is gone and past,
And all your loue is but a blast.
   And can you thus breake your behest 5
In dede and can you so?
Did you not sweare you loude me best,
And can you now say no?
Remember me poore wight in payne,
And for my sake turne once agayne. 10
   Alas poore Dido now I fele
Thy present paynful state,
When false Eneas did hym stele
From thee at Carthage gate.
And left thee sleapyng in thy bedde, 15
Regardyng not what he had sayd.
   Was neuer woman thus betrayed,
Nor man so false forsworne,
His faith and trouth so strongly tayed,
Vntruth hath alltotorne: 20
And I haue leaue for my good will,
To waile and wepe alone my fill.
   But since it will not better be,
My teares shall neuer blyn:
To moist the earth in such degree, 25
That I may drowne therin:
That by my death all men may saye,
Lo women are as true as they.
   By me all women may beware,
That see my wofull smart, 30
To seke true loue let them not spare,
Before they set their hart.
Or els they may become as I,
Which for my truth am like to dye.

## [223] The louer yelden into his ladies handes, praieth mercie.  35

*I*N fredome was my fantasie
  Abhorryng bondage of the minde,

                    But

[ 173 ]

But now I yelde my libertie,
And willingly my selfe I binde.
Truely to serue with all my hart,
Whiles life doth last not to reuart.                                    5
  Her beauty bounde me first of all
And forst my will for to consent:
And I agree to be her thrall,
For as she list I am content.
My will is hers in that I may,                                          10
And where she biddes I will obey.
  It lieth in her my wo or welth,
She may do that she liketh best,
If that she list I haue my helth,
If she list not in wo I rest.                                           15
Sins I am fast within her bandes,
My wo and welth lieth in her handes.
  She can no lesse then pitie me,
Sith that my faith to her is knowne,
It were to much extremitie,                                             20
With cruelty to vse her owne.
Alas a sinnefull enterprice,
To slay that yeldes at her deuice.
  But I thinke not her hart so harde,
Nor that she hath such cruell lust:                                     25
I doubt nothing of her reward,
For my desert but well I trust,
As she hath beauty to allure,
So hath she a hart that will recure.

[224] That nature which worketh al thinges                              30
      for our behofe, hath made wo-
        men also for our comfort
              and delite.

*A*Mong dame natures workes such perfite lawe is wrought,
    That things be ruled by course of kinde in order as they ought   35
And serueth in their state, in such iust frame and sorte,
    That slender wits may iudge the same, & make therof report.
Beholde what secrete force the winde dothe easely showe,
    Which guides the shippes amid the seas if he his bellowes blow.
                                                                  The

The waters waxen wilde where blustering blastes do rise,
  Yet seldome do they passe their bondes for nature that deuise.
The fire which boiles the leadc and trieth out the golde:
  Hath in his power both help and hurt if he his force vnfolde.          5
The frost which kilth the fruite doth knit the brused bones:
  And is a medecin of kind prepared for the nones.
The earth in whose entrails the foode of man doth liue,
  At euery spring and fall of leafe what plesure doth she giue.
The aier which life desires and is to helth so swete                    10
  Of nature yeldes such liuely smelles that cōfortes euery sprete.
The sonne through natures might doth draw away the dew,
  And spredes y̆ flowers where he is wōt his princely face to shew
The Mone which may be cald the lanterne of the night,
  Is halfe a guide to traueling men such vertue hath her light.         15
The sters not vertuelesse are bewtie to the eies,
  A lodes man to the mariner a signe of calmed skies.
The flowers and fruitefull trees to man doe tribute pay,
  And when they haue their duety done by course they fade away.
Eche beast both fishe and foule, doth offer lief and all,              20
  To norishe man and do him ease yea serue him at his call.
The serpentes venemous, whose vglye shapes we hate,
  Are soueraigne salues for sondry sores, & nedefull in their state.
Sith nature shewes her power, in eche thing thus at large,
  Why should not man submit hymself to be in natures charge           25
Who thinkes to flee her force, at length becomes her thrall,
  The wysest cannot slip her snare, for nature gouernes all.
Lo, nature gaue vs shape, lo nature fedes our lyues:
  Thē they are worse thē mad I think, against her force y̆ striues.
Though some do vse to say, which can do nought but fayne,              30
  Women were made for this intent, to put vs men to payne.
Yet sure I think they are a pleasure to the mynde,
  A ioy which man can neuer want, as nature hath assynde.


[225] when aduersitie is once fallen,
        it is to late to beware.                                        35


*T*O my mishap alas I fynde
  That happy hap is daungerous:
And fortune worketh but her kynd
To make the ioyfull dolorous.

                                                        But

But all to late it comes to minde,
To waile the want that makes me blinde,
   Amid my mirth and pleasantnesse,
Such chaunce is chaunced sodainly,              5
That in dispaire without redresse,
I finde my chiefest remedy.
No new kinde of vnhappinesse,
Should thus haue left me comfortlesse.
   Who wold haue thought that my request,      10
Should bring me forth such bitter frute:
But now is hapt that I feard lest,
And all this harme comes by my sute,
For when I thought me happiest,
Euen then hapt all my chiefe vnrest.          15
   In better case was neuer none
And yet vnwares thus am I trapt,
My chiefe desire doth cause me mone,
And to my harme my welth is hapt,
There is no man but I alone,             20
That hath such cause to sigh and mone.
   Thus am I taught for to beware
And trust no more such pleasant chance,
My happy happe bred me this care,
And brought my mirth to great mischance.    25
There is no man whom happe will spare,
But when she list his welth is bare.


[226] Of a louer that made his one=
      lye God of his
         loue.               30


*A*L you that frendship do professe,
   And of a frende present the place:
Geue eare to me that did possesse,
As frendly frutes as ye imbrace.
And to declare the circumstaunce,        35
There were them selues that did auaunce:
To teache me truely how to take,
A faithfull frende for vertues sake.
                  But

But I as one of little skill,
To know what good might grow therby,
Vnto my welth I had no will,
Nor to my nede I had none eye,     5
But as the childe dothe learne to go,
So I in time did learne to know.
Of all good frutes the worlde brought forth,
A faythfull frende is thing most worth.
    Then with all care I sought to finde,     10
One worthy to receiue such trust:
One onely that was riche in minde,
One secrete, sober, wise, and iust.
Whom riches coulde not raise at all,
Nor pouertie procure to fall:     15
And to be short in few wordes plaine,
One such a frend I did attaine.
    And when I did enioy this welth,
Who liued Lord in such a case,
For to my frendes it was great helth,     20
And to my foes a fowle deface,
And to my selfe a thing so riche
As seke the worlde and finde none sich
Thus by this frende I set such store,
As by my selfe I set no more.     25
    This frende so much was my delight
When care had clene orecome my hart,
One thought of her rid care as quite,
As neuer care had caused my smarte
Thus ioyed I in my frende so dere     30
Was neuer frende sate man so nere,
I carde for her so much alone,
That other God I carde for none.
    But as it dothe to them befall,
That to them selues respect haue none:     35
So my swete graffe is growen to gall,
Where I sowed mirthe I reaped mone
This ydoll that I honorde so,
Is now transformed to my fo.
That me most pleased me most paynes,     40
And in dispaire my hart remaines.
    And for iust scourge of such desart,
Thre plages I may my selfe assure,

Z.i.          First

[ 177 ]

First of my frende to lose my parte,
And next my life may not endure,
And last of all the more to blame,
My soule shall suffer for the same,                               5
Wherfore ye frendes I warne you all,
Sit faste for feare of such a fall,

## [227] Vpon the death of sir Antony
## Denny.

*D* Eath and the kyng did as it were contende,                    10
   Which of them two bare Denny greatest loue.
The king to shew his loue gan farre extende,
Did him aduaunce his betters farre aboue.
Nere place, much welthe, great honour eke him gaue,
To make it knowen what power great princes haue.                  15
   But when death came with his triumphant gift,
From worldly cark he quite his weried ghost,
Free from the corps, and straight to heauen it lift,
Now deme that can who did for Denny most.
The king gaue welth but fadyng and vnsure,                        20
Death brought him blisse that euer shall endure.

## [228] A comparison of the louers
## paines.

*L* Yke as the brake within the riders hande,
   Dothe strayne the horse nye woode with griefe of payne,   25
Not vsed before to come in such a bande,
Striueth for griefe, although god wot in vayne.
To be as erst he was at libertie,
But force of force dothe straine the contrary.
   Euen so since band dothe cause my deadly griefe,        30
That made me so my wofull chaunce lament,
Like thing hath brought me into paine and mischiefe,
Saue willingly to it I did assent.
To binde the thing in fredome which was free,
That now full sore alas repenteth me.                             35
                                      Of

## [229] Of a Rosemary braunche sente.

SVche grene to me as you haue sent,
  Such grene to you I sende agayn:
A flowring hart that wyll not feint,
For drede of hope or losse of gaine:
A stedfast thought all wholy bent,
So that he maye your grace obtain:
As you by proofe haue alwaies sene,
To liue your owne and always grene.

## [230] To his loue of his constant hart.

AS I haue bene so will I euer be,
  Vnto my death and lenger yf I might.
Haue I of loue the frendly lokyng eye,
Haue I of fortune the fauour or the spite,
I am of rock by proofe as you may see:
Not made of waxe nor of no metall light,
As leefe to dye, by chaunge as to deceaue,
Or breake the promise made. And so I leaue.

## [231] Of the token which his loue sent him.

THe golden apple that the Troyan boy,
  Gaue to Venus the fayrest of the thre,
Which was the cause of all the wrack of Troy,
Was not receiued with a greater ioye,
Then was the same (my loue) thou sent to me,
It healed my sore it made my sorowes free,
It gaue me hope it banisht mine annoy:
Thy happy hand full oft of me was blist,
That can geue such a salue when that thou list.

**Z.ii.**                    Manhod

[ 179 ]

5

10

15

20

25

30

## [232] Manhode auaileth not without
## good Fortune.

*T*Ho Cowerd oft whom deinty viandes fed,
  That bosted much his ladies eares to please,         5
By helpe of them whom vnder him he led
Hath reapt the palme that valiance could not cease.
The vnexpert that shoores vnknowen neare sought,
Whom Neptune yet apaled not with feare:
In wandryng shippe on trustlesse seas hath tought,      10
The skill to fele that time tv long doth leare.
The sportyng knight that scorneth Cupides kinde,
With fayned chere the payned cause to brede:
In game vnhides the leden sparkes of minde,
And gaines the gole, where glowyng flames should spede,    15
Thus I see proufe that trouth and manly hart,
May not auayle, if fortune chaunce to start.

## [233] That constancy of all vertues
## is most worthy.

*T*Hough in the waxe a perfect picture made,        20
  Dothe shew as fayre as in the marble stone,
Yet do we see it is estemed of none,
Because that fire or force the forme dothe fade.
Wheras the marble holden is full dere,
Since that endures the date of lenger dayes.       25
Of Diamondes it is the greatest prayse,
So long to last and alwayes one tappere.
Then if we do esteme that thing for best,
Which in perfection lengest time dothe last:
And that most vayne that turnes with euery blast     30
What iewell then with tonge can be exprest.
Like to that hart where loue hath framed such fethe,
That can not fade but by the force of dethe.

## [234] A comfort to the complaynt
## of Thestilis.
                                    35

                                    Thestilis

*T*Hestilis thou sely man, why dost thou so complaine,
　If nedes thy loue will thee forsake, thy mourning is in vaine.
For none can force the streames against their course to ronne,
Nor yet vnwillyng loue with teares or wailyng can be wonne.　　　5
Cease thou therfore thy plaintes, let hope thy sorowes ease,
The shipmen though their sailes be rent yet hope to scape the seas
Though straunge she seme a while, yet thinke she will not chaūge
Good causes driue a ladies loue, sometime to seme full straunge.
No louer that hath wit, but can forsee such happe,　　　10
That no wight can at wish or will slepe in his ladies lappe.
Achilles for a time fayre Brises did forgo,
Yet did they mete with ioye againe, then thinke thou maist do so.
Though he and louers al in loue sharpe stormes do finde,
Dispaire not thou pore Thestilis though thy loue seme vnkinde.　　　15
Ah thinke her graffed loue can not so sone decay,
Hie springes may cease from swellyng styll, but neuer dry away
Oft stormes of louers yre, do more their loue encrease:
As shinyng sunne refreshe the frutes whē rainyng gins to cease.
When springes are waxen lowe, then must they flow againe,　　　20
So shall thy hart aduaunced be, to pleasure out of paine.
When lacke of thy delight most bitter griefe apperes,
Thinke on Etrascus worthy loue that lasted thirty yeres,
Which could not long atcheue his hartes desired choyse,
Yet at the ende he founde rewarde that made him to reioyce.　　　25
Since he so long in hope with pacience did remaine,
Can not thy feruent loue forbeare thy loue a moneth or twaine.
Admit she minde to chaunge and nedes will thee forgo,
Is there no mo may thee delight but she that paynes thee so?
Thestilis draw to the towne and loue as thou hast done,　　　30
In time thou knowest by faythfull loue as good as she is wonne.
And leaue the desert woodes and waylyng thus alone,
And seke to salue thy sore els where, if all her loue be gonne.

[235] The vncertaine state of
a louer.　　　35

*L* Yke as the rage of raine,
　Filles riuers with excesse,
And as the drought againe,
Dothe draw them lesse and lesse.

**Z.iii.**　　　　　　　So

[181]

So I bothe fall and clyme,
With no and yea sometime.
  As they swell hye and hye,
So dothe encrease my state,                    5
As they fall drye and drye
So doth my wealth abate,
As yea is mixt with no,
So mirthe is mixt with wo.
  As nothing can endure,                       10
That liues and lackes reliefe,
So nothing can stande sure,
Where chaunge dothe raigne as chiefe.
Wherfore I must intende,
To bowe when others bende.                     15
  And when they laugh to smile,
And when they wepe to waile,
And when they craft, begile,
And when they fight, assayle,
And thinke there is no chaunge,                20
Can make them seme to straunge.
  Oh most vnhappy slaue,
What man may leade this course,
To lacke he would faynest haue,
Or els to do much worse.                       25
These be rewardes for such,
As liue and loue to much.


[236] The louer in libertie smileth at
them in thraldome, that some-
time scorned his                               30
bondage.


*A*T libertie I sit and see,
  Them that haue erst laught me to scorne:
Whipt with the whip that scourged me,
And now they banne that they were borne.       35
  I see them sit full soberlye,
And thinke their earnest lokes to hide:
Now in them selues they can not spye,
That they or this in me haue spied.

I see them sittyng all alone,
Markyng the steppes ech worde and loke:
And now they treade where I haue gone
The painfull pathe that I forsoke.
    Now I see well I saw no whit, 5
When they saw well that now are blinde
But happy hap hath made me quit,
And iust iudgement hath them assinde.
    I see them wander all alone, 10
And trede full fast in dredfull dout:
The selfe same pathe that I haue gone,
Blessed be hap that brought me out.
    At libertie all this I see,
And say no worde but erst among: 15
Smiling at them that laught at me,
Lo such is hap marke well my song.

## [237] A comparison of his loue wyth the faithfull and painful loue of Troylus to Creside. 20

I Read how Troylus serued in Troy,
    A lady long and many a day,
And how he bode so great anoy,
For her as all the stories saye. 25
That halfe the paine had neuer man,
Which had this wofull Troyan than.
    His youth, his sport, his pleasant chere,
His courtly state and company,
In him so straungly altred were, 30
With such a face of contrary.
That euery ioye became a wo,
This poyson new had turned him so.
    And what men thought might most him ease
And most that for his comfort stode, 35
The same did most his minde displease,
And set him most in furious mode,
For all his pleasure euer lay,
To thinke on her that was away,

His

# Songes.

His chamber was his common walke,
Wherin he kept him secretely,
He made his bedde the place of talke,
To heare his great extremitie.                                    5
In nothing els had he delight,
But euen to be a martyr right.
   And now to call her by her name
And straight therwith to sigh and throbbe:
And when his fansyes might not frame,                           10
Then into teares and so to sobbe,
All in extreames and thus he lyes
Making two fountayns of his eyes.
   As agues haue sharpe shiftes of fittes
Of colde and heat successiuely:                                 15
So had his head like chaunge of wittes:
His pacience wrought so diuersly.
Now vp, now downe, now here, now there,
Like one that was he wist not where.
   And thus though he were Pryams sonne                         20
And commen of the kinges hie bloude,
This care he had er he her wonne.
Till shee that was his maistresse good,
And lothe to see her seruaunt so,
Became Phisicion to his wo.                                     25
   And toke him to her handes and grace,
And said she would her minde apply,
To helpe him in his wofull case,
If she might be his remedy.
And thus they say to ease his smart,                            30
She made him owner of her hart.
   And truth it is except they lye,
From that day forth her study went,
To shew to loue him faithfully,
And his whole minde full to content.                            35
So happy a man at last was he,
And eke so worthy a woman she.
   Lo lady then iudge you by this,
Mine ease and how my case dothe fall,
For sure betwene my life and his,                               40
No difference there is at all.
His care was great so was his paine,
And mine is not the lest of twaine.

                                                          For

For what he felt in seruice true
For her whom that he loued so,
The same I fele as large for you,
To whom I do my seruice owe,                5
There was that time in him no payne,
But now the same in me dothe raine.
    Which if you can compare and waye,
And how I stande in euery plight,
Then this for you I dare well saye,           10
Your hart must nedes remorce of right
To graunt me grace and so to do,
As Creside then did Troylus to.
    For well I wot you are as good
And euen as faire as euer was shee,         15
And commen of as worthy bloode,
And haue in you as large pitie.
To tender me your owne true man,
As she did him her seruaunt than.
    Which gift I pray God for my sake,        20
Full sone and shortly you me sende,
So shall you make my sorowes slake,
So shall you bring my wo to ende.
And set me in as happy case,
As Troylus with his lady was.              25

## [238] To leade a vertuous and honest life,

*F*Lee frō the prese & dwell with sothfastnes
   Suffise to thee thy good though it be small,
For horde hath hate and climyng ticklenesse
Praise hath enuy, and weall is blinde in all       30
Fauour no more, then thee behoue shall.
Rede well thy self that others well canst rede,
And trouth shall the deliuer it is no drede.
    Paine thee not eche croked to redresse      35
In hope of her that turneth as a ball,
Great rest standeth in litle busynesse,
Beware also to spurne against a nall,
Striue not as doth a crocke against a wall,

              **Aa.i.**                Deme

Deme first thy selfe, that demest others dede
And trouth shall the deliuer, it is no drede.
    That the is sent, receiue in boxomnesse,
The wrestling of this world axith a fall:           5
Here is no home, here is but wildernesse.
Forth pilgrame forth beast out of thy stall,
Looke vp on high, giue thankes to god of all:
Weane well thy lust, and honest life ay leade,
So trouth shall the deliuer, it is no dreade.       10

### [239] The wounded louer deter
### mineth to make sute
### to his lady for
### his recure.

Sins Mars first moued warre or stirred men to strife,    15
  Was neuer seen so fearce a fight, I scarce could scape with life.
Resist so long I did, till death approched so nye,
To saue my selfe I thought it best, with spede away to fly.
In daunger still I fled, by flight I thought to scape
From my dere foe, it vailed not, alas it was to late.     20
For venus from her campe brought Cupide with hys bronde,
Who sayd now yelde, or els desire shall chace the in euery londe.
Yet would I not straite yelde, till fansy fiersly stroke,
Who from my will did cut the raines and charged me w̃ this yoke
Then all the dayes and nightes mine eare might heare the sound,   25
What carefull sighes my heart would steale to fele it self so bound
For though within my brest, thy care I worke he sayd,
Why for good wyll didest thou behold her persing iye displayde.
Alas the fishe is caught, through baite, that hides the hoke,
Euen so her eye me trained hath, and tangled with her loke.   30
But or that it be long, my hart thou shalt be faine,
To stay my life pray her furththrowe swete lokes whā I cõplaine
When that she shall deny, to doe me that good turne,
Then shall she see to asshes gray, by flames my body burne.
Desearte of blame to her, no wight may yet impute,     35
For feare of nay I neuer sought, the way to frame my sute.
Yet hap that what hap shall, delay I may to long,
Assay I shall for I here say, the still man oft hath wrong.
                           The

[240] The louer shewing of the continuall
paines that abide within his brest
determineth to die because he
can not haue redresse.                                    5

*T*He dolefull bell that still dothe ring,
    The wofull knell of all my ioyes:
The wretched hart dothe perce and wringe,
And fils mine eare with deadly noyes.
    The hongry vyper in my brest,                        10
That on my hart dothe lye and gnawe:
Dothe dayly brede my new vnrest,
And deper sighes dothe cause me drawe.
    And though I force bothe hande and eye,
On pleasant matter to attende:                           15
My sorowes to deceaue therby,
And wretched life for to amende.
    Yet goeth the mill within my hart,
Which gryndeth nought but paine and wo:
And turneth all my ioye to smart,                        20
The euill corne it yeldeth so.
    Though Venus smile with yeldyng eyes,
And swete musike both play and singe:
Yet doth my sprites fele none of these,
The clacke dothe at mine eare so ringe.                  25
    As smallest sparckes vncared for,
To greatest flames dothe sonest growe,
Euen so did this myne inwarde sore,
Begin in game and ende in wo.
    And now by vse so swift it goeth,                    30
That nothing can mine eares so fil:
But that the clacke it ouergoeth,
And plucketh me backe into the myll.
    But since the mill will nedes about,
The pinne wheron the whele dothe go:                     35
I wyll assaye to strike it out,
And so the myll to ouerthrow.

**Aa.ii.**                         The

## [241] The power of loue ouer gods them selues.

*F*Or loue Appollo (his Godhead set aside)　　　　　5
　Was seruant to the kyng of Thessaley,
Whose daughter was so pleasant in his eye,
That bothe his harpe and sawtrey he defide.
And bagpipe solace of the rurall bride,
Did puffe and blowe and on the holtes hy,
His cattell kept with that rude melody,　　　　　10
And oft eke him that doth the heauens gyde.
Hath loue transformed to shapes for him to base
Transmuted thus sometime a swan is he,
Leda taccoye, and eft Europe to please,
A milde white bull, vnwrinckled front and face,　　15
Suffreth her play tyll on his backe lepeth she,
Whom in great care he ferieth through the seas.

## [242] Of the sutteltye of craftye louers.

*S*Vch waiward waies haue some when folly stirres their braines　20
　To fain & plaine full oft of loue when lest they fele his paynes.
And for to shew a griefe such craft haue they in store,
That they can halt and lay a salue wheras they fele no sore.
As hounde vnto the fote, or dogge vnto the bow,
So are they made to vent her out whom bent to loue they know　25
That if I should discribe on hundred of their driftes
Two hūdred witts beside mine owne I should put to their shiftes
No woodman better knowes how for to lodge his dere
Nor shypman on the sea that more hath skill to guide the stere
Nor beaten dogge to herd can warer chose his game,　　　30
Nor scholeman to his fansy can a scholer better frame.
Then one of these which haue olde Ouids art in vre,
Can seke the wayes vnto their minde a woman to allure.
As rounde about a hiue the bees do swarme alway,
So rounde about ẙ house they prease wherin they seke their pray.　35
And whom they so besege, it is a wonderous thing,
What crafty engins to assault these wily warriers bring.
The eye as scout and watch to stirre both to and fro,

　　　　　　　　　　　　　　　　　Dothe

Doth serue to stale her here & there where she doth come and go,
The tonge doth plede for right as herauld of the hart:
And both the handes as oratours do serue to point theyr part.
So shewes the countinaunce then with these fowre to agree,     5
As though in witnes with the rest it wold hers sworne be.
But if she then mistrust it would turne black to whyte,
For that the woorrier lokes most smoth whē he wold fainest bite.
Then wit as counsellor a help for this to fynde:
Straight makes ẙ hand as secretayr forthwith to write his minde     10
And so the letters straight embassadours are made,
To treate in hast for to procure her to a better trade.
Wherin if she do think all this is but a shewe,
Or but a subtile masking cloke to hyde a craftye shrewe.
Then come they to the larme, then shew they in the fielde,     15
Then muster they in colours strange that wayes to make her yeld
Then shoote they batrye of, then compasse they her in,
At tilte and turney oft they striue this selly soule to win.
Then sound they on their Lutes then strain they forth their sōge,
Then romble they with instrumentes to laye her quite a long.     20
Then borde they her with giftes then doe they woe and watche,
Then night and day they labour hard this simple holde to catche.
As pathes within a woode, or turnes within a mase:
So then they shewe of wyles & craftes they can a thousand wayes

[243] Of the dissembling louer.     25

*G*Irt in my giltlesse gowne as I sit here and sow,
   I see that thynges are not in dede as to the outward show.
And who so list to loke and note thinges somewhat nere:
Shall fynd wher playnesse semes to haūt nothing but craft appere
For with indifferent eyes my self can well discerne,     30
How some to guide a ship in stormes seke for to take the sterne.
Whose practise yf were proued in calme to stere a barge,
Assuredly beleue it well it were to great a charge.
And some I see agayne sit styll and saye but small,
That could do ten tymes more than they that saye they can do all.     35
Whose goodly giftes are such the more they vnderstande,
The more they seke to learne and knowe & take lesse charge in hād
And to declare more plain the tyme fletes not so fast:
But I can beare full well in minde the songe now soūge and past.
The authour wherof came wrapt in a craftye cloke:     40

**Aa.iii.**     With

[ 189 ]

With will to force a flamyng fire where he could raise no smoke.
If power and will had ioynde as it appeareth plaine,
The truth nor right had tane no place their vertues had ben vain.
So that you may perceiue, and I may safely se,                    5
The innocent that giltlesse is, condemned should haue be.

## [244] The promise of a constant louer.

*A*S Lawrell leaues that cease not to be grene,
     From parching sunne, nor yet from winters thretta:
As hardened oke that fearth no sworde so kene,               10
As flint for toole in twaine that will not frette.
As fast as rocke or piller surely set
So fast am I to you and aye haue bene.
Assuredly whom I can not forget,
For ioy, for paine, for torment nor for tene.               15
For losse, for gayne, for frownyng, nor for thret.
But euer one, yea bothe in calme or blast,
Your faithfull frende, and will be to my last.

## [245] Against him that had slaundered
## a gentlewoman with                                         20
## him selfe

*F*Alse may he be, and by the powers aboue,
     Neuer haue he good spede or lucke in loue.
That so can lye or spot the worthy fame,
Of her for whom thou .R. art to blame.                       25
For chaste Diane that hunteth still the chase,
And all her maides that sue her in the race.
With faire bowes bent and arrowes by their side,
Can saye that thou in this hast falsely lied.
For neuer honge the bow vpon the wall,                       30
Of Dianes temple no nor neuer shall.
Of broken chaste the sacred vowe to spot,
Of her whom thou doste charge so large I wot.
But if ought be wherof her blame may rise,
It is in that she did not well aduise                        35
To marke the right as now she dothe thee know,
False of thy dedes false of thy talke also.
Lurker of kinde like serpent layd to bite,

                                                        As

As poyson hid vnder the suger white.
What daunger suche? So was the house defilde,
Of Collatiue: so was the wife begilde.
So smarted she, and by a trayterous force, 5
The Cartage quene so she fordid her corse.
So strangled was the R. so dcpe can auoyde,
Fye traytour fye, to thy shame be it sayd,
Thou dunghyll crowe that crokest agaynst the rayne,
Home to thy hole, brag not with Phebe agayne. 10
Carrion for the and lothsome be thy voyce,
Thy song is fowle I wery of thy noyce.
Thy blacke fethers, which are thy wearyng wede.
Wet them with teares and sorowe for thy dede.
And in darke caues, where yrkesome wormes do crepe, 15
Lurke thou all daye, and flye when thou shouldest slepe.
And neuer light where liuyng thing hath life,
But eat and drinke where stinche and filthe is rife.
For she that is a fowle of fethers bryght,
Admit she toke some pleasure in thy sight. 20
As fowle of state sometimes delight to take,
Fowle of meane sort their flight with them to make.
For play of winge or solace of their kinde:
But not in sort as thou dost breke thy mynde.
Not for to treade with such foule fowle as thou, 25
No no I swere and I dare it here auowe.
Thou neuer settest thy fote within her nest,
Boast not so broade then to thine owne vnrest.
But blushe for shame for in thy face it standes,
And thou canst not vnspot it with thy handes. 30
For all the heauens against thee recorde beare,
And all in earth against thee eke will sweare.
That thou in this art euen none other man,
But as the iudges were to Susan than.
Forgers of that where to their lust them prickt, 35
Bashe, blaser then the truth hath thee conuict.
And she a woman of her worthy fame,
Vnspotted standes, and thou hast caught the shame.
And there I pray to God that it may rest,
False as thou art, as false as is the best, 40
That so canst wrong the noble kinde of man,
In whom all trouth furst floorist and began.
And so hath stande till now the wretched part,

Hath

Hath spotted vs of whose kinde one thou art.
That all the shame that euer rose or may,
Of shamefall dede on thee may light I saye.
And on thy kinde, and thus I wishe thee rather,                    5
That all thy sede may like be to their father.
Vntrue as thou, and forgers as thou art,
So as all we be blamelesse of thy part.
And of thy dede. And thus I do thee leaue,
Still to be false, and falsely to deceaue.                         10

## [246] A praise of maistresse
## Ryce.

*I* Heard when Fame with thundryng voice did sommon to appere
   The chiefe of natures children all that kinde had placed here.
To view what brute by vertue got their liues could iustly craue,   15
And bade thē shew what praise by truth they worthy were to haue
Wherwith I saw how Venus came and put her selfe in place,
And gaue her ladies leue at large to stand and pleade their case.
Eche one was calde by name arowe, in that assemble there,
That hence are gone or here remaines in court or otherwhere.       20
A solemne silence was proclaimde, the iudges sate and heard,
What truth could tell or craft could faine, & who should be preferd.
Then beauty stept before the barre, whose brest and neck was bare
With heare trust vp and on her head a caule of gold she ware.
Thus Cupides thralles began to flock whose hongry eyes did say     25
That she had stayned all the dames that present were that day.
For er she spake ẘ whispring words, the prease was filde through-
And fansy forced common voyce therat to geue a shoute.      (out
Which cried to fame take forth thy trump, & sound her praise on hie
That glads the hart of euery wight that her beholdes with eye.     30
What stirre and rule (quod order than) do these rude people make,
We holde her best that shall deserue a praise for vertues sake.
This sentence was no soner said but beauty therewith blusht,
The audience ceased with the same, and euery thing was whusht.
Then finenesse thought by trainyng talke to win that beauty lost.  35
And whet her tonges with ioly wordes, and spared for no cost.
Yet wantonnesse could not abide, but brake her tale in haste,
And peuishe pride for pecockes plumes wold nedes be hiest plast.
And therwithall came curiousnesse and carped out of frame.
                                                            The

The audience laught to here the strife as they beheld the same.
Yet reason sone appesde the brute, her reuerence made and don,
She purchased fauour for to speake and thus her tale begoon,
Sins bountye shall the garland were and crowned be by fame,            5
O happy iudges call for her for she deserues the same.
Where tēperance gouernes bewtyes flowers & glory is not sought
And shamefast mekenes mastreth pride & vertue dwels in thought
Byd her come forth and shew her face or els assent eche one,
That true report shall graue her name in gold or marble stone.        10
For all the world to rede at will what worthines doth rest,
In perfect pure vnspotted life which she hath here possest.
Then skill rose vp and sought the preace to find if y̆ he might
A person of such honest name that men should praise of right.
This one I saw full sadly sit and shrinke her self a side,            15
Whose sober lokes did shew what gifts her wiefly grace did hide
Lo here (quod skill, good people all) is Lucrece left aliue,
And she shall most excepted be that lest for praise did striue.
No lenger fame could hold her peace, but blew a blast so hye,
That made an eckow in the ayer and sowning through the sky.           20
The voice was loude & thus it sayd come Rise with happy daies,
Thy honest life hath wonne the fame & crowned thee with praies.
And when I heard my maistres name I thrust amids the throng.
And clapt my handes and wisht of god y̆ she might prosper long.

## [247] Of one vniustly                                              25
## defamed.

*I*Ne can close in short and cunning verse,
  Thy worthy praise of bountie by desart:
The hatefull spite and slaunder to reherse.
Of them that see but know not what thou art,                          30
For kind by craft hath wrought thee so to eye,
That no wight may thy wit and vertue spye.
But he haue other fele then outward sight,
The lack wherof doth hate and spite to trie
Thus kind thy craft is let of vertues light:                          35
See how the outward shew the wittes may dull:
Not of the wise but as the most entend,
Minerua yet might neuer perce their scull,
That Circes cup and Cupides brand hath blend.
                                   𝕭𝕭.𝕚.            Whose

Whose fonde affects now sturred haue their braine,
So dothe thy hap thy hue with colour staine.
Beauty thy foe thy shape doubleth thy sore,
To hide thy wit and shewe thy vertue vayne,                    5
Fell were thy fate, if wisdome were not more.
I meane by thee euen G. by name,
Whom stormy windes of enuy and disdaine,
Do tosse with boisteous blastes of wicked fame.
Where stedfastnesse as chiefe in thee dothe raigne,          10
Pacience thy setled minde dothe guide and stere,
Silence and shame with many resteth there.
Till time thy mother list them forth to call,
Happy is he that may enioye them all.

## [248] Of the death of the late county    15
## of Penbroke.

Y Et once againe my muse I pardon pray,
   Thine intermitted song if I repete:
Not in such wise as when loue was my pay,
My ioly wo with ioyfull verse to treat.                       20
   But now (vnthanke to our desert be geuen,
Which merite not a heauens gift to kepe)
Thou must with me bewaile that fate hath reuen,
From earth a iewell laied in earth to slepe.
   A iewell, yea a gemme of womanhed,                         25
Whose perfect vertues linked as in chaine:
So did adorne that humble wiuelyhed,
As is not rife to finde the like againe.
   For wit and learnyng framed to obey,
Her husbandes will that willed her to vse                     30
The loue he bare her chiefely as a staye,
For all her frendes that would her furtherance chuse.
   Well sayd therfore a heauens gift she was,
Because the best are sonest hence bereft:
And though her selfe to heauen hence did passe,              35
Her spoyle to earth from whence it came she left.
   And to vs teares her absence to lament,
And eke his chance that was her make by lawe:
Whose losse to lose so great an ornament,
Let them esteme which true loues knot can draw.              40
                                              That

# [249] That eche thing is hurt of it selfe.

W Hy fearest thou thy outward foe,
   When thou thy selfe thy harme doste fedc,      5
Of griefe, or hurt, of paine, of wo,
Within eche thing is sowen the sede.
  So fine was neuer yet the cloth,
No smith so harde his yron did beate:
But thone consumed was with mothe,      10
Thother with canker all to fret.
  The knotty oke and weinscot old,
Within dothe eat the silly worme:
Euen so a minde in enuy rold,
Always within it self doth burne.      15
  Thus euery thing that nature wrought,
Within it self his hurt doth beare:
No outward harme nede to be sought,
Where enmies be within so neare.

# [250] Of the choise of a wife.      20

*T*He flickeryng fame that flieth from eare to eare.
  And aye her strength encreaseth with her flight
Geues first the cause why men to heare delight,
Of those whom she dothe note for beauty bright.
And with this fame that flieth on so fast,      25
Fansy dothe hye when reason makes no haste
  And yet not so content they wishe to see
And thereby knowe if fame haue sayd aright.
More trustyng to the triall of their eye,
Then to the brute that goes of any wight.      30
Wise in that poynt that lightly will not leeue,
Vnwise to seke that may them after greue.
  Who knoweth not how sight may loue allure,
And kindle in the hart a hotte desire:
The eye to worke that fame could not procure,      35
Of greater cause there commeth hotter fire.
For ere he wete him self he feleth warme,
The fame and eye the causers of his harme.
                  **Bb.ii.**        Let

Let fame not make her knowen whom I shall know,
Nor yet mine eye therin to be my guide:
Suffiseth me that vertue in her grow,
Whose simple life her fathers walles do hide.          5
Content with this I leaue the rest to go,
And in such choise shall stande my welth and wo.

## [251] Descripcion of an vngodlye
## worlde.

  WHo loues to liue in peace, and marketh euery change,          10
Shal hear such news frō time to time, as semeth wōderous strāge.
  Such fraude in frendly lokes, such frendshippe all for gayne:
Such cloked wrath in hatefull harts, which worldly men retayne.
  Such fayned flatteryng fayth, amongs both hye and low:
Such great deceite, such subtell wittes, the pore to ouerthrowe.          15
  Such spite in sugred tonges, such malice full of pride:
Such open wrong such great vntruth, which can not go vnspied.
  Such restlesse sute for roumes, which bringeth men to care:
Such slidyng downe  from slippry seates, yet can we not beware.
  Such barkyng at the good, such bolstrynge of the yll:          20
Such threatnyng of the wrathe of God, such vyce embraced styll.
  Such striuynge for the best, such climyng to estate:
Such great dissemblyng euery where, such loue all mixt wyth hate
  Such traynes to trap the iust, such prollyng faultes to pyke:
Such cruell wordes for speakyng truth, who euer hearde the like.          25
  Such strife for stirryng strawes, such discord dayly wrought,
Such forged tales dul wits to blind, such matters made of nought
  Such trifles tolde for trouth, such credityng of lyes,
Such silence kept when foles do speake, such laughyng at the wise
  Such plenty made so scarce, such criyng for redresse,          30
Such feared signes of our decay, which tong dares not expresse.
  Such chaunges lightly markt, such troubles still apperes,
Which neuer were before this time, no not this thousand yeres.
  Such bribyng for the purse, which euer gapes for more,
Such hordyng vp of worldly welth, such kepyng muck in store.          35
  Such folly founde in age, such will in tender youth,
Such sundry sortes among great clarkes, & few y̆ speake the truth
  Such falshed vnder craft, and such vnstedfast wayes,
Was neuer sene within mens hartes, as is found now adayes.
                                  The

The cause and ground of this is our vnquiet minde,
Which thinkes to take those goods away which we must leue be-
   Why do men seke to get which they cannot possesse,    (hinde.
Or breke their slepes w&#773; carefull thoughtes & all for wretchednes.    5
   Though one amonges a skore, hath welth and ease a while,
A thousand want which toyleth sore and trauaile many a mile.
   And some although they slepe, yet welth falles in their lap,
Thus some be riche and some be pore as fortune geues the hap,
   Wherfore I holde him wise which thinkes himself at ease,    10
And is content in simple state both god and man to please.
   For those that liue like gods and honored are to day,
Within short time their glory falles as flowers do fade away.
   Vncertein is their lifes on whom this world will frowne,
For though they sit aboue y&#771; starres a storm may strike the&#773; downe    15
   In welth who feares no fall may slide from ioy full sone,
There is no thing so sure on earth but changeth as the Mone.
   What pleasure hath the riche or ease more then the pore,
Although he haue a plesant house his trouble is the more.
   They bowe and speake him fayre, which seke to suck his blood,    20
And some do wishe his soule in hell and all to haue his good.
   The coueting of the goodes doth nought but dull the spirite,
And some men chaunce to tast the sower that gropeth for the swete
   The riche is still enuied by those which eate his bred,
With fawning spech and flattering tales his eares are dayly fed.    25
   In fine I see and proue the riche haue many foes,
He slepeth best and careth lest that litle hath to lose.
   As time requireth now who would avoide much strife,
Were better liue in pore estate then leade a princes life.
   To passe those troblesome times I see but little choise,    30
But help to waile with those that wepe & laugh when they reioise
   For as we se to day our brother brought in care,
To morow may we haue such chance to fall with him in snare,
   Of this we may be sure, who thinkes to sit most fast,
Shal sonest fal like wethered leaues that cannot bide a blast.    35
   Though that the flood be great, the ebbe as lowe doth ronne,
When euery man hath playd his part our pagent shalbe donne.
   Who trustes this wretched world I hold him worse then mad,
Here is not one that fereth god the best is all to badde.
   For those that seme as saintes are deuilles in their dedes:    40
Though y&#771; the earth bringes forth some flowers it beareth many
   I se no present help from mischief to preuaile,    (wedes.
But flee the seas of worldly cares or beare a quiet sayle.

**B.iii.**                 For

For who that medleth least shall saue him selfe from smart,
Who styrres an oare in euery boat shal play a folish part.

## [252] The dispairyng louer la-
### menteth. 5

WAlkyng the pathe of pensiue thought,
 I askt my hart how came this wo.
Thine eye (quod he) this care me brought.
Thy minde, thy witte, thy will also
Enforceth me to loue her euer, 10
This is the cause ioye shall I neuer.
  And as I walkt as one dismayde,
Thinkyng that wrong this wo me lent:
Right, sent me worde by wrath, which sayd,
This iust iudgement to thee is sent: 15
Neuer to dye, but diyng euer,
Till breath thee faile, ioy shalt thou neuer.
  Sithe right doth iudge this wo tendure,
Of health, of wealth, of remedy:
As I haue done so be she sure, 20
Of fayth and trouth vntill I dye.
And as this payne cloke shall I euer,
So inwardly ioye shall I neuer.
  Gripyng of gripes greue not so sore,
Nor serpentes styng causeth such smarte, 25
Nothing on earth may payne me more,
Then sight that perst my wofull hart.
Drowned with cares styll to perseuer,
Come death betimes, ioye shall I neuer.
  O libertie why doest thou swarue, 30
And steale away thus all at ones:
And I in pryson like to sterue,
For lacke of fode do gnaw on bones.
My hope and trust in thee was euer,
Now thou art gone ioye shall I neuer. 35
  But styll as one all desperate,
To leade my life in miserie:
Sith feare from hope hath lockt the gate,
Where pity should graunt remedye.

Dispaire

Dispaire this lotte assignes me euer,
To liue in payne.  Ioie shall I neuer.

## [253] An epitaph of maister Henry williams.

5

*F*Rom worldly wo the mede of misbeliefe,
　From cause of care that leadeth to lament,
From vaine delight the grounde of greater griefe,
From feare from frendes, from matter to repent,
From painfull panges last sorow that is sent. 　　　　10
From drede of death sithe death dothe set vs free,
With it the better pleased should we be.
　This lothsome life where likyng we do finde,
Thencreaser of our crimes: dothe vs beriue,
Our blisse that alway ought to be in minde. 　　　　15
This wyly worlde whiles here we breath aliue,
And fleshe our fayned fo, do stifely striue
To flatter vs assuryng here the ioye,
Where we alas do finde but great annoy.
　Vntolde heapes though we haue of worldly welth, 　　20
Though we possesse the sea and frutefull grounde,
Strength, beauty, knowledge, and vnharmed helth,
Though at our wishe all pleasure do abound.
It were but vaine, no frendship can be founde,
When death assaulteth with his dredfull dart. 　　　25
No raunsome can stay the home hastyng hart.
　And sithe thou hast cut the liues line in twaine,
Of Henry, sonne to sir Iohn Williams knight,
Whose manly hart and prowes none coulde stayne.
Whose godly life to vertue was our light, 　　　　30
Whose worthy fame shall florishe long by right.
Though in this life so cruell mightest thou be,
His spirite in heauen shall triumph ouer thee.

## [254] Against a gentlewoman by whom he was refused.

35

*T*O false report and flying fame,
　While erst my minde gaue credite light,

Bel-

[ 199 ]

Beleuyng that her bolstred name
Had stuffe to shew that praise did hight.
I finde well now I did mistake,
Vpon report my grounde to make. 5
   I hearde it sayd such one was she,
As rare to finde as parragon,
Of lowly cheare of heart so free,
As her for bounty could passe none.
Such one so faire though forme and face, 10
Were meane to passe in seconde place.
   I sought it neare thinkyng to finde,
Report and dede both to agree:
But chaunge had tride her suttell minde,
Of force I was enforced to see, 15
That she in dede was nothing so,
Which made my will my hart forgo.
   For she is such as geason none,
And what she most may bost to be:
I finde her matches mo then one, 20
What nede she so to deale with me?
Ha flering face with scornefull harte,
So yll rewarde for good desert?
   I will repent that I haue done,
To ende so well the losse is small, 25
I lost her loue, that lesse hath wonne,
To vaunt she had me as her thrall.
What though a gyllot sent that note,
By cocke and pye I meant it not.

# [255] An epitaphe written by w.G. 30
## to be set vpon his owne
### graue.

*L*O here lieth G. vnder the grounde,
  Emong the greedy wormes:
Which in his life time neuer founde, 35
But strife and sturdy stormes.
   And namely through a wicked wife,
As to the worlde apperes:

                              She

She was the shortnyng of his life
By many daies and yeres.
  He might haue liued long god wot,
His yeres they were but yong:                 5
Of wicked wiues this is the lot,
To kill with spitefull tong.
  Whose memory shall still remaine,
In writyng here with me:
That men may know whom she hath slaine.    10
And say this same is she.

## [256] An aunswere.

*I*F that thy wicked wife had spon the thred,
  And were the weauer of thy wo:
Then art thou double happy to be dead,     15
  As happily dispatched so.
If rage did causelesse cause thee to complaine,
  And mad moode mouer of thy mone:
If frensy forced on thy testy braine:
  Then blist is she to liue alone.     20
So, whether were the ground of others griefe,
  Because so doutfull was the dome:
Now death hath brought your payne a right reliefe,
  And blessed be ye bothe become:
She that she liues no lenger bounde to beare    25
  The rule of such a frowarde hed:
Thou that thou liuest no lenger faine to feare
  The restlesse ramp that thou hadst wedde.
Be thou as glad therfore that thou art gone,
  As she is glad she dothe abide.    30
For so ye be a sonder, all is one:
  A badder match can not betide.

## [257] Against women either good or badde.

*A* Man may liue thrise Nestors life,    35
  Thrise wander out Vlisses race:

𝔆𝔠.𝔦.              Yet

Yet neuer finde Vlisses wife.
Such chaunge hath chanced in this case.
   Lesse age will serue than Paris had,
Small peyn (if none be small inough)                 5
To finde good store of Helenes trade.
Such sap the rote dothe yelde the bough.
   For one good wife Vlisses slew
A worthy knot of gentle blood:
For one yll wife Grece ouerthrew                10
The towne of Troy. Sith bad and good
Bring mischiefe: Lord, let be thy will,
To kepe me free from either yll.

## [258] An answere.

_T_He vertue of Vlisses wife                          15
  Dothe liue, though she hath ceast her race,
And farre surmountes old Nestors life:
But now in moe than then it was.
Such change is chanced in this case.
   Ladyes now liue in other trade:              20
Farre other Helenes now we see,
Than she whom Troyan Paris had.
As vertue fedes the roote, so be
The sap and frute of bough and tree.
   Vlisses rage, not his good wife,             25
Spilt gentle blood. Not Helenes face,
But Paris eye did rayse the strife,
That did the Troyan buildyngs race.
Thus sithe ne good, ne bad do yll:
Them all, O Lord, maintain my will,            30
To serue with all my force and skyll.

## [259] The louer praieth his seruice to be accepted and his defaultes par- doned.

                                          35

Pro-

*P* Rocryn that some tyme serued Cephalus,
   With hart as true as any louer might,
Yet her betyd in louyng this vnright.
That as in hart with loue surprised thus,          5
She on a daye to see this Cephalus,
Where he was wont to shrowde him in the shade,
When of his huntyng he an ende had made.
Within the woddes with dredfull fote she stalketh,
So busily loue in her hedde it walketh.       10
That she to sene him may her not restrayne.
This Cephalus that heard one shake the leaues,
Vprist all egre thrustyng after pray,
With darte in hande him list no further dayne,
To see his loue but slew her in the greues,     15
That ment to him but perfect loue alway.
   So curious bene alas the rites all,
Of mighty loue that vnnethes may I thinke,
In his high seruice how to loke or winke,
Thus I complaine that wrechedest am of all.    20
To you my loue and souerayne lady dere,
That may myne hart with death or life stere
As ye best list. That ye vouchsafe in all
Mine humble seruice. And if that me misfall,
By negligence, or els for lacke of witte,     25
That of your mercy you do pardon it,
And thinke that loue made Procrin shake the leaues,
When with vnright she slayne was in the greues.

## [260] Description and praise of
## his loue.             30

*L* Yke the Phenix a birde most rare in sight
   With golde and purple that nature hath drest:
Such she me semes in whom I most delight,
If I might speake for enuy at the least.
Nature I thinke first wrought her in despite,    35
Of rose and lillye that sommer bringeth first,

𝕮𝖙.𝖎𝖎.          In

In beauty sure excedyng all the rest,
Vnder the bent of her browes iustly pight:
As polisht Diamondes, or Saphires at the least:
Her glistryng lightes the darkenesse of the night.    5
Whose little mouth and chinne like all the rest.
Her ruddy lippes excede the corall quite.
Her yuery teeth where none excedes the rest.
Faultlesse she is from fote vnto the waste.
Her body small and straight as mast vpright.    10
Her armes long in iust proporcion cast,
Her handes depaint with veines all blew and white.
What shall I say for that is not in sight?
The hidden partes I iudge them by the rest.
And if I were the forman of the quest,    15
To geue a verdite of her beauty bright,
Forgeue me Phebus, thou shouldst be dispossest,
Which doest vsurpe my ladies place of right.
Here will I cease lest enuy cause dispite.
But nature when she wrought so fayre a wight,    20
In this her worke she surely did entende,
To frame a thing that God could not amende.


[261] An answere to a song before im-
printed beginnyng. To
walke on doutfull    25
grounde.


*T*O trust the fayned face, to rue on forced teares,
  To credit finely forged tales, wherin there oft appeares
  And breathes as from the brest a smoke of kindled smart,
Where onely lurkes a depe deceit within the hollow hart,    30
  Betrayes the simple soule, whom plaine deceitlesse minde
Taught not to feare that in it self it self did neuer finde.
  Not euery tricklyng teare doth argue inward paine:
Not euery sigh dothe surely shewe the sigher not to fayne:
  Not euery smoke dothe proue a presence of the fire:    35
Not euery glistring geues the golde, that gredy folke desire:
  Not euery wailyng word is drawen out of the depe:

                                           Not

Not griefe for want of graunted grace enforceth all to wepe.
   Oft malice makes the minde to shed the boyled brine:
And enuies humor oft vnlades by conduites of the eyen.
   Oft craft can cause the man to make a semyng show     5
Of hart with dolour all distreined, where griefe did neuer grow.
   As cursed Crocodile most cruelly can toll.
With truthlesse teares, vnto his death, the silly pitiyng soule.
   Blame neuer those therfore, that wisely can beware
The guillful man, that suttly sayth him selfe to dread the snare.   10
   Blame not the stopped eares against the Syrenes song:
Blame not the mind not moued w̅ mone of falsheds flowing tong.
   If guile do guide your wit by silence so to speake,
By craft to craue and faine by fraude the cause ẙ you wold breake:
   Great harme your suttle soule shall suffer for the same:   15
And mighty loue will wreke the wrong so cloked with his name.
   But we, whom you haue warnde, this lesson learne by you:
To know the tree before we clime, to trust no rotten bowe,
   To view the limed bushe, to loke afore we light,
To shunne the perilous bayted hoke, and vse a further sight.   20
   As do the mouse, the birde, the fishe, by sample fitly show,
That wyly wittes and ginnes of men do worke the simples wo:
   So, simple sithe we are, and you so suttle be,
God help the mouse, the birde, ẙ fishe, & vs your sleights to fle.

[262] The constant louer la-
menteth.

SYns fortunes wrath enuieth the welth,                                    5
  Wherin I raygned by the sight:
Of that that fed mine eyes by stelth,
With sower swete, dreade, and delight.
Let not my griefe moue you to mone,
For I will wepe and wayle alone.                                          10
    Spite draue me into Borias raigne,
Where hory frostes the frutes do bite,
When hilles were spred and euery playne:
With stormy winters mantle white.
And yet my deare such was my heate,                                       15
When others frese then did I swete.
    And now though on the sunne I driue,
Whose feruent flame all thinges decaies,
His beames in brightnesse may not striue,
With light of your swete golden rayes,                                    20
Nor from my brest this heate remoue,
The frosen thoughtes grauen by loue.
    Ne may the waues of the salt floode,
Quenche that your beauty set on fire,
For though mine eyes forbere the fode,                                    25
That did releue the hote desire.
Such as I was such will I be,
Your owne, what would ye more of me.

[263] A praise of sir Thomas wyate thelder
for his excellent learning.                                               30

IN the rude age when knowledge was not rife,
  If Ioue in Create and other were that taught,
Artes to conuert to profite of our life,
Wende after death to haue their temples sought,
If vertue yet no voyde vnthankefull time,                                 35
                                                             Failed

Failed of some to blast her endles fame,
A goodly meane both to deterre from crime:
And to her steppes our sequele to enflame,
In dayes of truth if wyates frendes then wayle,                    5
The only det that dead of quick may claime:
That rare wit spent employd to our auaile.
Where Christ is taught we led to vertues traine.
His liuely face their brestes how did it freat,
Whose cindres yet with enuye they do eate.                        10

## [264] ¶ A song written by the earle of Sur-<br>rey by a lady that refused to<br>daunce with him.

*E*Che beast can chose hys fere according to his minde,
 And eke can shew a frendly chere like to their beastly kinde.    15
 A Lion saw I late as white as any snow,
Which semed well to lead the race his port the same did show.
 Vpon the gentle beast to gaze it pleased me,
For still me thought he semed well of noble blood to be.
 And as he praunced before, still seking for a make,               20
As who wold say there is none here I trow will me forsake.
 I might parceiue a wolfe as white as whales bone,
A fairer beast of fresher hue beheld I neuer none.
 Saue that her lokes were coy, and froward eke her grace,
Vnto the which this gentle beast gan him aduance apace.            25
 And with a beck full low he bowed at her feete,
In humble wise as who would say I am to farre vnmete.
 But such a scornefull chere wherwith she him rewarded,
Was neuer sene I trow the like to such as well deserued.
 With that she start aside welnere a fote or twaine,               30
And vnto him thus gan she say with spite and great disdaine.
 Lyon she sayd if thou hadst knowen my mind before,
Thou hadst not spent thy trauail thus nor al thy paine forlore.
 Do way I let the wete thou shalt not play with me,
Go range about where thou mayst finde some meter fere for the:     35
 With that he bet his taile, his eyes began to flame,
I might perceiue hys noble hart much moued by the same.
 Yet saw I him refraine and eke his wrath aswage,
And vnto her thus gan he say when he was past his rage.
                                                        Cruell

## Songes

Cruell, you do me wrong to set me thus so light,
Without desert for my good will to shew me such despight.
   How can ye thus entreat a Lion of the race,
That with his pawes a crowned king deuoured in the place:      5
   Whose nature is to pray vpon no simple food,
As long as he may suck the fleshe, and drink of noble blood.
   If you be faire and fresh, am I not of your hue?
And for my vaunt I dare well say my blood is not vntrue.
   For you your self haue heard it is not long agoe,      10
Sith that for loue one of the race did end his life in woe
   In tower strong and hie for his assured truthe,
Where as in teares he spent his breath, alas the more the ruthe.
   This gentle beast likewise whom nothing could remoue,
But willingly to lese his life for losse of his true loue.      15
   Other there be whose liues doe lingre still in paine,
Against their willes preserued ar that would haue died faine.
   But now I doe perceue that nought it moueth you,
My good entent, my gentle hart, nor yet my kind so true.
   But that your will is such to lure me to the trade,      20
As other some full many yeres to trace by craft ye made.
   And thus behold our kyndes how that we differ farre.
I seke my foes: and you your frendes do threten still with warre.
   I fawne where I am fled: you slay that sekes to you,
I can deuour no yelding pray: you kill where you subdue.      25
   My kinde is to desire the honoure of the field:
And you with blood to slake your thirst on such as to you yeld.
   Wherfore I would you wist that for your coyed lokes,
I am no man that will be trapt nor tangled with such hokes.
   And though some lust to loue where blame full well they might      30
And to such beasts of currant sort that should haue trauail bright.
   I will obserue the law that nature gaue to me,
To conquer such as will resist and let the rest goe fre.
   And as a faucon free that soreth in the ayre,
Which neuer fed on hand nor lure, nor for no stale doth care,      35
   While that I liue and breath such shall my custome be,
In wildnes of the woodes to seke my pray where pleseth me.
   Where many one shal ruse, that neuer made offense.
This your refuse against my power shall bode them ne defence.
   And for reuenge therof I vow and swere therto,      40
I thousand spoiles I shall commit I neuer thought to do.
   And if to light on you my luck so good shall be,
I shall be glad to fede on that that would haue fed on me.
                                           And

And thus farewell vnkinde to whom I bent and bow,
I would ye wist the ship is safe that bare his sailes so low.
    Sith that a lions hart is for a wolfe no pray,
With bloody mouth go slake your thirst on simple shepe I say.          5
    With more dispite and ire than I can now expresse,
Which to my pain though I refraine the cause you may wel gesse.
    As for because my self was aucthor of the game,
It bootes me not that for my wrath I should disturbe the same.


[265] The faithfull louer declareth his paines          10
        and his vncertein ioies, and with
            only hope recomforteth
                somwhat his wo=
                    full heart.


*I*F  care do cause men cry, why do not I complaine?          15
    If eche man do bewaile his wo, why shew I not my paine?
    Since that amongest them all I dare well say is none,
So farre from weale, so full of wo, or hath more cause to mone.
    For all thynges hauing life sometime haue quiet rest.
The bering asse, the drawing oxe, and euery other beast.          20
    The peasant and the post, that serue at al assayes,
The shyp boy and the galley slaue haue time to take their ease,
    Saue I alas whom care of force doth so constraine
To waile the day and wake the night continually in paine,
    From pensiuenes to plaint, from plaint to bitter teares,          25
From teares to painfull plaint againe: and thus my life it wears.
    No thing vnder the sunne that I can here or se,
But moueth me for to bewaile my cruell destenie.
    For wher men do reioyce since that I can not so,
I take no pleasure in that place, it doubleth but my woe.          30
    And when I heare the sound of song or instrument,
Me thinke eche tune there dolefull is and helpes me to lament.
    And if I se some haue their most desired sight,
Alas think I eche man hath weal saue I most wofull wight.
    Then as the striken dere withdrawes him selfe alone,          35
So doe I seke some secrete place where I may make my mone.
    There do my flowing eyes shew forth my melting hart,
So y̆ the stremes of those two welles right wel declare my smart

Dd.i.                    And

And in those cares so colde I force my selfe a heate,
As sick men in their shaking fittes procure them self to sweate,
   With thoughtes that for the time do much appease my paine.
But yet they cause a ferther fere and brede my woe agayne.     5
   Me thinke within my thought I se right plaine appere,
My hartes delight my sorowes leche mine earthly goddesse here.
   With euery sondry grace that I haue sene her haue,
Thus I within my wofull brest her picture paint and graue.
   And in my thought I roll her bewties to and fro,     10
Her laughing chere her louely looke my hart that perced so.
   Her strangenes when I sued her seruant for to be,
And what she sayd and how she smiled when that she pitied me.
   Then comes a sodaine feare that riueth all my rest
Lest absence cause forgetfulnes to sink within her brest.     15
   For when I thinke how far this earth doth vs deuide.
Alas me semes loue throwes me downe I fele how that I slide.
   But then I thinke againe why should I thus mistrust,
So swete a wight so sad and wise that is so true and iust.
   For loth she was to loue, and wauering is she not.     20
The farther of the more desirde thus louers tie their knot.
   So in dispaire and hope plonged am I both vp an doune,
As is the ship with wind and waue when Neptune list to froune.
   But as the watry showers delay the raging winde,
So doth good hope clene put away dispayre out of my minde.     25
   And biddes me for to serue and suffer pacientlie,
For what wot I the after weale that fortune willes to me.
   For those that care do knowe and tasted haue of trouble,
When passed is their woful paine eche ioy shall seme them double.
   And bitter sendes she now to make me tast the better,     30
The plesant swete when that it comes to make it seme the sweter.
   And so determine I to serue vntill my brethe.
Ye rather dye a thousand times then once to false my feithe.
   And if my feble corps through weight of wofull smart.
Do fayle or faint my will it is that still she kepe my hart.     35
   And when thys carcas here to earth shalbe refarde,
I do bequeth my weried ghost to serue her afterwarde.

Finis.

*and Sonettes.*

*Other Songes and sonettes written
by sir Thomas wiat the elder*

[266] *Of his loue called.
Anna.* 5

WHat word is that, that changeth not,
Though it be turned and made in twaine:
It is mine Anna god it wot.
The only causer of my paine:
My loue that medeth with disdaine. 10
Yet is it loued what will you more,
It is my salue, and eke my sore.

[267] That pleasure is mixed with
euery paine.

V Enemous thornes that are so sharp and kene, 15
Beare flowers we se full fresh and faire of hue:
Poison is also put in medicine.
And vnto man his helth doth oft renue.
The fier that all thinges eke consumeth cleane
May hurt and heale: then if that this be true. 20
I trust sometime my harme may be my health,
Sins euery woe is ioyned with some wealth.

[268] A riddle of a gift geuen by
a Ladie.

A Lady gaue me a gift she had not, 25
And I receyued her gift which I toke not,
She gaue it me willingly, and yet she would not,
and I receiued it, albeit, I could not,
If she giue it me, I force not,
And if she take it againe she cares not. 30
Conster what this is and tell not,
For I am fast sworne I may not.

𝔇𝔇.ii.                    That

[ 211 ]

[269] That speaking or profering
bringes alway
speding.

S Peake thou and spede where will or power ought helpthe,     5
  Where power dothe want will must be wonne by welth.
For nede will spede, where will workes not his kinde,
And gayne, thy foes thy frendes shall cause thee finde.
For sute and golde, what do not they obtaine,
Of good and bad the triers are these twaine.     10

[270] He ruleth not though he raigne ouer
realmes that is subiect to
his owne lustes.

I F thou wilt mighty be, flee from the rage
  Of cruell wyll, and see thou kepe thee free     15
From the foule yoke of sensuall bondage,
For though thy empyre stretche to Indian sea,
And for thy feare trembleth the fardest Thylee,
If thy desire haue ouer thee the power,
Subiect then art thou and no gouernour.     20
  If to be noble and high thy minde be meued,
Consider well thy grounde and thy beginnyng:
For he that hath eche starre in heauen fixed,
And geues the Moone her hornes and her eclipsyng:
Alike hath made the noble in his workyng,     25
So that wretched no way thou may bee,
Except foule lust and vice do conquere thee.
  All were it so thou had a flood of golde,
Vnto thy thirst yet should it not suffice.
And though with Indian stones a thousande folde,     30
More precious then can thy selfe deuise,
Ycharged were thy backe: thy couitise
And busye bytyng yet should neuer let,
Thy wretchid life ne do thy death profet.
                                  Whe-

[271] whether libertie by losse of life,
or life in prison and thral⸗
dome be to be pre⸗
ferred.                                                    5

*L* Yke as the birde within the cage enclosed,
 The dore vnsparred, her foe the hawke without,
Twixt death and prison piteously oppressed,
Whether for to chose standeth in doubt,
Lo, so do I, which seke to bryng about,                     10
Which should be best by determinacion,
By losse of life libertie, or lyfe by pryson.
  O mischiefe by mischiefe to be redressed.
Where payne is best there lieth but little pleasure.
By short death better to be deliuered,                     15
Than bide in paynefull life, thraldome, and dolore.
Small is the pleasure where much payne we suffer.
Rather therfore to chuse me thinketh wisdome,
By losse of life libertye, then life by prison.
  And yet me thinkes although I liue and suffer,           20
I do but wait a time and fortunes chance:
Oft many thinges do happen in one houre.
That which oppressed me now may me aduance.
In time is trust which by deathes greuance
Is wholy lost.  Then were it not reason,                   25
By death to chuse libertie, and not life by pryson.
  But death were deliuerance where life lengthes paine.
Of these two euyls let se now chuse the best:
This birde to deliuer that here dothe playne,
What saye ye louers? whiche shall be the best?            30
In cage thraldome, or by the hawke opprest.
And whiche to chuse make plaine conclusion,
By losse of life libertie, or life by pryson.


# F I N I S.

Imprinted at London in flete strete
within Temple barre, at the sygne of the
hand and starre, by Richard Tottel
the fift day of June.
An. 1557.

*Cum priuilegio ad impri-
mendum solum.*

POEMS ADDED IN THE SECOND EDITION (*B*)

OF

*SONGES AND SONETTES*

July 31, 1557

[272] The louer declareth his paines
to excede far the paines
of hell.

*T*He soules that lacked grace,                    5
  Which lye in bitter paine:
Are not in such a place,
As foolish folke do faine.
  Tormented all with fire,
And boile in leade againe,                         10
With serpents full of ire,
Stong oft with deadly paine.
  Then cast in frosen pittes:
To freze there certaine howers:
And for their painfull fittes,                     15
Apointed tormentours.
  No no it is not so,
Their sorow is not such:
And yet they haue of wo,
I dare say twise as much.                          20
  Which comes because they lack
The sight of the godhed,
And be from that kept back
Where with are aungels fed
  This thing know I by loue                 25
Through absence crueltie,
Which makes me for to proue
Hell pain before I dye.

There is no tong can tell
My thousand part of care
Ther may no fire in hell,
With my desire compare.                    5
   No boyling leade can pas
My scalding sighes in hete:
Nor snake that euer was,
With stinging can so frete
   A true and tender hert,      10
As my thoughtes dayly doe,
So that I know but smart,
And that which longes thereto.
   O Cupid Venus son,
As thou hast showed thy might.             15
And hast this conquest woon,
Now end the same aright.
   And as I am thy slaue,
Contented with all this:
So helpe me soone to haue                   20
My parfect earthly blisse.

## [273] Of the death of sir Thomas wiate the elder.

*L* O dead he liues, that whilome liued here,
  Among the dead that quick go on the ground.    25
Though he be dead, yet doth he quick apere,
By liuely name that death cannot confound
His life for ay of fame the trump shall sound.
Though he be dead, yet liues he here aliue.
Thus can no death from Wiate, life depriue.      30

## [274] That length of time consumeth all thinges.

*VV* Hat harder is then stone, what more then water soft?
  Yet with soft water drops, hard stones be persed softe.
    What geues so strong impulse,     35
    That stone ne may withstand?
    What geues more weake repulse,
    Then water prest with hand?

Yet weke though water be,
It holowith hardest flint:
By proofe wherof we see,
Time geues the greatest dint.                                        5

## [275] The beginning of the epistle of Pene=
### lope to Vlisses,made in=
### to verse.

*O* Lingring make Vlisses dere, thy wife lo sendes to thee,
  Her driry plaint write not againe, but come thy selfe to me.    10
Our hatefull scourge that womans foe proud Troy now is fordon
We bye it derer, though Priam slaine, and all his kingdome won.
O that the raging surges great that lechers bane had wrought,
When first with ship he forowed seas, and Lacedemon sought,
In desert bed my shiuering coarse then shold not haue sought rest,  15
Nor take in griefe the cherefull sunne so slowly fall to west.
And whiles I cast long rūning nightes, how best I might begile,
No distaff should my widowish hand haue weary made the while.
When dread I not more daungers great then are befall in dede:
Loue is a carefull thing God wot, and passing full of drede.     20

## [276] The louer asketh pardon of his passed
### follie in loue.

*Y*Ou that in play peruse my plaint, and reade in rime the smart,
  Which in my youth with sighes full cold I harbourd in my hart.
Know ye that loue in that fraile age, draue me to that distresse,  25
When I was halfe an other man, then I am now to gesse.
Then for this worke of wauering words where I now rage now
Tost in the toyes of troublous loue, as care or cōfort grew.      (rew
I trust with you that loues affaires by proofe haue put in vre:
Not onely pardon in my plaint, but pitie to procure.             30
For now I wot that in the world a wonder haue I be,
And where to lōg loue made me blinde, to late shame makes me se.
Thus of my fault shame is the fruite, and for my youth thus past,
Repentance is my recompence, and this I learne at last.
Looke what the world hath most in price, as sure it is to kepe,   35
As is the dreame which fansie driues, while sence and reason slepe.

## [277] The louer sheweth that he was striken by loue on good friday.

IT was the day on which the sunne depriued of his light,
To rew Christs death amid his course gaue place vnto ẏ night       5
When I amid mine ease did fall to such distemperate fits,
That for the face that hath my hart I was bereft my wits.
I had the bayte, the hooke and all, and wist not loues pretence,
But farde as one that fearde none yll, nor forst for no defence.
Thus dwelling in most quiet state, I fell into this plight,       10
And that day gan my secret sighes, when all folke wept in sight.
For loue that vewed me voide of care, approcht to take his pray,
And stept by stelth from eye to hart, so open lay the way.
And straight at eyes brake out in teares, so salt that did declare,
By token of their bitter taste that they were forgde of care.     15
Now vaunt thee loue which fleest a maid defenst w̃ vertues rare,
And wounded hast a wight vnwise, vnweaponed and vnware.

## [278] The louer describeth his whole state vnto his loue,and promising her his faith‹ full good will:assureth him‹       20 self of hers again.

THe Sunne when he hath spred his raies,
And shewde his face ten thousand waies,
Ten thousand thinges do then begin,
To shew the life that they are in.                                25
The heauen shewes liuely art and hue,
Of sundry shapes and colours new,
And laughes vpon the earth anone.
The earth as cold as any stone,
Wet in the teares of her own kinde:                               30
Gins then to take a ioyfull minde.
For well she feeles that out and out,
The sunne doth warme her round about.
And dries her children tenderly,
And shewes them forth full orderly.                               35
The mountaines hye and how they stand,
The valies and the great maine land.
The trees, the herbes, the towers strong,
The castels and the riuers long.

And euen for ioy thus of this heate,
She sheweth furth her pleasures great.
And sleepes no more but sendeth forth
Her clergions her own dere worth.
To mount and flye vp to the ayre,
Where then they sing in order fayre.
And tell in song full merely,
How they haue slept full quietly,
That night about their mothers sides.
And when they haue song more besides,
Then fall they to their mothers breastes,
Where els they fede or take their restes.
The hunter then soundes out his horne,
And rangeth straite through wood and corne.
On hilles then shew the Ewe and Lambe,
And euery yong one with his dambe.
Then louers walke and tell their tale,
Both of their blisse and of their bale.
And how they serue, and how they do,
And how their lady loues them to.
Then tune the birdes their armonie.
Then flocke the foule in companie.
Then euery thing doth pleasure finde,
In that that comfortes all their kinde.
No dreames do drench them of the night,
Of foes that would them slea or bite.
As Houndes to hunt them at the taile,
Or men force them through hill and dale.
The shepe then dreames not of the Woulf,
The shipman forces not the goulf
The Lambe thinkes not the butchers knife,
Should then bereue him of his life.
For when the Sunne doth once run in,
Then all their gladnes doth begin.
And then their skips, and then their play
So falles their sadnes then away.
And thus all thinges haue comforting,
In that that doth them comfort bring.
Saue I alas, whom neither sunne,
Nor ought that God hath wrought and don,
May comfort ought, as though I were
A thing not made for comfort here.

For beyng absent from your sighte,
Which are my ioy and whole delight
My comfort and my pleasure to,
How can I ioy how should I do? 5
May sick men laugh that rore for paine?
Ioy they in song that do complaine?
Are martirs in their tormentes glad?
Do pleasures please them that are mad?
Then how may I in comfort be, 10
That lacke the thing should comfort me.
The blind man oft that lackes his sight,
Complaines not most the lacke of light.
But those that knewe their perfectnes,
And then do misse ther blisfulnes, 15
In martirs tunes they syng and waile,
The want of that which doth them faile.
And hereof comes that in my braines,
So many fansies worke my paines
For when I wayghe your worthynes, 20
Your wisdome and your gentlnes,
Your vertues and your sundry grace,
And minde the countenaunce of your face,
And how that you are she alone,
To whom I must both plaine and mone. 25
Whom I do loue and must do still.
Whom I embrace and ay so wil,
To serue and please you as I can,
As nay a wofull faithful man.
And finde my selfe so far you fro. 30
God knowes what torment, and what wo,
My rufull hart doth then imbrace.
The blood then chaungeth in my face.
My synnewes dull, in dompes I stand.
No life I fele in fote nor hand, 35
As pale as any clout and ded,
Lo sodenly the blood orespred,
And gon againe it nill so bide.
And thus from life to death I slide
As colde sometymes as any stone, 40
And then againe as hote anone.
Thus comes and goes my sundry fits,
To geue me sundri sortes of wits.

Till that a sigh becomes my frende,
And then to all this wo doth ende.
And sure I thinke that sigh doth roon,
From me to you where ay you woon.                    5
For well I finde it easeth me,
And certes much it pleaseth me,
To think that it doth come to you,
As would to God it could so do.
For then I know you would soone finde,              10
By sent and sauour of the winde.
That euen a martirs sigh it is,
Whose ioy you are and all his blis.
His comfort and his pleasure eke,
And euen the same that he doth seke.                15
The same that he doth wishe and craue,
The same that he doth trust to haue.
To tender you in all he may,
And all your likinges to obey,
As farre as in his powre shall lye:                 20
Till death shall darte him for to dye.
But wealeaway mine owne most best,
My ioy, my comfort, and my rest.
The causer of my wo and smart,
And yet the pleaser of my hart.                     25
And she that on the earth aboue:
Is euen the worthiest for to loue.
Heare now my plaint, heare now my wo,
Heare now his paine that loues you so.
And if your hart do pitie beare,                    30
Pitie the cause that you shall heare.
A dolefull foe in all this doubt,
Who leaues me not but sekes me out,
Of wretched forme and lothsome face,
While I stand in this wofull case:                  35
Comes forth and takes me by the hand,
And saies frende harke and vnderstand.
I see well by thy port and chere,
And by thy lokes and thy manere,
And by thy sadnes as thou goest,                    40
And by the sighes that thou outthrowest:
That thou art stuffed full of wo,
The cause I thinke I do well know.

[ 223 ]

# Songes

A fantaser thou art of some,
By whom thy wits are ouercome.
But hast thou red old pamphlets ought?
Or hast thou known how bokes haue taught                    5
That loue doth vse to such as thow,
When they do thinke them safe enow.
And certain of their ladies grace:
Hast thou not sene oft times the case,
That sodenly there hap hath turnde,                        10
As thinges in flame consumde and burnde?
Some by disceite forsaken right.
Some likwise changed of fansy light.
And some by absence sone forgot.
The lottes in loue. why knowest thou not?                  15
And tho that she be now thine own:
And knowes the well as may be knowne.
And thinkes the to be such a one,
As she likes best to be her own.
Thinkes thou that others haue not grace,                   20
To shew and plain their wofull case.
And chose her for their lady now,
And swere her trouth as well as thow.
And what if she do alter minde?
Where is the loue that thou wouldest finde?                25
Absence my frende workes wonders oft.
Now bringes full low that lay full loft.
Now turnes the minde now to and fro,
And where art thou if it were so?
If absence (quod I) be marueilous,                         30
I finde her not so dangerous.
For she may not remoue me fro,
The poore good will that I do owe
To her, whom vnneth I loue and shall.
And chosen haue aboue them all,                            35
To serue and be her own as far,
As any man may offer her.
And will her serue, and will her loue,
As lowly as it shall behoue.
And dye her own if fate be so.                             40
Thus shall my hart nay part her fro.
And witnes shall my good will be,
That absence takes her not from me.

[ 224 ]

But that my loue doth still encrease,
To minde her still and neuer cease.
And what I feele to be in me,
The same good will I think hath she.                    5
As firme and fast to biden ay,
Till death depart vs both away.
And as I haue my tale thus told,
Steps vnto me with countenance bold:
A stedfast frende a counsellour,                       10
And namde is Hope my comfortour.
And stoutly then he speakes and saies:
Thou hast sayde trouth withouten nayes.
For I assure thee euen by othe,
And theron take my hand and trothe.                    15
That she is one the worthiest,
The truest and the faithfullest.
The gentlest and the meekest of minde:
That here on earth a man may finde,
And if that loue and trouth were gone,                 20
In her it might be found alone.
For in her minde no thought there is,
But how she may be true iwis.
And tenders thee and all thy heale,
And wisheth both thy health and weale.                 25
And loues thee euen as farforth than,
As any woman may a man,
And is thine own and so she saies,
And cares for thee ten thousand waies.
On thee she speakes, on thee she thinkes,              30
With thee she eates, with thee she drinkes.
With thee she talkes, with thee she mones,
With thee she sighes, with thee she grones.
With thee she saies farewell mine own.
When thou God knowes full farre art gon.               35
And euen to tell thee all aright,
To thee she saies full oft good night.
And names thee oft, her owne most dere,
Her comfort weale and al her chere.
And telles her pelow al the tale,                      40
How thou hast doon her wo and bale,
And how she longes and plaines for the,
And saies why art thou so from me?

Am I not she that loues the best?
Do I not wish thine ease and rest?
Seke I not how I may the please?
Why art thou then so from thine ease?                          5
If I be she for whom thou carest,
For whom in tormentes so thou farest:
Alas thou knowest to finde me here,
Where I remaine thine owne most dere,
Thine own most true thine owne most iust,                     10
Thine own that loues the styl and must.
Thine own that cares alone for the,
As thou I thinke dost care for me.
And euen the woman she alone,
That is full bent to be thine owne.                            15
What wilt thou more? what cāst thou craue?
Since she is as thou wouldest her haue.
Then set this driuell out of dore,
That in thy braines such tales doth poore.
Of absence and of chaunges straunge,                          20
Send him to those that vse to chaunge.
For she is none I the auowe,
And well thou maiest beleue me now.
When hope hath thus his reason said,
Lord how I fele me well apaide.                                25
A new blood then orespredes my bones,
That al in ioy I stand at ones.
My handes I throw to heuen aboue,
And humbly thank the god of loue.
That of his grace I should bestow,                            30
My loue so well as I it owe.
And al the planets as they stand,
I thanke them to with hart and hand.
That their aspectes so frendly were,
That I should so my good will bere.                           35
To you that are the worthiest,
The fairest and the gentillest.
And best can say, and best can do,
That longes me thinkes a woman to.
And therfore are most worthy far,                             40
To be beloued as you ar.
And so saies hope in all his tale,
Wherby he easeth all my bale.

For I beleue and thinke it true,
That he doth speake or say of you.
And thus contented lo I stand,
With that that hope beares me in hand:             5
That I am yours and shall so be,
Which hope I kepe full sure in me.
As he that all my comfort is,
On you alone which are my blis.
My pleasure chief which most I finde,          10
And euen the whole ioy of my minde.
And shall so be vntill the death,
Shall make me yeld vp life and breath.
Thus good mine own, lo here my trust.
Lo here my truth and seruice iust.          15
Lo in what case for you I stand.
Lo how you haue me in your hand.
And if you can requite a man,
Requite me as you finde me than.

## [279] Of the troubled comon welth re-     20
## stored to quiet by the mighty
## power of god.

*T*He secret flame that made all Troy so hot,
  Long did it lurke within the wooden horse.
The machine huge Troyans suspected not,       25
The guiles of Grekes, nor of their hidden force:
Till in their beds their armed foes them met,
And slew them there, and Troy on fire set.
  Then rose the rore of treason round about,
And children could of treason call and cry.      30
Wiues wroūg their hands, ẙ hole fired town through
When ẙ they saw their husbands slain them by. (out,
And to the Gods and to the skies they shright,
Vengeance to take for treason of that night.
  Then was the name of Sinon spred and blowne,   35
And wherunto his filed tale did tend.
The secret startes and metinges then were knowne,
Of Troyan traitours tending to this end.
And euery man could say as in that case:
Treason in Anthenor and Eneas.         40

[ 227 ]

But all to long such wisdome was in store,
To late came out the name of traytour than,
When that their king the aultar lay before
Slain there alas, that worthy noble man.　　5
Ilium on flame, the matrons crying out,
And all the stretes in streames of blood about.
　But such was fate, or such was simple trust,
That king and all should thus to ruine roon,
For if our stories certein be and iust:　　10
There were that saw such mischief should be doon
And warning gaue which compted were in sort,
As sad deuines in matter but of sport.
　Such was the time and so in state it stoode,
Troy trembled not so careles were the men.　　15
They brake y̆ wals, they toke this hors for good,
They demed Grekes gone, they thought al surety
Whē treason start & set the town on fire,　　(then.
And stroied Troians & gaue Grekes their desire.
　Like to our time, wherin hath broken out,　　20
The hidden harme that we suspected least.
Wombed within our walles and realme about,
As Grekes in Troy were in the Grekish beast.
Whose tempest great of harmes and of armes,
We thought not on, till it did noyse our harmes.　　25
　Then felt we well the piller of our welth,
How sore it shoke, then saw we euen at hand,
Ruin how she rusht to confound our helth,
Our realme and vs with force of mighty band.
And then we heard how treason loud did rore:　　30
Mine is the rule, and raigne I will therefore.
　Of treason marke the nature and the kinde,
A face it beares of all humilitie.
Truth is the cloke, and frendship of the minde,
And depe it goes, and worketh secretly,　　35
Like to a mine that creepes so nye the wall,
Till out breakes sulphure, and oreturneth all.
　But he on hye that secretly beholdes
The state of thinges: and times hath in his hand,
And pluckes in plages, and them againe vnfoldes.　　40
And hath apointed realmes to fall and stand:
He in the midst of all this sturre and rout,
Gan bend his browes, and moue him self about.

[ 228 ]

As who should say, and are ye minded so?
And thus to those, and whom you know I loue.
Am I such one as none of you do know?
Or know ye not that I sit here aboue, 5
And in my handes do hold your welth and wo,
To raise you now, and now to ouerthrow?
  Then thinke that I, as I haue set you all,
In places where your honours lay and fame:
So now my selfe shall giue you eche your fall, 10
Where eche of you shall haue your worthy shame.
And in their handes I will your fall shalbe,
Whose fall in yours you sought so sore to see.
  Whose wisdome hye as he the same foresaw,
So is it wrought, such lo his iustice is. 15
He is the Lord of man and of his law,
Praise therfore now his mighty name in this,
And make accompt that this our ease doth stand:
As Israell free, from wicked Pharaos hand.

[280] The louer to his loue:hauing for= 20
    saken him,and betaken her
       self to an other.

*T*He bird that somtime built within my brest,
  And there as then chief succour did receiue:
Hath now els where built her another nest, 25
And of the old hath taken quite her leaue.
To you mine oste that harbour mine old guest,
Of such a one, as I can now conceiue,
Sith that in change her choise doth chiefe consist,
The hauke may check, that now comes fair to fist. 30

[281] The louer sheweth that in dis=
    sembling his loue openly
      he kepeth secret his
        secret good will.

*N*Ot like a God came Iupiter to woo, 35
  When he the faire Europa sought vnto.

An other forme his godly wisdome toke,
Such in effect as writeth Ouides boke.
As on the earth no liuing wight can tell.
That mighty Ioue did loue the quene so well. 5
For had he come in golden garmentes bright,
Or so as men mought haue starde on the sight:
Spred had it bene both through earth and ayre,
That Ioue had loued the lady Europa fayre.
And then had some bene angry at the hart, 10
And some againe as ielous for their part.
Both which to stop, this gentle god toke minde,
To shape him selfe into a brutish kinde.
To such a kinde as hid what state he was,
And yet did bring him what he sought to passe. 15
To both their ioyes, to both their comfort soon,
Though knowen to none, til al the thing was don
In which attempt if I the like assay,
To you to whom I do my selfe bewray:
Let it suffice that I do seke to be, 20
Not counted yours, and yet for to be he.

## [282] The louer disceiued by his loue repenteth him of the true loue he bare her.

*I*That Vlysses yeres haue spent, 25
    To finde Penelope:
Finde well that folly I haue ment,
To seke that was not so.
Since Troylous case hath caused me,
From Cressed for to go. 30
  And to bewaile Vlysses truth,
In seas and stormy skies,
Of wanton will and raging youth,
Which me haue tossed sore:
From Scilla to Caribdis cliues, 35
Vpon the drowning shore.
  Where I sought hauen, there found I hap,
From daunger vnto death:
Much like the Mouse that treades the trap,
In hope to finde her foode, 40

And bites the bread that stops her breath,
So in like case I stoode.
   Till now repentance hasteth him
To further me so fast:
That where I sanke, there now I swim,      5
And haue both streame and winde:
And lucke as good if it may last,
As any man may finde.
   That where I perished, safe I passe,      10
And finde no perill there:
But stedy stone, no ground of glasse,
Now am I sure to saue,
And not to flete from feare to feare,
Such anker hold I haue.      15

[283] The louer hauing enioyed his loue, humbly
    thanketh the god of loue: and auowing
       his hart onely to her faithfully
        promiseth, vtterly to for⸗
         sake all other.      20

*T*Hou Cupide God of loue, whom Venus thralles do serue,
  I yeld thee thankes vpon my knees, as thou dost well deserue.
By thee my wished ioyes haue shaken of despaire,
And all my storming dayes be past, and weather waxeth faire.
By thee I haue receiued a thousand times more ioy,      25
Then euer Paris did possesse, when Helen was in Troy.
By thee haue I that hope, for which I longde so sore,
And when I thinke vpon the same, my hart doth leap therefore.
By thee my heapy doubtes and trembling feares are fled,
And now my wits ỹ troubled wer, with plesant thoughts are fed.      30
For dread is banisht cleane, wherein I stoode full oft,
And doubt to speake that lay full low, is lifted now aloft.
With armes bespred abrode, with opende handes and hart,
I haue enioyed the fruite of hope, reward for all my smart.
The seale and signe of loue, the key of trouth and trust,      35
The pledge of pure good will haue I, which makes the louers iust
Such grace sins I haue found, to one I me betake,
The rest of Venus derlinges all, I vtterly forsake.

And to performe this vow, I bid mine eyes beware,
That they no straungers do salute, nor on their beauties stare.
My wits I warn ye all from this time forth take hede,
That ye no wanton toyes deuise my fansies new to fede. 5
Mine eares be ye shit vp, and heare no womans voyce,
That may procure me once to smile, or make my hart reioyce.
My fete full slow be ye and lame when ye should moue,
To bring my body any where to seke an other loue,
Let all the Gods aboue, and wicked sprites below, 10
And euery wight in earth acuse and curse me where I go:
If I do false my faith in any point or case,
A sodein vengeance fall on me, I aske no better grace.
Away then sily rime present mine earnest faith,
Vnto my lady where she is, and marke thou what she saith. 15
And if she welcome thee, and lay thee in her lap,
Spring thou for ioy, thy master hath his most desired hap.

## [284] Totus mundus in maligno
### positus.

*C*Omplaine we may: much is amisse: 20
Hope is nye gone to haue redresse:
These daies ben ill, nothing sure is:
Kinde hart is wrapt in heauinesse.
   The sterne is broke: the saile is rent:
The ship is geuen to winde and waue: 25
All helpe is gone: the rocke present.
That will be lost, what man can saue?
   Thinges hard, therefore are now refused.
Labour in youth is thought but vaine:
Duty by (will not) is excused. 30
Remoue the stop the way is plaine.
   Learning is lewd, and held a foole:
Wisdome is shent, counted to raile:
Reason is banisht out of schoole:
The blinde is bold, and wordes preuaile. 35
   Power, without care, slepeth at ease:
Will, without law, runth where he list:
Might without mercy can not please.
A wise man saith not, had I wist.

When power lackes care and forceth not:
When care is feable and may not:
When might is slouthfull and will not:
Wedes may grow where good herbes cannot.
    Take wrong away, law nedeth not: 5
For law to wrong is bridle and paine.
Take feare away, law booteth not.
To striue gainst streame, it is but vaine.
    Wyly is witty: brainsicke is wise: 10
Trouth is folly: and might is right:
Wordes are reason: and reason is lies:
The bad is good: darknesse is light.
    Wrong to redresse, wisdome dare not.
Hardy is happy, and ruleth most. 15
Wilfull is witlesse, and careth not,
Which end go first, till all be lost.
    Few right do loue, and wrong refuse.
Pleasure is sought in euery state.
Liking is lust: there is no chuse. 20
The low geue to the hye checke mate.
    Order is broke in thinges of weight.
Measure and meane who doth not flee?
Two thinges preuaile: money, and sleight.
To seme is better then to be. 25
    The bowle is round, and doth downe slide,
Eche one thrusteth: none doth vphold.
A fall failes not, where blinde is guide.
The stay is gone: who can him hold?
    Folly and falshed prayeth apace. 30
Trouth vnder bushell is faine to crepe.
Flattry is treble, pride singes the bace.
The meane the best part scant doth pepe.
    This firy plage the world infectes.
To vertue and trouth it geues no rest: 35
Mens harts are burnde with sundry sectes,
And to eche man his way is best.
    With floods and stormes thus be we tost,
Awake good Lord, to thee we crye.
Our ship is almost sonk and lost. 40
Thy mercy help our miserye.
    Mans strength is weake: mans wit is dull:
Mans reason is blinde. These thinges tamend,

Thy hand (O Lord) of might is full,
Awake betime, and helpe vs send.
  In thee we trust, and in no wight:
Saue vs as chickens vnder the hen.            5
Our crokednesse thou canst make right,
Glory to thee for aye.   Amen.

## [285] The wise trade of
## lyfe.

DO all your dedes by good aduise,         10
  Cast in your minde alwaies the end.
Wit bought is of to dere a price.
The tried, trust, and take as frend,
For frendes I finde there be but two:
Of countenance, and of effect.          15
Of thone sort there are inow:
But few ben of the tother sect.
Beware also the venym swete
Of crafty wordes and flattery.
For to deceiue they be most mete,       20
That best can play hypocrisy.
Let wisdome rule your dede and thought:
So shall your workes be wisely wrought.

## [286] That few wordes shew wisdome,
## and work much quiet.       25

WHo list to lead a quiet life,
  Who list to rid him self from strife:
Geue eare to me, marke what I say,
Remember wel, beare it away.
Holde backe thy tong at meat and meale,     30
Speake but few wordes, bestrow them well.
By wordes the wise thou shalt espye,
By wordes a foole sone shalt thou trye.
A wise man can his tong make cease,
A foole can neuer holde his peace.     35
Who loueth rest of wordes beware.
Who loueth wordes, is sure of care.

For wordes oft many haue ben shent:
For silence kept none hath repent.
Two eares, one tong onely thou hast,
Mo thinges to heare then wordes to wast.                   5
A foole in no wise can forbeare:
He hath two tonges and but one eare.
Be sure thou kepe a stedfast braine,
Lest that thy wordes put thee to paine.
Words wisely set are worth much gold:                     10
The price of rashnesse is sone told.
If time require wordes to be had,
To hold thy peace I count thee mad.
Talke onely of nedefull verities:
Striue not for trifling fantasies.                        15
With sobernesse the truth boult out,
Affirme nothing wherin is dout.
Who to this lore will take good hede,
And spend no mo words then he nede,
Though he be a fole and haue no braine,                   20
Yet shall he a name of wisdome gaine
Speake while time is or hold thee still.
Words out of time do oft things spyll.
Say well and do well are thinges twaine,
Twise blest is he in whom both raigne.                    25

## [287] The complaint of a hot woer, delayed with doutfull cold answers.

*A* Kinde of coale is as men say,
  Which haue assaied the same:
That in the fire will wast away,                           30
  And outward cast no flame.
Vnto my self may I compare,
  These coales that so consume:
Where nought is sene though men do stare,                  35
  In stede of flame but fume.
They say also to make them burne,
  Cold water must be cast:
Or els to ashes will they turne,

And half to sinder wast.
As this is wonder for to se,
  Cold water warme the fire,
So hath your coldnesse caused me,               5
  To burne in my desire.
And as this water cold of kinde,
  Can cause both heat and cold,
And can these coales both breake and binde,
  To burne as I haue told.                 10
So can your tong of frosen yse,
  From whence cold answers come:
Both coole the fire and fire entice,
  To burne me all and some.
Like to the corne that standes on stake,      15
  Which mowen in winter sunne:
Full faire without, within is black:
  Such heat therin doth runne.
By force of fire this water cold,
  Hath bred to burne within,             20
Euen so am I, that heat doth hold,
  Which cold did first begyn.
Which heat is stint when I do striue,
  To haue some ease sometime:
But flame a fresh I do reuiue,           25
  Wherby I cause to clime.
In stede of smoke a sighing breath:
  with sparkes of sprinkled teares,
That I should liue this liuyng death,
  Which wastes and neuer weares.       30

## [288] The answer.

*Y*Our borrowd meane to moue your mone, of fume ẘouten flame
  Being fet from smithy smokyng coale: ye seme so by the same.
To shew, what such coales vse is taught by such as haue assayd,
As I, that most do wish you well, am so right well apayd.      35
That you haue such a lesson learnd, how either to maintaine,
Your fredome of vnkindled coale, vpheaped all in vaine:
Or how most frutefully to frame, with worthy workmans art,
That cunnyng pece may passe there fro, by help of heated hart.
Out of the forge wherin the fume of sighes doth mount aloft,     40

That argues present force of fire to make the metall soft,
To yelde vnto the hammer hed, as best the workman likes.
That thiron glowyng after blast in time and temper strikes.
Wherin the vse of water is, as you do seme to say,                    5
To quenche no flame, ne hinder heat, ne yet to wast away:
But, that which better is for you, and more deliteth me,
To saue you from the sodain waste, vaine cinderlike to be.
Which lastyng better likes in loue, as you your semble ply,
Then doth the bauen blase, that flames and fleteth by and by.        10
Sith then you know eche vse, wherin your coale may be applide:
Either to lie and last on hoord, in open ayre to bide,
Withouten vse to gather fat by fallyng of the raines,
That makes the pitchy iucye to grow, by sokyng in his veines,
Or lye on fornace in the forge, as is his vse of right,              15
Wherin the water trough may serue, and enteryeld her might
By worke of smithes both hand and hed a cūnyng key to make,
Or other pece as cause shall craue and bid him vndertake:
Do as you deme most fit to do, and wherupon may grow,
Such ioy to you, as I may ioy your ioyfull case to know.            20

## [289] An other of the same.

Stay gentle frend that passest by,
  And learne the lore that leadeth all:
From whence we come with hast to hye,
To liue to dye, and stand to fall.                                   25
  And learne that strength and lusty age,
That wealth and want of worldly woe,
Can not withstand the mighty rage,
Of death our best vnwelcome foe.
  For hopefull youth had hight me health,                     30
My lust to last till time to dye,
And fortune found my vertue wealth:
But yet for all that here I lye.
  Learne also this, to ease thy minde:
When death on corps hath wrought his spite,                          35
A time of triumph shalt thou finde,
With me to scorne him in delight.
  For one day shall we mete againe,
Maugre deathes dart in life to dwell.
Then will I thanke thee for thy paine,                               40
Now marke my wordes and fare thou well.

## [290] The answere.

W Hom fansy forced first to loue,
   Now frensy forceth for to hate:
Whose minde erst madnesse gan to moue,     5
Inconstance causeth to abate.
No minde of meane, but heat of braine
Bred light loue: like heate, hate againe
   What hurld your hart in so great heat?
Fansy forced by fayned fame.     10
Belike that she was light to get.
For if that vertue and good name
Moued your minde, why changed your will,
Sithe vertue the cause abideth still.
   Such, Fame reported her to be     15
As rare it were to finde her peere,
For vertue and for honestie,
For her free hart and lowly cheere.
This laud had lied if you had sped,
And fame bene false that hath ben spred.     20
   Sith she hath so kept her good name.
Such praise of life and giftes of grace,
As brute self blusheth for to blame,
Such fame as fame feares to deface:
You sclaunder not but make it plaine,     25
That you blame brute of brutish traine.
   If you haue found it looking neere,
Not as you toke the brute to be.
Bylike you ment by lowly cheere,
Bountie and hart that you call free,     30
But lewd lightnesse easy to frame,
To winne your will against her name.
   Nay she may deme your deming so,
A marke of madnesse in his kinde,
Such causeth not good name to go:     35
As your fond folly sought to finde.
For brute of kinde bent ill to blase,
Alway sayth ill, but forced by cause.
   The mo there be, such as is she,
More should be gods thank for his grace.     40

The more is her ioy it to see.
Good should by geason, earne no place,
Nor nomber make nought, that is good.
Your strange lusting hed wants a hoode.     5
  Her dealing greueth you (say ye)
Byside your labour lost in vaine.
Her dealing was not as we see,
Sclaunder the end of your great paine,
Ha lewd lieng lips, and hatefull hart,     10
What canst thou desire in such desart.
  Ye will repent, and right for done.
Ye haue a dede deseruing shame.
From reasons race farre haue ye ronne.
Hold your rayling, kepe your tong tame.     15
Her loue, ye lye, ye lost it not.
Ye neuer lost that ye neuer got.
  She reft ye not your libertie,
She vaunteth not she had your thrall.
If ought haue done it, let it lye,     20
On rage that reft you wit and all.
What though a varlets tale you tell:
By cock and pye you do it well.


[291] The louer complaineth his fault,that
    with vngentle writing had dis-     25
       pleased his lady.


*A*H loue how waiward is his wit what pāges do perce his brest
  Whom thou to wait vpon thy will hast reued of his rest.
The light, the darke, the sunne, the mone, the day & eke the night,
His dayly dieng life, him self, he hateth in despight,     30
Sith furst he light to looke on her that holdeth him in thrall,
His mouing eyen his moued wit he curseth hart and all,
From hungry hope to pining feare eche hap doth hurle his hart,
From panges of plaint to fits of fume from aking into smart.

Eche moment so doth change his chere not with recourse of ease,
But with sere sortes of sorrowes still he worketh as the seas.
That turning windes not calme returnde rule in vnruly wise,
As if their holdes of hilles vphurld they brasten out to rise.          5
And puffe away the power that is vnto their king assignde
To pay that sithe their prisonment they deme to be behinde.
So doth the passions long represt within the wofull wight,
Breake downe the banks of all his wits & out they gushen quite.
To rere vp rores now they be free from reasons rule and stay,          10
And hedlong hales thunruled race his quiet quite away.
No measure hath he of his ruth, no reason in his rage,          (age
No bottom groūd where stayes his grief, thus weares away his
In wishing wants, in wayling woes.  Death doth he dayly call,
To bring release when of relief he seeth no hope at all.          15
Thence comes that oft in depe despeire to rise to better state,
On heauen and heauenly lampes he layeth the faute of al his fate.
On God and Gods decreed dome cryeth out with cursing breath,
Eche thing that gaue and saues him life he damneth of his death.
The wōbe him bare, y̆ brests he suckt, ech star y̆ with their might,          20
Their secret succour brought to bring the wretch to worldly light
Yea that to his soules perile is most haynous harme of all,
And craues the cruellest reuenge that may to man befall:
Her he blasphemes in whom it lieth in present as she please,
To dampne him downe to depth of hell, or plant in heauens ease.          25
Such rage constrainde my strained hart to guide thunhappy hand
That sent vnsitting blots to her on whom my life doth stand.
But graunt O God that he for them may beare the worthy blame
Whom I do in my depe distresse finde guilty of the same,
Euen that blinde boy that blindly guides the fautles to their fall,          30
That laughes when they lament that he hath throwen into thral.
Or Lord, saue louring lookes of her, what penance els thou please
So her contented will be wonne I count it all mine ease.
And thou on whō doth hang my will, with hart, with soul & care,
With life and all that life may haue of well or euell fare:          35
Graunt grace to him that grates therfore with sea of saltish brine
By extreme heat of boylyng brest distilled through his eyen.
And with thy fancy render thou my self to me againe,
That dayly then we duely may employ a painelesse paine.

To yelde and take the ioyfull frutes that herty loue doth lend,
To them that meane by honest meanes to come to happy end.

[292] The louer wounded of Cupide,
    wisheth he had rather ben       5
        striken by death.

*T*He blinded boy that bendes the bow,
  To make with dint of double wound:
The stowtest state to stoupe and know:
The cruell craft that I haue found.      10
  With death I would had chopt a change,
To borow as by bargain made:
Ech others shaft when he did range,
With restlesse rouyng to inuade,
  Thunthralled mindes of simple wightes,    15
Whose giltlesse ghostes deserued not:
To fele such fall of their delightes,
Such panges as I haue past God wot.
  Then both in new vnwonted wise,
Should death deserue a better name,    20
Not (as tofore hath bene his guise)
Of crueltie to beare the blame.
  But contrary be counted kinde,
In lendyng life and sparyng space:
For sicke to rise and seke to finde,    25
A way to wish their weary race
  To draw to some desired end,
Their long and lothed life to rid.
And so to fele how like a frend,
Before the bargain made he did.    30
  And loue should either bring againe,
To wounded wightes their owne desire:
A welcome end of pinyng payne,
As doth their cause of ruthe require:

Or when he meanes the quiet man,
A harme to hasten him to grefe:
A better dede he should do then,
With borrowd dart to geue relefe.                    5
　　That both the sicke well demen may,
He brought me rightly my request:
And eke the other sort may say,
He wrought me truely for the best.
　　So had not fancy forced me,                     10
To beare a brunt of greater wo:
Then leauing such a life may be,
The ground where onely grefes do grow.
　　Vnlucky likyng linkt my hart,
In forged hope and forced feare:                     15
That oft I wisht the other dart,
Had rather perced me as neare.
　　A fayned trust, constrayned care,
Most loth to lack, most hard to finde:
In sunder so my iudgement tare,                      20
That quite was quiet out of minde.
　　Absent in absence of mine ease,
Present in presence of my paine:
The woes of want did much displease,
The sighes I sought did greue againe.                25
　　Oft grefe that boyled in my brest,
Hath fraught my face with saltish teares,
Pronouncyng proues of mine vnrest,
Whereby my passed paine appeares.
　　My sighes full often haue supplied,              30
That faine with wordes I wold haue said:
My voice was stopt, my tong was tyed,
My wits with wo were ouerwayd.
　　With tremblyng soule and humble chere,
Oft grated I for graunt of grace:                    35
On hope that bounty might be there,
Where beauty had so pight her place.
　　At length I found, that I did fere,
How I had labourde all to losse,
My self had ben the carpenter,                       40
That framed me the cruell crosse.
　　Of this to come if dout alone,
Though blent with trust of better spede:

So oft hath moued my minde to mone,
So oft hath made my hart to blede.
   What shall I say of it in dede,
Now hope is gone mine olde relefe:             5
And I enforced all to fede,
Vpon the frutes of bitter grefe?

## [293] Of womens changeable will.

*I*Wold I found not as I fele,            10
  Such changyng chere of womens will,
By fickle flight of fortunes whele,
By kinde or custome, neuer still.
   So shold I finde no fault to lay,
On fortune for their mouyng minde,       15
So should I know no cause to say
This change to chance by course of kinde.
   So should not loue so work my wo,
To make death surgeant for my sore,
So should their wittes not wander so,      20
So should I reck the lesse therfore.

## [294] The louer complayneth the losse of his ladye.

*N*O ioy haue I, but liue in heauinesse,
  My dame of price bereft by fortunes cruelnesse,    25
My hap is turned to vnhappinesse,
Vnhappy I am vnlesse I finde relesse.
   My pastime past, my youthlike yeres are gone,
My mouthes of mirth, my glistring daies of gladsomnesse:
My times of triumph turned into mone.      30
Vnhappy I am vnlesse I finde relesse.
   My wonted winde to chaunt my cherefull chaunce,
Doth sigh that song somtime the balades of my lesse:
My sobbes, my sore and sorow do aduaunce.
Vnhappy I am vnlesse I finde relesse.      35
   I mourne my mirth for grefe that it is gone,
I mourne my mirth wherof my musing mindefulnesse:

Is ground of greater grefe that growes theron,
Vnhappy I am vnlesse I finde relesse.
   No ioy haue I: for fortune frowardly:
Hath bent her browes hath put her hand to cruelnesse:     5
Hath rest my dame, constrayned me to crye,
Vnhappy I am vnlesse I finde relesse.

## [295] Of the golden meane.

*T*He wisest way, thy bote, in waue and winde to guie,
   Is neither still the trade of middle streame to trie:     10
Ne (warely shunnyng wrecke by wether) aye to nie,
          To presse vpon the perillous shore.
Both clenely flees he filthe: ne wonnes a wretched wight,
In carlish coate: and carefull court aie thrall to spite,
With port of proud astate he leues: who doth delight,     15
          Of golden meane to hold the lore.
Stormes rifest rende the sturdy stout pineapple tre.
Of lofty ruing towers the fals the feller be.
Most fers doth lightenyng light, where furthest we do se.
          The hilles the valey to forsake.     20
Well furnisht brest to bide eche chanses changing chear.
In woe hath chearfull hope, in weal hath warefull fear,
One self Ioue winter makes with lothfull lokes appear,
          That can by course the same aslake.
What if into mishap thy case now casten be?     25
It forceth not such forme of luck to last to thee.
Not alway bent is Phebus bow: his harpe and he,
          Ceast siluer sound sometime doth raise.
In hardest hap vse helpe of hardy hopefull hart.
Seme bold to beare the brunt of fortune ouerthwart.     30
Eke wisely when forewinde to full breathes on thy part,
          Swage swellyng saile, and doubt decayes.

## [296] The praise of a true
## frende.

*W* Ho so that wisely weyes the profite and the price,     35
   Of thinges wherin delight by worth is wont to rise.
Shall finde no iewell is so rich ne yet so rare,
That with the frendly hart in value may compare.

What other wealth to man by fortune may befall,
But fortunes changed chere may reue a man of all.
A frend no wracke of wealth, no cruell cause of wo,
Can force his frendly faith vnfrendly to forgo.                    5
  If fortune frendly fawne, and lend thee welthy store,
Thy frendes conioyned ioy doth make thy ioy the more.
If frowardly she frown and driue thee to distresse,
His ayde releues thy ruthe, and makes thy sorow lesse.
  Thus fortunes pleasant frutes by frendes encreased be,      10
The bitter sharp and sowre by frendes alayde to thee.
That when thou doest reioyce, then doubled is thy ioy,
And eke in cause of care, the lesse is thy anoy.
  Aloft if thou do liue, as one appointed here,
A stately part on stage of worldly state to bere:             15
Thy frende as only free from fraud will thee aduise,
To rest within the rule of mean as do the wise.
  He seeketh to foresee the peril of thy fall.
He findeth out thy faultes and warnes thee of them all.
Thee, not thy luck he loues, what euer be thy case,          20
He is thy faithfull frend and thee he doth embrace.
  If churlish cheare of chance haue thrown thee into thrall,
And that thy nede aske ayde for to releue thy fall:
In him thou secret trust assured art to haue,
And succour not to seke, before that thou can craue.         25
  Thus is thy frende to thee the comfort of thy paine,
The stayer of thy state, the doubler of thy gaine.
In wealth and wo thy frend, an other self to thee,
Such man to man a God, the prouerb sayth to be.
  As welth will bring thee frendes in louring wo to proue,   30
So wo shall yeld thee frendes in laughing wealth to loue.
With wisedome chuse thy frend, with vertue him retaine:
Let vertue be the ground, so shall it not be vaine.

## [297] Of the vanitie of mans
## lyfe.                                                       35

*V*Aine is the fleting welth,
    Whereon the world stayes:
Sithe stalking time by priuy stelth,
Encrocheth on our dayes.
  And elde which creepeth fast,                               40
To taynte vs with her wounde:

[ 245 ]

Will turne eche blysse vnto a blast,
Which lasteth but a stounde.
  Of youth the lusty floure,
Which whylome stoode in price:      5
Shall vanish quite within an houre,
As fire consumes the ice.
  Where is become that wight,
For whose sake Troy towne:
Withstode the grekes till ten yeres fight,   10
Had rasde their walles adowne.
  Did not the wormes consume,
Her caryon to the dust?
Did dreadfull death forbeare his fume
For beauty, pride, or lust?      15

## [298] The louer not regarded in earꓫ nest sute, being become wiꓫ ser, refuseth her profred loue.

*D*O way your phisike I faint no more,   20
The salue you sent it comes to late:
You wist well all my grief before,
And what I suffred for your sake.
Hole is my hart I plaine no more,
A new the cure did vndertake:   25
Wherfore do way you come to late.
  For whiles you knew I was your own,
So long in vaine you made me gape,
And though my fayth it were well knowne,
Yet small regard thou toke therat,   30
But now the blast is ouerblowne.
Of vaine phisicke a salue you shape,
Wherfore do way you come to late.
How long or this haue I bene faine,
To gape for mercy at your gate,   35
Vntill the time I spyde it plaine,
That pitie and you fell at debate.
For my redresse then was I faine:
Your seruice cleane for to forsake,

Wherfore do way you come to late.
　For when I brent in endlesse fire,
Who ruled then but cruell hate?
So that vnneth I durst desire　　　　　　　　　5
One looke, my feruent heate to slake.
Therfore another doth me hyre,
And all the profer that you make,
Is made in vayne and comes to late.
　For when I asked recompence,　　　　　　　10
With cost you nought to graunt God wat:
Then said disdaine to great expence,
It were for you to graunt me that.
Therfore do way your rere pretence,
That you would binde that derst you brake,　　15
For lo your salue comes all to late.

[299] The complaint of a woman
　　rauished, and also mor=
　　　tally wounded.

*A* Cruell Tiger all with teeth bebled,　　　　20
　A bloody tirantes hand in eche degre,
A lecher that by wretched lust was led,
(Alas) deflowred my virginitee.
And not contented with this villanie,
Nor with thoutragious terrour of the dede,　　25
With bloody thirst of greater crueltie:
Fearing his haynous gilt should be bewrayed,
By crying death and vengeance openly,
His violent hand forthwith alas he layed
Vpon my guiltles sely childe and me,　　　　30
And like the wretch whom no horrour dismayde,
Drownde in the sinke of depe iniquitie:
Misusing me the mother for a time,
Hath slaine vs both for cloking of his crime.

[300] The louer being made thrall by　　　　35
　loue, perceiueth how great
　　a losse is libertye.

*A*H libertie now haue I learnd to know,
　By lacking thee what Iewell I possest,
When I receiued first from Cupids bow
The deadly wound that festreth in my brest.　　5
　So farre (alas) forth strayed were mine eyes,
That I ne might refraine them backe, for lo:
They in a moment all earthly thinges despise,
In heauenly sight now are they fixed so.
　What then for me but still with mazed sight,　　10
To wonder at that excellence diuine:
Where loue (my freedome hauing in despight)
Hath made me thrall through errour of mine eyen,
For other guerdon hope I not to haue,
My foltring toonge so basheth ought to craue.　　15

## [301] The diuers and contrarie passions of the louer.

*H*Olding my peace alas how loud I crye,
　Pressed with hope and dread euen both at ones,
Strayned with death, and yet I cannot dye.　　20
Burning in flame, quaking for cold that grones,
Vnto my hope withouten winges I flye.
Pressed with dispayre, that breaketh all my bones.
Walking as if I were, and yet am not.
Fayning with mirth, most inwardly with mones.　　25
Hard by my helpe, vnto my health not nye.
Mids of the calme my ship on rocke it rones.
I serue vnbound, fast fettred yet I lye.
In stede of milke that fede on marble stones,
My most will is that I do espye:　　30
That workes my ioyes and sorowes both at ones.
In contrairs standeth all my losse and gaine:
And lo the giltlesse causeth all my paine.

## [302] The testament of the hawthorne.　　35

*I*Sely Haw whose hope is past,
　In faithfull true and fixed minde:

To her whom that I serued last,
Haue all my ioyefulnes resignde,
Because I know assuredly,
My dying day aprocheth nye.                                    5
  Dispaired hart the carefull nest,
Of all the sighes I kept in store:
Conuey my carefull corps to rest,
That leaues his ioy for euermore.
And when the day of hope is past,                            10
Geue vp thy sprite and sigh the last.
  But or that we depart in twaine,
Tell her I loued with all my might:
That though the corps in clay remaine,
Consumed to asshes pale and white.                          15
And though the vitall powres do ceasse,
The sprite shall loue her natrelesse.
  And pray my liues lady dere,
During this litle time and space,
That I haue to abiden here,                                   20
Not to withdraw her wonted grace,
In recompensing of the paine,
That I shall haue to part in twaine.
  And that at least she will withsaue,
To graunt my iust and last request:                         25
When that she shall behold his graue,
That lyeth of lyfe here dispossest,
In record that I once was hers,
To bathe the frosen stone with teares.
  The seruice tree here do I make,                            30
For mine executour and my frende:
That liuing did not me forsake,
Nor will I trust vnto my ende,
To see my body well conueyde,
In ground where that it shalbe layde.                        35
  Tombed vnderneth a goodly Oke,
With Iuy grene that fast is bound:
There this my graue I haue bespoke,
For there my ladies name do sound:
Beset euen as my testament tels:                             40
With oken leaues and nothing els.
  Grauen wheron shalbe exprest,
Here lyeth the body in this place,

Of him that liuing neuer cest
To serue the fayrest that euer was,
The corps is here, the hart he gaue
To her for whom he lieth in graue.                                    5
    And also set about my hersse,
Two lampes to burne and not to queint,
Which shalbe token, and rehersse
That my good will was neuer spent.
When that my corps was layd alow,                                    10
My spirit did sweare to serue no mo.
    And if you want of ringing bels,
When that my corps goth into graue:
Repete her name and nothing els,
To whom that I was bonden slaue.                                     15
When that my life it shall vnframe,
My sprite shall ioy to heare her name.
    With dolefull note and piteous sound,
Wherwith my hart did cleaue in twaine:
With such a song lay me in ground,                                   20
My sprite let it with her remayne,
That had the body to commend:
Till death therof did make an end.
    And euen with my last bequest,
When I shall from this life depart:                                 25
I geue to her I loued best,
My iust my true and faithfull hart,
Signed with the hand as cold as stone:
Of him that liuing was her owne.
    And if he here might liue agayne,                               30
As Phenix made by death anew:
Of this she may assure her plaine,
That he will still be iust and trew.
Thus farewell she on liue my owne.
And send her ioy when I am gone.                                    35

## [303] The louer in dispeire lamen=
## teth his case.

*A* Dieu desert, how art thou spent?
    Ah dropping teares how do ye washe?
Ah scalding sighes, how be ye spent?                                40

To pricke them forth that will not hast,
Ah payned hart thou gapst for grace,
Euen there where pitie hath no place.
  As easy it is the stony rocke,                                5
From place to place for to remoue,
As by thy plaint for to prouoke:
A frosen hart from hate to loue,
What should I say such is thy lot,
To fawne on them that force the not.                          10
  Thus maist thou safely say and sweare,
That rigour raighneth and ruth doth faile,
In thanklesse thoughts thy thoughts do wear
Thy truth, thy faith, may nought auaile,
For thy good will why should thou so,                         15
Still graft where grace it will not grow.
  Alas pore hart thus hast thou spent,
Thy flowryng time, thy pleasant yeres.
With sighing voyce wepe and lament:
For of thy hope no frute apperes,                             20
Thy true meanyng is paide with scorne,
That euer soweth and repeth no corne.
  And where thou sekes a quiet port,
Thou dost but weigh agaynst the winde,
For where thou gladdest woldst resort,                        25
There is no place for thee assinde.
Thy desteny hath set it so
That thy true hart should cause thy wo.


## [304] Of his maistresse .m.B.

*I*N Bayes I boast whose braunch I beare,                       30
  Such ioy therin I finde:
That to the death I shall it weare,
  To ease my carefull minde.
In heat, in cold, both night and day,
  Her vertue may be sene:                                      35
When other frutes and flowers decay,
  The bay yet growes full grene.
Her berries fede the birdes full oft,
  Her leues swete water make:

Her bowes be set in euery loft,
  For their swete sauours sake.
The birdes do shrowd them from the cold,
  In her we dayly see: 5
And men make arbers as they wold,
  Vnder the pleasant tree.
It doth me good when I repayre,
  There as these bayes do grow:
Where oft I walke to take the ayre, 10
  It doth delight me so.
But loe I stand as I were dome,
  Her beauty for to blase:
Wherwith my sprites be ouercome,
  So long theron I gase. 15
At last I turne vnto my walk,
  In passing to and fro:
And to my self I smile and talk,
  And then away I go.
Why smilest thou say lokers on, 20
  What pleasure hast thou found?
With that I am as cold as stone,
  And ready for to swound.
Fie fie for shame sayth fansy than,
  Pluck vp thy faynted hart: 25
And speke thou boldly like a man,
  Shrinke not for little smart.
Wherat I blushe and change my chere,
  My senses waxe so weake:
O god think I what make I here, 30
  That neuer a word may speake.
I dare not sigh lest I be heard,
  My lokes I slyly cast:
And still I stand as one were scarde,
  Vntill my stormes be past. 35
Then happy hap doth me reuiue,
  The blood comes to my face:
A merier man is not aliue,
  Then I am in that case.
Thus after sorow seke I rest, 40
  When fled is fansies fit.
And though I be a homely gest,
  Before the bayes I sit,

Where I do watch till leaues do fall,
   When winde the tree doth shake:
Then though my branch be very small,
   My leafe away I take.              5
And then I go and clap my hands,
   My hart doth leape for ioy.
These bayes do ease me from my bands,
   That long did me annoy:
For when I do behold the same,
   Which makes so faire a show:      10
I finde therin my maistresse name,
   And se her vertues grow.

## [305] The louer complaineth his harty loue not requited.

                                      15

WHen Phebus had the serpent slaine,
   He claymed Cupides boe:
Which strife did turne him to great paine,
The story well doth proue.
For Cupide made him fele much woe,    20
In sekyng Dephnes loue.
   This Cupide hath a shaft of kinde,
Which wounded many a wight:
Whose golden hed had power to binde,
Ech hart in Venus bandes.         25
This arrow did on Phebus light,
Which came from Cupides handes.
   An other shaft was wrought in spite,
Which headed was with lead:
Whose nature quenched swete delight,   30
That louers most embrace.
In Dephnes brest this cruell head,
Had found a dwellyng place.
   But Phebus fonde of his desire,
Sought after Dephnes so:        35
He burnt with heat, she felt no fire,
Full fast she fled him fro.
He gate but hate for his good will,
The gods assigned so.

My case with Phebus may compare,
His hap and mine are one,
I cry to her that knowes no care,
Yet seke I to her most:                                                5
When I approche then is she gone,
Thus is my labour lost.
   Now blame not me but blame the shaft,
That hath the golden head,
And blame those gods that with their craft                              10
Such arrowes forge by kinde.
And blame the cold and heauy lead,
That doth my ladies minde.

## [306] A praise of .m.M.

*I*N court as I behelde, the beauty of eche dame,                       15
  Of right my thought frō all the rest should .M. steale the same.
But, er I ment to iudge: I vewed with such aduise.
As retchlesse dome should not inuade: the boundes of my deuise.
And, whiles I gased long: such heat did brede within,
As Priamus towne felt not more flame, whē did the bale begin.          20
By reasons rule ne yet by wit perceue I could,
That .M, face of earth yfound: enioy such beauty should.
And fansy doubted that from heauen had Venus come,
To norish rage in Britaynes harts, while corage yet doth blome,
Her natiue hue so stroue, with colour of the rose,                     25
That Paris would haue Helene left, and .M. beauty chose.
A wight farre passyng all, and is more faire to seme,
Then lusty May the lodg of loue: that clothes the earth in grene.
So angell like she shines: she semeth no mortall wight,
But one whom nature in her forge, did frame her self to spight.        30
Of beauty princesse chiefe: so makelesse doth she rest,
Whose eye would glad an heauy wight: and pryson payne in brest,
I waxe astonied to see: the feator of her shape,
And wōdred that a mortal hart: such heauenly beames could scape
Her limmes so answeryng were: the mould of her faire face,            35
Of Venus stocke she semde to spring, the rote of beauties grace.
Her presens doth pretende: such honour and estate,
That simple men might gesse her birthe: if folly bred debate.
Her lokes in hartes of flint: would such affectes imprese,
As rage of flame not Nilus stremes: in Nestors yeres encrease.        40

Within the subtill seat, of her bright eyen doth dwell,
Blinde Cupide with the pricke of paine: that princes fredom sell.
A Paradice it is: her beauty to behold,
Where natures stuffe so full is found, that natures ware is sold,     5

## [307] An old louer to a yong
## gentilwoman.

*Y*E are to yong to bryng me in,
   And I to old to gape for flies:
I haue to long a louer bene,     10
If such yong babes should bleare mine eyes,
But trill the ball before my face,
I am content to make you play:
I will not se, I hide my face,
And turne my backe and ronne away.     15
   But if you folowe on so fast,
And crosse the waies where I should go,
Ye may waxe weary at the last,
And then at length your self orethrow.
I meane where you and all your flocke,     20
Deuise to pen men in the pound:
I know a key can picke your locke,
And make you runne your selues on ground.
   Some birdes can eate the strawie corne,
And flee the lime that fowlers set,     25
And some are ferde of euery thorne,
And so therby they scape the net.
But some do light and neuer loke,
And seeth not who doth stand in waite,
As fish that swalow vp the hoke,     30
And is begiled through the baite.
   But men can loke before they leape,
And be at price for euery ware,
And penyworthes cast to bye good cheape,
And in ech thyng hath eye and care.     35
But he that bluntly runnes on hed,
And seeth not what the race shal be:
Is like to bring a foole to bed,
And thus ye get no more of me.

## [308] The louer forsaketh his vnkinde loue.

*F*Arewell thou frosen hart and eares of hardned stele,
   Thou lackest yeres to vnderstand the grefe that I did fele.   5
The gods reuenge my wrong, with equall plage on thee,
When plesure shal prick forth thy youth, to learn what loue shalbe.
Perchance thou prouest now, to scale blinde Cupides holde,
And matchest where thou maist repent, when al thy cards are told
But blush not thou therfore, thy betters haue done so,   10
Who thought they had retaind a doue, when they but caught a cro
And some do lenger time, with lofty lokes we see,
That lights at length as low or wors thē doth the betell bee.
Yet let thy hope be good, such hap may fall from hye:
That thou maist be if fortune serue, a princesse er thou dye.   15
If chance prefer thee so, alas poore sely man,
Where shall I scape thy cruell handes, or seke for succour than?
God shild such greedy wolues, should lap in giltlesse bloode,
And send short hornes to hurtful heads, ẙ rage like lyons woode.
I seldome se the day, but malice wanteth might,   20
And hatefull harts haue neuer hap, to wreke their wrath aright.
The madman is vnmete, a naked sword to gide,
And more vnfit are they to clime, that are orecome with pride.
I touch not thee herein, thou art a fawcon sure,
That can both soer and stoupe sometime, as men cast vp the lure.   25
The pecock hath no place, in thee when thou shalt list,
For some no soner make a signe, but thou perceuest the fist.
They haue that I do want, and that doth thee begilde,
The lack that thou dost se in me, doth make thee loke so wilde.
My luryng is not good, it liketh not thine eare,   30
My call it is not half so swete, as would to god it were.
Well wanton yet beware, thou do no tiryng take,
At euery hand that would thee fede, or to thee frendship make,
This councell take of him that ought thee once his loue,
Who hopes to mete thee after this among the saintes aboue.   35
But here within this world, if he may shonne the place,
He rather asketh present death, then to beholde thy face.

## [309] The louer preferreth his lady aboue all other.

*R* Esigne you dames whom tikelyng brute delight,
  The golden praise that flatteries tromp doth sown
And vassels be to her that claims by right,
The title iust that first dame beauty found.
Whose dainty eyes such sugred baits do hide,        5
As poyson harts where glims of loue do glide.
  Come eke and see how heauen and nature wrought,
Within her face where framed is such ioy:
As Priams sonncs in vaine the seas had sought,     10
If halfe such light had had abode in Troy.
For as the golden sunne doth darke ech starre,
So doth her hue the fayrest dames as farre.
  Ech heauenly gift, ech grace that nature could,
By art or wit my lady lo retaynes:       15
A sacred head, so heapt with heares of gold,
As Phebus beames for beauty farre it stayns,
A sucred tong, where eke such swetenesse snowes,
That well it semes a fountain where it flowes.
  Two laughyng eyes so linked with pleasyng lokes,   20
As wold entice a tygers hart to serue:
The bayt is swete but eager be the hookes,
For Dyane sekes her honour to preserue.
Thus Arundell sits, throned still with fame,
Whom enmies trompe can not attaynt with shame.   25
  My dased head so daunted is with heapes,
Of giftes diuine that harber in her brest:
Her heauenly shape, that lo my verses leaps,
And touch but that wherin she clowds the rest.
For if I should her graces all recite,      30
Both time should want, and I should wonders write.
  Her chere so swete, so christall is her eyes,
Her mouth so small, her lips so liuely red:
Her hand so fine, her wordes so swete and wise,
That Pallas semes to soiourne in her hed.     35
Her vertues great, her forme as farre excedes,
As sunne the shade that mortall creatures leades.
  Would God that wretched age would spare to race,
Her liuely hew that as her graces rare:
Be goddesse like, euen so her goddesse face,    40
Might neuer change but still continue faire
That eke in after time ech wight may see,
How vertue can with beauty beare degree.

## [310] The louer lamenteth that he would forget loue, and can not.

*A*Las when shall I ioy,                                              5
   When shall my wofull hart,
Cast forth the folish toy
That breadeth all my smart.
A thousand times and mo,
I haue attempted sore:                                               10
To rid this restlesse wo,
Which raigneth more and more.
   But when remembrance past,
Hath laid dead coales together:
Old loue renewes his blast,                                          15
That cause my ioyes to wither.
Then sodaynely a spark,
Startes out of my desire:
And lepes into my hart,
Settyng the coles a fire.                                            20
   Then reason runnes about,
To seke forgetfull water:
To quench and clene put out,
The cause of all this matter.
And saith dead flesh must nedes,                                     25
Be cut out of the core,
For rotten withered wedes,
Can heale no greuous sore.
   But then euen sodaynely,
The feruent heat doth slake:                                         30
And cold then straineth me,
That makes my bodies shake.
Alas who can endure,
To suffer all this paine,
Sins her that should me cure,                                        35
Most cruell death hath slaine.
   Well well, I say no more,
Let dead care for the dead,
Yet wo is me therfore,
I must attempt to lead,                                              40

One other kinde of life,
Then hitherto I haue:
Or els this paine and strife,
Will bring me to my graue.

# VARIANT READINGS AND MISPRINTS
## (*A–I*)

# VARIANT READINGS AND MISPRINTS

EDITIONS are referred to by the following letters, as is explained in more detail in the Introduction to volume II:

*A*, 1st edition, June 5, 1557
*B*, 2d edition, July 31, 1557 (British Museum copy)
*C*, 2d edition, July 31, 1557 (Capell copy)
*D*, 3d edition, 1559
*E*, 4th edition, 1565
*F*, 5th edition, 1567
*G*, 6th edition, 1574
*H*, 7th edition, 1585
*I*, 8th edition, 1587

The following list aims to include every verbal variant from *A* in *B–I* and from the additional poems (Nos. 272–310) of *B* in *C–I*, as well as all the misprints in *A–I* that I have observed in checking each of those texts three times (but very likely a number have been overlooked). Mere differences in spelling (like *account-accompt, on-one, perfet-perfect-parfit, slander-sclaunder, the-thee, then-than*) are not listed unless, for one reason or another, they seem to have a special interest; but wherever the spelling adds or omits what is, or what might be, an extra syllable, it is noted. In general no attention is paid, furthermore, to capitalization or punctuation (to do so would require a whole volume); to cases of faulty spacing, unless a different or a doubtful wording results, or unless they are corrected in my own text; to wrong fonts of type or broken letters, except occasionally for the texts of *A* and *B*; to undotted *i*'s (of which there are many bewildering instances), letters or words out of alignment, printers' lead-marks, changed indention, and the like. For a record of misprints in folio-numbers, key-words, and signature-marks see the descriptions of the editions given in the Introduction to volume II.

Readings at the left of the bracket are those of my own text: variations from them in any of the original editions are given at the right of the bracket. A reading followed by a letter and a plus-sign occurs in the edition represented by the letter and in all the subsequent sixteenth-century editions. Similarly, the letters *A* through *I* when connected by hyphens include all intervening editions. Concretely, *B+* represents every edition from *B* to *I* inclusive, as does also *B–I; DFI* shows that a reading is in the editions of 1559, 1567, 1587; *DEG+*, in the editions of 1559, 1565, 1574, 1585, 1587. Thus, an entry like "thy selfe with thine *F+* " indicates that *thy selfe with thine* is the reading, but not necessarily the exact spelling, in all the editions from 1567 to 1587 inclusive. Where the readings given from *G* and *H* are not duplicated in the Bodleian and the Grenville (British Museum) copies of the 1574 and 1585 editions, the readings of those copies are added with the symbols *G*¹ and *H*¹.

[ 263 ]

# VARIANT READINGS AND MISPRINTS

To make these collations was an utter weariness of the flesh, and their bulk proves somewhat embarrassing to the spirit. Most readers will, properly enough, pass them by with a glance; but a few students may find them of value. For they throw a flood of light on the degeneration of texts under the hands of Elizabethan printers; they are indispensable in identifying the texts followed in the reprints of the eighteenth and nineteenth centuries; and, conceivably, they may some day be of service in helping to date or to identify an undated or a fragmentary edition.

2.  1–2 The . . . Reader] To (¶To *C*) the reder *B+*
    4 workes] woorkers *BC*
    8 noble] *Om. F+*
    13 for] for the *G+*
    15 horders] s *defective in A:*    treasure] *Om. HI*
    17 presently] present *HI*
    19–20 remoued] remoned *D perhaps*
    21 frendes] s *defective (possibly a broken* r) *in A*
    22 work] workes *FGH*
    24 swete] *Om. HI*
3.  2 Descripcion] ¶Description *C,* Dcscription (*with* c *in a wrong font*) *H*
    4 rue] e *blurred out of C*
    6 furth] forth *C+*
    7 And] Twise *B+*
    8 despoiled] displayed *I*
    9 new] ones *B+*
    10 haue] *Om. F*
    14 warmth] warmeth *HI*
    15 in flame] inflame *D+*
    17 yeares] *Om. F+*
    20 harm] hart *F+*
    29 all] *Om. HI*
    34 trauailes] trauaile *G+*
    38 chere] chcre *G?:*    playn] *Partly torn in D*
    39 measure] m *inverted in E*
4.  4 knitteth] knitteh *D*
    10 ankerd] Ankards *HI:*    spretes] sprites *BCD,* spirites *E+*
    11 agazed] agazde *HI:*    sinke] sinck *D (with* c *badly blurred)*
    15 dothe] doeth *H*
    16 my fill] me still *I*
    17 this] s *blurred out of C*
    19 ,alas] 'alas *B*
    20 myne] my *HI:*    wounde] o *broken in A*
    23 Description]¶Description *C*
    26 soote] foote *B:*    season] seasons *FGH,* reasons *I:*    furth] forth *B+*
    29 make] matte *I*
    33 flote] flete *B+*
    34 sloughe] slougth *FG,* sloth *HI:*    slinges] flynges *E+*
    38 thus] this *G+*
5.  2 Description] ¶Description *C,* Decription *G:*    state] estate *E+*
    4 When] Wh en *AE*
    5 me causde to] had made me *B+*

5. 6 I loked] I¨ loked *B (C similarly has one dot over* I *and one over* o)
  15 persaunt] present *D+*
  19 blowen] blowne *B–H*
  21 that was their quest] of their request *B+*
  27 The . . . fed] To her for help my hart was fled *B+*
  28 me] m *inverted in D*
  32 nowe] no we *A:* brest] prest *HI*
  36 Description] ¶Description *C*
  37 affections] afflictions *HI*

6. 2 SVche] SVuch *E*
  3 accord] d *blurred out in H and Hı*
  4 is] in *B*
  6 He] H e *A:* makes the one] causeth thone *B+:* with] wlth *D*
  7 other] others *D+*
  8 flame] flames *F*
  12 calde] caldo *G*
  13 me] *Om. HI*
  15 paines] paine *HI:* were] where *E*
  16 this] the *HI*
  24 grene] greue *I*
  27 furth] forth *C+*
  31 thousand] thonsand *H (perhaps correct in Hı):* resoluing] esoluing
   *E:* all in] of his *D+*
  33 pleasures] pleasure *E+:* the] his *B+*
  34 track] trackt *D,* tracte *E–G,* trasse *H,* trase *I*
  36 transforme] trasfourme *E:* the] the the the *H*
  39 change] chaunce *E*
  42 my] the *D+*

7. 3 meash] mase *D+*
  4 with] ẁith *A*
  9 despeire of] d *badly blurred in C,* dispeired *D+*
  15 might] night *D*
  16 when] wen *E:* earth] yearth *E*
  17 tree] treee *I*
  19 woe] woes *B+:* dore] dur *D+*
  20 quod] quoth *HI*
  21 shalt] shall *F?*
  22 health] heath *H*
  23 space] place *E+*
  24 kindes] kinde *D+* (kuide *E apparently*)
  27 for] for for *E*
  28 furth] forth *G+*
  35 That] *Final* t *defective in H (correct in Hı):* that] the *I*

8. 2 brought] wrought *D+*
  3 at will, and] at wy l and *E*
  8 quod] quoth *HI*
  9 Vnwillingly] Vnwittingly *B+*
  12 of] of the *EF:* mine . . . so] did so my heart *HI*
  14 ye] I *B+*
  16 but] bnt *B:* mine] my *I:* empressed] expressed *B+*
  18 home] howe *DE*
  19 my] to *I*

# VARIANT READINGS AND MISPRINTS

8. 23 thus] this *F*+
   24 Complaint] ¶Complaint *C*
   28 with me he] he me with *HI*
   30 taught] thought *D*+
   32 refraine] restraine *B*+
   33 straight] straigh *C*, straigtht *G*
   34 cowarde] cowred *DE*, couered *F*+
   35 flight] delight *HI*

9.  3 dame] *Om. EF*
    4 hote . . . tastes] hotte is, that who tastes *B:*    the same] thesame *A*
    5 thawed] chawed *D–G*, chawsed *HI*
    6 kindled] kindeled *B*, kindlyd *C:*    fired] fixed *D*+
    7 hate] hart *BD*
    8 This] With *B:*    so opprest] ar supprest *B*
    9 That in] Feeleth *B:*    harborde] harbordes *HI:*    late] smart *B*
   11 so colde in] well of *B:*    founde] foude *D*
   14 of] *Om. DEF*
   16 My seruice thus is growen] Wherby my seruice growes *B:*    growen]
      growne *F*
   17 Description] Desctiption *D*, Deserption *F*
   22 Cambers] Camaers *HI:*    did geue] furst gaue *B:*    her] hei *D*
   23 Fostered] Fostred *BD*+
   25 she doth] did she *B*
   26 With] With a *B:*    where . . . costly] who tasteth ghostly *B:* tasteth]
      tasted *HI*
   29 Hampton] Hamton *D:*    for] *Om. HI*
   30 Windsor] winsor *HI*
   33 The . . . hurtfulnes] *Printed at the very bottom of sig. A5 as well as (with*
     *line 34 added) at the top of sig. A5ᵛ in H*

10.  2 flowring] floring *E*
   10 Enmy] Enemy *E*+
   12 taken] tak en *A*
   19 aboute] aboue *G*+
   21 not I] now I *G*, I now *HI*
   24 doubtfull] doleful *G*+:    ease] case *E*+
   25 doe] doth *G*+
   26 by and by] byandby *A*
   27 Geues] Giue *HI*
   30 eche] cche *A apparently*
   31 reuiueth] r *defective in A*
   32 pleasure] p *broken or in wrong font in A*
   33 Windsor] Winsore *G*+:    susteyned] susteinde *G*+
   35 The] Set *B:*    plot] plots *B:*    with] i *blurred out in D*
   36 blossomd] blossomed *EFG*, blossomes *HI:*    bowes] blowes *HI*

11.  4 hatelesse] hartelesse *DG*+
   11 me] m *apparently inverted in A*
   12 Vow] A vow *D*+
   13 be re-] bere- *C (in A the hyphen is perhaps doubled)*
   15 doth] do *B*
   18 or] or or *I*
   24 flood] fllood *C*
   31 alway] alwaies *HI*

12. 2 other] others *F*+
    5 But] For *B:*    mine] my *G*+:    mought] might *HI*
    6 Yet, sins] Sins that *B*
    7 tresses] tresse is *B*
    8 that] to *B:*    hid] hide *B*, had *D*+
  10 cornet] corner *BHI:*    me] my *B*
  11 a] of *B*
  17 taught] taugh *H*
  19 vnknowen] vnknowne *G*
  22 Of] Of al *EFG*
  23 Ladie] Garret *B*
  26 thy] the *D*+
  29 Prisoned] Prisoner *E*+:    he re-] here *F*+
  33 Windsor] Winsor *EGH:*    in] *Om. E*+
  35 feast] feastes *B:*    than] thtn *H:*    Priams] Priam *G*+
13. 9 palme] plaine *F*+:    where] were *C*
  10 gleames] gleaines *G apparently*
  11 and] aud *E*
  12 kept] kepes *F*+
  21 groues] grones *HI*
  22 pleasaunt] pleasaunce *D*
  23 ofte] of *HI:*    founde] fonnde *I*
  26 rayns] rayne *D:*    swift ybreathed] swyfty breathed *D*+
  27 houndes] hounde *E*+
  28 harte] harts *HI*
  31 yet] it *HI*
  35 kept] kepe *F*+
  36 night] nightes *B*
  40 Vpsupped] Vnsupped *HI*
  43 thy] this *E*+:    doest] dost *HI*
14. 3 Eccho] Eche *EF*, Eche stone *G*+
    7 greater] greate *D*
    8 my] mie *FG*
    9 comforteth] conforteth *E*
  10 the] *Om. G*+
  13 distrains] *First* i *blurred in C*, disdaines *HI*
  16 haue] hath *F*+
  20 boysteous] boystrous *HI*
  23 Appeasde] Appeased *D*+
  24 that] *Om. G*+:    those] these *HI*
  26 full] from *G*+
  28 ouerrone] ouercome *F*+
  31 longe] longs (s *apparently inverted*) *D*
  34 life] tyme *E*+
15. 2 care] fare *E*+
    3 fare] care *E*+
    6 sea] seas *E*+
  13 my] m *inverted in D*
  14 rememberance] remembrance *BFHI*
  22 that] which *HI*
  34 a] *Om. D*+
  35 And] *Torn in H (H*¹ *correct):*    flood] flouds *HI*

16.   3 waxe] ware *B*, waxt *D:*      calme] talme *D apparently*
     4 fro] from *E+*
   11 iniust] vniust *G+*
   12 mistaking] mista,/king *B*
   14 when] whem *G*
   20 vttering] vttringe *F+:*     plain] int *torn out in B*
   21 hym] haue *HI:*     attaint] t *torn in B*
   22 quod] quoth *HI*
   23 chaunce] chauuce *B*
   26 retchlesse] rechlesse *EFG*
   27 rufull] ruthfull *HI:*     thought] though *D*
   28 sayd] saieth *FG*, saith *HI*
   33 If] It *D:*     write thou] writethou *A*
   36 fordid] forbyd *F+*
17.   9 quod] $\varphi$ *E–H*, qd *I*
   10 Doest] Dost *E+*
   11 quoth] quod *D*, $\varphi$ *E–H*, qd *I*
   12 vnworthy] vnwor hy *D*
   13 sighe] sieghe *E*
   16 shalt] shall *EF*
   17 with] t *blurred out in C*
   19 quoth] quod *DE*, $\varphi$ *F–H*, qd *I*
   27 amid] and *H*, and in *I*
   28 befallen] befalled *E:*     Priam] Prian *HI*
   30 her] *Om. D+*
   31 no] not *I*
   33 lenger] longer *G+*
   37 turned] turnde *CDF+*
   38 welcome] weldome *H*
   40 to$^2$] for to *HI*
   42 hath] *Om. H*
18.   4 thousand] trousand *E*
   5 sprites] spirites *H*
   8 furies] furie *G+:*     restord] restored *HI*
   10 corse] corps *E+*
   12 Chreseids] Creseids *BCE*, Creseides *D*, Cresides *F+:*     Priams]
      Priamus *E*
   13 trew] trne *F*
   14 as] so *G+:*     belonged] belongeth *B+:*     couered] couerd *F*
   24 ye] yet *D*
   28 and] an d *A*
   30 I] *Blurred out in D:*     tembrace] to embrace *HI*
   32 well] will *D+:*     and sone] and he *HI* (andh e in *H*$^1$ *with* e *badly*
      *broken*)
   35 he] *Om. HI*
   38 semes] seme *F+*
   40 Another] And other *D*
19.   4 my$^2$] and *HI*
   8 saith] saieth *H*
   10 dischargen] discharged *E+*
   14 slake] slacke *EFG:*     gnawing] knawing *E+*
   22 me] *Om. DE*, dooe *F+*

19. 26 reproueth] teproueth *A*
    31 sayen] sayne *E+*
    33 darkest] darknest *G*
20. 10 her] hlr *H*
    13 the] che *D*
    15 well] *Om. HI*
    21 a] *Om. D*
    32 your] you *C*
    35 your] yonr *D*
    38 the in] in the *B+*
21. 8 such] your *D+*
    18 bought] t *inverted in H*
    19 mine] my *G+*
    22 suffreth] suffereth *HI*
    24 my] my well *BC:*      beloued] beleued *DE*
    28 thine] then *HI*
    29 all] ill *I*
    30 loued] loud *F+*
    31 fed] feed *HI*
    32 withstand] i *not impressed in D*
    33 held] heldest *D*, yeldest *EHI*, yeldst *FG:*      hand] haud *B*, hand *H*
22. 2 forsaken] forsakeu *D*
    3 forsaketh] fotsaketh *D apparently*
    8 glimsing] glsiming *A*, glisming *B*, glinsing *E+*
    12 auance] aduaunce *HI*
    14 fortunes] fortune *HI*
    18 Is] As *F+*
    22 can] cau *E*
    30 thousand] thousaud *H:*      troubles] troules *B*
    39 to] so *D*
23. 5 louer] r *barely impressed (not inked) in A*
    12 stremes] sltremes *A apparently (with initial* s *defective):*      consume]
            consumed *EF*
    15 when] wen *F*
    23 full] *Om. HI*
    32 of] of such *E+*
    33 Though] Thought *F*
24. 6 might] migt *C*
    8 estemed] estemde *CDFGI:*      pese] pece *F*
    10 iudged] iudgde *G*, iudge *HI*
    18 the] :he *D (or else a broken* t)
    19 blustring] blusteryng *BC:*      winde] win *B*
    23 chorlish] churlish *B+*
    26 would] will *G+*
    38 it] *Om. E+*
    41 constance of the] constancye of *D+*
25. 6-7 towarde] towards *D+*
    8 louers.] *The period is a large blot in A*
    9 carelesse] carelasse *D:*      walke] walkt *B*
    11 a] an *F+*
    17 suffreth] suffereth *HI*
    18 fed] feed *H:*      with] wlth *D*

25. 20 doth] doeth *H*
   21 seemd] seemed *HI*
   22 go] grow *B*+
   24 doth] doeth *H*
   28 weried] wery *E*+
   29 to] to. *A apparently*
   30 forthwith] forwith *E*, fo twith *F*
   38 powdred] powred *HI*

26.  5 be] by *G*+
    6 richesse] riches *E*+
   11 continuance] continnance *C*
   13 ioyned] ioynde *C*+
   18 Contented] Content *F*+ :    with thine owne] thy selfe with thine *F*+
   20 meane] manne *F*+
   24 shonning] shounyng *E*
   25 thy] the *HI*
   27 aduisdly] aduisedly *E*+
   28 with] wit *D*
   30 often] of ten *E*
   33 ouerthwartes] ouerthwarts *HI*
   36 Now ill] Nowil *D*, No will *E*+ :    Phebus] Phebns *I*
   37 vnbent] bent *HI*

27.  2 sailes] saile *D*
    3 hast] hall *E*+
    5 translated] trauslated *D*
    7 Persie] Perse *D*
    8 Asie] Asia *G*+
   11 sepulture] sepulchre *E*+
   16 a] *Om. HI*
   19 imprinted] inprinted *G*
   25 had] hath *G*+
   27 murdrers] murdres *D*, murderers *HI*
   28 thy] the *G*+
   30 Wepe] With *B*+
   32 temperd] tempered *HI*
   33 the place] *Om. HI*
   34 thy] the *D*+ :    corse] corps *E*+
   35 vapord] vapored *E*+
   36 Pyramus] Priamus *EF*

28.  3 W.] VVyat *D*, What *E*+
    4 encreased] encreaseth *D*+
   10 to²] the *I*
   12 vertue] verue *C*
   15 ryme] tyme *EF*
   17 vnparfited] imparfited *G*, imperfited *HI:*    for] for a *I*
   20 enflame] in flame *E*
   23 whose] wose *C:*    iudgement] indgement *G:*    affect] effect *HI*
   28 trouth] troth *GH:*    auance] aduaunce *HI*
   31 met] m *perhaps inverted in E*, meete *H*
   34 lose] lost *H*
   35 But] But when *D*+

28. 38 receiued] recyiued *H*
    39 this] chis *D*
    40 possesse] possede *D*
29. 2 Sardinapalus] Sardanapalus *B*+
    3 and] and his *I*
    6 filthy] filthly *DE:*   staynd] standes *HI*
    12 garlands] garland:s *D apparently*
    13 scace] scarce *F*+
    14 slouth] slougth *F:*   womanish] womanuish *H*
    15 sprite] spirit *H*
    17 appalled] appald *F*+
    18 Murthered] Murdred *F*+
    21 happiest] bappiest *H*
    24 Layd] Layed *E*+
    27 sighed] sight *D*+:   thought doth] thought dyd *BC*, thoughtes did
       *D*+
    28 thought] though *H*
    30 eke] ecke *G:*   bones] bone *HI:*   opprest] oppresse *G*
    31 and lye] *Om. HI*
    32 old man] oldman *AB:*   sees] see *H*
    33 boy] voy *E:*   liue] lynd *E:*   so much] somuch *A*
    34 three] *First* e *torn out in D*
30. 4 wytherd] withered *D*+
    5 so] to *E*+
    7 shuts] shittes *G:*   as] when *HI*
    8 Thy] The *D*+:   messengers] messenger *FG*
    9 belief] belife *BC*
    11 two] to *E*
    14 Wherat] Werat *E*
    18 est] cst *or a broken* e *in A*
    19 humiliasti] humilitasti *D*
    21 And] Aud *D:*   represt] erprest *H*, exprest *I*
    24 griefes] greef *HI*
    29 lingring] lingering *EFG*
    30 nought] naugh *H*
    34-35 *are combined into one line,* Vnto a wretch that hat (hath *E*+) so oft
       ben shed *D*+
    37 Exhortation] An exhortation *HI*
31. 2 Ratclif] Ratelife *F*+:   thy] they *E*, the *F*+:   rechlesse] retch-
       lesse *BCD*
    5 without] wihout *F*
    8 weried] waried *D*
    9 louer] loues *E*
    10 that] *Om. D:*   serued] reserued *D*
    11 alway] alwaies *HI:*   enmy] enemy *E*+
    14 forthwith] furth with *D*
    19 And] Aud *D*
    20 wandred] wandered *CEFG*
32. 2 louer] loue *F*
    5 The] The one *E*+:   my] me *F*
    7 with] whith *E*
    8 displaying] displayeth *F*+

[ 271 ]

32.  14 enterprise] enterprises *HI*
      22 neuer . . . loue] of your loue neuer *HI*
      24 date] daie *I*
      25 teares] toares *E apparently:*      continual] continually *F+:*      haue]
         hath *B+*
      29 boones] bones *D+*
      31 withouten] without *F+*

33.   5 yfiled] I filed *D*, yfild *F+*
      11 Of] O *blurred out in D:*      lost] last *B–F*
      14 is] *Om. E+*
      24 my] me *F*
      30 lightenyng] lightninge *G+*
      31 erryng] crying *B+*
      34 after] *Om. E+*
      35 noyse] noyise *H*

34.   5 mislead] m *inverted in D*
      10 my way do stop] doe stoppe my way *HI*
      11 lockyng] lacking *F+:*      my] wy *D*
      12 So] Go *GH*
      14 her] his *F+*
      15 that] thac *D*
      17 forth] furth *DE*
      25 By] Be *D*
      26 *Line om. in D+*
      27 dangerous] daugerous *H*
      36 do] to *F+*

35.   4 moneth] e *broken (looking like* c*) in A*, month *BCG*
       5 vnlucky] vnluckly *D*, vnluckelie *EF*
       8 do way] doway *ABC:*      your] our *D*
      17 eke] ere *HI*
      23 sighes] siges *H*, signes *I:*      with] wiih *D apparently*
      24 ioye] o *missing in C:*      my] may *D*
      26 slack] slake *G+*
      35 whose] wose *E*

36.   2 others] other *HI*
      13 chanceth] chaunced *C+*
      18 cloke] clocke *D*
      19 in] of *HI*
      21 me] I *I*
      28 diuersenesse] diuersenest *F:*      blamen] blame men *E+*

37.   2 so] no *E+*
       3 Against] Agaiust *I*
       9 may] my *D*
      11 hide] hid *I*
      13 eyn] eyen *B+*
      16 his] the *I*
      18 kept] kepe *G+:*      fro] from *G+*
      21 me] my *I*
      22 succour] soccour *F*
      23 standst] standes *CD*, standest *EFGI*, standeth *H:*      afraied] afraid
         *C+*
      30 *Between 30 and 31 H has an irregular and a needless double space*

[ 272 ]

37. 33 in] of *I*
    35 and] and and *H*
38.  2 arise] then rise *HI*
     3 and] *Om. F+*
     5 not] nat *FGH*
     8 eye] eyes *I*
    10 thus] *Om. B+*
    13 And my] Au dmy *H (an dmy H¹)*
    16 on] vppon *HI*
    18 nightes] night *HI:*    passe] e *badly blurred in A*
    21 readinesse] readuiesse *C apparently*
    23 An] And *E+*
    25 of¹] of of *D:*    teares] teare *FGH*
    27 Wrethed] Wretched *D+*
    29 comfort] m *perhaps inverted in C*
    31 douteous] doutful *B+*
    33 washeth] wastethe *F+*
    35 worldly] worldy *E*, wordly *FG*
39.  2 this] his *B+*
     4 *Line om. in HI*
     8 betwixt] bewixt *E:*    game] gaine *I*
     9 seldome] seldoine *E apparently*
    10 repentance] representance *E+*
    12 is] i *I*
    18 not] non *HI*
    19 sometyme] sometimes *HI*
    23 better] *Om. HI*
    24 thinne] thine *E+*
    25 loose] lost *I:*    shoulders] shouldiers *I*
    28 how] hou *E*
    30 turnde] tourned *E+:*    through] thorow *H*
    32 leaue] leaue to leaue *HI*
    36 To a] The *D+*
    37 nay] no *E+*
40.  9 yea] ye *EFG*
    10 *Line om. in D+*
    13 no more] nomore *AB*
    14 loue] louer *HI*
    17 kisse] kuse *A apparently because of broken type*
    18 offended] ed *blurred in C*
    21 you] thou *HI:*    the] h *broken*, e *badly spaced in H:*    is] it *I*
    25 Ielous] ielious *I*
    26 the] rhe *D*
    29 wandring] wandering *E+*
    30 rechlesse] retchles *G+*
41.  3 had] *Om. E+*
     4 loue] louer *F+*
     5 her] *Om. HI*
     6 nedes] uedes *D*
    18 Thought he] Though thee *B+:*    thing] things *I*
    20 he] be *F*
    28 your] my *G+*
42.  2 styll] s *defective in A*
     4 taste] raste *D apparently*

[ 273 ]

42. 7 suretie] suerte *C*
   8 haue] hath *C*+
   10 syr] for *E*+
   20 such] ruth *B*+:     doth] do *D*
   21 it] *Om. F*+
   30 Or] Or els *F*+
   31 sinke] sieke *H*, seeke *I*:     my] may *H*
   33 cloked] choked *I*
   37 by] *Om. HI*

43. 3 ben] be *HI*:     wonderous] d *indiscernible in D*
   4 fortune] t *indiscernible in D*:     play] plaies *HI*
   5 makst] makest *E*+
   6 *Line om. in D*+
   8 thy] all *I*:     hap²] hap hap *H*
   9 set] seet *H*
   10 sekest] seekst *EF*
   11 mayst] may *D*, mayest *H*:     so] lo *I*
   16 hindryng] hindering *E*+:     didst] diddest *HI*
   18 willes] wiles *E*+
   19 Wenyng] wenning *E*+:     didst] dist *E*
   20 didst] diddest *HI*:     begyle] begyile *D*
   21 thy] my *F*+:     wouldst] would *C*+:     me haue] haue me *F*+
   22 thy] *Om. B*+
   28 Finisht] Finishe *G*+
   33 fare] feare *I*
   34 he is] is he *FGI*
   35 Spied] Spieth *HI*
   38 a part] apart *C–F*

44. 2 astart] estart *E*+
   6 state] estate *HI*
   7 restfull place] restlesse state *HI*
   11 remembrer] rememberer *E*
   15 heate] theate *E*+
   16 paynes] pain *D*+
   17 cure] care *I*
   19 ouerthwart] ouerwhart *I*
   26 place] peace *HI*:     away] *Om. HI*
   35 sourse] course *D*+
   37 eschue] issue *HI*

45. 5 enmy] enemy *E*+
   6 causde] cause *HI*:     accited] acited *B–E*, assited *F*+
   8 mought] might *I*
   9 with] wich *D*
   10 dredeth] deadeth *I*
   11 alway] alwayes *I*
   14 fierly] firely *BC (possibly* fircly *in B)*, fyry *D*, sirely *F*
   20 wayes] waies is *E*+
   22 false lyer] falselier *H*
   23 forceable] forcible *HI*
   27 hath ytasted] haue I tasted *D*
   28 that] rhat *H*
   30 araced] eraced *F*+

45. 34 litle] title *D*
    35 nought] naugh *H*
    38 youthly] youthfull *I*
    39 tempered] tempred *I*
    40 euer] neuer *D*
46. 2 to] *Om. HI*
    8 thorough] through *B–FHI*, chrough *G*
    12 laborous] wery *HI*
    15 nother] neither *I*
    19 heauenly] hauenly *E:*    goddes] God *HI*
    20 note] not *EF*
    31 the same] thesame *A*
    32 and] aud *D*
    34 both] doth *D+:*    and] aud *D*
    35 tother] other *D+*
    36 aduersair] aduersarie *D+*
    37 thother] tother *EFG*, the other *HI*
    38 troth] trouth *DE*, trought *F*, trough *G:*    aloofe] allofe *EF*
    41 selleth] felleth *E+:*    makes] make *C+*
    42 my] any *D*
    43 shames] shame *HI*
47. 2 euermore] enermore *C*
    4 brought] brough *D*
    7 Where:as] Whereas *B+:*    daskard] dastard *D+:*    mought] might *G+*
    9 Hanniball] Haneball *H:*    troubelous] troublous *D*
    12 nurture] honour *B+:*    glorious] *Om. HI*
    13 honor] actes *B–H*, artes *I:*    bring them] lift them vp *B+*
    20 way] wayes *I*
    24 stirred] virred *D*
    25 causde] caused *E+*
    35 ginneth] giueth *HI*
    36 tell] sell *EF*
    38 wyse] wist *I*
    40 in his dede] indede *HI*
    41 Doutyng] Donbting *H*
    43 euer] euet *H*
48. 3 yet] ye *I*
    4 he] *Om. F*
    5 plain] plaim *HI*
    8 yet] it *HI*
    15 hath] had *HI*
    16 forgotten] forgotteu *D*
    17 her him] him her *D+*
    19, 21, 27 quod] quoth *HI*
    28 lenger] longer *E+*
    31 Souche] Such(e) *throughout E+*
    32 the same] thesame *A*
    33 no more] nomore *A*
    34 I] In *E*
    38 depe] deeper *E*
49. 2, 4 may] many *D+*

49. 4 moornyng] morning $E+$
    8 ouerthwart] ouerhtwart $EF$
    9 moorning] morning (m *inverted in E*) $EFG$
    18 chance] thance $I$
    20, 22 And] Aud $D$
    23 ere] or $E+$:    be long] belong $D$
    28 myne] my $I$
    29 fet] set $D+$
    30 sighes] sighe $E+$
    32 plaint] plaintes $HI$
    34 my] *Om.* $D$
50. 2 now] how $F+$
    7 that¹] the $I$
    8 A right] Aright $HI$
    9 lese] lesse $E+$
    11 they] thy $F$:    falsed] falshed $D–H$
    12 kynde] kende $F$
    13 prouerb] prourrbe $D$ *apparently:*    sayeth] saith $B–Gl$
    14 and] aud $D$: auance] aduance $G+$
    17 to] and $I$
    21 wreck] wreke $E$, wreake $I$
    28 troth] trouth $D+$
    33 euermore] euer $HI$
    34 loue] louer $I$
    35 her] his $I$
    37 hath] haue $HI$
    39 whilst] whilest $G+$
51. 7 the same] thesame $A$
    11 did] dit $G$
    15 pricked] prickt $EF$
    16 Cupide] Cupides $C$
    19 Behold] BBholde $I$
    23 thee] there $E+$
    25 the] *Om.* $F+$
    28 meueth] moueth $I$
    30 stroke] strocke $EF$
    31 him that] himthat $A$
    32 here] her $E+$
52. 2 vaileth] valleth $C$ *apparently:*    troth] trouth $E+$
    4 flee] fleee $F$
    5 craftinesse] carftinesse $B$
    6 crafty] craiftie $H$:    plain] p lain $A$
    7 and fayn] andfaine' $H$ *(and* fa i n $H¹$*)*
    8 disdain] disdaine' *with* e *broken in H (correct in* $H¹$*)*
    10 troth] trouth $E+$
    11 Deceaud] Deceaued $B+$
    13 trap] trapt $BC$, trape $D$
    18 Somtime] Sometimes $HI$
    21 to] and $I$:    Calais] Calas $BC$, Cales $D+$
    22 furth] forth $BCD$, *om.* $E+$
    23 whilom] wilome $E+$
    24 his] this $D–H$

52. 28 somtime] sometimes *HI*
    30 hath] had *HI*
    31 me] be *I:*      alowd] alowed *CE+*
    33 After] Afteer *D:*      that] ẙ *F+:*      broke] broken *HI*
53. 12 all to] alto *HI:*      breake] breske *D*
    16 without] withought *F*
    19 be] to be *I*
    21 *Line om. in I:*      promised] promysd *D*
    23 can⌋ cau *B*
    31 me] mo *C,* my *D:*      you] yon *G*
54.  4 which] wich *EF*
    16 my] thy *HI*
    17 mynde] mindes *B+*
    19 faultes] fautlesse *D+*
    21 glosse] glose *F+*
    23 train] retayne *E+*
    28 eares] cares *B+*
    32 wet] wot *D*
    33 may] might *HI*
55.  2 haue] hane *F*
     3 of] to *I*
     5 Yet] Ye *E+:*      that] not *C+*
    12 doth] do *HI*
    15 apart] a part *H*
    32 ye] you *I*
56.  3 winne] winnne *B*
    14 fet] set *E*
    16 nere] neare *BCD,* ner *EF*
    30 praieth] ptaieth *B,* praith *F:*      to] *Om. BC*
    36 ye] it *HI*
    38 Nor] For *B+*
57.  2 fantasy] fantise *D*
     6 them] thym *G*
    12 your] your our *F*
    14 knowne] knowen *E+*
    15 ne] now *B+*
    16 lamenteth] lamenth *C*
    21 your] youu *I apparently*
    23 length] lenth *C*
    24 The] My *B+:*      sweltyng] swelling *F+*
    32 hounde] houud *I*
    34 which] wich *E*
    36 my] me *HI:*      band] hand *F+:*      payne] payue *G*
    37 crye] cree *D*
58. 11 euer] euery *B+*
    26 to] vnto *B+*
    31 rathe] rash *HI*
    40 lokes] looke *F+*
59.  8 Sith] Sins *C+*
    13-14 his seruice] their desired welfare *HI*
    17 crye] cdy *G*
    20 fare] feare *I*

59. 21 lenger] longer *I*
    22 wasteful] watchfull *HI:*     tried] trie *D*+
    25 auayle] u *curiously defective in A*
    27 by] but *I*
    28 *Line om. in HI*
    29 eat] cat *H*, catch *I*
    35 lenger] longer *I*
    36 thurst] thrust *D*
    39 They] the *I*
60. 5 had] hath *D*+:     geuen] giued *D*
    10 countenance] countnance *CI*
    13 haue] hane *I*
    23 againe] a gaine *G*
    24 nere] neree *H*
    26 to sone] tosone *A:*     gaine] game *HI*
    28 To] So *H*
    31 haue] hath *FG*
    32 Ainst] Against *C*+
    33 yelden] yelding *E*+
    34 in thy] thy *B*, by *C*+
61. 2 thee hath] hath the *HI*
    13 enmy] enemy *E*+:     of] to *F*+
    28 myne] my *HI*
    32 day] nay *B*+
    34 nay] day *B*
    36 I] y *F*
62. 2 Now] New *EFG:*     sheweth] shewed *G*+
    3 wondersly] wonderously *G*+
    4 may] my *D*+
    11 haue¹] hane *B perhaps*
    12 hath] now hath *BCE*+, now haue *D*
    23 eare] care *HI*
    37 Although] Althought *H*
63. 3 Vnquit] Vnquiet *HI'*
    5 witherd] withered *B*+
    7 Playning] P *broken in A*
    21 and] aud *D*
    23 wondrous] wondrous a *FG*, wonderous a *HI*
    30 louer describeth] louerdcscribeth *D*
    36 out] oue (*or* ouc) *D apparently:*     proper] *Om. B*+
    37 Thorow] Through *HI*
    38 Directly downe into] And downe directly to *B*+
64. 2 wherof] wereof *H*
    10 through out] thoroughout *FG*
    18 do] doth *HI*
    19 lead] feade *E–H*, seade *I*
    20 his] i *in a wrong font in A*
    22 loke] loooke *H*
    24 mayst] maiest *F*+
    25 doest] dost *BCD:*     madest] made *E*+
    26 mayst] mayest *E*+
    29 in my] *Om. HI*

65.  6 slake] slacke *I*
     7 my] me *I*
     28 With all] withall *HI*
     33 complayne] complaine' *H apparently*
     34 sought] sough *E*
     37 it] yet *HI*
     42 neuer] nener *D*
66.  3 Lea] Leo *CD:*      cared] carde *E+*
     9 me] my *G:*      that] thar *D:*      mought] might *HI*
     13 But] Be *I*
     15 description] pescription *E*, prescription *F+*
     16 he] *Om. HI*
     22 The] Her *B+*
     23 be] by *FG*
     26 quiet] quietnes *E+:*      his] *Om. B+*
     29 With doubtful loue that but increaseth pain *B+*
     30 And] For *B+*
     31 and] *Om. F+*
     32 sea] *Om. HI:*      mountaine] monntaine *G*
     33 Temis] Temmes *C+*
     34 his] her *EF*
67.  5 And] Aud *G*
     6 Any thing] One drop of *B+*
     11 that²] *Om. D+*
     14 is] his *BCD*
     16 playneth] plainth *BCD:*      that] that very *B+*
     17 Still] So styl *B+:*      displeasure] dispeasure *A*
     18 away] *Om. D+*
     19 doth] doe *I*
     24 offred] offered *HI*
     27 som] from *E+:*      peace] place *I*
     28 my] *Om. D*
     31 vaine] vame *D*
     34 chase] chafe *D+*
     36 he] *Om. I*
68.  5 the] *Om. HI*
     6 these] those *I:* vnmesurable] vnmiserable *HI*
     14 boystous] boystrous *DHI*, boisteous *EFG*
     26 thought] thoughe *H:*      distayned] disdayned *I*
     27 if] *Om. D+:*      sparkelyng] speaking *E+*
     31 continually] conti nually *A*
     33 burnyng a] burning *BC*, burnid *D*, burned *E+:*      and] and if *B+:*
        fresyng] fre syng *A*
     34 by] I by *B+:*      I stroy] destroy *B+*
69.  2 renouncing] nenouncing *I*
     5 lore] loue *F+*
     6 endeuer] endure *HI*
     10 scape] seape *H:*      leuer] lieffer *E+*
     12 me] time *D+*
     16 lenger] longer *F+*
     17 The] Tthe *D*
     18 vnkinde] vukinde *B*

69. 24 repayd after] repayed on $B+$
    25 is there] there is $B+$:  none] no $I$:  nother] other $B+$
70. 2 brest] briest $I$
    4 hartes] hart es $A$:  it] he $D+$:  fare] feare $D+$
    6 watred] shatered $D+$
    9 somthing] somtime $B+$:  is in] in the $D+$
    11 force] sore $E+$
    13 no²] ne $EF$, me $G+$
    16 that] which $D+$:  of] af $D$
    23 beat] a *blurred and broken in* $A$
    34 can] cand $C$
    35 From] Fram $E$
    36 vnhappe] owne happe $G+$
    37 ioy] foe $I$
    39 to moorne] *Om.* $HI$:  do] doth $HI$
    40 by] my $I$
71. 10 which] with $BC$:  pities] p *imperfect in* $A$
    12 lest] last $I$:  yet I] I yet $HI$
    18 by] my $D+$
    20 assaile] now assaile $B+$
    22 brest] briest $I$
    24 loue] louer $F+$
    27 succours] succoure $EG+$, succcour $F$
    28 fate] fat $I$
    32 wight] weight $I$
72. 2 mayst] mayest $F+$
    3 Some] So me $D$, So $F+$:  pleasant] pleasaut $I$
    9 hides] hies $B+$
    22 thoughtes] thougtes $D$:  that] the $HI$
    26 leese] lose $E+$
    31 Pheb⁹ $AD-H$:  spere] sphere $D+$
    33 bate] hate $F+$
    35 sprong] sproug $H$:  did] dit $D$:  leaue] loue $E$
    37 this] his $E+$
    38 encrease] enrrease $D$ *apparently*
    41 it] is $HI$
    43 feares] teares $D+$
73. 2 redresse] redreste $D$
    3 These] Those $B+$:  wherein] weerein $H$
    5 doth] doe $HI$
    6 sits] fits $F+$:  myne] my $D+$:  absent] absence $HI$
    9 of] that $B+$:  those] these $D+$:  to] doe $D+$
    11 that toucheth me so] so toucheth (touched $HI$) me $B+$
    14 thing] things $HI$
    20 yet] it $HI$:  so²] to $D+$
    21 or els] orels $A$
    29 case] ease $D$
    30 those²] these $D+$
    31 of] f *blurred badly in* $A$
    32 pleasant] pleasaut $I$
    34 vndiscrete] vndiscrcte $D$ *apparently*
    35 me fro] fro me $B+$:  ragged] raged $F+$

VARIANT READINGS AND MISPRINTS

73. 37 if] of *D–H*
    41 restyng] restling *HI*
    43 that] the *D+*
74.  3 grief] i *blurred in A*
    11 thus] this *D+*
    13 a teare] teares *HI*
    14 my present] present my *I*
    15 hart²] start *DE*
    19 Spite] Spiie *G*
    21 shalt thou] shall you *B+*
    24 mine] my *HI*
    26 mine] my *D+*
    29 to heare] to heare to heare *I*
    30 moue] mone *D+*
    33 throwne] throwen *H*
75.  4 thee] they *F+*:    hath] haue *G+*
     6 thy] thee *BCD*
    11 when] wen *C*
    14 Or els] Orels *A*
    24 cruelty] cruelly *D+*:    to] do *I*
    30 mine] my *FG*
    32 knowne] knowen *HI*
76. 13 professe] prefesse *I*
    19 troth] trouth *D+*
    23 length] lenght *H*
    31–35 *Speech tags* (Louer., Lady.) *trimmed away in A except for a few letters; present in B+*
    32 inflamde] inflamed *CG+*
77.  3 alas, with] and rew my *B+*
     5 two] to *F+*
     6 Thou] Tho *E*
     7 wouldst] wouldest *E+*:    maist] maiest *HI*
     8 thy] the *B+*
     9 wordes] word *HI*
    10 forgot.] forgot˙ *A*
    15 drieues] driuest *F+*
    16 wouldest] wouldst *D*
    17 out.] *Period doubtful in A*
    19 Lo.] *Perhaps* Lo, *in A:*    wastes] wasteth *E+*
    23 should] shall *HI*
    27 treasure] treasnre *A*
    30 purpose] purppse *C*
    33 haue] had *HI*
    36 chance] chauce *D:*    dedly] dredly *D+*
78.  2 furor] fnror *D*
     3 my minde] minde minde *H*
     5 What] When *HI*
    12 thy] the *F+*
    13, 14 doest ] dost *HI*
    22 his] hs *A*
    24 and] nnd *G*
    25 altred] altered *B+*:    thy] they *E*

[ 281 ]

78. 26 Sometime] Sometimes *HI:*    that] and *D+:*    drieues] driuest *F+*
    27 Sometime] Somettme *I:*    leadst] leadest *E+*
    28 subiectes] subiecte *HI*
    31 the same] thesame *A*
    34 chosen] chosed *HI*
    35 secretely] secertly *B*
    36 the fee] thee free *D+*
79. 2 my] my my *E*
    8 troth] trouth *E+*
    10 that] what *G+*
    13 finde] finde    *A apparently*
    19 craue] traue *EF*
    29 Against] Againe *EF*
    30 nede] dede *HI*
    34 dede] *Final* e *defective in A*
    35 eschange] exchange *I*
80. 2 Vulcane] Vvulcane *A*
    9 enmy] enemie *E+*
    13 fetrers] fetters *B+*
    14 weares] weare *EF*
    16 iudge] iuge *C:*    mine] my *CHI*
    24 but] bnt *G*
    29 Stond] Stande *D+*
    30 astate] estate *C+*
    32 toyes] ioyes *D+*
81. 5 to] do *C:*    hardly] yardly *E,* yarely *F–H,* yearely *I*
    6 knowen] knowne *E–H*
    7 vnknowen] vnknowne *E–H*
    11 in] is *G+*
    12 lordly] worldly *B–EG+,* wordly *F*
    13 ioynde] ioyned *E+*
    15 fettred] fettered *D+*
    18 Carthage] Charthage *D*
    21 aduance] auance *D+*
    22 that] that that *D*
    23 vnpossest] vnposess *B+:*    in] now in *B+*
    27 that] the *I:*    thy] the *I*
    29 temmes] temmmes *C*
    30 welthy] whelthy *E*
    31 Brutus] Brutes *D*
    32 leanes] leaues *E+*
82. 11 the] *Om. HI*
    13 brest] briest *I*
    16 Returne] Retourue *G*
    19 of one] one of *B*
    22 Poins] Peines *H*
    23 My] Ny *D*
    27 thought] tought *D:*    endured] endurd *FG*
    28 caue] cause *D*
    29 furrowes] furrous *D–H,* furours *I:*    swimmed] swemmed *G+*
    31 worse then] then woorse *E*
    34 For] For = *A apparently*

83.  8 quod] quoth *HI:*     a] *Om. I*
    11 doth] doe *HI*
    17 boyle] boyld *D+:*     on²] *Om. DI*
    21 this] the *HI:*     iape] scape *I*
    23 so] *Om. I*
    25 doth] do *C*
    27 scrapes] scarpes *B*
    32, 35 quod] quoth *HI*
    37 fare] feare *E+*
    42 fare] feare *E+*
84.  5 had] *Om. E+:*     her¹] *Om. D*
     7 whither] whether *E+*
     8 The] Thy *E–H*
    10 And] Aud *B*
    15 made] m *inverted in D*
    16 power] poore *E+*
    17 semyng] seking *B+*
    19 worst] worse *BCDG+*, warse *EF:*     they] the *GH*
    21 blindes] blindnes *I*
    22 in] *Om. HI*
    24 you] yee *E+:*     no¹] nor *I:*     no³] nor *E+*
    25 although] althought *E*
    26 hawbart] halbart *D*, hawlbert *I*
    29 delite] delits *B+*
    30 shalt] shal *GH*
    35 Nor] For *E+:*     his] a *B+*
    36 conies] coneis *DE*, counies *H* (connies *H¹*):     riuers] riuer *HI*
    37 an] a *G+*
    39 misseke] mislike *D+*
    40 thine] their *I*
    42 euer] neuer *B+*
85.  5 feele] finde *I*
     6 Madde] Made *B+:*     ye] you *I*
     8 your] thy *B+*
     9 Henceforth] Hencefurth *EFG*
    27 not] not that *B+*
    35 my] my my *H*
    41 nice] vice *BCD*, vile *E+*
86.  2 can not] canuot *I:*     set] seth *EFG*, seeth *HI*
     5 crouch] crutche *E+*
    11 as] *Om. E+*
    13 paint] paine *F+*
    18 Ceasar] Caesar *D*, Caeser *E*
    20 Ceasars] Caesars *DE:*     if] of *F+*
    24 singyng] singging *F*
    29 manifolde] many folde *E–H*
    30 Topas] Copas *E+*
    33 Grinne] Grine *D*, Grimme *HI*
    36 these] those *G:*     would] could *D*
    38 much] muh *E*
    42 fall] be fall *HI*
87.  2–3 *are repeated in A only*

[ 283 ]

87.   4 dronkennesse] dronekennesse *F:*     felowship] fellowshep *H*
    10 suffreth] suffereth *B+*
    12 rayleth] sayleth *E+:*    rechlesse] retchlesse *HI:*    ech] euery *I*
    15 the] *Om. D+:*    a] *Om. I*
    16 not²] no *DE*
    18 mayst] maiest *HI*
    22 to] *Om. D+:*    stalke] stalbe *E*
    27 ordred] ordered *HI*
    29 Fraunce] Fraunee *D apparently*
    30 savry] sauery *B+*
    32 to seme] beseeme *HI*
    34 Flaunders] Flandrers *D,* Flaundres *EFG:*    deme] dimme *HI*
    38 poyson] pryson *E+*
    42 thou] you *HI*

88.   4 Bryan] Btian *G*
    15 that] thar *H*
    18 doest] dost *I*
    19 mightest] mightst *CI:*    home] whome *EF*
    20 noppy] nappy *B+*
    22 swine] swines *E:*    groines] grones *DI*
    25 sound] souud *D*
    28 moysture] moyster *B+*
    29 and] aud *G*
    33 doest] dost *HI*
    36 so] *Om. G+*
    39 trouth] trauth *G*
    40 goeth] goth *EFG*

89.   2 vertue] verrue *D:*    goeth] goes *HI*
    3 language] launguage *E*
    4 the] thy *B+*
    6 thy] my *D*
    9 it] yet *EFG*
    10 By which returne] But if thou can *B+*
    13 stall] stale *HI:*    landes] land *F+:*    feese] fee *E+*
    14 into] in *HI*
    16 Sometime] Sometimes *I*
    21 purse] putse *G*
    25 charge] paine *B+:*    deburs] disburse *B+*
    26 riueld] riueled *E+*
    29 thee] thou *F+:*    mayest] mayst *C+*
    31 Whilst] Whilest *G+:*    thine] thy *BCHI*
    32 se] se that *B+*
    33 thy²] *Om. B+*
    36 Auaunce] Aduance *HI*
    37 turne] trane *E+:*    it] thou it *B+*
    38 ware] wary *F+*
    41 nice] nece *I*
    42 his] *Om. HI*
    43 beares] heares *E*

90.   4 should] would *G+*
    7 Should] Sould *H*
    12 thing] guift *B+*

90. 14 coyne] qoyne *D*, quoyne *E+*
17 wanderyng] wandring *BCDG+*
18 Iunos] Aunos *E*, Amos *F+:*      stormes] storme *HI:*      light] t *defective in A*
19 Atlas] Itlas *E+:*      taught] tau ht *D:*      lastyng] lesting *F+*
20 lockes] lookes *I:*      golden] holden *F+*
21 quod] quoth *HI:*      he] be *H*
23 Or] Of *D+:*      thus] this *I:*      power] poure *D*
24 Repungnant] Repugnant *B+:*      mids] midst *I:*      earth] yearth *D*
25 liuing thinges] liuinges *E+*
30 which] as which *D:*      therin] them *HI*
31 his] the *I*
32 continuall] contiuuall *D*, continnall *I*
35 tother] other *G+*
36 the¹] that *H*
37 drawen] drawne *E+:*      from] *Om. HI:*      to thother] from the other *HI*
38 Toucheth] Touching *DI:*      centre] centrie *I*
39 discriyde] describde *E+*
40 thother] the other *E+:*      hight] high *HI*
91. 2 so] lo *G+*
3 about] aboue *I*
4 earth] *Om. HI*
6 But] Bnt *D:*      bene] be *HI*
7 those²] the *E+*
9 So] Go *G+:*      that] the *HI:*      repungnant] repugnant *B+*
11 pore] power *I*
12 nine] mine *G+*
13 hundred] hundered *D*, hundereth *EF*, hundreth *G+*
15 hundred] hundreth *I:*      threscore] threeschore *H*
18 seuenth] seaueth *I*
19 gatherth] gathereth *D+:*      sly] flie *I*
21 almost] almofi *I apparently:*      sixtene] fifteene *I*
22 bowt] bouwghe *D*, bought *E+:*      starre] Starres *I:*      Saturne] Sature *I*
23 &] aud *D*
26 benigne] beninge *F+*
28 fift] sixt *HI*
31 her] he *B+*
32 gouernd] gouerned *E+*
33 for²] so *I*
34 that¹] y *G+*
35 the¹] *Om. HI:*      that] the *I*
39 twenty] twanty *C:*      dayes] dai s *D:*      and²] nnd *G*
41 ful] fnll *D:*      out] *Om. HI*
43 seueral] seneral *G*
92. 2 layed] layd *B+*
3 and] aud *G:*      rowndes] rounde *I*
6 to the] to *B+*
7 Although] Althongh *D*, Althought *H*
8 the] their *D+*

92. 10 But] Bnt *D*:   we] me *E+*:   well] wil *GH*:   also ] alo *G+*:
   these¹] the *E+*:   mouinges ] mouing *D+*
   11 about] aboue *D*
   12 to the] tothe *A*
   13 T.] S.T. *D+*
93. 2 –97.3 *in A only*
   31 or els] orels *A*
94. 10 in case] incase *A*
95. 37 yf you] *Apparently one word in A*
96. 8 Or els] Orels *A*
   12 no man] noman *A*
   23 weddyng ] *The period is doubtfully present in A*
97. 4 The Muses] Of the ix. Muses *B+*
   5 lo] to *I*
   9 Clio] Clion *C+*:   solem] solempne *G*:   old] all *B+*
   12 like] *Om. HI*
   14 eare] eares *F+*
   15 Terpsichor] Terpescor *D+*
   19 Polymnie] Polymine *D+*
   20 renkes] rankes *B+*
   22 ninefolde] ninefolds *HI*
   23 blastes] blestes *G+*:   Euterpe] Eutrepe *B–G*, Eutrope *HI*
   24 hence] hence my *D+*
   25 mids] myddes *EFG*:   sprite] spirit *HI*
   27 the] *Om. HI*
   28 forth] furth *D*
   30 saiyng] sayinges *F+*
   31 sustaine] snstaine *G*
   35 In] Iu *D*
   36 uoide] *The u, which should be v, is probably an inverted* n *in A*
98. 3 Endures, defacyng] Eudures (*correct in* G¹) defaciug *G*
   6 ylswading] ill vading *G+*
   7 renown] renewne *E*
   8–104.6 *in A only*
   20 in case] incase *A*
99. 4 In case] Incase *A*
   5 You] o *defective in A*
   7 in case] incase *A*
100. 28 foūd] foñd *A*
101. 2 fansiefourm] fanslefourm *A*
   29 no mans] nomans *A*
   36 feruent] ferueut *A*
102. 23 sober mood] sobermood *A*
103. 6 Right so] Rightso *A*
104. 9 thou] thon *B*:   yclad] I clad *HI*
   12 fare] rare *HI*
   13 Mindes] *Second letter (perhaps* y*) unreadable in D*
   19 auncient] anncient *I*
   21 either] euery *I*
   24 known] knowen *H*
   26 No] Fo *H*:   brand] braud *H*
   27 to] so *E+*:   soft] sought *HI*

104.  28 the same] thesame *A*
    29 Iulie] Iuly *E*+:    too much] toomuch *AB*
    30 Nero] Fero *HI*
    31 well] let *I*
    32 ouermeek] onermeek *A*
105.   2 goom] gut *D*+:    prayzd] prazed *D*+
    3 Stands] Stande *D*+:    in] is *E*+:    balance] baslance *I apparently:*
       payzd] payzed *E*+
    7 the tother] the tothers *G*, ther others *H*, the others *I*
    8 medcines] medicines *D*+:    in] to *I*
  11 vnmeasurable] n *inverted in D*
  14 What] Whhat *G (correct in G*¹*)*
  15 &] *Om. HI:*    bate] hate *F*+
  17 with] *Om. F*+:    ynough] yuough *G*
  21 maym] meime *F*+
  22 fond] founde *G:*    pincheth] pinched *G*+
  23 no] ny *DE*
  24 Metrodorus] Metrodotus *F*+
  26 WHat] WHHat *G:*    you²] yon *H*
  27 courts] courte *HI:*    encreased] encreaseth *F*+
  28 beak] breake *G*+
  33 thing] rhing *G (correct in G*¹*)*
  35 that] the *HI*
106.  2–8 *in A only*
  12 decayd] decayed *D–G*
  14 lust] lnst *H*
  19 Thy] The *D*+:    wil] *Om. HI*
  21 mayst] maiest *H*
  23 leef] left *G*+
  24 pattern] patter *HI*
  27 Yea] Ye *D*+:    mayst] mayest *H:*    founde] fouede *G*
  29 bitter] bittter *D:*    diuided] duuded *A apparently*
  30 O] Of *HI:*    sprite] spirit *HI*
  32 Scipio] Cipio *I*
  33 egall] equall *I*
  34 Gesippus] Gisippus *D*+
  35 Menetus] Menethus *D–H (with second* e *almost blurred out in D),*
      Menetbus *I*
  36 Nisus] Nisup *G*
107.  2 Pirith] Pirch *G*+
    3 dayes] dayys *E*
    4 Atticus] Articus *G*, Artichus *HI*
    5 lo dothe lott] lo doth *EF*, doth *G*+
    6 shalt] shall *I:*    there] here *I*
    7 fayled] faileth *I*
    8 rare] sare *G:*    be holden] beholden *E*
  11 sayth] saieth *FG:*    hee)] he() *B:*    frendship] frendships *D*+
  13 Next] Vext *C:*    frendful] frendly *D*+
  14–115. 7 *in A only*
  21 full] sull *A*
  37 Strength] Stength *A*
108.  28 no mo] nomo *A*

110.  18  in] iu *A*
     27  no dout] nodout *A*
     33  heauenly] heanenly *A*
111.   4  world] wor ld *A*
114.  18  too far] toofar *A:*    too much] toomuch *A*
115.   9  first] fierst *G*
     10  Alexander] Alexauder *G*
     11  Persians] Parsians *HI*
     12  Now] No *HI*
     13  taratantars] dredfull trompets *B+*
     14  shafts] shaft *E+:*    the] y̆ *HI*
     17  gnawing] knawing *G+*
     18  Macedoins] Macedons *D+*
     18  hide] byde *E+*
     21  Moyst] Most *HI:*    bebledd] be bledd *B–H:*    bate] bare *I*
     22  while] when *HI:*    giue] gaue *D+*
     23  lightning] lightening *B+:*    gleaus] glaues *F+*
     24  and] by *I*
     26  preserues] preserurs *H*
     27  could] should *D+*
     30  soweth] sowing *HI:*    kindes] kynde *B+:*    cruel] *Om. HI*
     31  ycutt] cut *I:*    lyeth] lieih *G*
     32  through] thorough *FG*
     33  down] smites *B+:*    beats] wounds *B–E,* woūdes the *F+*
     34  shinand] shinyng *B+*
116.   4  celestiall] eclestiall *H*
     5  meetyng] meung *HI*
     8  forwarned] forwarneth *HI:*    derth] death *E+*
     11  autum] atumne *C*
     12  Whether] Whither *EF*
     13  tunes] times *HI:*    heauens] heauenly *G+:*    harmony] armony *E–H:*    can] *Om. I*
     16  that] y̆ᵉ *F+*
     19  what] whath *E:*    opposition] apposition *E+*
     22  this] his *E+:*    hemisphere] heauensphere *D–F,* heauenly sphere *G+*
     24  had] hath *D+*
     25  Threatned] Threatened *I*
     26  Hee] Hr *H*
     27  heeʳ] *Om. E+*
     28  Macedoins] Macedons *D+*
     29  desirous] desrious *C*
     31  now] not *I*
     33  Alisanders] Alexanders *B+*
     34  other] another *HI*
     36  sayth] saieth *F+*
     37  mothers] mothes *EF:*    thy] the *HI*
     38  emong] among *B+*
     41  learnings] learning *G+:*    laude] lande *C apparently*
     42  Martiall] martall *D*
117.  2–3  *These lines are transposed in HI*
     4  soft] sought *HI:*    woords] workes *CD*

[ 288 ]

117.  10  Longgatherd] Long gathered *C+*:      soon] some *DE*
    15  deep] d *defective in D*, kepe *E+*:      Auern] Anerne *G (correct in G¹)*
    19  greaue] geeue *H*
    20  quishes] pusshes *G+*
    21  reyled] rayled *C*, trayled *D+*
    22  perceyuing] perceiued *G+*
    23  in] iu *D*
    25  turnd] turned *G+*:      the] his *B+*
    26  balefull] baltfull *F.*
    27  Macedonian] Macedoniam  *C*,  Macedonians  *D+*:      chieftanes]
        chiefe captaines *HI*
    29  renk] reuk *B–G*, ruke *HI*
    31  Wherwith] wherwich *G*
    36  wayld] wilde *E+*:      such] snch *G (correct in G¹)*
    38  Alisander] Alexander *B+*
    41  feeld] filde *F*, fildc *G*:      subdeewd] subdued *B+*
118.  3  same¹] *Om. HI*
    4  he] ht *G*, hi *H*, him *I*
    5  daughters] daughter *HI*
    6  and] aud *A*
    12  haplesse] hoples *HI*
    14  reskued] reskned *D*:      ciuil] euel *D+*:      ciuil swoord] *Both words*
        *somewhat obscured by broken type in A*
    15  Wilt] Wil *HI*:      mine] my *HI*
    18  speakyng] *The* a *did not print in A:*      no more] nomore *A*
    19  Room] Rome *B–EHI*
    20  hee washt] bewasht *HI*
    23  rough] cought *E+*:      floods] flood *D+*
    24  stowrs] showres *B+*
    30  prone] proue *B+ (correct in H¹)*
    34  They] The *G+*
    38  fone] sonne *F+*:      aknow] acknow *D+*
    39  drawn] drawen *DEHI*
    40  in] and *HI*
119.  2  preserud] preserued *E*:      Room] Rome *D+*
    3  thundryng] thundering *E+*
    4  eek] cek *A possibly*:      eyger] tyger *E+*
    8  attempt] *Om. D+*
    9  tharmed] tharmd *HI*:      had] hath *HI*
    11  Rooms] Romes *B+*
    12  sayth] sith *C*, sayeth *DEH*
    17  In] I *D*:      all] *Om. G+*:      the] *Om. HI:*  gaynstriue] ganstriue *G+*
    19  Room] Rome *D+*:      ynough] yuough *H*
    20  suffreth] suffered *HI*
    22  thofspring] the ofspring *B+*
    24  fayl] fall *DE*
    25, 29  Room] Rome *D+*
    26  fortune] fortude *H*
    27  Antonius] Antonlus *H*
    30  hoped] hooped *D*
    32  preparde] prepared *HI*:      vnmoued] vnmoude *HI*
    36  the] that *I*:      forth] furth *CFG*, first *HI*

119. 38 with] with his *HI*
    39 sayth] saieth *G:*    and] aud *D*
    41 fild] fielde *GH*
    43 also doth hee of] doth he of also *HI*
120.  4 lothly] lothy *B+*
    6 Grayes] Graces *E+:*    wept] wepe *E+*
    7 weep] pepe *D+*
    8 hertpersyng] her persing *D*, here percing *E+:*    Pitho] Picho *G+*
    9 suffisde] luffisd *HI*
    10 spake] speake *G+:*    soote] foode *D+*
    13 no more] nomore *A*
    14 and] aud *D*
    15 stock] flocke *I*
    20 quoth] quod *E+*
121.  1 Vncertain auctours *AI*] Songes and Sonnettes of/ vncertain auctours *BC*, and Sonettes. of/ vncertaiue auctours *D*, and Sonettes./ vncertain auctours *E–H*
    3 to his loue] *Om. HI*
    4 pitye.] *Period badly blurred in A*
    5 hartes] hart *F+*
    7 his] *Om. I*
    9 lodged] logde *E*, lodgd *F–H:*    him] *Om. I*
    20 hath] doth *I*
    22 arrowes] arrowe *E+*
    24 wist] wisht *H*
    28 moue] mone *D*
    31 sight] sigh *D*
    33 a] no *D*
    36 learned] learnd *I*
    37 hath] ẙ *F+*
    39 hath] hat *E*
122.  2 *Line almost split in two in A by the wrinkling of the paper in printing*
    4 consent] content *G+*
    11 fortunes] fortune *E–H*
    13 No] Nor *HI*
    14 cannōs] cānop *E*
    16 hole] whote *EF*
    19 Full oft] Full of it *E*
    22 the] thy *F+:*    here] her *B+*
    23 thee] to thee *HI*
    24 mayst] maiest *HI:*    see] seee *E:*    earthly] earthtly *F:*    where] were *E*
    29 long] *Om. E+*
    36 set] let *HI*
    37 Deuerox] Deuorox *B+*
    38 Ferres] Feres *HI*
123.  3 as] a *E–H*
    4 worldly] wordly *G*
    13 in] it in *H*
    14 serued] serude *C*
    17 enmies] enemies *E+*
    22 did] doth *I*

123. 24 Death] Daath *H*
    25 brought] brough *DH:*    geue] *Om. HI*
    27 to] and *I*
    28 meane] meaue *I*
    30 ouerronne] ouercome *G+*
    32 by] my *BCD*
    33 is] as *E+*
    34 God for] *Om. F+*
    35 lose] loses *D*, looses *E+*
124.  5 enmy] enemy *E+*
    23 theyr] the *HI*
    25 this] his *F+*
    27 The] That *E+*
    28 strange] strannge *H*
    29 conflict] coflict *H*
    36 daweth] dawneth *F+*
    37 mo] they *HI*
    39 makes] m *inverted in A*
125.  2 dure] durc *G¹*
    6 of] of df *G*
    7 know] bring *HI*
    8 *Line om. in HI:*    bring] know *C*
    10 spring] sprng *I*
    11 his] hts *D*
    20 Wherfore] Therfore *G+*
    21 dissolude] dissolued *EHI:*    fleshy] fleshly *B+*
    22 armed] armde *B+*
    23 souldiers] *Om. D+*
    31 had] hath *F+*
    32 it] *Om. HI*
    35 thought] thoughe *H:*    barbd] barbed *E+*
    36 armd] armed *E*
    37 Or els] Orels *A*
    38 wandering] wandring *G*
126.  3 moued] moud *F+*
    4 Whereon] r *blurred out in B:*    stayde] staied *E+:*    thought]
       though *H*
    7 scornd] scorned *D:*    taught] taugh *DH*
    9 vayn most] *Om. D+*
    10 nature] uature *H*
    11 lackt] lacke *G*
    14 featurde] featured *E+:*    shape] sshape *D*
    16 deckt] decke *D*, decked *E+*
    18 some time] sometimes *HI:*    in] iu *H*
    19 how] *Om. D:*    bleard] bleared *E*
    20 enflamde] inflamed *D-EG+:*    a] *Om. D*
    22 set the] setthe (*with second* t *inverted*) *D*
    23 dispayre] despite *F+*
    26 marlians] Marlian *F+*
    29 renderyng] rendring *G+*
    31 And] Aud *D:*    seased] ceased *HI*
    32 there] thcre *D apparently*

126. 33 to] t *blurred in D*
    36 this] my *D+*
127. 2 stat[e of]] stat (*with final* t *hardly legible*) *A*, state *B*
    3 this] his *E+:*    wisheth] wasteth *E+*
    4 lenger] longer *E+*
    11 the] th e *A*
    13 mery] merier *D+*
    22 louer] loner *I*
    24 caught] canght *D*
    26 you] ye *C+*
    32 My] Me *H:*    large] lare *H*
    33 gate] gates *I* (*H probably* gats)
128. 7 thought] thonght *G*
    9 hede] hid *H:*    tauntes] tanntes *A:*    nor] or *HI*
    11 scorned] scornde *B+*
    12 fraudes] fraud *HI*
    13 smiled] smilde *F+*
    14 begiled] begylde *F+*
    17 fed] fede *GH:*    the] ehe *G*
    19 And] Aud *A*
    20 beheld] behilde *GH:*    laught] langht *D*
    24 liue] lliue *H*
    25 wait] waitc *D apparently*
    29 as] that *HI*
    31 know] knew *HI*
    33 euen] *Om. D+*
    42 so] *Om. HI*
129. 9 Fortune] Fottune *B apparently*
    12 Where] Vhere *H*
    14 taste] take *D*
    17 paines] payne *E+*
    18 clime] climes *F+*
    19 auanceth] aduaunceth *I*
    22 no] n *inverted in D:*    as] so *HI*
    25 haue] hath *E+*
    28 Yet] Let *G+*
    29 as] a *D+*
    30 neither] neuer *HI:*    nor] uor *G*
    40 cause] causes *D+*
130. 9 eke] *Om. E+*
    11 slaundring] slaūdering *F+*
    13 sound] sonnd *I*
    15 hath] heath *E*, haue *HI*
    16 to] in *F+:*    ruine] ruen *G+*
    17 pluck] pluckt *H:*    right] *Om. HI:*    doe] *Om. D:*    enhaunce]
        enchaunce *BC*
    20 on] in *I*
    22 trust] *Initial* t *poorly impressed in A*
    22–23 *Title in B+ is* The louer dredding to moue his sute for (fcr *D ap-*
        *parently*) dout of deniall, accuseth all women of disdaine and fickle-
        nesse
    23 calamaties] *First* a *almost invisible in A*

130. 25 depe] dcepe *I*
    26 footing] foating *EF.*
    26–131. 12 *In E various words are mutilated, perhaps by a fold in the paper*
        *in printing*
    29 put] pnt *G*
    31 on] in *HI*
    35 his] hid *F*, her *I*
    36 beastes] beast *HI*
131. 2 eyes.] *In A the period is much below the line*
    4 frutefull] hatefull *I*
    6 yea] yet *G*+
    7 vnknowne] vnknowen *HI*
    8 ouerthrowne] ouerthrowene *G*+
    9 kept] keept *H*
    11 a] my *HI*
    12 spied] spred *B*+:     flaming] flamming *G*+
    13 tormenteth] tormenth *E*
    16 The] Thd *F*
    18 Plutoes] Plntoes *I*
    19 fiery] flery *H:*     that] thal *H*
    24 Promethus] Prometheus *E*+
    25 Vultures] Vulturnes *E*+:     strayned] st rayned *A*
    33 my¹] m *inverted in A*
    36 sodeinly] sodaiuely *H*
132. 6 Yet] Ye *D–H*, yea *I:*     poyson] prison *HI*
    8 swete] swette *E*
    11 straunge] strauuge *A*
    13 no] to *D*+:     lenger] lynger *G*+
    16 seen] see *D*+
    19 saw] say *DE*
    22 sport] spot *D*+
    23 dothe] did *G*+
    24 wherby] werby *DE*, whererby *H*
    27 mo] more *HI*
    28 wrought] brought *F*+
    31 which] wich *DE*
    33 Harpelus] Harpalus *B*+
    38 And] As *B*+
133. 2 Harpalus] Harpalaus *F:*     prayed] prayd *B*+
    3 paramour] paromour *H*
    4 Harpalus] Harpalaus *F*
    9 Harpelus] Harpalus *B*+
    10 ioye] toy *I*
    12 twine] twiue *H perhaps*
    13 garlandes] garlants *F*+
    14 Couslippes] Cowsleps *H*, Cowslops *I*
    22 fardest] farthest *D*+
    24 waxt] wax *E–H*, wart *I*
    25 clot] clod *D*+
    26 consumed] cousumed *G*
    28 be] ben *HI*
    31 spent] shent *D*+

133. 32 forewatched] forwatcht *E*, forwacht *F+*
   34 semde] semed *DG+*:     hatched] hatchte *F+*
   36 were] w *inverted in G*
   38 alwaies he] he alwaies *HI*:     ware] bare *I*
134.  2 Harpelus] Harpalus *B+*
   3 Vnhappiest] V *inverted in H*
   6 wentest] wentst *DE*, wenest *F+*
  10 for] *Om. HI*:     conuert] couuert *D*
  13 wouldst] wouldest *D–G*
  17 reapes] reapest *E+*
  19 herken] harke *B+*
  23 pasture] pastures *D*
  24 begylde] beguile *H*
  25 face] makes *B+*
  32 with] mith *H*
  35 Phillida] Philiday *D*
  38 it] *Om. E+*
  41 in] iu *D*
  42 shape] shappe *E*
135.  6 brest] brests *H*
  11 loued] loud *FG*
  14 Write] *In A the* W *is in a font more like lower than upper case*
  15 This] Thus *H*:     chance] chauuce *G*
  16 Here] Heee *D*:     Harpelus] Harpalus *HI*
  17 Whom] By *B+*:     cruell loue] cruell *H*, crueltie *I*:     hath] now *B+*
  18 By] Whom *B+*
  19 Murdred with false] Hath murdred (murdered *HI*) with *B+*
  23 Wilfords] Wildfordes *EFG*:     ysponne] esponne *D+*
  25 breke] breake of *D*
  28 though²] thong *GH*:     him] m *inverted in G*
  36 lenger] longer *F+*:     partes may] partesmay *A*
136.  4 step] stepte *B+*
  6 Brittons] Brutons *H*, Brutans *I*
  7 lende] leud *H* (*correct in H¹*)
  10 him self] himselefe *I*
  13 wandryng] wandering *HI*:     wordly] worldly *B+*
  18 For] Yet *C+*
  23 so that] that so *D*
  24 heape] help *HI*:     hordst] hordest *C*
  29 shell] wel *D+*
  34 liekt] like *G+*
  36 throng] through *D+*:     throwen] throwne *G*
137.  2 Lorde] lood *GH*
  3 appayre] appeare *HI*
  6 Where] Whei (*apparently with the* i *undotted*) *B*, When *C*:     there] *Om. I*
  10 which] wich *E*, with *F+*:     sayth] faith *F+*
  11 Knocke and] Knocked *EFHI*, Kuocked *G*
  13 wandryng] wandering *H*, wanderiug *I*
  15 wandryng] wandering *FHI*
  16 Shalbe] Salbe *D* (*with the* l *blurred*):     receiued] receyude *FI*

137. 20 lone] loue $B+$
     21 threatened] threatned $D+$
     23 fulfilde] fulfiled $E+$
     25 my²] *Om. DE*
     26 forth] furth *EFG*
     31 do] to *C*
     32 hast] hath $F+$
     33 sprite] spirite $G+$
     35 telleth] telleh *D*
     39 oft] of *E*
138.  2 their] the $G+$
      4 that] the *E:*    smit] smir *E apparently:*    the] that $E+$
     12 the wo] *A colon or a printer's lead is between these words in A*
     15 my] m *inverted in G*
     19 changed] changde *BD*, change *C*
     20 so] fo *F*
     29 may] might *HI*
     37 brest] briest *I*
     41 alone] a loue *E*
     43 me] my *HI:*    mone] moue *E*
139.  3 wandering] wandring *D*
      4 tied] tyde $D+$
      8 forthwithall] furth withall *DEF*
      9 lenger] longer $E+$
     12 a] on *HI*
     13 and] with $G+$
     16 blinded] blinnded *D*
     21 *Line om. in HI*
     23 yet] *Om.* $D+$
     25 yere] yeres *HI*
     29 had] haue *HI*
     30 did] dit *C*
     33 harme] heart *I*
     41 so] to *HI*
140.  5 shapen] shaken *D*
     17 From] For *I*
     18 strange] starnge *D*
     21 chiefest] chiest *A*, chefist *BC*
     24 suffred] suffered *HI*
     34 oft] of *E*
     36 state] seate *HI*
     39 my] mine *HI*
     42 would] wonld *G*
     43 ye] you *HI*
141.  2 wisht] wish *HI:*    might] may *HI*
      3 bitter] e *inverted in G*
      6 lingred] lyngered *EFHI*, lengered *G*
     12 times] time *D*
     15 wight] whight *I*
     19 must] wust *G*
     20 me] mo *G*
     32 was for] this was *I*

141.  33 Thus] Thns *G*
  34 those] these *E+*
  35 I meane, those] Those shining *B–FHI,* Those shynig *G*
142.   3 iudgement] iugement *C*
  19 happe] hoppe *G,* hope *HI*
  29 forth] furth *DE*
  30 hast] hah *G*
  34 thinkyng] thrnking *G*
  35 many folde] manifolde *D+*
  36 And] Aud *B:*  mannes] mans *HI*
143.   3 his] her *E+*
   4 not] uot *A*
   9 behestes] behest *E+*
  14 enemy] enmy *DEFG:*  my] myne *BE*
  15 Mishappe I meane] Cruell mishappe *B+*
  19 the] the the *I*
  22 gone] quite gone *B+*
  26 welth] which *HI*
  30–31 O brittle ioye, O welth vnstable:/ O fraile pleasure, O slidyng blisse *BC; D+ om.* O slidyng . . . pleasure
  32 he] they *HI*
  33 length] lengh *F*
  37 knowen] knowne *HI*
144.   3 That] The *HI:*  all] *Om. D,* in *E+*
   4 songen] longen *D*
   5 mischiefe] misehief *F*
   6 wofull] wofnl *D*
   9 sprites] spirites *F+*
  12 enmy] enemy *G+:*  my] this *B+*
  13 ender] enner *H*
  16 the²] thy *HI*
  34 foes] foer *EF*
  40 no] *Om. E*
  41 no] not *F+*
145.   5 word] world *I*
  12 the] that *I*
  15 inpreaseth] impreaseth *F+*
  17 nere] nerer *B+:*  bewty] *Om. D+*
  19 bloodlesse] bloudish *I*
  28 yet] *Om. HI*
  30 Alway] Alwayes *I*
  32 all] *Om. D+*
  33 ready] doon *BCD,* done *E+*
  34 wilfull] wilfnl *G*
146.   3 And] Aud *D:*  in] in a *I*
  16 neuer] set *B+*
  17 walke] wake *F*
  18 Although] althought *G*
  22 all] at *G*
  23 witte] witt e *A*
  27 makes] make *B*
  28 lye] liue *E+*

146. 32 Iames wilford] Iames wilford knight *B–G*, Iohn VVilford, Knight *HI*
  33 forlet] forset *E+*
  34 compast] compasse *G+*
  36 his life to traine] to end his life *B+*
147.  2 sith] such *D*
   7 praise] fame *B+*
  10 trouth] troth *HI*
  12–13 of of *A only*
  17 say nay²] *Om. E+*
  18 wilt] shalt *E+*
  19 *Line om. in E+*
  20 so] to *DG+:*  sware] sweare *D*
  27 my] m *inverted in C*
  30 which] that *HI:*  now] yet *B+:*  to] two *EFG*
  31 liuely] liuery *E*
  33 trouth] troth *HI*
  36 trouth] thouth *D*, troth *HI*
148.  3 diseased] diseasde *B+*
   7 well] wels *D*
   8 thinges] thinghes *E*
   9 Nor] Not *D:*  denide] denied *E+*
  10 loued] beloued *E+*
  14 sprite] spirite *HI*
  15 wellyng] wailing *D+*
  17 on] ou *D:*  feares] teares *HI*
  24 feares] teares *HI*
  25 the eares] theares *C*
  30 to] to his *E+*
  33 sonne] suune *I*
  35 masheth] masketh *F+*
149.  3 after] apter *D:*  paynes] paine is *B+*
   8 doth] t *blurred in B*
  11 much] mnch *C*
  12 Should] Sould *A:*  it] in *D+*
  13 whall] Whale *HI*
  14 graine] gayne *E+*
  16 thexpence] the expence *HI*
  18 do] doth *B+*
  19 know] knew *I*
  21 spirites] sprites *B–G*
  25 teares] teare *D+*
  26 plant] paint *I:*  brest] briest *I*
  37 so] lo *G+*
  39 me] my *D+:*  ioy] ioyes *I*
  40 not] uot *G*
  43 Who] Whose *EFG*
150.  2 ensigne] ensing *FG*
   4 I folde] yfold *F+*
   5 through] throught *EF:*  Through dread] Though dead *I*
   8 Student] studient (Student *HI*) that plaied fast or (and *C*) lose *B+*
   9 Student] Student *B–G:*  plast] placed *D+*
  17 ¶] *Om. B+:*  meane] meanest *I*

150. 20 flattering] flattring *CHI*
    22 good] goood *D*
    23 crocked] croked *CD*, crooked *E+*
    24 lest²] gest *EFG*, guest *HI*
    25 wines] wins *HI:*    both,] both' *G*
    27 waiteth on] walteth ou *D*
    28 sickernes] sickerues *C*
    33 betwixt] betwix *G*
    34 auance] aduaunce *I*
    36 blustring] blustering *C*

151. 3 haue] hath *C*
    6 batrid] batered *D+:*    eft] oft *I*
    7 stand] stode *D+:*    stoden] stode *C*
    15 hory] hoyry *GH*
    18 to] in *D*
    21 ben] be *F+*
    26 doth] do *G+*
    28 ¶] *Om. B+*
    31 be] is *E+*
    32 eke] the *E+*
    35 discrye] espy *D+*
    39 and] aud *A*

152. 2 vnnocht] vnnoct *FGH*, vnnockt *I:*    to] of *E+*
    4 he] that he *HI:*    se,] *Followed a blurred mark in A, possibly a comma*
    10 lōg] well *I:*    disges] disgest *HI*
    14 bondage] bondnge *B*, bonding *D+*
    15 furth] forth *B+:*    that] ỹ *G+*
    17 my] y *unreadable in D*
    23 a] the *F+*
    26 boisterous] boisteous *EFG*
    33 armies] armes *F+:*    fight] sight *HI:*    the²] this *E+*
    35 Taspayre] Taspyre *B–G*, T'aspire *H*, To aspire *I:*    troned] throned *E+*
    36 saws] lawes *E+*
    37 peruert] t *blurred out in E*
    38 whence] wence *F:*    mayst] maiest *I*
    39 wādring] wādering *EFG:*    take] taye *C*, toke *E+*

153. 2 rise] rayse *E+*
    7 nature] natute *B*
    12 worldly] wotldly *D:*    fade] vade *B+*
    13 no] ne *BCD*
    15 haue] hath *G+*
    21 Zepharus] Zephirus *DF+*, Zephirius *E:*    blustering] blustring *DHI*
    25 furth] forth *B+*
    26 The] Then *B+:*    empties] emties *E:*    Autumn] Antumne *D*, Autunm *I apparently*
    28 done] doe *HI:*    so] *Om. I*
    31 haue lost] lost haue *F+*
    33 doth] do *G+*
    35 thy¹] the *HI*
    37 the] them *GH*, thē *I*
    38 surged] sugred *BCDHI*, surgred *EF*

154.  3 Theseus] Thes eus *A:*      Periothous] Perithous *B*+
      9 her] on *G*
     10 darkened] darkned *BCG*
     13 storme] streame *B*+
     14 forth] furth *D*
     20 my] me *BC*
     24 burnyng] burinng *D*, burniug *G*
     25 darte] durst *G*+
     33 snare] smare *F*
     37 carefull] carefnll *D*

155.  3 So] Do *BC:*      fraile] r *defective and unrecognizable in B*
      7 choise] chose *G*
      9 No ragyng] Nor aging *C*
     12 doolfull] dolefull *D*+
     13 compasse] compaste *G*
     14 stormes] storme *D*
     15 and] aud *D*
     19 reue] rue *C:*      fro] from *B*+
     31 precious] pcecious *D:*      stone] stoune *I*
     32 wishe] wisht *C*
     37 lampe] lambe *F*+

156.  6 nor] or *F*+
      8 is] is a *F*+
      9 trouth] troth *HI*
     11 you] ye *HI:*      sey] say *D*+
     16 comes] come *FG*
     18 redier] ruddier *D*+
     24 dothe] dethe (*with the first* e *inverted*) *A apparently*
     32 as] so *HI*
     40 geue] geue. *or* geue, *possibly in A*
     42 euer] *Om. D*+

157.  3 for] for the *F*+
      6 fate full sore] fatefull sore *D*
      7 comes] come *HI*
      8 caste] call *F apparently*
      9 the^r] che *G*
     12 haue they] they haue *HI*
     16 liues] liuest *D*+
     17 Eschue] Escheu *F:*      best] besT *in B only, completing the acrostic;*
            *initial letters of 4–17 spaced in AB only:*      thatched] patched *E*+
     22 is] in *E*+
     23 vnknowen] vnknowne *D*+
     34 berent] becrent *F apparently*
     35 crauyng] caruing *BC*
     37 And] Aud *H:*      enemies] enmies *C*

158.  7 liueth vnder] liues vnder the *BC*, restes vnder the *D*+
     13 myne] my *I*
     16 ⁋] *Om. D*+
     19 his] of his *F*+
     21 like] licke *C*
     24 play] pray *B*+
     33 mayst] maiest *HI:*      may,] may' *H*

[ 299 ]

158. 34 mayst] mayest *I*
    36 the] *Om. B+*
159.  4 seke] *First* e *blotted out in B*
    5 state] estate *G+*
   15 guyse] gulfe *HI:*     vncertain] vncectaine *I*
   18 they] thy *E*
  20 gyde] guyded *E+:*     fettred] fettered *CD*, freted *F+*
  21 grenes] grenesse *B–GI*, grennesse *H*
  25 labour] labonr *G*
  31 that] the *E+*
  32 demde] deemed *GH*
  37 calde] clad *HI:*     of] to *E+*
160.  4 trained] trainde *C–GI*
    6 tornay] turnay *D+*
  10 now] *Om. E+*
  11 his] this *I*
  14 mislikt] misliekt *B*, mislyked *D*
  16 doth] did *HI*
  19 ygraue] ygraud *F*, ygraued *G+*
  20 hateth] hated *D+:*     vertues] vertuous *D+*
  21 plast] placed *D*
  24 groweth] growth *I*
  28 praise] ptaise *G*
  30 truth] trust *HI:*    haue] hath *C:*    tryed] tride *B+*
  33 hire] heire *G*
  36 death] vertue *D+*
161.  2 youthfull] youthfnll *H (correct in H¹)*
    5 graue] grant *H*
  11 amids] amidst *HI*
  19 will be] wilbe be *F:*    be] me *C*
  21 will not] not will *E*
  25 How] Hhw *A*
  28 you] yon *G*
  36 portrayed] protrayed *E–H*
  37 lo here] behold *B+*
162.  2 in] into *DF+*
    5 But] Bu *E*
    7 euer] neuer *EFG*
    9 strength] steength *D:*    remaines] remaine *B*
  13 whilst] whilest *C*
  14 the] that *E+:*    do²] doth *B–G*
  15 spirite] sprite *B–G*
  18 Here] Her *I*
  23 loued] loues *HI*
  28 touche] though *E+*
  32 you] ye *E+*
  34 The] This *C*
  36 lamenteth] lamenting *G+:*    therfore] thererefore *F*
163.  2 thing] thinges *DI*
  22 Lieth] Lyes *B+*
  27 restyng] relling *G*
  30 my] me *I*

163. 31 eyen] eye *E*+:     watry] waterie *I*
    34 they] the *I*
    36 Thassault] The assault *HI*
164.  4 battry] battery *D*:     such] *Blurred in C*
    9 souldiours] souldiou s *B*
    12 siluer] sliuer *B apparently*
    14 band] hand *E*+
    16 powder] poulder *H*
    17 the fort] thē forth *E*+
    20 spence] expence *HI*:     powder] poulder *H*:     spared sparde *B*,
        espared *G*
    24 to] co *H*
    27 vp set] set vp *I*
    28 walked] walke *E*, walken *H*, walking *I*
    30 desire] dasire *G*
    31 his] her *C*
    32 of] or *D*
    34 Then] The *DEFHI*:     pikes] pickes *FG*
    35 holbarders] holbardes *DEFH*,     holbordes *G*, Holberds *I*
    37 dims] dimps *D*+
    38 the] now *D*+
    41 graunt] geaunt *G*
    43 And] aud *G*
165.  3 yelded] yeldded *G*, yeeld *H*
    4 bad] had *HI*
    6 wilde] mylde *D*+:     fet] set *DEFHI*
    8 quoth] quod *D–G*
    9 Hath] Had *HI*:     you] yon *G*
    13 youe] your *B*+
    15 let] lit *G*
    21 thinkes] thinges *F*
    23 be] are *D*+
    27 clawed] clawde *C*+:     cowche] crowch *B*+
    29 bene] beeue *I*
    30 delight] dlight *I*
    35 youthly] youthfull *I*:     rime] tyme *D*+
    37 toyes] ioyes *G*+:     time] rime *F perhaps*
166.  2 hedge] lodge *D*+
    9 shrowdyng] shreding *G*+
    17 did] do *HI*
    24 bared] barehead *D*+
    33 none] no *HI*
    36 wentworthes] Ventworths *HI*
167.  3 wolden] woulded *E–H*
    4 forth] furth *EFG*:     foile] foly *E*+
    5 matcht] match *BCD*
    8 that²] they *G*+
    9 distain] disdaine *HI*
    10 deliueryng] deliuering *G*
    14 purposeth] pnrposeth *A*
    18 slepes] steepes *I*
    19 in] iu *G*:     me] time *I*

167. 24 vnconstantly] vnconstanly *D*
    25 swaruyng] swering *BC*
    26 oft] of *B–G*, off *HI*
    27 Without] Withouten *D:*      knowen] knowne *C–G*
    29 thy] my *E+*
    30 bough] bongh *G*
    31 nothing] neuer *E+*
    32 or] ere *G+:*     blossoms] dlosomes *GH:*    to] *Om. B+*
    34 Thy] The *HI*
    35 sugred] surgred *GH*
    38 caterpiller] cater piller *ABC*
168.  2 thy] the *C+*
    3 thy] the *G+:*    pretended] pretented *BCD*, pretenced *E+*
    4 thou] *In A the word looks like* th:u
    8 haue] hane *G*
    12 portrayd] portraied *GI*, protraide *H*
    13 there] thether *I*
    24 grekish] gregish *C*
    25 lost] st *out of line in A and blurred in C*
    26 louer] louet *F*
    30 bereft] better *C+*
    31 sowen] sowne *D+:*    for] from *I*
    32 raineles] ramless *H*
    33 want] whan *E+*
    34 water] waters *C–F*
    35 Chameleon] Thameleon *BC*, Chamelon *E–H*, Camelion *I*
    37 repulsed] tepulsed *B apparently*
169.  2 plea-] *A has a blurred period instead of a hyphen*
    5 shinyng] shinning *I:*    here] *Om. D+*
    7 through] though *C–H*
    16 tottryng] tottering *DI*
    17 depraueres] depraures *D*
    20 doest] dost *DEF*, doth *G+*
    21 of²] *Om. HI:*    Petrarke] Petrake *D*, Petrarche *E+*
    23 Petrarke] Petrarche *EFHI*, Petarche *G*
    27 bones] boues *C*
    29 lighted] lightned *G+*
    30, 32 forth] furth *D–G*
170.  3 ther was] therwas *A*, therc was *D:*    Laura] Laure *BC*
    4 petrarke] Petrache *E*, Petrarche *F+*
    5 petrark] Petrak *DH*, Petrarch *I*
    8 petrarke] Petrarche *E+*
    10 I wote] Iiwote *G:*    where] were *G:*    file.] file.. *A apparently*
    13 line] lime *GH*, limme *I:*    proporsion] provorsion *B apparently*
    18 liude] liued *DG+*, liuid *EF*
    23 and] *Om. B+*
    25 The] *Om. B+*
    26 To] *Om. B+:*    tickle] Trikle *BCD*
    27 thou] Thon *G:*    ruth] truth *C+*
    28 delph] delpth *I*
    29 The] *Om. B+:*    sacke] Sarke *E+*

170.  30  so causels] causels *B*, causeles *C*+
      31  plante] plaint *DF*+
      32  Darke] *Om. B*+
      33  carieth] cariest *B*+
      34  Cruelty] Cruely *E*
      35  stubberne] stubbornely *HI*
      36  to] *Om. E*+
      37  Solleyn] n *out of line in A*
171.   2  Solleyn] Swollen *D*+:      stony] stone *E*+
       6  very] all *B*+
       7  and¹] annd *D:*      craftinesse] craftin esse *A*
       8  willow] *Om. HI*
       9  withouten] without *B*+
      10  The] *Om. B*+
      13  haddest] hadst *D*, hast *E*+:      not] no *D*
      14  that] *Om. B*+
      15  might] mought *BCEFG*, mough *D*, might *HI*
      16  From] Fro *G*+:      out] out of *B–G*
      20  were] where *E*
      25  astate] estate *C*+
      29  worldly] wordly *F*, worly *G*
      32  care] carc *G*
      34  hart] hearth *E*
      38  our] her *I*
172.   3  worldly] wordli *F*, wordly *G*
       7  money] moneys *DF*+
       9  heauen] heaneu *G*
      10  worldly] wordly *FG*
      13  and] aud *I*
      16  my] *Om. E*+:      I] I do *G*+
      17  one] once *I:*      releue] reliue *G*
      19  sight] sighe *G*
      20  in] on *D*+
      21  paragon] Haragon *H*
      22  forsaken] fotsaken *I*
      23  or] or of *I*
      30  lenger] longer *I*
      31  you] yon *I*
      33  this] thus *D*+
      36  *B*+ *after 36 add six lines:*
              And shal my faith haue such refuse
              In dede and shall it so,
              Is ther no choise for me to chuse
              But must I leue [leane *H*] you [yon *F*] so?
              Alas pore woman then alas,
              A werye life hence must I pas.
      39  a] *Om. D*+
173.   2  heard her] her heard *C*
       7  sweare] swoare *G:*      loude] loued *B–FHI*, loeud *G*
       9  wight] weight *I*
      13  false] salse *A*

[ 303 ]

173. 17 betrayed] betrayde *D*+
    19 trouth] troth *CDHI:*    strongly] strougly *I:*    tayed] tyed *BC,*
        tyde *D*+
    20 Vntruth] Vntroth *I:*    alltotorne] al ro torne *G*
    22 alone] at one *GH*, at once *I*
174. 8 And] Aud *D:*    agree] agrce *G (correct in G¹)*
    10 is] his *C*
    12 It] At *C*
    15 If] I *C*
    17 lieth] lye *D*+
    19 faith] fitte *D*+:    knowne] knowen *I*
    20 It were to] At to were *C*
    24 hart] har *C*
    30 That] The *D*
    35 ruled] rulde *D*+
    37 iudge] iuge *C*
    38 easely] easly *C*
    39 shippes] ship *I*
175. 2 waxen] wax en *A*
    3 bondes] bond es *A*, boundes *E*
    6 kilth] kils *B*+:    brused] bruied *D apparently*
    7 a] *Om. E*
    8 whose] wose *F*
    11 sprete] spirit *HI*
    15 vertue hath] vtrtue hate *G*
    16 not] nor *HI*
    17 the] *Om. E*
    19 they²] the *F*
    22 serpentes] serpens *C*
    24 nature] natures *G*
    28 nature²] natures *EF:*    our] ou *E:*    lyues] luies *B apparently*
    36 my] *Om. D*
176. 3 blinde] bliude *I*
    4 my] thy *G*+
    5 chaunce] chaunces *GH*
    11 forth] furth *D–G*
    15, 18 chiefe] chiefest *G*+
    25 mischance] mischunce *G*
    31 you] yon *A*
    36 that] thet *G:*    auaunce] aduance *DEFHI*
    37 to] *Om. F*
    38 faithfull] faithfnll *I:*    vertues] vertnes *B*
177. 14 pouertie] prouertie *EF*
    20 frendes] friend *I*
    22 And] Aad *A*
    23 sich] such *B*+
    27 orecome] ouercome *I*
    29 caused] causde *B*+
    30 my] me *E*
    36 growen] growne *H*
    38 honorde] honored *G*+
178. 14 him] he *I*

178. 15 knowen] known *B–H:*      power] powet *H*
     17 worldly] worthy *D*, wordly *FG*
     27 god wot] godwot *A*
     30 Euen] Enen *I*
     32 into] into my *I*
     33 did] do *G+*
     34 binde] blind *G+*
179. 6 flowring] florishing *D+:*      heart] beart *G*
     10 by] my *G+*
     16 eye,] eye' *D*
     17 the fauour or the spite] fauour or despite *B+*
     24 golden] golded *H*
     29 sore] ore *F*
     31 of] *Om. HI*
     32 when that] $\overset{t}{y}$ when *G+*
180. 2 *An old hand in C has crossed out the entire poem (cf. 181.34)*
     4 Tho] The *B+*
     5 eares] cares *E*, eare *I*
     6 them] *Om. HI*
     7 valiance] valance *DE*, variance *I:*      cease] crase *EF*
     8 vnknowen] vnknowne *GH*
     9 apaled] appalled *D+*
     10 wandryng] wandering *EFHI:*      trustlesse] tristles *HI*
     11 fele] sele *EF*, sell *G+:*      to] so *HI*
     16 trouth] troth *E+:*      manly] malice *F+*
     17 chaunce] chauuce *G*
     20 Though] Thuoghe *E*
     26 it] *Om. F+*
     29 lengest] longest *F+:*      dothe] do *D+*
     30 And] Aud *I*
     32 framed] framde *D+*
     33 cannot] tannot *G*
     34–35 An answere of comfort *B+*
181. 7 sailes] saile *E+*
     8 she] sshe *D*
     11 That] Tat *D*
     12 Achilles] Archilles *GH*
     13 maist] maiest *HI*
     14 stormes] storme *F*
     19 gins] giues *I:*      to] do *E*
     21 thy] my *G+*
     27 moneth] month *D+*
     29 mo] more *D:*      paynes] paine *EF*, paineth *G+*
     30 Thestilis] Thistilis *DGH*
     32 and] aud *D*
     33 where] were *B*
     34 of] of of *B:*      *poem crossed out in C (cf. 180.2)*
     36 Lyke] Llyke *F*
182. 6 they] thy *G:*      and] aud *I*
     17 waile,] waile' *G*
     21 to] so *HI*
     24 he] that he *G+*

182.  39 spied] spide *B+*
183.   6 whit] white *I*
       8 quit] quite *F+*
       9 iudgement] iugement *C*
      15 but] bnt *D*
      16 laught] laugh *CEI*
      17 is] a *I*
      24 bode] boode *D*
      25 her] here *G+:*      stories] story *G+*
      29 and] aud *D*
      30 altred] altered *D+*
      33 turned] turnde *B–F*
      37 in] iu *G*
184.   3 secretely] seretely *A*
       8 her²] the *I*
       9 to] co *H:*      throbbe] shrobbe *G+*
      10 fansyes] fansie *I*
      14 shiftes] shitftes *I*
      19 that] he *F+*
      20 Pryams] Prians *G*
      21 And] aud *G:*      commen] common *H:*      the] thei (*with* i *inverted*) *G*
      22 her] were *FG*, was *HI*
      23 shee] he *I*
      35 full] for *F+*
      37 she] was she *E+*
185.   3 so] to *F–H*
       5 seruice] sernice *I*
       7 the] that *HI*
      14 well] *Om. HI*
      16 commen] common *D*
      19 her] his *F+:*      seruaunt] au *blurred out of E*
      22 you] yon *D:*      slake] slacke *G+*
      24 as] a *I*
      25 Troylus] Troylous *I*
      28 prese] praise *I:*   &] aud *D*
      30 For] Gor *C:*      climyng] climming *E+:*      ticklenesse] ficklenes *E+*
      34 trouth] troth *I*
      35 eche] ach *HI*
      39 not] uot *D:*      crocke] crcoke *A*, croke *FG*, crooke *HI*
186.   3 trouth] troth *I*
       4 in] it in *E+*
       5 axith] asketh *B+*
       7 forth] forth, forth *BC*
       9 and] and and *D*, an *I*
      11 deter] *No hyphen in A*
      16 fight] sight *GI*
      17 approched] approchd *FG*
      19 flight] fiight *A apparently*
      21 For] From *G+*
      22 londe] lande *D+*
      24 did] hath *HI:*      charged] chardg *F+*
      25 eare] eares *HI:*      might] may *HI*

186. 27 brest] briest *I*
    28 didest] didst *B+*
    32 furththrowe] forththrow *B–H*, forth through *I*
    34 she] *Om. G+*
    35 wight] whight *EF:*    yet] it *HI*
    37 what] *Om. HI:*    delay] decay *G+*
    38 oft] still *HI*
187.  2 the] *Om. F+*
     3 paines] *Perhaps followed by a broken comma in A:*    brest] briest *I*
     7 The] She *H*
   10 brest] briest *I*
   11 gnawe] knaw *FG*
   13 dothe] do *G+*
   15 matter] matters *HI*
   18 goeth] goe *I*
   20 turneth] turned *E+*
   21 yeldeth] eldeth *HI*
   22 Though] Thus *I*
   23 both] doth *B+*
   24 sprites] spirits *F+*
   25 clacke] clarke *BDE:*    eare] eares *I*
   26 sparckes] parkes *E+*
   27 flames] games *F+:*    dothe] do *B+*
   28 did] do *I*
   35 whele] wele *GH:*    dothe] do *HI*
188.  4 aside] asside *G*
     5 Was] Whose *I*
     7 and] and his *E+:*    defide] deade *E+*
     9 on] od *F+*
   12 base] basse *G+*
   13 swan] swast *I*
   14 taccoye] taccoe *C*, toccoy *G+*
   15 vnwrinckled] vnwricckled *HI*
   16 Suffreth] Suffereth *HI:*    his] the *I:*    lepeth] lepte *D+*
   17 the seas] heseas *D (t blurred out)*
   20 Such] Susch *E*
   21 paynes] paine *I*
   24 or] as *HI*
   27 beside] besides *HI*
   29 Nor] No *HI*
   30 Nor] No *G+:*    warer] water *F+:*    game] gaine *E+*
   31 scholeman] seholeman *D:*    fansy] fantasie *E+*
   32 Then] The *I:*    these] those *G+*
   34 alway] alwaies *HI*
   35 ẙ] ỹ *B+ (and so possibly A itself)*
   36 wonderous] wondrous *H*
   37 What] W *blurred out in A*
189.  2 stale] state *E+*
     3 herauld] he told *I*
     4 part] pact *HI*
     5 countinaunce] rountenaunce *G*
     6 hers] her *HI*

189.   7 mistrust] mistrnst *G*
      10 makes] make *G*+:      secretayr] secretarie *G*+
      11 And] Aud *D*
      14 craftye] craft ye *A*
      15 larme] larum *D*
      16 that] y̆ *HI (and perhaps G)*
      17 they¹] the *I:*      then] them *F*+
      21 borde] brode *D*
      22 catche] cacth *H*
      25 An answer in (iu *D*) the behalfe of a woman of an vncertain aucthor *B*+
      26 giltlesse] guitlesse *H*
      28 list ] ist *blurred out in B*
      32 stere] stir *HI*
      35 can] could *HI*
      36 giftes] gifces *D apparently:*      the] they *FG*
      39 can] cam *D*
190.   2 flamyng] flamming *G*
      3 ioynde] ioined *DE*
      4 The] Thē *C*+
      5 I] *Om. HI:*      may²] may right *I:*      safely] falsly *EFGH,* plainely *I*
      10 fearth] feareth *B*+
      11 As] A *E*+:      frette] frete *BEFG,* freete *D,* freate *CHI*
      12 fast] sast *D*
      15 For] Nor *HI:*      nor] no *E*
      17 or] and *B*+
      22 he] *Om. B*+:      be] be and be *HI*
      23 or] and *HI*
      26 Diane] Diana *G*+
      29 hast] haste *EFG:*      lied] lide *B*+
      32 broken] brokeu *D*
      33 doste] doeste *D*
      34 may] might *E*+
      35 in] *Om. G*+
      36 marke] make *I*
      37 of¹] in *I:*      dedes] dede *B*+
      38 layd] layed *D*
191.   2 hid] did *G*+:      suger] sugred *I*
      4 Collatiue] Collatine *D*+
      6 Cartage] Carthage *E*+:      fordid] forbid *HI*
      7 R. so depe can auoyde] Rodopeian maide *B*+
      9 crokest] crokst *D–G,* crocks *HI:*      agaynst] againe *G*+
      12 noyce] voice *HI*
      15 yrkesome] yeeksome *H:*      wormes] wormms *FG:*      crepe] crye *E*+
      16 shouldest] sholdst *E*+
      19 a] *Om. HI*
      25 treade] trade *E*+
      26 I²] *Om. B*+
      28 Boast] oa *defective in A:*      thine] thy *HI*
      35 prickt] pricke *D*
      42 furst] fiest *D:*      floorist] floorisht *B*+
      43 the] thy *B*+
192.   2 spotted] spottted *D*

192.　4 shamefall] shamefull *B+*
　　　6 their] thy *H*, the *I*
　　　7 Vntrue] Vntrrue *I*
　　　8 we] *Om. E+*
　　12 Ryce] R. *B+*
　　13 thundryng] thundering *I*
　　14 had] hath *B+*
　　15 To] The *G+:*　　what] was *HI*
　　19 arowe] a howe *H:*　　assemble] assemblie *D+*
　　20 or¹] and *HI*
　　21 solemne] solembe *H*, solempne *I:*　　silence] silenee *G*
　　25 began] begau *H*
　　27 prease] pase *C*
　　28 common] commmon *D*
　　30 with] wiih *G*
　　32 praise] e *blurred out in A*
　　34 The . . . same] The noise did cease, the hall was stil *B+:*　　whusht]
　　　　whust *E+*
　　35 finenesse] sinenesse *C perhaps:*　　trainyng] trainig *I:*　　that] the *I*
　　36 tonges] tonge *B+*
　　37 wantonnesse] watonnesse *D*, wantounes *I*
　　38 plumes] l *inverted in G*, prumes *H*
　　39 curiousnesse] curioulnesse *I apparently*
193.　3 reason] reasou *I:*　　appesde] appeased *E+*
　　　4 for] or *B:*　　and] aud *I*
　　　5 be by] by the *I*
　　　8 mastreth] mastereth *HI:*　　vertue] vtue *E*
　　12 she] he *E+*
　　13 preace] praise *I*
　　14 of²] a *G+*
　　17 quod] quoth *I:*　　Lucrece] Lucres *E+*
　　18 excepted] accepted *D+:*　　praise] loue *I*
　　19 lenger] longer *I*
　　20 That, eckow] ha *and* ck *are torn out of B:*　　sowning] swoning *F+:*
　　　　through] thorough *H*
　　21 Rise] R. *B+*
　　22 Thy] The *HI:*　　fame] same *EFG*
　　23 heard] h *torn in B:*　　maistres] maisters *G*
　　28 Thy] the *F+*
　　29 slaunder] sclauunder *G*
　　30 know] kow *D*
　　31 wrought] taught *HI*
　　33 haue] hath *F+*
　　35 thy] by *C+*
　　37 entend] ented *D*
　　38 Minerua] Minyrua *H*
　　39 and] aud *D:*　　hath] haue *I*
194.　2 their] the *E+*
　　　5 hide] hede *D+:*　　vertue] vertues *I*
　　　9 boisteous] boisterous *D+*
　　11 setled] suttle *E+*
　　15 death] dearh *D:*　　county] countisse *B+*

[ 309 ]

194. 19 pay] pray *E*+
    20 ioyfull] ioyfil *D*
    22 merite] merits *HI*
    24 laied] laide *C*+:    to] fo *G*
    25 a] *Om. HI*:    womanhed] womanhod *D*
    29 learnyng framed] fearning, ramed *H*, learning, ramed *I*
    30 willed] willled *E:*    her] here *EFG*
    32 furtherance] furderance *HI:*    chuse] chose *E*+
    33 heauens] heauen *HI*
    34 Because] By cæuse *E*
    35 And] Aud *D:*    though] sought *G:*    *By a curious error HI have here,*
        And sought her selfe to heauen hence be refte.
        And sought her selfe to heauen hence did passe.
    38 And] Add *D*
195. 5 doste] doth *G*+
    6 or] of *I:*    of²] or *B*+
    9 yron] yrou *D*
    10 with] by *I*
    15 doth] do *H*
    19 enmies] enemies *B*+
    21 fame] flame *D*
    22 encreaseth] encceaseth *A:*    with] *Om. E*+
    23 heare] her *G*+
    27 so] *Om. HI*
    28 if] *Om. HI*
    30 wight] weight *D*
    31 that] the *HI*
    32 Vnwise] Wnwise *H:*    seke] se *D:*    may] way *I*
    36 greater] great *I*
    37 he] here he *HI:*    him self] him himselfe *E*+
196. 3 Nor] Not *GHI*
    5 Whose] Wose *F:*    fathers] father *HI*
    7 my] in *E*+
    8 Descripcion] Descriptiou *I*
    10 in] in perfect *I*
    11 semeth wōderous] seme right wōdrous *B*+
    14 flatteryng] flattring *D–G:*    amongs] among *HI*
    15 deceite] dyspite *HI*
    17 vnspied] vnspide *B*+
    18 sute] suites *HI*
    19 slippry] slippery *C*+
    20 bolstrynge] bolstering *D*
    21 embraced] embrast *G*+
    22 to] to such *HI*
    25 hearde] beard *H*
    26 stirryng] sturriug *D*
    27 to] do *E*+
    29 silence] scilence *FGH*
    35 worldly] wordly *FG*
    37 speake] speakes *GH:*    truth] troth *I*
    39 mens] two *HI*

197.   3 thinkes] thinke *G*+
     4 which] that *G*+
     5 carefull] carefnl *G*
     6 amonges] amongest *FG*, amongst *H*, among *I*
    12 are] is *I*
    13 do] doth *FG*
    15 starres] starre *FG*, stares *H:*    may] wil *E*+:    strike] cast *E*+
    17 so] *Om. HI:*    on] on the *I*
    20 seke] scke *D apparently*
    22 spirite] sprite *D*+
    25 flattering] flattring *CEF*
    26 In fine] I find *E*+
    27 that] $\overset{e}{y}$ *G*
    33 may we] we may *I*
    35 wethered] withered *B*+
    37 playd] played *EFG:*    shalbe] wylbe *D*+
    40 that] $\overset{e}{y}$ *G*
    41 bringes] bring *HI:*    forth] furth *CD:*    many] may *I*
    42 present] preseut *D*
    43 worldly] wordly *FG:*    cares] care *C*+
198.   2 that] y *G:*    medleth] meddeleth *HI:*    selfe] sesfe *A*
    8 Thine] Thnie *H:*    quod] quoth *HI:*    brought] thought *F*+
    10 Enforceth] Enforce *GH*, Enforced *I*
    12 walkt] walke *D*+
    27 wofull] *Om. HI*
    30 doest] dost *BCDHI*
    38 lockt] locke *D*
199.   2 assignes] assigned *E–H*, assinde *HI*
    3 Ioie] Ioee *A*
    4 maister] M. *HI*
    6 worldly] wordly *H:*    mede] ende *C*+
    9 from¹] for *B*+:    from²] r *broken in A*
    10 last] *A may have* sast:    that] $\overset{e}{y}$ *F*
    14 crimes] trimes *I apparently*
    15 alway] alwaies *F*+
    17 fo] to *E–H*
    18 here] her *G*, vs *HI*
    22 vnharmed] warmed *E*+:    helth] hclth *Á apparently*
    23 our] a *B*+:    do] doth *HI*
    27 hast] *Om. B*+
    28 sonne] sonue *G:*    Iohn] Iohan *G*
    32 this] his *E*+
    33 spirite] sprite *C–G*
    37 While erst] Whilist *BC*, whylest *D*+
200.   5 grounde] gounde *A*
    7 As] a *F*
    9 for] of *I*
    10 so faire] sofaire *A*, were faire *B*+
    12 neare] neare, and *B*+
    14 chaunge] channge *D:*    had] hath *I:*    tride] tried *B*+
    15 to] for to *HI*
    18 as] a *G*+

200. 22 flering] fliering *D–G*
 27 vaunt] want *E*+
 29 meant] meane *E*+
 30–32 written . . . graue] made by w. G. lying on his death bed, to be (de *D*) set vpon his owne tombe *B*+
 37 through] thorough *EF*
201.  5 they] the *E*
  6 is] i *obliterated in A*
 17 to] *Om. D*
 18 mad] made *G*+
 20 blist] blisse *G*+
 22 so] sd *I*
 25 lenger] longer *B*+
 27 lenger] longer *F*+
 31 ye be] be ye *G*+: sonder] snnder *G apparently*
 32 can] cad *A*
202.  4 had] *Om. HI*
 10 yll] *Om. HI*
 16 though] thought *E*
 19 change] chaunce *E*+: chanced] canced *C*
 24 frute] rote *B*, roote *C*+
 28 buildyngs] buildyng *B*+
 29 good] godd *G*
 30 my] me *HI*
203.  3 hart] har *G:* true] tuue *F apparently*
  4 this] his *EFG*, is *HI:* vnright] vpright *HI*
  5 surprised] surpressed *HI*
  9 she] forth *B*+
 11 to] so *FGH:* sene] see *D*+: her] *Om. D*
 13 Vprist] Vprest *HI:* thrustyng] thursting *E*+
 14 no] to *E*+
 16 alway] alwaies *HI*
 17 rites] rightes *F*+
 20 wrechedest] wretchedst *B*+: am] am I *H*
 22 myne] my *B*+
 23 That] tthat *G*
 24 that] *Om. B*+
 26 *Line om. in E*+
 27 thinke] thiuk *H*
 29 Description] Descreption *F*
 32 That nature hath with gold and purple drest *B*+
 36 that] y̔ͤ *F*+
204.  3 browes] bowes *E*+: iustly] iusty *D:* pight] plight *I*
  4 polisht] *Om. B*+: Saphires] Saphers *F*+
  5 glistryng] glistering *DHI:* lightes] light *F*+
  7 excede] excedes *G*+
 11 iust] full *E*+
 15 theᴵ ] ihe *D*
 17 shouldst] shouldest *G*+
 18 doest] dost *C*+
 19 Here] her *G*
 20 wight] weight *I*

204. 23–26 to . . . grounde] *Om. B*+
    28 oft] of *E*+
    29 breathes] breates *E*+:    brest] briest *I*
    30 within] wtthin *D*
    31 plaine] paine *I*
    33 Not] Nor *I:*    tricklyng] tricking *GH*
    34 Not] Nor *I*
    35 Not] Nor *G*+
    36 glistring] glistering *DH*
205. 4 enuies] enuious *C:*    humor] humors *I:* conduites] condntes *I*
    5 Oft] Ofr *D*
    6 distreined] distreinde *C*+
    7 toll] toyle *I*
    8 silly] sile *H*
    10 sayth] saieth *FGH,* sayles *I:*    dread] draw *I*
    12 moued] moud *F*+
    16 loue] Ioue *I:*    cloked] clothed *D*+
    17 lesson] lessor *AE*
    18 we] ye *HI:*    no] to *F*+
    19 light] lihgt *G*
    21 do] doth *G*+:    mouse] moule *E:*    sample] samply *BC*
    23 so] to *D*
206. 1–2 *in A only*
    7 mine] my *G*+
    11 draue] drawe *D:*    Borias] Boreas *D*+
    14 winters] winter *HI*
    18 thinges] thing *EFG*
    26 the] t *obliterated in D*
    29–30 Of the same *B*+
    31 the] thr *D*
    34 Wende] Weud *C apparently:*    temples] temple *E*+
    35 yet no] it on *HI*
207. 3 deterre] deferre *E*+
    4 our] her *G*+
    7 employd] employed *D*+
    11 ⟨⟨⟩ *Om. B*+
    11–12 Surrey] Surreie *EF*
    12 by] to *D*
    20 praunced] prauncd *FG,* pranncd *H,* pranned *I*
    25 aduance] auance *D–G*
    26 her feete] herfeete *A*
    29 sene] none *I*
    30 welnere] well nie *HI*
    32 knowen] knowne *HI*
    35 mayst] maiest *BH*
208. 2 you] yon *H*
    7 noble] nobles *HI*
    9 blood] blooud *E*
    11 in] for *HI*
    14 likewise] so dyed *B*+
    16 Other] O *blurred out of D*
    21 to] *Om. D*

208. 24 fled] fed *E+*
    28 wist] wish *HI*
    29 with] wich *F apparently*
    31 should] would *B+*
    32 that] which *HI*
    38 ruse] rue *B+*
    39 This] Thus *B+:*    bode] bote *BCE+*, boote *D:*    ne] no *B+*
    41 I¹] A *B+*
    43 fed] feed *H*
209. 3 ye] you *CHI:*    sailes] saile *F+*
    5 thirst] thrist *D*
    9 bootes] botes *E–H:*    not] nat *E*
    10 The] ¶ The *C*
    12 recomforteth] recomforted *HI*
    16 I not] not I *BCD*
    17 amongest] amongst *B–G*
    19 haue] hath *C+*
    21 and] aud *G:*    serue] serues *B+*
    22 and] aud *B*
    23 doth so] so doth *EFG*
    26 teares] yeares *GH:*    it] *Unrecognizable in D*
    30 in] iu *H:*    my] mine *HI*
    31 sound] soun *D*
210. 2 colde] could *E+*
    3 self] selues *HI*
    4 do] dooth *HI*
    5 brede] bred *H*
    7 goddesse] goddes *H*
    10 bewties] bewtie *HI*
    11 louely] lyuely *E+:*    looke] looks *HI*
    13 smiled] smylde *E+*
    14 riueth] rueth *E+*
    18 then] when *E+:*    thinke] th nke *D*
    21 desirde] desyre *F+:*    tie] trye *E+*
    22 an] and *C+*
    23 is] in *G+:*    waue] wane *G:*    when] where *HI*
    24 watry] watery *B+*
    25 clene] eleane *F*
    27 the] that *F+*
    28 care] cars *H*, cares *I*
    29 eche] *Om. HI*
    32 And] Aud *D*
    33 Ye] yea *FGH*
    34 feble] dedly *E+*
    35 kepe] kept *E+*
    37 I do] Ado *D*
    38 Finis] *Om. B+*
211. 2–3 *in A only*
    4 called.] called *B+*
    6 that²] *Om. I*
    7 turned] turnde *C+*
    15 thornes] thrones *B:*    kene] kyne *E–H*

211.  30 take] takes $G+$
212.   5 ought] ough $F$:      helpthe] helpth $B$, helpeth $C+$
      10 the] *Om. HI*
      15 wyll] well $H$
      17 thy] thyne $B+$
      18 Thylee] Thisce $HI$
      19 the] thy $HI$
      21 meued] moued $D+$
      22 thy[1]] the $HI$
      23 heauen] heanen $A$
      26 thou may] may thou $B+$
      29 Vnto] V *inverted in H:*      thirst] thrist $G$:      it] *Om. EFG*, neuer $HI$
      32 thy[1]] thy thy $D$
      34 Thy] The $HI$
213.   1 Son[ett]es] *Torn in A*
       9 to] tho $E$, the $F+$:      chose] choise $I$
      10 which] wich $E$
      11 should] shoule $E$
      13 mischiefe[1,2]] michief $E$
      16 paynefull] painefnll $I$
      18, 26, 28, 32 chuse] chose $E–H$
      19 life by] by life $HI$
      23 oppressed] opprest $B+$
      27 lengthes] lengthens $D+$
      28 euyls] ylles $B+$
      30 the] *Om. I*
      32 And] In $HI$
      34 FINIS.] *Om. B+*
217.   2–259.5 *in B+, not A*
       4 of] in $I$
      14 certaine] cherin $G+$
      21 they] thy $H$
      24 are aungels] Angels are $HI$
      28 pain] paines $HI$
218.   7 hete] hart $HI$
       9 so frete] set free $I$
      13 longes] long $I$
      14 Venus] Venns $B$
      15 hast] has $E$
      19 Contented] Coutented $H$
      22 Thomas] Thoms $H$
      23 elder] eldet $D$ *apparently*
      25 go] goes $D–G$
      26 he[2]] the $D$
      30 Wiate,] *The point may be a semicolon in B*
      34 softe] oft $D+$
      35 What] WHat $B$
219.   4 wherof] therof $E+$
       6 beginning] beginnieg $I$
       9 Lingring] Lingering $E+$:      sendes] lends $HI$
      10 write] writ $D$
      11 that] ẙ $F+$

[315]

219. 12 it] ir *D apparently:*      derer] dere *E+:*      though Priam] through
           Priams *HI:*      kingdome] kingnome *E*
       13 bane] bande *E+*
       14 he] the *F+:*      forowed] sorowed *E+*
       15 coarse] course *HI*
       18 should] shonld *H:*      hand] *Om. HI*
       24 harbourd] harboured *HI:*      hart.] *Period very doubtful in B*
       26 then] that *E+*
       27 rew] *Om. HI*
       31 haue I] I haue *I*
       34 this] thus *C+*
       36 while] whiles *D+*
220.   4 depriued] depr iued *B*
        5 amid] & *E+*
        8 wist] wisht *HI*
        9 farde] fearde *HI*
       10 in] in this *HI*
       12 his] hi s *B*
       14 brake] braste *E+*
       15 forgde] forged *D,* forge *EFG*
       16 which] whi h *D,* wich *E:*      fleest] seest *I:*      rare] race *H*
       23 shewde] shewed *G+*
       24 thousand] tousand *E*
       28 laughes] langhes *D*
       31 then] theu *H*
       36 mountaines] meuntaines (*first* e *inverted*) *I apparently*
       38 towers] towners *E*
221.   3 furth] forth *D+:*      pleasures] pleasure *HI*
        5 clergions] clergious *F*
       10 night] nighe *E,* might *G:*      mothers] mother *DEF*
       12 breastes] brest *H*
       13 their] t *inverted in D*
       14 soundes] souudes *D*
       15 And] Aud *D*
       17 And] Aud *D:*      dambe] dame *D,* damme *E+*
       21 lady] Ladies *I:*      loues] lones *G*
       25 that²] ha *torn in B, om. F+*
       26 of] oft *EF*
       27 them] then *DEF*
       28 taile *C+*] t *not recognizable in B*
       29 them through] thorough *HI*
       30 Woulf] woull *H*
       32 not] no *D*
       36 then²] *Om. F+*
       38 thus] then *HI*
       39 that²] *Om. D*
       43 A] An *E*
222.   4 comfort] c *badly broken in B*
        6 for] with *D+*
        7 song] songes *G*
        8 martirs] martiers *E–H*
        9 pleasures] pleasure *DE*

222. 12 man] *Om. HI*
    14 their] iheire *G*
    16 martirs] martiers *G*
    17 The] They *E:*    that] the *EF*
    18 braines] braine *HI*
    19 worke] workes *HI:*    paines] paine *I*
    20 wayghe] h *badly broken in B*, waight *D–G*, waite *HI*
    22 your] o *defective (or some other letter) in I*
    23 the] your *I*
    24 she] the *H apparently:*    alone] al one *E*
    26–27 Whom] *The* w *is in a different font that resembles lower case rather than capitals; so also at* 227.7, 32, 236.22, 23, 237.13, 35, 37, 238.5, 242.29, 244.21, *etc.*
    29 nay] may *C+*
223.  2 sigh] sight *FGH*
    4 that] the *E+:*    sigh] sight *H*
    5 ay] as *E+*
    12 sigh] sight *E*
    13 all] *Om. D+*
    15 And] Aud *H:*    euen] *Om. HI*
    22 wealeaway] well a way *HI:*    mine] my *HI*
    26 And] Aud *D*
    31 Pitie] *Second* i *inverted in G*
    32 dolefull] doefull *F*
    33 sekes] seke *D–H*
    35 stand] stond *EFG*
    37 and] aud *D*
    39 manere] maners *F+*
    41 the] thy *HI*
    42 full] fu ll *B*
224.  4 ought] oustt *D*, oft *E+*
    5 known] knowen *C+*
    6 such] snch *H*
    7 enow] enough *HI*
    9 oft] of *C*
    16 thine] thy *F+*
    17 knowne] knowen *HI*
    18 *Entire line repeated in G*
    20 thou] *Om. HI:*    others] other *I*
    21 plain] paine *G+*
    22 chose] choose *I*
    23 trouth] troth *I*
    25 wouldest] wouldst *HI*
    28 and] now *E–H*
    30 absence] basence *B*
    32 remoue] m *inverted in H*
    33 good] d *torn away in B*
    39 As] and *D+*
    43 her] *Om. HI*
225.  2 doth] do *HI*
    3 and] aud *D*
    4 And] Aud *B*

225.   8 told] rold *B apparently*
    10 a] and *I*
    11 namde] named *D+*
    15 trothe] trouth *H*
    21 might] mought *H*
    23 how] now *I*
    34 she] *Om. H*
    35 knowes] knowest *D+*
    39 her] *Om. E–H*
226.   3 Do I] *An* h *or a broken* b *is inserted crosswise between these words in B:*
       thine] thy *HI*
    7 tormentes] torment *HI:*     farest] fearest *HI*
    9 owne] *Om. DE*
    10 most²] must *G*
    11 loues] loue *E+*
    17 is] i s *B:*     wouldest] wouldst *I*
    18 driuell] dr iuell *B:*     of] of the *E+*
    19 poore] puore *D*
    21 those] thos e *B*
    23 maiest] maie st *B*, maist *EFG*
    28 handes] hande *D+*
    30 should] shonld *G*
    37 gentillest] gentilliest *H*
    42 so] *Om. D+:*     his] this *D+*
227.   5 that²] *Om. HI*
    10 *Line om. in I*
    12 the] that *E+*
    14 mine] my *D+*
    19 me¹] *Om. HI*
    27 armed] arme *GH*, armde *I:*     met] mete *G+*
    31 yͤ hole] that who *HI*
    32 them by] thereby *HI*
    35 Sinon] Simon *HI*
    37 startes] states *D+:*   metinges] meeting *HI:*   knowne] knowen *HI*
228.   3 came] come *D+:*   name] nam e *B*
    7 in] aud *D*, and *E+*
    9 ruine] rniue *D*
    11 should] to *I*
    13 sad] said *D+:*     matter] matters *HI*
    15 so] *Om. E+*
    17 demed] deemd *I*
    24 harmes] harnes *F*
    29 band] hande *D+*
    36 creepes] creepe *HI*
    38 on hye] only *I*
    42 and] aud *I*
    43 browes] browe *E+:*     moue] mouo *G (correct in G¹)*
229.   3 those] chose *F+*
    5 ye] yet *H apparently:*     not] no *E*
    6 in] *Om. D+*
    7 and now] *Om. D+*
    13 yours] your *HI*

229. 14 he] e *blurred out in B*
     17 his] is *E*
     23 within] with *I*
     24 then] the *HI*
     27 mine¹] my *D+*
     30 fist] fiist *B*
     31 louer sheweth] louershewetb *D*
     36 sought] sough *E*
230.  2 An] And *E*
      3 in] *Om. G+*
      5 That] The *D*
      9 loued] louen *E*
     10 And] d *inverted in D*
     11 ielous] iewels *D+*
     13 into] inio *G*
     15 he] *Om. HI*
     16 ioyes] ioie *HI*
     22 disceiued] deceiued *D+*
     23 the] *Om. D+*
     25 haue] hath *CD*
     29 Troylous] Troylus *D+*
     32 skies] skie *HI*
231.  3 case] ease *E*
      4 hasteth] hasted *D+*
      5 me] m *inverted in D*
     23 haue] hane *H*
     24 waxeth] wexeth *EFG*
     25 receiued] receiud *FG:*     times] ttmes *B*
     26 was] war *D*
     27 haue I] I haue *G+:*     longde] longed *HI:*     so] *Om. I*
     30 fed] fled *HI*
     31 banisht] banish *GH*
     33 opende] opened *DF+*
     34 enioyed] enioyd *EF:*     fruite] frite *E:*     for] of *I*
     36 I] *Om. H:*     iust] lust *D+*
232.  2 mine] my *D+*
      3 do] did *D:*     on] in *HI*
      4 ye] you *HI*
      5 toyes] toye *D apparently*
      6 Mine] My *D+:*     shit] shut *D+*
     10 sprites] pirites *D*
     13 A] And *G+*
     15 thou] t *blurred out in B*
     28 refused] refusd *FG*
     29 youth] youih *I*
     30 excused] excusd *HI*
233.  4 might] night *E–H*
      6 wrong] worng *H*
      8 booteth] boteth *DH*
      9 gainst] against *D+*
     10 Wyly] Will *E+*
     12 are] is *D+*

233. 13 good] good and *F*+
15 is] his *C*
26 bowle] bonle *I*
29 can] cane *D*
32 Flattry] Flattery *DG*+
33 doth] do *HI*
34 This] The *G*+
36 burnde] bunrde *F*
38 floods] flo ds *D*
40 sonk] song *GH*
41 mercy] meccy *H*
43 blinde] blnde *I*

234. 5 chickens] cheekens *FG*, cheikens *H*
11 minde] mide *C:*      alwaies the end] *Om. E*+
12 bought] bonght *H (correct in H¹)*
16 inow] enough *HI*
17 tother] other *I*
21 play] pleade *HI*
31 bestrow] bestow *C*+
33 sone shalt thou] thou shalt soone *I*

235. 4 Two] To *D*
12 require] requirt *G*
19 mo] more *G*+:      he] is *G*+
23 thinges] times *H*, time *I*
25 blest] blist *E*+
26 hot] whot *F*+
30 assaied] assayde *F*+
34 These] Those *F*+
35 sene] seeene *E:*      stare] start *H*
37 say] *Om. HI*

236. 12 answers] answere *I*
15 stake] sta ke *D*, stacke *E*+
16 mowen] women *G*+
30 wastes] walles *F*+
32 borrowd] borowed *D*+
33 fet] set *DF*+:      coale] coales *D*+:      same] flame *HI*
34 shew] vew *D:*      coales] coale *D–H*,      a coale *I*
35 am] and *E*+
37 vnkindled] vnkindeled *F:*      vpheaped] vnheaped *F*+
39 there fro] therefore *F*+
40 Out] Ont *G:*      doth] do *G*+

237. 7 is] *Om. H*
9 lastyng] lusting *HI*
10 flames] flameth *HI:*      fleteth] flitteth *E*+:      and²] and and *H*
11 your] our *D*+
12 lie] lyue *D:*      on] an *G*+
14 iucye] iuyce *D*+
16 trough] through *G*+:      enteryeld] entryelde *GH*, entry yelde *I*
17 key] kay *D*+
24 whence] whenee *B*
26 that] the *G*+
30 hight] light *G*+

[ 320 ]

237.　34 thy] my *D*
　　　41 wordes] word *HI*
238.　 3 forced] forceth *E+*:　　loue] lone *H*
　　　 7 but] dut *B*
　　　 8 heate] *Om. E+*
　　　15 her] here *GH*
　　　16 rare] farre *G+*
　　　19 laud] land *E+*:　　sped] spred *HI*
　　　20 spred] speed *H*, sped *I*
　　　23 blusheth] blusseth *D*
　　　28 toke] take *F+*
　　　32 winne] winde *G+*
　　　38 sayth] saieth *G*
　　　40 thank] thanks *HI*
239.　 3 by] be *D*
　　　 7 Byside] Beside *C*, Besides *D+*
　　　10 Ha] He *D*
　　　18 libertie] liberrie *I*
　　　19 vaunteth] vaunceth *I:*　　not] *Om. E+*:　　your] yow *D+*
　　　20 ought] oft *E+*
　　　30 life] like *D+*
　　　32 moued] mouing *E–H*, moning *I*
　　　33 hope] hoapte *E:*　　pining] pinning *I:*　　hurle his] hurt the *I*
　　　34 plaint] pla nt *D*
240.　 4 That] Not *D+*:　　returnde] returned *D+*
　　　 6 their] the *G+*
　　　 7 that] the *HI*
　　　 9 they] thy *H*
　　　10 vp rores] vp vprores *HI*
　　　11 his quiet] the vnquiet *HI*
　　　12 ruth] tuth *GH*
　　　14 wayling] wailig *D:*　　doth] *Om. HI*
　　　16 oft] of *E+*
　　　18 with] of *I*
　　　19 him life] himselfe *G+*
　　　20 brests] brest *I:*　　y̧] y̧ *I apparently*
　　　21 the] y̧ *HI*
　　　22 soules] soule *HI*
　　　24 blasphemes] blasphe mes *B*, basphemes *D:*　　present] presence *I*
　　　25 dampne] damne *E+*:　　plant] plaint *G+*
　　　27 her] hys *E+*
　　　30 that] the *HI:*　　fautles] faultrers *D–G*, faulterers *HI*
　　　31 throwen] trowen *H*
　　　32 Or] O *I*
　　　33 contented] conteuted *D*
　　　35 fare] feare *H*
　　　37 through] thorough *F*
241.　 4 of] by *HI*
　　　 6 striken] sticken *G*, sticked *H*
　　　 7 The] The blind *HI:*　　blinded] blinde *D*
　　　 9 and] aud *E*
　　　11 had] haue *G+*

[ 321 ]

241. 13 others] other *E+*
     14 rouyng] rauing *I*
     15 Thunthralled] Thuuthralled *I*
     16 Whose] Wose *F*
     19 both] b *blurred badly in B*:    wise,] wise' *D*
     24 lendyng] leading *G+*
     28 life] time *D+*
     34 doth their] *Final* h *and initial* t *torn in B*
242.  5 borrowd] borowed *D+*
      6 demen] demed *F+*
      7 brought] brounght *G*
     14 Vnlucky] Vulucky *H*
     16 wisht] wish *HI*
     18 constrayned] coustrained *D*
     20 iudgement] iugemeut *E*:    tare] tore *EF*
     21 quite] quiet *DG+*:    quiet] quite *DI*
     25 sighes] sighen *E–H*
     26 Oft] Of *E+*
     29 paine] paines *CHI*:    appeares] appeare *HI*
     30 supplied] supplide *HI*
     31 That] Than *E–H*, Then *I*
     32 voice] i *inverted in G*
     33 ouerwayd] ouerwaied *D*, ouerwayld *E+*
     34 tremblyng] treembling *H*
     37 so] *Om. HI*
     39 labourde] laboured *HI*
243.  5 hope] hape *E*:    mine] my *I*
      8 womens] womans *F+*
     11 changyng] changin *H*:    womens] womans *E+*
     13 or] of *CI*
     15 minde] mindes *HI*
     17 to] so *HI*:    chance] chauncde *I*
     19 surgeant] surgeon *CE+*
     20 their] her *G+*
     28 yeres] yere *EFG*
     29 mouthes] monthes *D–G*, month *H*, mouth *I*:    glistring] glistering
        *D+*:    gladsomnesse] gladsounesse *C apparently*
     30 times] tyme *E+*
     34 and sorow do] my sorrowes doth *HI*
     36 mourne] *Badly blurred in B*:    it] *Om. G+*
244.  5 cruelnesse] *Blurred out of F*
      7 finde] fiinde *F*
      9 thy] the *HI*
     12 the] *Om. D+*
     13 Both] Beth *(with* e *inverted) B*:    he] be *H*, by *I*
     14 carlish] calish *D+*
     15 proud] pround *H*:    astate] estate *D+*
     17 rifest] rife st *B*, riefest *EFG*
     19 lightenyng] lightning *E+*:    furthest] furdest *I*
     20 valey] vallies *HI*
     21 chanses] chauuces *I*
     23 self] selue *F+*:    makes] make *D*:    appear] appeares *HI*

244. 30 ouerthwart] ouertwart *H*
    35 that] y̆ *G perhaps*, thou *HI*
    37 is so] so is *GH*
245.  3 fortunes] fortues *H*
    11 frendes] frenees *E*, ftyndes *G*
    12 doest] dost *G*+:    doubled] double *I*
    13 is] of *G*+
    19 out] ou *D*:    thee] them *HI*
    22 thrown] throwen *HI*:    into thrall] *Om. HI*
    23 thy¹] they *GH*:    releue] receiue *G*+
    24 thou] that *HI*:    art] are *HI*
    27 thy] my *G*+
    30 louring] louinge *E*+
    32 chuse] chose *E*+
    40 elde] yelde *D*
246.  2 turne] true turne *E–H*, tnrne *I*:    vnto] into *HI*
    3 Which] whice *D*:    lasteth] lasteeh *G*, tasteth *I*:    stounde]
       staunde *D*+
    7 consumes] cosumes *D*
    11 Had] Han *GH*
    12 wormes] walles *HI*
    18 her] his *G*+:    profred] profered *D*
    20 phisike] phisske *B*
    23 suffred] suffed *E*, suffered *HI*
    29 knowne] kuowen *D*, knowen *E*+
    31 ouerblowne] ouerblowe *HI*
    34 or] to *C*
    35 haue] hane *H*
247.  3 brent] brant *H*, burnt *I*
    6 slake] slacke *EFG*
    11 With] Which *D–G*
    14 do way] doway *B*
    15 derst] erst *C*+
    19 wounded] woundcd *D apparently*
    20 all] *Om. G*+:    bebled] be bled *D*, be bleed *E*
    21 hand] had *E*
    23 deflowred] deflorwed *D*
    24 this] my *I*
    25 the] ᵗ *G*
    27 his] with *D*
    29 layed] laid *HI*
    31 the] that *EG*:    horrour] honor *I*
248.  2 now] *Om. E*+:    learnd] learned *C*+
    5 festreth] festereth *H*
    6 strayed] strained *G*+
    9 sight] sigh *G*+:    fixed] vexed *I*
    11 excellence] excellent *HI*
    12 hauing] haning *I*
    13 mine] my *I*:    eyen] eyes *E*+
    14 I] and *I*
    15 basheth] bashed *G*+
    16 contrarie] conttary *G*

[ 323 ]

248.  22  withouten] without *C*, whithouten *E*, withouteu *I*
       23  with] weth *H*
       26  my²] *Om. HI:*     health] help *D:*     nye] me *H*
       28  fettred] fettered *HI*
       29  fede] fed *G+*
       32  contrairs] contraries *D+*
249.   4  assuredly] assurely *FG*
        7  I] that *D+*
        8  Conuey] Conney *G*
      17  natrelesse] nathelesse *C–H*, nethelesse *I*
      24  that] tha t *B:*     withsaue] witsaue *C+*
      31  mine] my *D+*
      35  shalbe] shold be *D+*
      41  nothing] noting *F*
250.   2  him] h im *B:*     liuing] liyng *E*, lying *FGH*
       4  the] that *G+*
       5  *Line om. in HI*
       6  my] his *G+*
      11  spirit] sprite *D*
      12  you] thou *HI:*     ringing] ringging *FG*
      13  goth] goeth *D+*
      15  bonden] bounden *D+*
   17, 21  sprite] spirit *HI*
      25  this] my *G+*
      27  and] a nd *B*
      28  the] *Om. C*
      30  here] *Om. E+*
      32  she] ye *C*
251.   3  payned] painted *G+:*     gapst] gapest *I*
      11  maist] maiest *HI*
      14  truth] ruth *D:*     auaile] awaile *H*
      16  graft] graffe *DG+*
      20  no] ne *GH*
      23  sekes] sekest *D+*
      25  gladdest] gladliest *F+:*     woldst] would *G*
      31  therin] threin *F*
      33  carefull] carelesse *E+*
      37  The bay] Thy bate *I:*     yet] it *HI*
      38  Her] Het *H*
      39  make] makes *I*
252.   2  be set] beset *E+*
       3  their] her *I*
       6  make] makes *I*
      10  Where] Whete *F apparently*
      13  Her] He *FG*
      14  sprites] spirit *HI*
      21  found] foun *D*
      23  swound] sound *E+*
      24  sayth] saieth *D*
      25  faynted] fained *DG+*
      27  little] any *I*
      33  slyly] sely *G+*

252. 39 I am] am I *I*
    42 a] *Om. HI*
253. 7 doth] did *I*
    8 bands] bauds *C*, handes *E–H*
    20 fele] selfe *E+*
    21, 32, 35 Dephnes] Daphnes *D*, Daphnis *E+*
    28 wrought] wronght *G*, brought *I*
    31 most] m *inverted in D*, must *GH*
    36 felt] fele *GH*
    39 assigned] assignde *HI*
254. 7 my] my la *E*
    8 shaft] shaftes *HI*
    16 my] me *C+*
    18 retchlesse] ritchelesse *G+*
    20 Priamus] Priams *HI*
    22 yfound] I found *H*, I finde *I*
    23 And] As *G+*
    25 natiue] nature *D*
    26 haue] hane *G*
    28 the$^1$] be *F+*
    29 mortall] mortalll *E*
    30 forge] forgde *H*
    31 princesse] princes *HI*
    32 would] whould *I:*    heauy] heauen *G+:*    brest] briest *I*
    33 astonied] astoned *G:*    feator] featur(e) *DEHI*, fature *FG*
    39 affectes] effectes *D+*
    40 in] *Om. E+*
255. 6 An] And *F*
    9 And] Aud *D*
    12 before] bcfore *G*
    19 length] lenght *EF*
    23 selues] selfe *G+*
    27 they] the *EF*
    31 begiled] begild *D*
    35 hath] haue *G+*
    39 ye] yc *G apparently*
256. 4 hardned] hardened *E+*
    5 did] do *G+*
    6 plage] plauge *H*
    9 maist] maiest *HI*
    10 thy] the *HI*
    12 lenger] linger *D+*
    15 maist] maiest *H*
    16 chance] chanuce *G*
    20 the] that *I*
    21 wreke] wrecke *EFG*
    23 orecome] ouercome *I*
    26 shalt] shall *EFG*
    27 For] From *G+:*    a] in *E–H*
    28 doth] hath *D+*
    29 dost] doest *D–G:*    thee] thy *D+*
    30 luryng] lnring *H:*    liketh] laketh *D*

# VARIANT READINGS AND MISPRINTS

256. 31 it¹] *Om. HI*
    32 yet] it *HI:*    no] not *CHI*
    33 thee²] thy *I*
    36 within] with n *D*
257.  3 praise] prise *EFG,* price *HI:*    that] the *E+:*    flatteries] flatterers
        *D+:*    sown] sound *C+*
     5 title] tittle *GH*
     6 sugred] surgred *GH*
     7 poyson] poisons *HI:*    glims] glimes *E+*
     9 where] wherein *HI:*    is] in *D*
  11 had²] *Om. F+*
  13 the] in the *G+:*    dames] dame *F+*
  16 heares] heartes *D+*
  18 sucred] sugred *DEFI,* surged *G,* surgred *H*
  20 Two] Twe *B apparently*
  22 be] is *G+*
  25 enmies] enimies *HI*
  26 daunted] dainted *D*
  27 that] the *E+*
  37 shade] shades *G+*
258.  7 the] thy *G+:*    toy] ioy *EF*
  15 his] her *I*
  30 slake] slacke *F*
  32 bodies] bodie *C+*
259.  2 One] Onc *G*
   5 me] my *C:*    my] me *C:*    me to] to me *D+:*    graue] graee *C*

# VARIATIONS FROM *A* AND *B* IN ARBER'S REPRINT (1870)

# VARIATIONS FROM *A* AND *B* IN ARBER'S REPRINT (1870)

ARBER's reprint is described in the Introduction to volume II. The following list aims to include only his unauthorized variations from *A* and *B* in spelling and punctuation. He silently corrects misprints, expands contractions, changes indention, gives headlines (as at 93.1, 121.1) in large capitals, and otherwise deviates in typography; but to enumerate these variations has seemed unnecessary. In numerous cases he has put a false reading into his text of *A*, in a foot-note calling attention to the "correct reading," which he claims to have found in *B*: these cases of imaginary errors in *A* I have indicated by adding an asterisk to Arber's incorrect readings, which are given at the right of the brackets.

| | | |
|---|---|---|
| 3. | 13 | with] with the* |
| 4. | 15 | whiche] which |
| 5. | 23 | the] The |
| 6. | 3 | accord.] accord, |
| | 5 | strok.] strok, |
| | 16 | turne] turne, |
| | 27 | come] came* |
| | 38 | splene] splene, |
| 7. | 21 | swete] sweete |
| | 37 | about,] about. |
| | 39 | receaue] receue |
| 8. | 8 | quod] quoth |
| | 21 | more,] more. |
| | 23 | befall,] befall. |
| | 26 | LOue,] LOue |
| | 32 | shadowe,] shadowe |
| | 38 | remoue.] remoue, |
| 10. | 2 | to day] to-day |
| | 10 | moste] most |
| 11. | 3 | mynde] minde |
| 12. | 24 | gyftes] gyfts |
| 13. | 4 | suche] such |
| | 6 | longe] long |
| | 19 | youth.] youth, |
| 14. | 19 | Grekes] Greekes |
| | 24 | yeres] years |
| | 36 | Therfore] Therefore |
| 17. | 10 | despight?] despight: |
| | 18 | he] hee |
| 18. | 7 | hath] had* |
| | 13 | treew] trew |
| | 31 | now] nowe |
| | 40 | cumne] cumme |

| | | |
|---|---|---|
| 19. | 2 | sonne.] sonne, |
| | 9 | brest,] brest. |
| | 14 | mind.] mind, |
| | 40 | coulde] could |
| 20. | 8 | lawe] loue* |
| | 38 | the in] in the *(See the Variant Readings)* |
| 21. | 18 | dearely] dearly |
| | 28 | see] se |
| 22. | 40 | farewel] Farewel |
| 23. | 16 | whose] Whose |
| | 35 | or] Or |
| 24. | 12 | which] Which: night,] night. |
| | 16, 19 | where] Where |
| | 41 | minde.] minde, |
| | 43 | want] Want |
| 25. | 11 | how] howl |
| | 20 | Yet] Ye |
| | 21 | seemd] seemed |
| | 33 | Lorde] Lord |
| 26. | 32 | cliues,] cliues. |
| 27. | 6, 22 | sir.] sir: w.] W. |
| 28. | 34 | manhodes, shape] manhodes shape, |
| 29. | 34 | how] h ow |
| 30. | 4 | wytherd] wythered |
| | 13 | define.] define |
| | 14 | Wherat] Whereat |
| | 27 | this] his* |
| 31. | 10 | fansy,] fansy |
| 32. | 20–21 | affection] affection. |
| | 26 | in] on* |
| | 33 | If] It |

32. 34 wene,] wene.
33. 33 bearyng] learnyng*
35. 30 place,] place
    34 hart] heart
36. 16 any] my*
38.  5 scape] scrape
39.  3 perceaueth] preceaueth
     4 Wherby] Whereby
40. 12 obtayn] obtain
    23 hart] heart
41. 19 thy] the*
43. 33 fleeth,] fleeth
44.  9 hart] heart
    12 wherin] wherein
    25 hart] heart
    36 raine.] raine,
45.  2 wiates] Wiates
    16 suffred] suffered
    31 frailnesse,] frailnesse;
    34 litle] little
46. 14 distresse,] distresse.
    29 olde] old
    34 parauenture] perauenture
47. 19 facion,] facion
    27 ,he] he
48. 19 by,²] by
    21 he.)] he)
49. 16 began,] began
    18 some] from
    21 Then,] Then
    29 fet] set
51. 21 othe] oathe
52.  4 doublenesse?] doublenesse
    31 alowd] allowd
    34 willowe] willow
55. 32 fayn] fain
    35 bare,] bare.
    39 syde.] syde
56.  2 guide,] guide.
     3 it no] in to*
    16 are] ar
57. 27 vnfaynedly,] vnfaynedly.
60. 30 kinde] kind
61. 36 I.] I, (*A doubtful*)
64. 18 do] to
65. 12 alwayes] always
    15 say] say.
    33 complayne] complaine
67.  9 minde.] minde
    16 playneth:] playneth,
    20 then] than
68. 26 distayned:] distayned,

69. 14 theron] thereon
    18 loue,] loue.
    27 desyre.] desyre,
    28 fault.] fault:
70.  9 and] And
    32 wherto] whereto
    38 assinde.] assinde,
    39 relent,] relent.
71. 10 dart.] dart,
72.  7 end.] end
    29 thē] them (*instead of* then)
    32 ,me.] me,
    44 delight.] delight,
73. 16 *Arber has a misleading double space after this line*
    28 doutfull] doubtfull
    36 At] As
74. 22 first he] he first
75. 20 welth,] welth
    22 serue,] serue
76.  4 a loft:] a loft,
     8 serue] serue,
    27 deserued] diserued
    31–35 Arber has "Louer.", "La." *before these lines: see the Notes and the Variant Readings*
77. 10 not:] not,
    18 forbere.] forbere,
    24 doute] doubte
    29 why] Why
    35 holde:] holde?
    38 vnkinde] vnkind
78. 13 doest] dost
    34 see,] See
80.  4 naught:] naught
     9 enmy] enemy
    10 wiat] Wiat
    24 onely] onley
    30 reioyce.] reioyce,
81. 23 vnpossest.] vnpossest,
82.  6 faythfully] faithfully
     9 self] selfe
    16 milke] milk
    33 barly] barley
83. 18 hath] hath, (*A has a broken lead, not a comma*)
    33 loude?] loude
    34 well.] well,
    37 dranke] drank
84. 35 Nor] For
85. 19 Courtiers] courtiers

87. 27 ordred] ordered
88. 35 Now] Nowe
    37 frendes] friends
89. 26 skynne] skinne
    43 beares] bears
90. 17 Troian] Tro ian: knight] Knight
    18 whō] Whom
    25 nourse] nurse
91. 12 nine] mine
    19 gatherth] gathereth*
    35 order.] order
    37 tread] treade
    41 ful] full
92. 9 east ²] west
93. 2, 4 trueloue] true loue
    23 by:] by,
94. 10 hed:] hed,
    16 dreed?] dreed:
    17 auaunt.] auaunt,
95. 3 wold] would
    31 bee.] bee,
96. 7 pan?] pan?)
    9 soone] soon
    34 great:] great,
97. 2 say:] say
    5 king] King
    12 dothe] doth
    14 eare] earr
    26 dothe] doth
98. 18 cankred] cankered
    22 dothe] doth
99. 9 moste] most
    28 beast:] beast.
    29 Salomon] Solomon
100. 25 whō Britan] whom Britain
     26 Bothe] Both
     37 nill] will
101. 2 fansiefourm] fansie fourm
     11 yblest:] yblest,
     13 frendships] friendships
     14 tyme] time
     15 mark] marke: depaynt] depaynt,
     17 Of.] Of
     24 dere.] dere,
     28 woork,] woork
102. 7 conntrey] countrey
     12 ryfe] ryte
     32 now] nowe: yere,²] yere
     33 chere] cher e
     35 wit] with

103. 7 howrs] howrs,
     29 ỹ] ye
104. 12 mark] marke
     14 you?] you:
105. 2 prayzd] prayzed
     4 chcre,] chere.
     8 medcines] medicines
     12 Possidonius,] Possidonius
     28 wee] we
     35 dye:] dye,
106. 4 lābes] babes
     17 no²] so
     23 dothe] doth:    led.] led:
     29 fowl] fowle
     35 Menetus] Menclus*
107. 23 forow] sorow
     37 drawes] draws
108. 3 wilford] Wilford
     6 body] bo dy
     11 wight.] wight
109. 4 nor] not
     14, 22 w.] W.
110. 8 so conioynd] conioyned
     16 dere:] dere?
     18 complaintes] complaints
     36 reneew] renew
111. 14 moother] mother
     21 laws,] laws.
112. 2 face.] face
     4 go?] go.
     23 bad,] bad
     38 coomfort] comfort
113. 24 still.] still
     28 dwell,] dwell.
     34 the²] Om.
114. 23 bright,] bright
     28 And] And, (*A has a lead-mark, not a comma*)
     38 fine,] fine.
     39 Shelley] Shelly
115. 9 the] Om.
     35 hee³] he
116. 16 heauen:] heauen,
     19 makes] markes*
     20 dothe] doth
     41 bothe] both
117. 6 death,] deathe
     32 seg.] seg
     40 prayse] prase
118. 4 honour] honor: procurde,] procurde.
     10 Therfore] Therefore

118.  30 prone] proue
119.   2 preserud] preserued
       9 safegard] safeguard
      22 know:] knowe
      31 man,] man
      32 vnmoued.] vnmoued,
      34 Be] Bee
      37 swoords] swords
      39 styll?] styll:
      42 heap,] heap
120.   2 paynt.] paynt:
      19 labour spare:] lab our
         spare.
121.   6 his¹] this
      20 hath] had
      38 say.] say,
122.   2 time,] time
      15 had] hath
      26 self] selfe
123.   2 skye?] skye
      19 frenship] frienship
124.   9 quiet] quite
      38 snow] snowe
125.  14 ioy,] ioy.
      32 hand] hande
      33 secrete] secret
      36 armd] armed
126.  18 fawnd] fawned
127.  24 in] tn
128.  20 therat] thereat
129.   4 flee:] flee.
130.  10 fynde] finde
      23 calamaties] calamities
      26 dothe] doth
      31 bushe] rushe*
131.   5 than¹] then
132.  13 saw,] saw
      16 birde] bride*
      24 come,] come.
      28 a parfite] aparfite
      29 said] said,
133.  30 most] moste
134.   6 by] my
135.  20 wilfordes] Wilfordes
136.   8 in] of
      13 wordly] worldly
137.  10 call] call, (*A has a lead-mark,
         not a comma*)
      33 sprite] spirite
138.  16 feele.] feele
      24 began] began,
      29 greue.] greue,

138.  31 law] law, (*A has a lead-mark,
         not a comma*)
      41 syt] sit
139.  32 that] and
      41 forgo] forgo.
140.  21 chiefest] chist (*A has* chiest)
141.  21 lyfe,] lyfe
144.  11 more,] more.
      40 syng] sing: more:] more,
145.  10 white] White
      29 abacke] aback.
      32 winne,] winne.
146.   5 where] Where
      29 dothe] doth
      32 sir] Sir: wilford] Wilford
      34 whose] who
147.  12–13 of of] of
      30 which] whiche
148.  36 meane] mean
149.   7 obtayne,] obtayne.
      10 share.] share,
      12 grief] griefe: gall,] gall.
      34 swim.] swim,
150.  25 betwene] between
151.   3 mindes.] mindes,
       6 the] The
      12 sendith] sendeth
152.   3 That] Than
       4 tyme] time
      10 hept] kept
      16 flye,] flye: lighteth] lyghteth
      38 mayst] mayest
153.  14–15 *Arber transposes these
         lines**
      16 apere.] apere
      26 worne.] worne:
      28 whiche] which
154.  30 brier,] brier.
      34 disceitfull] deceitfull
155.  17 were] wert
      26 be gon,] begon.*
      34 eyes,] eyes.
      36 hart] harte
156.   6 nor] or
      12 farre,] farre
157.  20 a] is a
158.   2 griefe] grief
       7 liueth] liued
      12 all] my*
      20 god,] got
159.  15 state,] state
160.  15 Peragon.] Peragon

161.  12 dothe] doth
      15 lyfe] life
162.   3 wepyng] weepyng
       6 soft] softe
163.  37 Thassault] Th[e] assault
164.  34 with] wiht
165.   4 bad] had*: blow] blowe: re-
         trete,] retrete. (*A doubtful*)
      13 youe] your
      22 leaue] leeue
      35 youthly] youthly,
      38 wrincles] wrinckles
166.   2 now,] now
       7 prouide.] prouide,
       8 spade,] spade
      14 leaue] leue
      36 wentworthes] Wentworthes
167.  30 bough,] bough.
168.  12 portrayd] portrayed
      28 hand] hande
      38 desyre] desyre.
169.   4 worlde,] worlde.
      15 delights] delightes
      23 poets] Poets
170.   4 paragone,] paragone.
       5 petrark] Petrark
      17 parfit] parfite
      27 thou] Thou
      29 selfe] self: change,] change.
      31 prouoke,] prouoke.
171.  10 graunge,] graunge
      15 mught] might*
      26 which] Which
172.   4 knowe] know
       7 which] Which
      15 gladde,] gladde.
      17 imbracing] embracing
173.   5 breake] break
175.   2 blastes] blasts
       5 hurt] hurte
      11 cōfortes] comforts
      19 they haue] theyhaue
      34 when] When
177.  33 none.] none
      39 fo.] fo,
178.   7 fall,] fall.
      11 loue.] loue,
      25 Dothe] Doth: griefe] greife
180.   9 feare:] feare;
181.   6 sorowes] sorrowes
      20 then] then, (*A has a lead-
         mark, not a comma*)

182.  13 chiefe.] chiefe,
183.  11 dredfull] dredful
      18 wyth] with
      37 mode,] mode.
      38 lay,] lay
      39 away,] away.
184.   3 secretely,] se[c]retely. (*See
         the Variant Readings*)
       4 talke,] talke.
       9 therwith] therewith
      17 diuersly.] diuersly:
185.  22 sorowes] sorrowes
      27 life,] life.
186.   3 the] thee
       9 Weane] Wean e
      36 sute.] sute,
187.   5 haue] haue his
      16 therby,] therby:
      25 both] doth
      35 go:] go,
188.  10 melody,] melody.
      11 gyde.] gyde,
189.  40 authour] author
190.  12 piller] pillar
      17 or] and
      21 selfe] selfe.
192.   4 shamefall] shamefull
      17 Wherwith] Wherewith
      27 whispring] whispering
193.  25 vniustly] uniustly
      31 eye,] eye.
      39 blend.] blend
194.  12 there.] there,
      15 Of] On
      16 Penbroke] Pembroke
195.   7 the] a
      10 mothe,] mothe.
      21 eare.] eare,
196.   8 vngodlye] vngodly
      11 news] newes:    strāge]
         stra nge
      13 harts] hartes
      23 wyth] with
      24 faultes] faults
      27 nought] nought,
197.   5 wretchednes] wretche nes
       9 hap,] hap.
      23 tast] taste
      26 riche] rich
      28 avoide] auoide
      30 troblesome] troublesome
      33 morow] morrow

197. 37 playd] played: shalbe] shall
be
199. 5 williams] Williams
16 aliue,] aliue
17 striue] striue.
26 home hastyng] homehastyng
32 thou] though*
200. 30 w] W
202. 29 yll:] yll,
203. 31 birde] bride
204. 28 wherin] wherein
31 minde] minde.
205. 22 wo:] wo.
206. 6 Wherin] Wherein
25 fode,] fode
29 wyate thelder] Wyate th[e]
elder
34 sought,] sought.
207. 27 vnmete.] vnmete,
35 the:] the
208. 13 ruthe.] ruthe,
209. 7 pain] pain,
36 doe] do
210. 17 slide.] slide,
22 doune,] doune
24 delay] delaye
33 feithe.] feithe
211. 2 sonettes] Sonettes
3 wiat] Wiat: elder] elder.
4 called.] called
10 disdaine.] disdaine
21 health,] health.
23 geuen] giuen
28 and] And
212. 5 helpthe,] helpthe
8 finde.] finde
213. 2 whether] Whether
27 paine.] paine
217. 27 proue] proue.
218. 23 wiate] Wiate
30 Wiate,] Wiate; (*See the Vari-
ant Readings*)
36 ne] we
219. 3 holowith] holoweth
25 distresse,] distresse.
27 rew] rew.
33 is] in
220. 7 hart] heart
9 defence.] defence,
13 way.] way,
15 care.] care,
16 rare,] rare.

220. 22 hath] had
24 thinges] things
221. 28 hunt] hunte
42 were] ware
222. 16 syng] sing
20 wayghe] waygne
40 stone,] stone
223. 5 woon.] woon,
7 me,] me.
29 so.] so,
34 and] aud
224. 15 loue.] loue,
41 fro.] fro,
225. 13 nayes.] nayes,
15 trothe.] trothe,
17 faithfullest.] faithfullest,
31 drinkes.] drinkes,
33 grones.] grones,
226. 3 wish] wishe
35 bere.] bere,
227. 14 Thus] Thou: here] beare
20 comon] common
30 cry.] cry,
228. 20 wherin] wherein
23 beast.] beast,
40 againe] again
229. 20 loue:] loue
23 somtime] sometime
28 conceiue,] conceiue.
230. 4 tell.] tell,
9 had] *Om.*
12 gentle] ientle
13 kinde.] kinde,
27 that] what
34 me] we
35 Scilla] Sicilla
231. 11 finde] find
18 hart] heart
22 deserue.] deserue,
24 faire.] faire,
30 plesant] pleasant
232. 5 new] newe
25 winde] wind
26 present.] present,
233. 4 slouthfull] slothfull
19 state.] state,
22 weight.] weight,
33 best] beast
234. 11 end.] end
18 swete] swete.
235. 2 ben] been
17 wherin] wherein

236.   2 sinder] sinder,
    4 Cold] Colde
    19 cold,] cold
    26 Wherby] Whereby
    28 with sparkes] With sparkles
    33 same.] same,
    37 vpheaped] vnheaped
237.   2 metall] metal
    16 Wherin] Wherein
    22 passest] passeth
    30 had] that
    31 dye,] dye.
    33 lye.] lye
238.   20 ben] been
239.   15 kepe] keep
    21 you] your
    27 brest] brest,
240.   25 ease.] ease,
    26 thunhappy] the unhappy
    27 vnsitting] vnfitting:   stand.]
      stand,
    29 finde] find
    32 Or] O:  els] else
    37 brest] breast
242.   5 borrowd] borrowed:   geue]
      gaue
    9 best.] best,
    25 againe.] againe,
    32 stopt,] stopt
    33 ouerwayd] ouerwayed
243.   3 hart] heart:  blede.] blede,
    14 lay,] lay.
    29 gladsomnesse:] gladsomnesse
    30 mone.] mone,
    37 wherof] whereof
244.   2 theron,] theron.
    18 be.] be,
    30 beare] bear
245.   8 distresse,] distresse:
    18 peril] perill
    29 be.] be,
    35 lyfe] life
246.   2 vnto] into

246.   11 their] the
    23 suffred] suffered
    28 gape,] gape.
247.   21 degre] degree
248.   2 learnd] learned
    3 possest, ] possest.
    4 bow] bow,
    24 not.] not,
    28 fettred] fettered
    32 gaine:] gaine,
    36 past,] past.
249.   15 asshes] ashes
    16 powres] powers
    35 layde.] layde,
250.   4 hart] hert
    23 therof] thereof
251.   27 so] so,
    31 therin] therein
    39 leues] leaues
252.   14 Wherwith] Wherewith
    27 smart.] smart,
    31 speake.] speake,
    43 sit,] sit.
253.   9 annoy:] annoy.
    35 so:] so.
254.   3 one,] one.
    5 most:] most.
    17 ment] meant
    22 M,] M.
    26 chose.] chose,
    29 wight,] wight.
    32 wight:] wight,
    34 scape] scape.
    38 birthe:] birthe,
255.   5 sold,] sold.
    25 that] the
    34 cheape,] cheape.
256.   13 lights] light: betell bee.] betel
      bee,
    37 then] than: beholde] behold
257.   23 sekes] seeks
258.   14 coales] coles

# INDEX OF FIRST LINES

# INDEX OF FIRST LINES

References are to poem-numbers. A prefixed asterisk indicates that the poem appears in the first edition (*A*) only, italics that the poem is not in *A* but is in all later editions (*B–I*). Lines in brackets are readings that appear in an edition later than *A*, and only such bracketed readings are included as are necessary to make the index readily usable for *B–I* no less than for *A*. Authority for the bracketed insertions will be found in the appropriate entries of the Variant Readings and Misprints.

*A cruel tiger all with teeth bebled* . . . . . . . . . . . . . . 299
A face that should content me wondrous well . . . . . . . . . . . . 93
*A heavy heart with woe increaseth every smart . . . . . . . . . . 138
*A kind of coal is as men say* . . . . . . . . . . . . . . . . . . 287
A lady gave me a gift she had not . . . . . . . . . . . . . . . . 268
A man may live thrice Nestor's life . . . . . . . . . . . . . . . 257
A spending hand that alway poureth out . . . . . . . . . . . . . . 126
A student at his book so placed . . . . . . . . . . . . . . . . . 193
Accused though I be without desert . . . . . . . . . . . . . . . . 74
*Adieu desert how art thou spent* . . . . . . . . . . . . . . . . 303
*Ah liberty now have I learned to know* . . . . . . . . . . . . . 300
*Ah love how wayward is his wit what pangs* . . . . . . . . . . . 291
Alas madame for stealing of a kiss . . . . . . . . . . . . . . . . 54
Alas so all things now do hold their peace . . . . . . . . . . . . 10
Alas that ever death such virtues should forlet . . . . . . . . . 189
*Alas when shall I joy* . . . . . . . . . . . . . . . . . . . . . 310
All in thy look my life doth whole depend . . . . . . . . . . . . 90
All you that friendship do profess . . . . . . . . . . . . . . . . 226
Although I had a check . . . . . . . . . . . . . . . . . . . . . . 21
Among Dame Nature's works such perfect law is wrought . . . . . . 224
As cypress tree that rent is by the root . . . . . . . . . . . . . 215
As I have been so will I ever be . . . . . . . . . . . . . . . . . 230
As laurel leaves that cease not to be green . . . . . . . . . . . 244
As oft as I behold and see . . . . . . . . . . . . . . . . . . . . 24
*As this first day of Janus' youth restores unto the year . . . . 145
At liberty I sit and see . . . . . . . . . . . . . . . . . . . . . 236
Avising the bright beams of those fair eyes . . . . . . . . . . . 51
Because I still kept thee fro lies and blame . . . . . . . . . . . 48
Behold love thy power how she despiseth . . . . . . . . . . . . . 69
Behold my picture here well portrayed for the nonce . . . . . . . 208
Bewail with me all ye that have professed . . . . . . . . . . . . 209
Brittle beauty that nature made so frail . . . . . . . . . . . . . 9
By fortune as I lay in bed my fortune was to find . . . . . . . . 180
*By heaven's high gift in case revived were . . . . . . . . . . . 137
Caesar when that the traitor of Egypt . . . . . . . . . . . . . . 45
*Charis the fourth Pieris the tenth the second Cypris Jane . . . . 139
*Complain we may much is amiss* . . . . . . . . . . . . . . . . . 284
Cruel and unkind whom mercy cannot move . . . . . . . . . . . . . 220
Death and the king did as it were contend . . . . . . . . . . . . 227
*Deserts of nymphs that ancient poets show . . . . . . . . . . . . 141
Desire alas my master and my foe . . . . . . . . . . . . . . . . . 112
Disdain me not without desert . . . . . . . . . . . . . . . . . . 79

# INDEX OF FIRST LINES

Divers thy death do diversely bemoan . . . . . . . . . . . . . . . 30
*Do all your deeds by good advice* . . . . . . . . . . . . . . . 285
*Do way your physic I faint no more* . . . . . . . . . . . 298
Driven by desire I did this deed . . . . . . . . . . . . 122
Each beast can choose his fere according to his mind . . . . . . . . 264
Each man me tell'th I change most my device. . . . . . . . . . . . 46
Each thing I see hath time which time must try my truth . . . . . . 206
Ever my hap is slack and slow in coming . . . . . . . . . . . 94
Experience now doth show what God us taught before . . . . . . . . 200
False may he be and by the powers above . . . . . . . . . . 245
Farewell love and all thy laws for ever . . . . . . . . . . . . 99
Farewell the heart of cruelty . . . . . . . . . . . . . . . . 61
*Farewell thou frozen heart and ears of hardened steel* . . . . . . . . . . 308
Flee from the press and dwell with soothfastness. . . . . . . . . . . 238
For love Apollo his godhead set aside . . . . . . . . . . . . . 241
For shamefast harm of great and hateful need . . . . . . . . . . . 114
For that a restless head must somewhat have in ure . . . . . . . . . 204
For Tully late a tomb I gan prepare . . . . . . . . . . . . . 167
For want of will in woe I plain . . . . . . . . . . . . . . . 80
*For Wilford wept first men then air also . . . . . . . . . . . 157
From these high hills as when a spring doth fall . . . . . . . . . 63
From Tuscan came my lady's worthy race . . . . . . . . . . . 8
From worldly woe the meed of misbelief . . . . . . . . . . . . 253
Full fair and white she is and White by name . . . . . . . . . . . 186
Girt in my guiltless gown as I sit here and sew . . . . . . . . . . 243
Give place ye lovers here before . . . . . . . . . . . . . . . 20
Give place you ladies and be gone . . . . . . . . . . . . . . 199
Go burning sighs unto the frozen heart . . . . . . . . . . . . . 103
Good ladies ye that have your pleasures in exile . . . . . . . . . . 19
*Gorgeous attire by art made trim and clean . . . . . . . . . . . 146
He is not dead that sometime had a fall . . . . . . . . . . . . 72
*Holding my peace alas how loud I cry* . . . . . . . . . . . . . 301
How oft have I my dear and cruel foe . . . . . . . . . . . . . 96
I find no peace and all my war is done . . . . . . . . . . . . . 49
I heard when Fame with thund'ring voice did summon to appear . . . . 246
I lent my love to loss and gaged my life in vain . . . . . . . . . . 195
I loathe that I did love . . . . . . . . . . . . . . . . . . 212
I ne can close in short and cunning verse . . . . . . . . . . . . 247
I never saw my lady lay apart . . . . . . . . . . . . . . . . 13
I read how Troilus served in Troy . . . . . . . . . . . . . . 237
I see that chance hath chosen me . . . . . . . . . . . . . . . 113
I see there is no sort . . . . . . . . . . . . . . . . . . . 210
*I silly haw whose hope is past* . . . . . . . . . . . . . . . 302
*I that Ulysses' years have spent* . . . . . . . . . . . . . . 282
*I would I found not as I feel* . . . . . . . . . . . . . . . 293
If amorous faith or if an heart unfeigned . . . . . . . . . . . . 98
If care do cause men cry why do not I complain . . . . . . . . . 265
If ever man might him avaunt . . . . . . . . . . . . . . . 81
If ever woful man might move your hearts to ruth . . . . . . . . . 168
[If every man might him avaunt] . . . . . . . . . . . . . . . 81
If it were so that God would grant me my request . . . . . . . . . 221
If right be racked and overrun . . . . . . . . . . . . . . . 170

# INDEX OF FIRST LINES

If that thy wicked wife had spun the thread . . . . . . . . . . . . 256
If thou wilt mighty be flee from the rage . . . . . . . . . . . . . . 270
If waker care if sudden pale color . . . . . . . . . . . . . . . . 44
Imps of King Jove and Queen Remembrance lo . . . . . . . . . . . 133
*In Bays I boast whose branch I bear* . . . . . . . . . . . . . . . 304
*In court as I beheld the beauty of each dame* . . . . . . . . . . . 306
In court to serve decked with fresh array . . . . . . . . . . . . . 119
In Cypris springs whereas Dame Venus dwelt . . . . . . . . . . . . 7
In doubtful breast whiles motherly pity . . . . . . . . . . . . . . 123
In faith I wot not what to say . . . . . . . . . . . . . . . . . 60
In freedom was my fantasy . . . . . . . . . . . . . . . . . . . 223
In Greece sometime there dwelt a man of worthy fame . . . . . . . . 172
In seeking rest unrest I find . . . . . . . . . . . . . . . . . 198
In the rude age when knowledge was not rife . . . . . . . . . . . 263
In winter's just return when Boreas gan his reign . . . . . . . . . 18
In working well if travail you sustain . . . . . . . . . . . . . . 134
It burneth yet alas my heart's desire . . . . . . . . . . . . . . 109
It is no fire that gives no heat . . . . . . . . . . . . . . . . 188
It may be good like it who list . . . . . . . . . . . . . . . . 58
*It was the day on which the sun deprived of his light* . . . . . . . 277
Laid in my quiet bed in study as I were . . . . . . . . . . . . . 33
Like as the bird within the cage enclosed . . . . . . . . . . . . 271
Like as the brake within the rider's hand . . . . . . . . . . . . 228
Like as the lark within the merlion's foot . . . . . . . . . . . . 173
Like as the phoenix a bird most rare in sight . . . . . . . . . . . 260
Like as the rage of rain . . . . . . . . . . . . . . . . . . . 235
Like unto these unmeasurable mountains . . . . . . . . . . . . . 97
*Lo dead he lives that whilom lived here* . . . . . . . . . . . . . 273
Lo here lieth G. under the ground . . . . . . . . . . . . . . . 255
Lo here the end of man the cruel sisters three . . . . . . . . . . . 182
Love fortune and my mind which do remember . . . . . . . . . . . 95
Love that liveth and reigneth in my thought . . . . . . . . . . . 6
*Lovers men warn the corps beloved to flee . . . . . . . . . . . . 130
Lux my fair falcon and thy fellows all . . . . . . . . . . . . . . 92
Madame withouten many words . . . . . . . . . . . . . . . . 53
*Man by a woman learn this life what we may call . . . . . . . . . 158
Martial the things that do attain . . . . . . . . . . . . . . . . 27
Marvel no more although . . . . . . . . . . . . . . . . . . . 65
*Methought of late when Lord Maltravers died . . . . . . . . . . . 164
Mine old dear enemy my froward master . . . . . . . . . . . . . 64
Mine own John Poins since ye delight to know . . . . . . . . . . . 125
*Mirror of matrons flower of spouselike love . . . . . . . . . . . . 159
Mistrustful minds be moved . . . . . . . . . . . . . . . . . . 108
[My dame withouten many words] . . . . . . . . . . . . . . . . 53
My galley charged with forgetfulness . . . . . . . . . . . . . . 50
My heart I gave thee not to do it pain . . . . . . . . . . . . . 100
My love to scorn my service to retain . . . . . . . . . . . . . . 75
My lute awake perform the last . . . . . . . . . . . . . . . . 87
My mother's maids when they do sew and spin . . . . . . . . . . . 124
My Ratcliff when thy rechless youth offends . . . . . . . . . . . 35
My youthful years are past . . . . . . . . . . . . . . . . . . 207
Nature that gave the bee so feat a grace . . . . . . . . . . . . . 88

# INDEX OF FIRST LINES

Nature that taught my silly dog God wot . . . . . . . . . . . . . 202
*No image carved with cunning hand no cloth of purple dye . . . . . . 148
*No joy have I but live in heaviness* . . . . . . . . . . . . . . . 294
*Not like a God came Jupiter to woo* . . . . . . . . . . . . . . . 281
*Now blithe Thalia thy feastful lays lay by . . . . . . . . . . . . 160
Now clattering arms now raging broils of war . . . . . . . . . . . . 165
*Now flaming Phoebus passing through his heavenly region high . . . . 142
[Ny mother's maids when they do sew and spin] . . . . . . . . . . 124
O evil tongues which clap at every wind . . . . . . . . . . . . . 177
O happy dames that may embrace . . . . . . . . . . . . . . . . . 17
*O ling'ring make Ulysses dear thy wife lo sends to thee* . . . . . . . 275
O loathsome place where I . . . . . . . . . . . . . . . . . . . 23
O Petrarch head and prince of poets all . . . . . . . . . . . . . 218
O temerous tauntress that delights in toys . . . . . . . . . . . . 217
Of all the heavenly gifts that mortal men commend . . . . . . . . . 154
Of Carthage he that worthy warrior . . . . . . . . . . . . . . . 120
Of purpose Love chose first for to be blind . . . . . . . . . . . . 110
Of thy life Thomas this compass well mark . . . . . . . . . . . . 28
Once as methought Fortune me kissed . . . . . . . . . . . . . . 86
*One is my sire my sons twice six they be . . . . . . . . . . . . 136
Pass forth my wonted cries . . . . . . . . . . . . . . . . . . . 77
Perdy I said it not . . . . . . . . . . . . . . . . . . . . . . . 91
*Phoebe twice took her horns twice laid them by . . . . . . . . . . 129
Phyllida was a fair maid . . . . . . . . . . . . . . . . . . . . 181
Procris that sometime served Cephalus . . . . . . . . . . . . . . 259
*Resign you dames whom tickling bruit delight* . . . . . . . . . . . 309
Resound my voice ye woods that hear me plain . . . . . . . . . . 59
Right true it is and said full yore ago . . . . . . . . . . . . . . 57
Set me whereas the sun doth parch the green . . . . . . . . . . . 12
Shall I thus ever long and be no whit the near . . . . . . . . . . 190
She sat and sewed that hath done me the wrong . . . . . . . . . 67
Sighs are my food my drink are my tears . . . . . . . . . . . . . 116
Since fortune's wrath envieth the wealth . . . . . . . . . . . . . 262
Since love will needs that I shall love . . . . . . . . . . . . . . 107
Since Mars first moved war or stirred men to strife . . . . . . . . . 239
Since thou my ring mayst go where I ne may . . . . . . . . . . . 203
*Sith Blackwood you have mind to wed a wife . . . . . . . . . . . 131
Sith singing gladdeth oft the hearts . . . . . . . . . . . . . . . 185
Sith that the way to wealth is woe . . . . . . . . . . . . . . . 192
*Sith Vincent I have mind to wed a wife . . . . . . . . . . . . . 132
So cruel prison how could betide alas . . . . . . . . . . . . . . 15
So feeble is the thread that doth the burden stay . . . . . . . . . 104
*So happy be the course of your long life . . . . . . . . . . . . . 143
Some fowls there be that have so perfect sight . . . . . . . . . . 47
Some men would think of right to have . . . . . . . . . . . . . 82
Sometime I fled the fire that me so brent . . . . . . . . . . . . . 71
Speak thou and speed where will or power ought help'th . . . . . . 269
Stand whoso list upon the slipper wheel . . . . . . . . . . . . . 118
*Stay gentle friend that passest by* . . . . . . . . . . . . . . . 289
Such green to me as you have sent . . . . . . . . . . . . . . . 229
Such is the course that Nature's kind hath wrought . . . . . . . . 84
Such vain thought as wonted to mislead me . . . . . . . . . . . 41

# INDEX OF FIRST LINES

Such wayward ways hath love that most part in discord . . . . . . . . 4
Such wayward ways have some when folly stirs their brains . . . . . . 242
Sufficed not madame that you did tear . . . . . . . . . . . . . . . 105
Tagus farewell that westward with thy streams . . . . . . . . . . . 121
Th' Assyrian king in peace with foul desire . . . . . . . . . . . . . 32
The ancient time commended not for naught . . . . . . . . . . . . 150
The answer that ye made to me my dear . . . . . . . . . . . . . . 83
*The bird that sometime built within my breast* . . . . . . . . . . . 280
*The blinded boy that bends the bow* . . . . . . . . . . . . . . . 292
[The coward oft whom dainty viands fed] . . . . . . . . . . . . . . 232
The doleful bell that still doth ring . . . . . . . . . . . . . . . . . 240
The doubtful man hath fevers strange . . . . . . . . . . . . . . . 191
The enemy of life decayer of all kind . . . . . . . . . . . . . . . 85
The fancy which that I have serued long . . . . . . . . . . . . . . 36
The flaming sighs that boil within my breast . . . . . . . . . . . . 101
The flickering fame that flieth from ear to ear . . . . . . . . . . . 250
The furious gun in his most raging ire . . . . . . . . . . . . . . . 73
The golden apple that the Trojan boy . . . . . . . . . . . . . . . 231
The golden gift that nature did thee give . . . . . . . . . . . . . . 14
The great Macedon that out of Persia chased . . . . . . . . . . . . 29
*The issue of great Jove draw near you Muses nine . . . . . . . . . 155
The lenger life the more offence . . . . . . . . . . . . . . . . . . 174
The life is long that loathsomely doth last . . . . . . . . . . . . . 171
The lively sparks that issue from those eyes . . . . . . . . . . . . 40
The long love that in my thought I harbor . . . . . . . . . . . . . 37
[The longer life the more offence] . . . . . . . . . . . . . . . . . 174
*The noble Henry he that was the Lord Maltravers named . . . . . . . 163
[The one long love that in my thought I harbor] . . . . . . . . . . . 37
The pillar perished is whereto I leant . . . . . . . . . . . . . . . . 102
The plague is great where fortune frowns . . . . . . . . . . . . . . 176
The restful place renewer of my smart . . . . . . . . . . . . . . . 62
The restless rage of deep devouring hell . . . . . . . . . . . . . . 179
*The secret flame that made all Troy so hot* . . . . . . . . . . . . . 279
The shining season here to some . . . . . . . . . . . . . . . . . . 216
The smoky sighs the bitter tears . . . . . . . . . . . . . . . . . . 214
The soote season that bud and bloom forth brings . . . . . . . . . . 2
*The souls that lacked grace* . . . . . . . . . . . . . . . . . . . . 272
The storms are past these clouds are overblown . . . . . . . . . . . 34
The sun hath twice brought forth his tender green . . . . . . . . . . 1
*The sun when he hath spread his rays* . . . . . . . . . . . . . . . 278
The virtue of Ulysses' wife . . . . . . . . . . . . . . . . . . . . . 258
The wand'ring gadling in the summer tide . . . . . . . . . . . . . 55
The winter with his grisly storms ne lenger dare abide . . . . . . . . 197
*The wisest way thy boat in wave and wind to guy* . . . . . . . . . . 295
*The worthy Wilford's body which alive . . . . . . . . . . . . . . . 156
Therefore when restless rage of wind and wave . . . . . . . . . . . 166
Thestilis a silly man when love did him forsake . . . . . . . . . . . 201
Thestilis thou silly man why dost thou so complain . . . . . . . . . 234
They flee from me that sometime did me seek . . . . . . . . . . . . 52
*Thou Cupid god of love whom Venus' thralls do serve* . . . . . . . . 283
Though coward oft whom dainty viands fed . . . . . . . . . . . . . 232
Though I regarded not . . . . . . . . . . . . . . . . . . . . . . 25

# INDEX OF FIRST LINES

Though in the wax a perfect picture made . . . . . . . . . . . . 233
Throughout the world if it were sought . . . . . . . . . . . . . 117
To false report and flying fame . . . . . . . . . . . . . . . . 254
To live to die and die to live again . . . . . . . . . . . . . . 213
To love alas who would not fear . . . . . . . . . . . . . . . . 222
To my mishap alas I find . . . . . . . . . . . . . . . . . . . 225
To this my song give ear who list . . . . . . . . . . . . . . . 175
To trust the feigned face to rue on forced tears . . . . . . . . . 261
To walk on doubtful ground where danger is unseen . . . . . . . 178
*To you madame I wish both now and eke from year to year . . . . . 144
*To you this present year full fair and fortunable fall . . . . . . . . 147
Too dearly had I bought my green and youthful years . . . . . . . 22
Unstable dream according to the place . . . . . . . . . . . . . 42
Unto the living Lord for pardon do I pray . . . . . . . . . . . . 184
Unwarely so was never no man caught . . . . . . . . . . . . . 89
*Vain is the fleeting wealth* . . . . . . . . . . . . . . . . . 297
Venemous thorns that are so sharp and keen . . . . . . . . . . . 267
Vulcan begat me Minerva me taught . . . . . . . . . . . . . . 115
W. resteth here that quick could never rest . . . . . . . . . . . 31
Walking the path of pensive thought . . . . . . . . . . . . . . 252
Was never file yet half so well yfiled . . . . . . . . . . . . . . 39
*What cause what reason moveth me what fancy fills my . . . . . . . 140
*What harder is than stone what more than water soft* . . . . . . . . 274
What man hath heard such cruelty before . . . . . . . . . . . . 68
What needs these threat'ning words and wasted wind . . . . . . . 56
What one art thou thus in torn weed yclad . . . . . . . . . . . 149
What path list you to tread what trade will you assay . . . . . . . 151
What race of life run you what trade will you assay . . . . . . . . 152
What rage is this what furor of what kind . . . . . . . . . . . . 111
[What resteth here that quick could never rest] . . . . . . . . . . 31
*What sweet relief the showers to thirsty plants we see . . . . . . . 128
What thing is that which I both have and lack . . . . . . . . . . 187
What vaileth troth or by it to take pain . . . . . . . . . . . . . 70
What word is that that changeth not . . . . . . . . . . . . . . 266
When Audley had run out his race and ended were his days . . . . . 205
When Cupid scaled first the fort . . . . . . . . . . . . . . . . 211
When Dido feasted first the wandering Trojan knight . . . . . . . 127
When dreadful swelling seas through boisterous windy blasts . . . . . 196
When first mine eyes did view and mark . . . . . . . . . . . . 106
*When Phoebus had the serpent slain* . . . . . . . . . . . . . 305
*When princes' laws with reverend right do keep the . . . . . . . . 153
When raging love with extreme pain . . . . . . . . . . . . . . 16
When summer took in hand the winter to assail . . . . . . . . . . 5
When Windsor walls sustained my wearied arm . . . . . . . . . . 11
When youth had led me half the race . . . . . . . . . . . . . . 3
Where shall I have at mine own will . . . . . . . . . . . . . . 66
Who crafty casts to steer his boat . . . . . . . . . . . . . . . 194
Who justly may rejoice in aught under the sky . . . . . . . . . . 169
*Who list to lead a quiet life* . . . . . . . . . . . . . . . . . 286
Who list to live upright and hold himself content . . . . . . . . . 183
Who loves to live in peace and marketh every change . . . . . . . 251
*Who would believe man's life like iron to be . . . . . . . . . . . 135

# INDEX OF FIRST LINES

*Whom fancy forced first to love* . . . . . . . . . . . . . . . . . . . . 290
*Whoso that wisely weighs the profit and the price* . . . . . . . . . . . 296
Why fearest thou thy outward foe . . . . . . . . . . . . . . . . 249
*Why Nicholas why dost thou make such haste . . . . . . . . . . 161
With Petrarch to compare there may no wight . . . . . . . . . . . 219
Within my breast I never thought it gain . . . . . . . . . . . . . 76
Wrapped in my careless cloak as I walk to and fro . . . . . . . . . 26
[Wyatt resteth here that quick could never rest] . . . . . . . . . . . 31
*Ye are too young to bring me in.* . . . . . . . . . . . . . . . . . 307
Ye that in love find luck and sweet abundance . . . . . . . . . . . 43
*Yea and a good cause why thus should I plain . . . . . . . . . . . 162
Yet once again my muse I pardon pray . . . . . . . . . . . . . . 248
Yet was I never of your love aggrieved . . . . . . . . . . . . . . 38
*You that in play peruse my plaint and read in rhyme the smart* . . . . . 276
*Your borrowed mean to move your moan of fume withouten flame* . . . . . 288
Your looks so often cast . . . . . . . . . . . . . . . . . . . . . . 78